The Bread of Life

olic Bible Study

Cycle A

DEACON KEN & MARIE FINN

"The Paraclete, the Holy Spirit whom the Father will send in my name, will instruct you in everything, and remind you of all that I have told you." *John 14:26*

THE BREAD OF LIFE CATHOLIC BIBLE STUDY

Cycle A

THE BREAD OF LIFE CATHOLIC BIBLE STUDY

Cycle A

DEACON KEN AND MARIE FINN

QUEENSHIP PUBLISHING COMPANY
P.O. Box 42028
Santa Barbara, CA 93140-2028
Phone: (800) 647-9882 FAX: (805) 569-3274

I have concluded that the materials presented in
this work are free of doctrinal or moral errors.

Bernadeane Carr, STL
Censor Librorum
7 July 1992

In accord with 1983 CIC 827 § 3, permission to
publish this work is hereby granted.

+ Robert E. Brom
Bishop of San Diego
15 July 1992

Published by:
    Queenship Publishing
    P.O. Box 42028
    Santa Barbara, CA 93140-2028
    Phone: (800) 647-9882 FAX: (805) 957-1631

ISBN 0-882972-31-7 (Volume A)

Acknowledgments

Our special thanks to all those who have helped Marie and me in the writing of this bible study.

To the many translators, Josefina, Rosa, Javier, MaryLou, Stella, Carmen, Luis & Magdelina, Maria, Larry & Myrna, Frances, we say thank you.

To all the Word Processor operators, Jean, Grace, Debbie, Nicole, Paul, Jerry, Deacon Tom, Bob, Joe, Steve, we say thank you.

To Marianne and Paul, for their work on the cover, we say thank you.

To all those who helped with the mailing, Ray & MaryJane, Marlene, Bob & Rosemary, Rick & Leonore, Greg & Laura, Eunice, Eloise, Marlene, Glen, Geri, Julie, and the students from St. Mary's and St. Timothy's, we say thank you.

To all the proofreaders, Nap, Alice, Marlene, Ernie, Roberto, Martha, Diane, Geraldine, Cathy, Helen, Larry, Phyllis, the women of St. Mary's and St. Timothy's Bible Study, we say thank you.

To all the board members and advisors of St. Dismas Guild, Bob, Greg, Carol, Terry, Fred, Ed, we say thank you.

To our Pastors, Fr. Fred & Fr. Ramon, we say thank you.

To our children and their spouses, Mom, sisters & brothers, we say thank you for all your love and support.

To all those we have not named that have donated or contributed, time, talent, or treasure, we say thank you.

To the Holy Spirit for using all of us to bring His Holy Word to the many who are longing to know Our Heavenly Father and His Son Jesus, and have fellowship with Him, we say thank you.

Dedicated to the memory of

Grace Dinger

Whose death from cancer took place during the final days of writing this book. Grace's life was a total commitment to the word of God.

"THERE ARE DIFFERENT GIFTS BUT THE SAME SPIRIT; THERE ARE DIFFERENT MINIS-TRIES BUT THE SAME LORD; THERE ARE DIFFERENT WORKS BUT THE SAME GOD WHO ACCOMPLISHES ALL OF THEM IN EVERYONE." 1 CORINTHIANS 12:4-6

Introduction

In this work are excerpts from the documents of Vatican II, one of which is a Decree on the Apostolate of Lay People. That document was written by some 2500 bishops in 1965. The council of bishops have challenged the Christian laity by encouraging them in their role of becoming disciples of Jesus Christ.

The church was founded to spread the Kingdom of Christ over all the earth for the glory of God the Father to make men partakers in redemption and salvation, and through them to establish the rich relationship of the entire world to Christ.

Christ sent by the Father, is the source of the Church's whole apostolate; "Whoever dwells in me and I in him bears much fruit, for separated from me you can do nothing (John 15:5)". Only the light of faith and the meditation on the Word of God can enable us to find everywhere and always the God "In whom we live and exist" (Acts 17:28). The Church's mission is concerned with the salvation of men; and men win salvation through the grace of Christ and faith in him. The apostolate of the Church therefore, and of each of its members, aims primarily at announcing to the world by word and action the message of Christ and communicating to it the grace of Christ. The principal means of bringing this about is the ministry of the Word and of the sacraments.

There is a famine today that is raging across this great land of ours. There is a deep hunger and thirst for the healing Word of the lord Jesus Christ. Many people in our society are looking for false gods to heal their wounded lives. Many of our people are looking for status, power, success, wealth, good jobs, and they look to their peers for recognition and approval. When this fails many try to find the solution in drugs, alcohol, sex, money, good works, philosophies, morality, even political systems. None have worked, nor will they ever work. Our society can not live together in love and peace until there is a spiritual change which only God's Word can produce.

Today much of mankind is still reluctant to admit that the only way that man can get back to God is through his son Jesus Christ. All of the many varied hurting experiences of the people in the world can only be changed when we begin to acknowledge that the world itself cannot satisfy our deeply personal needs. We need to come to the realization that man indeed does live by everything that proceeds out of the mouth of God (Deuteronomy 8:3).

Jesus has come into our world to end the famine that ravages the human heart. Therefore with humility, boldness, and energy, we must personally hear the Word, pray the Word, study the Word, proclaim the Word, and live the Word of the Lord Jesus Christ.

Guidelines for those leading
the Bread of Life Catholic Bible Study.

The opening prayer may be spontaneous or planned. Include John 14:26, which is, "The Paraclete, the Holy Spirit whom the Father will send in my name, will instruct you in everything, and remind you of all that I told you."

Reread the application from the previous week. Ask each person in turn how they fulfilled the application. Begin by sharing your own application.

<u>Write</u> answers to the application and the questions, including the personal questions. Keep the answers brief. If answers are not written down, pass to the next person.

Answers written in the quiet of our own home give the Holy Spirit an opportunity to speak to us directly and reveal His truths to us. We are more open to hearing and responding to the Holy Spirit. We build community when we share in the group what He has revealed to us.

First Day – Read the two questions and answer them yourself. Then have each person (only those who have written down their answers) respond to the questions.

Second Day – Read the first reading, have each person answer a question. Read the commentary for that day. (Have those comfortable at reading read a paragraph at a time.) Note: The answers to the personal questions should be written down.

Third and Fourth Day – Same as above

Fifth Day – Read the psalm and ask the two questions (giving your answer). Have those who have written down their answers share.

Read the application, then remind everyone to do the lesson for the following week.

The closing prayer can be spontaneous or planned. Follow the lead of the Holy Spirit.

Schedule

Liturgical Colors

Violet – Advent and Lenten Seasons
White – Christmas and Easter Season
Green – Sundays in Ordinary Time
Red – Palm and Pentecost Sundays

Before You Begin

Before you begin reading and studying God's Holy Word, always pray and ask God to speak to you through his Holy Spirit.

God's Word tells us "The Paraclete, the Holy Spirit whom the Father will send in my name, will instruct you in everything and remind you of all that I told you." (John 14:26)

It is imperative that you both understand <u>and</u> believe that scripture. The Holy Spirit is your teacher. There is one teacher, one Father, one God. For you to grow and become more like Jesus every day of your life.... you must be in submission to his teaching. His teaching can come to you in different ways.

1. By a revelation directly to you from God. In your quiet time alone with God in prayer many times God will speak to you. Sometimes we don't hear him because we are so busy talking and asking him for things. "Be still and know that I am God".

2. Through the Scriptures. God speaks to us and shows us how to live our lives according to his plan in his Holy Word.

3. Through the Church. (Church meaning the people of God) Every time the priest, deacon, or readers proclaim the Word of God there is a message for you personally.

As you take time each day to do this study in preparation for the celebration of Mass on Sunday the Lord is able to teach you and help you in dealing with your everyday relationships with the people you come in contact with. The key to this study is in training you to listen to what God is saying to <u>you</u>. When the priest or deacon give their homily at Mass and you listen carefully to what God is saying to you as he speaks through them, you will each day become more alert to his teaching through others. As you obey and follow his way in your life you will find a transformation taking place within you and you will find the joy and peace of knowing your God by loving others.

Our prayer for you is that you come to know the loving, just God that we have come to know through his Word and find the joy and peace that is yours in him.

In Jesus' name,

Deacon Ken & Marie

Deacon Ken & Marie Finn

FIRST SUNDAY OF ADVENT – CYCLE A

BEFORE YOU BEGIN

Pray and ask God to speak to you through His Holy Spirit. "THE PARACLETE, THE HOLY SPIRIT WHOM THE FATHER WILL SEND IN MY NAME, WILL INSTRUCT YOU IN EVERYTHING, AND REMIND YOU OF ALL THAT I TOLD YOU." (JOHN 14:26)

FIRST DAY   **Reread last week's readings.**

1. What was a helpful or new thought from the readings or from the homily you heard on Sunday?

2. From what you learned, what personal application did you choose to apply to your life this week?

SECOND DAY   **READ ISAIAH 2:1-5**   **FIRST READING**

("Come, let us climb the Lord's mountain.")

1. Who saw something concerning Judah and Jerusalem and whose son was he? Isaiah 2:1

2. What will happen to the mountain of the Lord's house, who will come towards it, and when will this happen? Isaiah 2:2

3. What will the people say who come to it? Isaiah 2:3

4. Who is to instruct us in his ways, in whose paths are we to walk, and from where will instruction come? Isaiah 2:3

5. Where is Zion? 1 Kings 8:1, Joel 4:17, 21

6. In days to come, from where will the Word of the Lord come? Isaiah 2:3

7. Where does the Word of God come from today? John 1:1,14

8. How do we know he is speaking to us if he is not walking and talking with us as he did with the apostles two thousand years ago? John 16:7

9. In days to come, how will there be a judgment? And what will end? Isaiah 2:4

10. What are we to walk in and who is the light of the world? Isaiah 2:5, John 8:12

Personal – How are you anticipating with joy our Lord's coming? Do your family and friends know that Jesus will come again? How are you preparing for his coming and how is your family preparing for it?

THIRD DAY	READ ROMANS 13:11-14	SECOND READING

("Let us cast off deeds of darkness and put on the armor of light.")

1. What is the summation of all the commandments? Romans 13:9-10

2. When should we wake from sleep? Romans 13:11

3. When will our salvation be completed? Revelations 1:7, 1 Thessalonians 5:2

4. What does it mean to "accept the faith? " Write out the following verses:
   John 3:16 & John 14:6

5. What does verse 12 of Romans 13 say about the day and night, what must we cast off and what must we put on? Romans 13:12

6. What is the armor of light? (Light representing Jesus, John 8:12) List all of the armor that we are to put on: Ephesians 6:10-17
   Helmet –
   Breastplate –
   Belt –
   Footgear –
   Shield –
   Sword –

7. According to Romans how are we to live and how are we not to live? Romans 13:13

Personal – According to verse 13, what is one of the major reasons for divorce today? What is one of the major causes of automobile accidents? What is one of the major causes of abortion today? What is one of the major causes of division in our churches today?

8. To put on the Lord Jesus Christ, how must we conduct ourselves? 1 John 2:6

9. For what are we not to make provision? Romans 13:14

10. How do we not give in to the desires of the flesh? Galatians 5:13

Personal – Do you know Jesus well enough through his Word to walk as he did? In what way can you better learn about him?

FOURTH DAY	READ MATTHEW 24:37-44	GOSPEL

("Stay awake, therefore, you cannot know the day your Lord is coming.")

1. Who is the Son of Man? Matthew 1:18, 23

2. What will he repeat? Matthew 24:37, Gen 7:11-23

3. What were the people doing in the days before the flood and what did the flood do to them? Matthew 24:38-39

4. What will happen when Jesus comes again? Matthew 24:40-41

5. What must we do, why must we do this, and what must we not allow? Matthew 24:42-43

6. Who are the thieves? John 10:1, 8

7. What do the thieves come to do? John 10:10

8. What must we be before the Son of Man comes? Matthew 24:44

9. How can we be best prepared? John 8:31

Personal - In what way are you living according to his teachings? How do you know his teachings?

FIFTH DAY   **READ PSALM 122:1-9**

("We will go up to the house of the Lord.")

Read and meditate on Psalm 122:1-9.

What is the Lord saying to you personally through the Psalm?

How can you apply this to your life?

SIXTH DAY   **READ ALL OF THE COMMENTARY**

ISAIAH 2:1-5

The emphasis in this passage is peace through obedience to God. This is the only kind of peace that will be permanent. The temple is mentioned, not so much because of its architecture, but because of the presence of God in the Old Testament scripture. The temple was a symbol of religious authority, and all worship was centralized through the temple. The temple was a symbol of God's holiness, and it was the setting for many of the great visions of the prophets. The temple was a symbol of God's covenant with Israel.

The temple was a symbol of God's forgiveness and it prepared the people for the coming of their long-awaited Messiah. The temple was a testimony to human effort and creativity, and finally, above all else, the temple was a place of prayer. Isaiah was prophesying what was going to happen to Jerusalem, and that was that Jerusalem would not only be freed of her bondage, but that she would become a leader to all nations.

The new Jerusalem is a city of God where there will be no more tears, no more sorrow, no more crying, no more pain and no more death. Have you ever wondered what heaven will be like? The Holy City, or New Jerusalem is described in scripture (Rev. 21) as a place where God dwells among his people amid the absence of pain, sorrow and death.

This is a tremendous comfort for us, because no matter what we may be going through, it is not the last word. God has written that last chapter and he has promised us that if we believe in his Son (Jesus), we will not perish but have eternal life (John 3:16). We are told in this passage that a wonderful day of peace will come when we are taught God's laws and then obey them. We know that sin causes war, conflict, sickness, and disruption.

We are encouraged to begin to obey God, not in the next world but rather, in today's world. He has given us his Word for direction and guidance. We will not have to wait until we die to enjoy the benefits of his love, we will begin to enjoy them immediately. We will become changed and that change will affect our family, friends, and fellow co-workers. We must never forget God made a covenant with us. He will never break his promise, and his promise is to be with us until the end of time. (Matt. 28:20).

ROMANS 13:11-14

In this message, Paul really stresses the urgency of changing our lives before Jesus Christ comes back again. No man knows when God will rise and bid him go. The time grows shorter, for we are every day one day nearer that time. Paul stresses that we too must have all things in our life ready. St Augustine, in his story "Confessions" tells of finding conversion in the last verses of this passage. He wondered how long it was going to take to end his life of sinfulness.

With his Word God had spoken to St. Augustine and he will speak to us if we will let him. We do not search for God; he is already searching for us. God's Word can always find the human heart, no matter how much darkness surrounds it. Let Jesus come into your heart right now and put on the clothes of light and the armor of right living.

In Roman society, a young man put down the clothes of his childhood and put on the toga, a sign of an adult, with its rights and responsibilities. Paul is saying we have laid aside the clothes of the law and now we are putting on Christ's clothes of righteousness. We are to do the same, we are to cast off and throw away our rotten garments of sin and put on the clothes of grace. Paul was appealing to the commitment the believers had made in their baptism (2:12). They understood baptism to symbolize the death and burial of the old way of life, followed by resurrection to a new life in Christ. When we think of our old life in sin as being dead, we then have a powerful motive to resist sin in our lives today. Today we must consider ourselves dead and unresponsive to the deadly desires of sins of attitude as well as to sins of the flesh. Attitudes lead to action, just like hatred can lead to murder. Jealousy can lead to fighting, and lust can lead to adultery. We must be ourselves, as clean on the inside as we are on the outside when Christ returns again.

MATTHEW 24:37-44

The message in today's Gospel is to be alert, and be prepared for Jesus' return to earth. We call this special time Advent as we prepare for the celebration of the birth of the Christ Child on Christmas Day. As we prepare for this blessed day in our Christian calendar, we need to especially remember that what we are celebrating is the anticipation of Christ coming again on this earth to bring the "Good News" to all who have believed in him. As we are told in today's passage, we are fortunate not to know when that special day comes because we might become lazy in our work for Christ. Some would probably keep on sinning right up to the end and then try to turn to God in the nick of time.

Our goal in life is not just to get to heaven; we also have a commission (Matt. 28:19) right here on earth. We must continue on in our life, living out the reality of God's presence until we see the triumphant return of our Savior. Our Lord's second coming will be instantaneous and there will be no time for last minute repentance or bargaining. The choice we have already made today will determine our destiny. Have you made a choice today to let Jesus Christ become the Lord of your life? In today's passage, Jesus is not telling us about his return to put fear or doubt in our heart. He is not trying to get us into making all kinds of predictions. He is warning us to be prepared. He is giving us a warning of love, because he wants no man or woman to perish.

The bottom line in today's message is: Will you be found faithfully doing his work on the day of his return? We have those who say we can work our way to heaven alone, and others who say we need only faith to be saved. A story was told of a man in a rowboat taking passengers from the dock to the waiting ship. He had painted on one oar "Faith" and on the other oar "Works." When he used only the oar that said "Faith," the boat went in a circle to the left. When he used only the oar marked "Works," the boat still went into a circle, only this time to the right. When he used both oars the boat went ahead to its desired goal. Jesus wants us, in faith, to continue our good works until he comes again in glory.

Application

In the first reading, we saw the emphasis being placed on obedience. The second reading stressed the urgency of changing our lives, and the Gospel tells us to be alert and prepared.

This week, be alert and prepared to do battle against temptation and sin by being obedient to those who are placed in authority over us. Therefore, let us curb our tongue when we are in conversations at work, school or in the privacy of our own home. The example you provide will allow your co-workers, classmates and family to see the gifts and fruits of the Spirit in your life.

SECOND SUNDAY OF ADVENT - CYCLE A

BEFORE YOU BEGIN:

Pray and ask God to speak to you through His Holy Spirit. "THE PARACLETE, THE HOLY SPIRIT WHOM THE FATHER WILL SEND IN MY NAME, WILL INSTRUCT YOU IN EVERYTHING, AND REMIND YOU OF ALL THAT I TOLD YOU." (JOHN 14:26)

FIRST DAY   **Reread last week's readings.**

1.   What was a helpful or new thought from the readings or from the homily you heard on Sunday?

2.   From what you learned, what personal application did you choose to apply to your life this week?

SECOND DAY   **READ ISAIAH 11:1-10**   **FIRST READING**

("The Spirit of the Lord shall rest upon him.")

1.   What shall sprout from the stump of Jesse and of whom is Jesse the father? Isaiah 11:1, 1 Samuel 16:11-13

2.   Who is the sprout? Luke 3:23-33

3.   What shall rest upon him? Isaiah 11:2

4.   Who baptized Jesus and what happened when he was baptized? Mark 1:9-11

5.   What seven things did the Spirit give Jesus? Isaiah 11:2-3

6.   How does he not judge? Isaiah 11:3

7.   Whom does he judge, whom does he strike and how? Isaiah 11:4

8.   What is the band around his waist and the belt upon his hips? Isaiah 11:5

9.   What will then happen? Isaiah 11:6-9

10.   On that day, of what will the earth be full? Isaiah 11:9

11.   What is the root of Jesse set up as, who shall seek him out and why? Isaiah 11:10

Personal - In what way did you have the power of God's Spirit rush on you as Jesus did when John baptized him. How old were you? Jesus was about 30 years old. Luke 3:23

THIRD DAY   **READ ROMANS 15:4-9**   **SECOND READING**

("Welcome one another, then, as Christ welcomed you, for the glory of God.")

1. Why was everything written before our time and what do we derive from this instruction? Romans 15:4

2. What do the words from the scriptures give us? Romans 15:4

3. By whom is Scripture inspired and for what is it useful? 2 Timothy 3:16

4. Of what is God the source and what does he enable us to do? Romans 15:5

5. What does this enable us to do with one heart and voice? Romans 15:6

Personal – In what way are you learning patience from God's Word?

6. What are we to do with one another; why and for what reason? Romans 15:7

Personal – In what way have you accepted those in your family, at work, etc. right where they are? In what way have you been encouraging them in their walk? How have you recognized God's patience toward you?

7. Why did Christ become a minister of the circumcised? Romans 15:8

8. Why do the Gentiles glorify God? Romans 15:9

9. What two things does scripture say we shall do? Romans 15:9

FOURTH DAY   **READ MATTHEW 3:1-12**   **GOSPEL**

("He it is who will baptize you in the Holy Spirit and fire.")

1. Who made his appearance in the desert of Judea, what was he doing and what was his theme? Matthew 3:1-2

2. Who spoke the same message as John? Matthew 4:17

3. When Jesus sent the 12 apostles out for the lost sheep of Israel, what did he tell them to announce? Matthew 10:7

4. How was John dressed and who was going out to him? Matthew 3:4-5

5. What were they doing as they were being baptized by John and to what does repentance lead? Matthew 3:6, Mark 1:4

6. What did John say to the Pharisees and Sadducees who were stepping forward for the baptism, what did he ask them to do, and on what did he tell them not to pride themselves? Matthew 3:7-9

Personal – What evidence can you produce that shows you have repented of the sin of unbelief?

7.   What would be the reason for cutting down a tree? Matthew 3:10

Personal – What kind of fruit are you producing? Ask family, friends or co-workers to evaluate you and have them tell you what kind of fruit they see coming from you.

8.   Why does John baptize in water and how does he see himself next to the one who will follow him? Matthew 3:11

9.   Who is the one to whom John is referring and how will he baptize us? John 1:14-17, Matthew 3:11

10.   What is in his hand and what will he do with it? What will he gather and what will he burn? Matthew 3:12

11.   Who are the ones he will gather and who are the ones who will go into the unquenchable fire? Matthew 12:31-37, Jeremiah 15:7

Personal – Evaluate yourself before you began reading God's Word and now. What changes do you see in yourself?

FIFTH DAY   **READ PSALM 72:1-2, 7-8, 12-13, 17**

("In him all the tribes of the earth shall be blessed.")

Read and meditate on Psalm 72:1-2, 7-8, 12-13, 17

What is the Lord saying to you personally through the Psalm?

How can you apply this to your life?

SIXTH DAY   **READ ALL OF THE COMMENTARY**

ISAIAH 11:1-10

This passage tells us about a new shoot that would grow from the stump of the tree called the royal line of David. The new shoot would be called the Messiah and he would be greater than the original tree (David) and would bear much fruit. This coming Messiah, the perfect king, perfect priest and spiritual king would come from David's line to reign over Israel. He was given the name of "The Lord of Righteousness" (Jeremiah 23:6).

All of us long for fair treatment from others but sadly all of us do not give that fair treatment to others. We hate those who base their judgments on the way people look, talk or even by the color of their skin. We see or read about people being judged on false evidence or hearsay and we hate it. Yet, many times, we ourselves are quick to judge others using those same standards. Christ is the only one who is clothed in truth. He is the only one who is not prejudiced. Jesus is the only one who can be a perfectly fair judge. We need to give our hearts to him completely. Only then can we learn to be as truthful and fair to others as we would want them to be to us.

Today the need to be truthful is needed more than at any other time in history because we are surrounded by so much distortion and outright lies. Satan is the father of lies and he lies to us in his presentation of pornography, drugs, homosexuality and abortion. Peace in the Lord Jesus Christ is the only answer to deceit and conflict, whether it be in a family or a nation. The passage goes on to show wild animals living at peace with one another. Even more incredible is for hostile people to live at peace with one another.

Only in Jesus Christ can hostilities be laid to rest as true love prevails; this is the peace that surpasses all understanding (Philippians 4:7). A golden age was predicted in this passage and it still is to come today and it will when Jesus Christ reigns over the entire earth. We can, until that time, carry out our commission and live to bring others to Jesus Christ, our Lord and Savior (Matthew 28:19).

ROMANS 15:4-9

The deeper the hunger and thirst is to know God's Word in scripture, the more our attitude towards the past, present and future will be affected. Scripture has shown over and over that God has continually kept his promise of salvation to those who believe in him. The more we know of scripture, the more we know about what God has done for us. This leads to a greater confidence in what he will do for us in the days ahead.

Our daily study of the holy scripture followed by prayerful reflection and action will increase our trust that God's will is the best choice for us. We are being called to accept Jesus as our Lord and Savior and this means being in harmony with his teachings and sharing his values and perspectives. We cannot hope to live in harmony with others until we first learn patience, steadiness, and encouragement from Jesus.

We can be in harmony with others only when we have the attitude of Christ (Philippians 2:2-11). We need to develop an attitude of love toward other Christians as well. As we become more capable of maintaining this attitude of love for people of all cultures throughout each day, we will learn how to live in harmony with each other. To live in harmony means to love and respect each other regardless of creed, race or color and regardless of being rich or poor, young or old, sickly or well.

We are called to welcome each other warmly into the church. This means we are to love one another as he has loved us (John 15:12). We are called to affirm each other, and forgive one another. We are called to repent of our sinful actions towards God and man (Mark 1:15). Repentance means to change our lives completely. We are called to make our beloved church not only a haven for saints but a hospital for sinners. Jesus said to us on the cross, "I thirst" (John 19:28) and we are called to satisfy that thirst by loving one another and living in harmony with all of God's creation.

MATTHEW 3:1-12

John came onto the scene like the thundering voice of Almighty God. He courageously spoke out against wrongdoing wherever he saw it. He spoke out against the evil doings of King Herod, living with his brother's wife and against the ritualistic formalism of the self-righteous Sadducees and Pharisees. John spoke out against evil in the state, in the church and in the crowd on the streets. John not only denounced men for the evil they had done, but challenged them to be what could be in accordance with the moral standards of God. Many thought John the Baptist was in reality Elijah who had returned to herald the coming of the

Messiah (King) (Malachi 4:5). John was preparing the way for the King. The preacher, the teacher with the booming prophetic voice, points not at himself, but at God.

John was recognized as a prophet, because he had in him that special authority which clings to the man who comes into the presence of men out of the presence of God. John strongly warns the people that being just the descendants of Abraham does not guarantee their entrance into heaven. To the Israelite, this was an incredible statement because Abraham was unique in his goodness and in his favor with God. John was warning the people that they could not live on the spiritual deeds of the past. He told them that a degenerate age cannot hope to claim salvation for the sake of a heroic past. An evil son cannot hope to plead on the merits of a righteous Father.

We need to reflect on John's presence and his message of warning to our own society. Do we as a people live in obedience to the teachings of Jesus Christ? Do we love one another as he loved us (John 15:12)? Do we practice in our daily living the message that we preach in our churches? Do we expect to be saved because we belong to a certain type of denomination? Do we really believe that Jesus Christ is the only bridge to salvation? The silence of God's voice in today's world of violence, pornography, abortion and drugs is deafening.

The message of John, calling out to the people to make way and prepare themselves for the coming of the Lord, is no less urgent today. John's promise to the people that the baptism of the Holy Spirit would fill them with the fire of love and power was like a measure of cool water given to a man thirsting in the desert (Isaiah 44:3). The Spirit of God is the Spirit of Power. When the Spirit of God enters into a man, his weakness is clothed with the power of God. His tired, lack-lustre, appearance of defeat of life is gone, and a new surge of life enters him. Do you really believe this?

Application

The first reading tells us only the truth can set us free and the truth is Jesus (John 8:32). The second reading reveals scripture has shown over and over that God has kept his promise of salvation to those who believe in him. The Gospel tells us to prepare ourselves, for the kingdom of God is at hand.

This week, let us practice what we preach by keeping a list of the things that we have done throughout the day. Then at evening time, reflect on how close your actions match your words. Try this for one week and get ready for a miracle.

THIRD SUNDAY OF ADVENT – CYCLE A

BEFORE YOU BEGIN:

Pray and ask God to speak to you through His Holy Spirit. "THE PARACLETE, THE HOLY SPIRIT WHOM THE FATHER WILL SEND IN MY NAME, WILL INSTRUCT YOU IN EVERYTHING, AND REMIND YOU OF ALL THAT I TOLD YOU." (JOHN 14:26)

FIRST DAY   **Reread last week's readings.**

1.   What was a helpful or new thought from the readings or from the homily you heard on Sunday?

2.   From what you learned, what personal application did you choose to apply to your life this week?

SECOND DAY   **READ ISAIAH 35:1-6, 10**   **FIRST READING**

("They will meet with joy and gladness.")

1.   What will exult and bloom and for what reason? Isaiah 35:1-2

2.   What is the response to seeing the glory of the Lord? Isaiah 35:2

3.   What are we to do with hands that are feeble and knees that are weak? Isaiah 35:3

4.   What are we to say to those whose hearts are frightened? Isaiah 35:4

5.   Why should we not fear? Is 35:4 41:10 and Zechariah 8:13

6.   What will happen to the eyes of the blind and the ears of the deaf? Isaiah 35:5

7.   What will happen to the lame and the tongue of the dumb? Isaiah 35:6

8.   Who will return and what will they enter Zion doing? Isaiah 35:10

9.   With what will they be crowned, and what will flee from them? Isaiah 35:10

Personal – In what way do those in your family, or your friends or co-workers, see joy and rejoicing in your life? How can you, in a joyful way, show your appreciation for what God has done for you?

THIRD DAY **READ JAMES 5:7-10** **SECOND READING**

("Steady your hearts, because the coming of the Lord is at hand.")

1. What must we be until the coming of the Lord? James 5:7

2. What does the farmer do? James 5:7

3. What must you do and for what reason? James 5:8

4. What does 1 Corinthians 13:4 say about patience?

5. What must you not do and for what reason? James 5:9

6. Who stands at the gate? James 5:9

7. Who is the one to judge us? 1 Corinthians 4:5

8. For what has God set Jesus apart? Acts 10:37-42

9. Who are our models in suffering hardship? James 5:10

10. In whose name did the prophets speak? James 5:10

Personal – In what way have you suffered hardship for speaking the name of Jesus? In what way have you been a model to your family, friends or work associates? How does patience fit into your life? Reflect on this.

FOURTH DAY **READ MATTHEW 11:2-11** **GOSPEL**

("The poor have the good news preached to them.")

1. Where was John when he heard about the works Christ was performing and whom did he send to ask Jesus a question? Matthew 11:2

2. What was John's message and why was he in prison? Matthew 3:1-2 14:3-4

3. What was the question John sent his disciples to ask Jesus? Matthew 11:3

4. What was Jesus' reply, especially noting who has the good news preached to them? Matthew 11:4-5

5. What two things did Jesus say to report to John and who is blest? Matthew 11:4, 6

6. To whom does the reign of God belong? Luke 6:20

Personal – In what way are you being blest by what you hear and see going on around you?

7. As the messengers went off, about whom did Jesus speak to the crowds, and what question did he ask them as to what they were looking for? Matthew 11:7-9

8. As what did Jesus affirm John and what did scripture say about John? Matthew 11:9-10

9. What did Jesus say history has done? Matthew 11:11

10. Whom does Jesus consider greater than John the Baptist? Matthew 11:11

Personal – In what way has Jesus affirmed you by the actions you have taken in dealing with those around you?

FIFTH DAY   **READ PSALM 146:6-10**

("The Lord sets captives free.")

Read and meditate on Psalm 146:6-10.

What is the Lord saying to you personally through the Psalm?

How can you apply this to your life?

SIXTH DAY   **READ ALL OF THE COMMENTARY**

ISAIAH 35:1-6, 10

Isaiah has delivered a message of judgment on all of the nations in almost all of the thirty-four previous chapters. His message includes Judah and Israel consistently rejecting the God of Abraham, Jacob and Moses. There were times of relief and restoration in the history of the chosen people but these seemed to be only at the most crucial times. A small remnant of faithful believers prevailed during these times of God's wrath and judgment.

We see in this passage Isaiah bringing to the people a vision of hope, beauty and encouragement. The people are shown a God of judgment, but also are shown a God of incredible mercy. We see a God that is perfect in his love and complete in his hatred of sin. God has shown his love for all of these he has created through his never ending mercy. Many have failed to respond to his love because of the temptations of the world. He has in his all encompassing love extended his full range of mercy on all who have repented and come back to him. We too enjoy the benefits of his mercy, and we too will be part of the final kingdom, which is described so beautifully in this passage.

This will be the kind of world you and I can look forward to after the judgment, when all of creation will rejoice in God. The talk and times of tribulation end with the beginning of this passage. Life after the final judgment will be peaceful and joyful because we will be "home" praising the living God forever and ever. Even now as we read this, Jesus Christ, our Lord and Savior, is preparing a place for us (John 14:1-6) and he is preparing the road for us. He will walk with us on this road "home". This road will run from the desert of suffering to the blessings of eternal life. It can be traveled only while following God. Our Lord

Jesus will never stop pointing the way for us. He is always beside us as we go. Let us follow that vision. Let our highway be holy. Let us all respond to God's call and lead others on to God's holy highway to heaven.

JAMES 5:7-10

To understand this passage one has to realize that the early church lived in expectation of the immediate second coming of Jesus Christ. James is exhorting the people to be patient for the few short years that remain. He tells about the farmer who has to wait patiently for the early and late rains in order for his crops to mature. The farmer needs much patience to wait until nature does her work, and the Christian needs much patience in his life until Christ comes again. During this time between planting and harvesting, they must confirm their faith, by affirming and helping each other in all the circumstances. A farmer depended greatly on his neighbors to help him at harvest time and support was needed, not criticism.

Today we do not have as many farmers, but we still are busy planting the seeds of life. We too must be ready to help our neighbor, not only in times of harvest, but also in times of disaster. The early church was mistaken in thinking that Jesus would return within a generation, but the call to support and love one another is still a major part of the Christian walk. It is interesting to note that both the Christians and the farmers must live by faith. Many people blame others when things begin to go wrong in their life (Genesis 3:12, 13). Our reluctance to own up to our own share of responsibility causes many to strike out and blame others. This method is easier and more visible, but it is also destructive and sinful.

We need to reflect on what is being said in this passage and apply it to our own lives. What is being said is that before any of us judges others we should be very much aware that Christ, the ultimate judge, will come to evaluate us (Matthew 7:1-5). Our patience needs to be in our ability to put the needs of others before our own. We also need to pray for courage; that will sustain us in the battle against sin. It is only as we go through the trials and sufferings that we gain the grace and courage of patience. History has shown us how much the prophets of the Old and New Testament have patiently suffered for the love of Jesus Christ. We who are called to the Christian walk can expect our cross of suffering which we in faith and patience will carry everywhere that the people cry out "I thirst."

MATTHEW 11:2-11

John the Baptist's career had ended in shambles. He was now in prison, put there by King Herod. John never sought to soften the truth and was incapable of seeing evil without taking a stand against it. King Herod stole his brother's wife and lived with her in sin. John spoke out fearlessly and Herod took his revenge. John reflected while in prison about whether Jesus really was the Messiah. John thought that his role was to be out preaching to the people and preparing them for Jesus. How could he do this while in jail? Sounds kind of familiar, doesn't it?

Many times in our lives we think that we are being blocked from doing what we think is the best way to go. We may be stopped by poor health, old age or even lack of natural ability to do what we think the Lord is calling us to do. Jesus answered John's doubts by telling him to look around and see what was being done in the community. The blind were able to see, the deaf able to hear. Lepers were being cured and people were being raised from the dead and preaching the good news. Jesus' answer to John was the kingdom of God is at hand (Mark 1:15). Jesus' identity was obvious to John when he heard the answer that Jesus sent him.

We too need to reflect on our own salvation and our own level of doubt. We need only to look at the evidence in scripture and the changes in our own life. We have seen how he has forgiven us of our sins and when we doubt, we do not need to turn from him. In fact, when we have feelings of doubt then we should turn completely to him. We need to observe John and see who and what he was. He was a man who lived in the desert and was very close to the earth. He had no fancy clothes and he ate no exotic food. Some of the people thought he was mad, yet they flocked to hear and see him. He spoke with authority and humility. He was abrasive to the lawless and in total submission to Christ. Today John's style would probably be laughed out of town because his message was too simple and too clear. John's basic message was "Repent, the kingdom of God is at hand" (Mark 1:15).

Many people today do not want to repent because "repent" means a complete change of life. We are all sinners (Romans 3:23) and we are all called to repent. Fall on your knees and be still and listen to our God (Psalm 46:10). Then ask him to create in you a new clean heart that is filled with clean thoughts and desires (Psalm 51:10). John's message was "Good News" and that was that Jesus was the long awaited Messiah and he had come to begin God's personal reign on earth. Jesus offered freedom to the poor, the oppressed, and the hopeless, and he does no less than that even today. So repent and be of good cheer, for the kingdom of God is surely at hand.

Application

The first reading shows a God that is just and merciful. The second reading tells us that patience is a godly virtue, and the Gospel reveals a call to repentance now!

This week, let your actions speak for themselves in your home, work, and school area. Patience and kindness are clear signs of love. To repent means to change. Start being humble and patient today. Let others be the first in line, the first to eat, the first to speak. Be the first to give and give freely. Your witness will be a tremendous sign that "the kingdom of God is at hand."

FOURTH SUNDAY OF ADVENT - CYCLE A

BEFORE YOU BEGIN:

Pray and ask God to speak to you through His Holy Spirit. "THE PARACLETE, THE HOLY SPIRIT WHOM THE FATHER WILL SEND IN MY NAME, WILL INSTRUCT YOU IN EVERYTHING, AND REMIND YOU OF ALL THAT I TOLD YOU." (JOHN 14:26)

FIRST DAY   **Reread last week's readings.**

1.   What was a helpful or new thought from the readings or from the homily you heard on Sunday?

2.   From what you learned, what personal application did you choose to apply to your life this week?

SECOND DAY   **READ ISAIAH 7:10-14**   **FIRST READING**

("Therefore the Lord himself will give you this sign.")

1.   To whom did the Lord speak and through whom did he speak? Isaiah 7:10 & Isaiah 7:3

2.   Who is Ahaz? Isaiah 7:1

3.   For what was Ahaz to ask God? Isaiah 7:11

4.   What was Ahaz's answer to this question? Isaiah 7:12

5.   What did Isaiah say to Ahaz? Isaiah 7:13

6.   What did the Lord give Ahaz? Isaiah 7:14

7.   What was the sign he gave him? Isaiah 7:14

8.   What did the Pharisees and teachers of the law say to Jesus, and what was his answer? Matthew 12:38-40

9.   What was the sign given to the shepherds? Luke 2:12, 16-17

PersonalTHIRD DAY   **READ ROMANS 1:1-7**   **SECOND READING**

("Through him we have been favored with apostleship.")

1.   Who was sending greetings and how does he refer to himself? Romans 1:1

2.   What is he called to be and for what is he set apart? Romans 1:1

3. Where is recorded what he promised long ago through his prophets? Romans 1:2

4. Whom is the Gospel concerning, from whom did he descend and how did he descend from him? Romans 1:3

5. How was he made Son of God? Romans 1:4

6. For what two reasons have you been called? Romans 1:5

7. What are we to spread concerning his name? Acts 4:12

8. To whom have we been called to belong? Romans 1:6

9. To whom was Paul speaking? Romans 1:7

10. To what did he say they had been called and what does he greet them with from God our Father and the Lord Jesus Christ? Romans 1:7

Personal – In what way do you see yourself called to spread the name of Jesus just as Paul was? How can you become an apostle for Jesus to your family and friends?

FOURTH DAY   **READ MATTHEW 1:18-24**   **GOSPEL**

("She is to have a son and you are to name him Jesus because he will save his people from their sins.")

1. How did the birth of Jesus Christ come about? Matthew 1:18

2. Through the power of whom was Mary found to be with child? Matthew 1:18

3. Who was Joseph and what kind of a man was he? Matthew 1:19

4. What was Joseph's intention, how did the angel of the Lord appear to him, and what did he say to him? Matthew 1:19-20

5. When was another time an angel appeared to Joseph in a dream, what did he tell him to do, and what was his response? Matthew 2:13-14

6. What did the angel say Mary would have, what was she to name him, and for what reason? Matthew 1:21

7. Why did all this happen, who was the prophet, and what did he say? Matthew 1:22, Isaiah 7:14

8. What does his name mean and what did Joseph do when he awoke? Matthew 1:23-24, Isaiah 8:8, 10

9. As Joseph recognized God speaking to him through an angel, what did his obedience show? John 14:21

10.   What did he not do before Mary bore a son, and what did Joseph name the child? Matthew 1:25

11.   What do the following scriptures say about the name of Jesus? John 14:13, Acts 2:21 and 4:12, Philippians 2:9-10

Personal – When and where do you experience the presence of God the most in your life? What do you need to do to experience "Immanuel, God is with you" more completely in your life? How often do you think, feel, experience and call upon the name of Jesus in your everyday life?

FIFTH DAY   **READ PSALM 24:1-6**

("He shall receive a blessing from the Lord.")

Read and meditate on Psalm 24:1-6.

What is the Lord saying to you personally through the Psalm?

How can you apply this to your life?

SIXTH DAY   **READ ALL OF THE COMMENTARY**

ISAIAH 7:10-14

This passage shows us the incredible generosity of God in his urging Ahaz to ask him for a sign. This sign would show Ahaz that God wanted to protect him and crush his enemies. The King refused and appeared almost righteous by stating that he would not test God with a sign. The truth of the matter was that God had told him to ask but Ahaz was not really sure what God would say. Many of us use the same excuse, saying that we do not want to bother God with our puny problems. This keeps us from being realistic and communicating honestly with him.

We need to seriously remember and hold fast to the scripture in 1 Corinthians 2:9: "Eye has not seen, ear has not heard, nor has it so much as dawned on man what God has prepared for those who love him." God loves us so much that he is constantly giving us signs of his presence and love. We need to reflect for a moment on how many times he has been present to us in the form of other people who are in our lives. God gave Ahaz and all of us the greatest sign of all time. He stated that a child shall be born to a virgin and she shall call him "Immanuel." This means "God is with us" and he will always be with us even to the end of time (Matt. 28:20). This was a great prophecy of the Messiah.

Jewish people waited for over seven hundred years and when Christ was born in a lowly cave and took on the role of a helpless infant, the sign of all signs was ignored and missed by the non- believers. There are many people in the world today who are non- believers and who are looking for a sign. You are that sign, you are called to be that light. You are called to be an ambassador for God. They will know God is present by the sign of the way we love one another.

ROMANS 1:1-7

This passage was written by Paul who had not yet been to Rome. It was unthinkable to hear a Roman citizen call himself a slave; and yet, that is what Paul called himself, a slave to Jesus Christ. Paul chose to be completely obedient and dependent on his beloved Jesus. We need to reflect on our own attitude toward Christ. Is Christ your Master? Are you dependent on and obedient to Jesus Christ? Paul tells about Jesus being part of the Jewish royal line and being born and then dying and rising from the dead. Paul believed totally that Jesus was the promised Messiah, and the resurrected Lord. Paul tells the Romans of his agreement with the teaching of all scripture and of the traditional oral teaching of the apostles. Paul really emphasizes that God's grace is an undeserved privilege and that it is also accompanied by a responsibility to share God's forgiveness with others. This is our responsibility, to witness to the world. God may never call you to witness overseas, but he is calling you to witness where you are now. Rome was the capital of the world. The city was wealthy, literary, and artistic. It was a cultural center but in terms of morality, it was dying. Many great cities in the world are facing that same fate today. Christianity was at odds with many elements in the Roman culture.

The Romans trusted in their military power to protect them against their enemies. Does this type of thinking sound familiar? Christians were being exhorted to hold fast to their views on morality. We might well look around our own society and see whether the traditional family values such as sanctity of life, marriage, and chastity are being threatened by a godless way of life. Paul showed his love toward the Roman church by expressing God's love for them, and we need to do just that too. We need to reach out and affirm our church leaders and tell them that we love them and support them in this ministry. We need to witness to Jesus' commandment to "Love one another as I have loved you" (John 13:34).

MATTHEW 1:18-24

This passage addresses why a virgin birth is so important to the people of the Christian faith. Because Jesus was born of a woman, he was fully human. Also being the Son of God, he was both fully human and divine. We can relate totally with Jesus because he was human and he was like us and because he experienced every kind of temptation we experience today. In his whole life, Jesus never committed a sin. Because of this he understands our weakness and he offers us his forgiveness.

We can approach God with a reverence and yet boldness when we pray because we know that he truly understands our complete needs. We do not need to feel uncomfortable when we go before the Lord in prayer, as he loves us so much and he has been where we are now, and has the ability to help us. We need to understand the importance of the virgin birth in order to accept the situation that surrounded the birth of Jesus Christ. Mary was betrothed to Joseph when she became pregnant, and Joseph was confronted with only a few options to resolve the issue of his bride-to-be being pregnant, but not by him.

The Jewish marriage was the culmination of three stages. The first was when the couple became engaged, generally after their families agreed to their union. Later on, when a public announcement was made, the couple became "betrothed." This was considered binding and broken only by divorce or death. There was no sexual relationship allowed however, until after the couple was married. The "betrothal" time was planning where to live, stocking the place with furniture, etc. Mary's pregnancy displayed an apparent unfaithfulness that carried a severe social stigma. Joseph had a right according to Jewish law either to divorce her or to have her stoned in front of her father's house (Deut. 22:23, 24). Joseph was told in a dream to follow God's will and to take Mary for his wife. He was told by the Lord that Mary had conceived this child by the power of the Holy Spirit. Reflect for a moment how you would react to this type of a situation. Joseph chose to obey God's command to marry her in spite of the obvious humiliation that they both experienced through the towns people. Joseph's actions revealed several admirable qualities that the young men of today would do well to emulate. He displayed a stern principle, discretion and sensitivity. He was very responsive to God and displayed tremendous self-discipline.

Joseph took God's option and that was to marry Mary. God shows us that if we obey him, he will show us more options on how to live according to his will than we think possible. We must never forget that God took on the limitations of humanity so he could live and die for the salvation of all who believe in him.

Application

The first reading shows us that God wants us to communicate (prayer) with him so that he can shower us with his incredible generosity. The second reading tells us that obedience and dependency on Jesus Christ is the only way to freedom. The Gospel reveals that boldness and reverence are what he wants from us in prayer.

Get down on your knees and thank Christ for coming to earth so that he could die on the cross for your sins. Then ask him to take control of your life and ask the members of your family to join you as you fall on your knees and give him praise and adoration for coming to be with you. That is why they called him "Immanuel."

HOLY FAMILY – CYCLE A

BEFORE YOU BEGIN:

Pray and ask God to speak to you through His Holy Spirit. "THE PARACLETE, THE HOLY SPIRIT WHOM THE FATHER WILL SEND IN MY NAME, WILL INSTRUCT YOU IN EVERYTHING, AND REMIND YOU OF ALL THAT I TOLD YOU." (JOHN 14:26)

FIRST DAY   **Reread last week's readings.**

1.   What was a helpful or new thought from the readings or from the homily you heard on Sunday?

2.   From what you learned, what personal application did you choose to apply to your life this week?

SECOND DAY   **READ SIRACH 3:2-6, 12-14**   **FIRST READING**

("He who honors his father atones for sins.")

1.   Where does the Lord place a father over his children, and what does he confirm over sons? Sirach 3:2

2.   What happens to him who honors his father? Sirach 3:3

3.   What do we store up when we revere our mother? Sir 3:4

4.   By what is the man gladdened who honors his father and what happens when he prays? Sirach 3:5

5.   What will happen to him who reveres his father? Sir 3:6, Exodus 20:12

6.   What is he doing who brings comfort to his mother? Sir 3:6

7.   What are we to do and what are we not to do when our father gets old? Sirach 3:12

8.   To whom are we to listen, for what reason, and whom are we not to despise? Proverbs 23:22

9.   How are we to treat our father even if his mind fails? Sirach 3:13

10.   What will not be forgotten and as what will it serve? Sirach 3:14

Personal – In what way do you listen to and honor both your earthly father and your heavenly Father? In what way has your earthly father become a burden to you in his old age? Compare your relationship with your heavenly Father and your earthly father and repent where necessary.

| THIRD DAY | READ COLOSSIANS 3:12-21 | SECOND READING |

("You children obey your parents in everything as the acceptable way in the Lord.")

1. With what five things are we to clothe ourselves, and for what reason?
   Colossians 3:12

2. What are these five qualities called, according to Galatians 5:22?

3. What are we to do with one another, what are we to do over any grievance we
   may have for anyone and why are we to forgive? Colossians 3:13

4. What did Jesus say as he was dying on the cross and to whom was he speaking?
   Luke 23:34

5. In the Lord's Prayer, what are we saying and what is the Father saying?
   Matthew 6:12-15

Personal - How have you sinned and received the forgiveness of God? In what way is that reflected by the way you forgive others when they have hurt you?

6. What virtue do we put on over all the rest? Colossians 3:14

7. What must reign in our hearts, of what are we members, what are we called, and
   to what must we dedicate ourselves? Colossians 3:15

8. What must dwell in us, how are we to treat one another and how are we to sing
   gratefully to God? Colossians 3:16

9. Whatever we do, in speech or action, in whose name are we to do it, and to
   whom are we to give thanks? Col 3:17

10. How are husbands to act towards their wives and how are wives to act towards
    their husbands? Colossians 3:18-19

11. How are children to act towards their parents and fathers towards children?
    Colossians 3:20-21

Personal - What do you think is the biggest cause of break-up in the family today? How do you think this can be remedied? In what way are you obeying or disobeying what God says in Colossians 3:18-21? Reflect on this and make changes where necessary. Remember, we receive grace from the sacrament of reconciliation.

| FOURTH DAY | READ MATTHEW 2:13-15, 19-23 | GOSPEL |

("Get up, take the child and his mother, and set out for the land of Israel.")

1. After the astrologers left, how did the angel of the Lord appear to Joseph and what
   was his command? Matthew 2:13

2. How did Joseph respond to his command? Matthew 2:14

3. How long did he stay in Egypt and what did the Lord say through the prophet Hosea? Matthew 2:15, Hosea 11:1

4. After Herod's death, what happened to Joseph? Matthew 2:19

5. What other time did Joseph have a dream and was given instructions by the Lord? Matthew 1:20

6. What was the command given him? Matthew 2:20

7. How did Joseph respond to this command? Matthew 2:21

8. What had Joseph heard, causing him to fear to return to Bethlehem? Matthew 2:22

9. How was he warned, and to what region did he go? Matt 2:22

10. In what town did they settle and what was fulfilled? Matthew 2:23

Personal - Joseph listened and responded to the Word of God. in what ways have you heard the Lord speak to you and you obeyed? What ways has he spoken to you personally? List all the ways God speaks to us.

FIFTH DAY   **READ PSALM 128:1-5**

("Happy are those who fear the Lord and walk in his ways.")

Read and meditate on Psalm 128:1-5.

What is the Lord saying to you personally through the Psalm?

How can you apply this to your life?

SIXTH DAY   **READ ALL OF THE COMMENTARY**

Today we are celebrating the special Feast of the Holy Family. We see in our reading how the power and love of holy families can change a dark world into a community of light.

SIRACH 3:2-6, 12-14

Sirach was a pious, learned Jew who lived in the second century B.C. He wrote a collection of sayings to help others live their lives in accordance with God's Holy Word. In today's passage he speaks of family. He shows us that the family unit has been honored as the foundation of the human race. The foundation of the family was traditionally the father and he had the place of honor. The father was given the right to be respected and obeyed by his family. The mother also shares the authority with the father in the home. The authority of both parents, in accordance with God's word, is to be respected by their children.

This passage really applies very strongly to today's families because the family structure is under a severe attack by Satan through certain groups and different aspects of our society's values. Children who respect their parents are not only doing God's will, but also are storing up spiritual rewards for themselves. Over the centuries it has been shown that children who respect their parents generally have children who will respect them. We see that prayer is very important for a family's growth and that all prayer is answered. The call to love, honor and respect our parents carries with it a promise of God's blessing. A long life was a sign of God's blessing in the Hebrew world and it signified that we were dedicated to God's will.

Children are called to give their aging parents loving care and the child who has learned to respect his parents is respecting God. No matter how feeble, mentally or physically, one's parents may become, it is the children's privilege and responsibility to care for them. This is not some social health care's program slogan, instead, it is a clear statement of responsibility that is in accordance with God's Holy Word. God wants love, kindness, respect, honor, sacrifice, comfort, safety, etc.

COLOSSIANS 3:12-21

Paul wrote this letter while imprisoned in Rome. He was told by a follower of his called Epaphras, that recent converts to the Christian faith were being disturbed by false teachers. Paul's letter spells out some very practical rules for Christian living. We are told to clothe ourselves with compassion, kindness, lowliness, meekness and patience. Paul is telling them that these virtues must be secure in their hearts in order for the community to live out the Christian vision. Forgiveness was a main virtue of a Christian, and this is what separated him from the non-believer. God wiped out all our sins in baptism and is constantly waiting to wash away the sins of a repentant sinner in the sacrament of reconciliation. We also must imitate God and be willing to forgive a repentant brother or sister.

Paul again shows us as a body, and with Christ as the head, and as the source of unity, harmony and peace. We hear that it is not enough to know the doctrine of Christ, rather we must live it and our lives must be witnesses of good-bearing fruit. Today, as then, we are called to help each member of the family of God. Paul deals with the family by telling the wife to be subject to the spiritual authority of her husband. Children are called to obey their parents. Paul tells the husband to "love your wife." This may sound common today, but in Paul's times, wives were not considered much more than "chattel" or prized goods. Wives had no rights and a wife was the property of the husband. Paul's call to "love your wife" brings her into equality and a full sharing in the authority of the family. Paul finally tells fathers not to provoke their children. The authority of a father comes from God and this authority is to lead, to love, and to serve his family, not to drive them into the ground. A loving father leads his children by serving them in the name of the Lord. A loving father puts on the mind of Christ (Philippians 2:2-5).

MATTHEW 2:13-15, 19-23

Herod's actions were those of a desperate person. He killed all the Jewish boys under the age of two, in a desperate attempt to prevent this so-called newborn king from taking his throne away. Herod was not successful because his act was a twisted human act. Jesus was a king by divine action. We need to see in this that no one can distort or prevent God's plan. People hurt only themselves in trying to do so.

Joseph received from God a second dream. His first dream revealed to him that Mary was carrying in her body the "Messiah" (1:20). His second dream showed him how to protect his family and to leave immediately for Egypt. Joseph's heart was open because he was prepared in his relationship with God. He continued to be open and receptive to God's guidance. We need to ask ourselves whether we are open to God's guidance, and would we move like Joseph did, if God called us to do so.

The trip to Egypt was in itself not so unusual, because many colonies of Jews lived there. The trip was about 12 days traveling on hard roads with cold lonely nights and very little comfort. There is an interesting parallel between the Holy Family's flight to Egypt and Israel's history. When Israel was young, she went to Egypt, as Joseph, Mary and Jesus did. God led Israel out (Hosea 11:1) and God brought the Holy Family back. God continues to save his people even today.

Today's Gospel shows how strong love and obedience are tied together. We also see that the foundation of a family is the father. Joseph's loyalty and protection of Mary and Jesus were directly connected to his being obedient to God's command. Joseph is a role model that all husbands and fathers can imitate. God's wish is that all families be holy and all holy families be in complete obedience to God's Holy Word. How holy is your family?

Application

The first reading tells us that the human family has been honored as the foundation of the human race. The second reading reveals to us the danger of false teachers being as real today as it was in his time. The Gospel shows us that no one can distort or prevent God's plan.

Fathers, take some time each day to read God's Holy Word and see what it is saying about the family. **Parents**, give your children the example of obedience by being obedient to God in your manner of talk. No bickering, no nagging, no slandering, and no gossip. **Children,** obey your parents in everything and speak to them with respect, kindness and joy. God wants you to have a Holy Family, too.

EPIPHANY OF THE LORD - CYCLE A

BEFORE YOU BEGIN

Pray and ask God to speak to you through His Holy Spirit. "THE PARACLETE, THE HOLY SPIRIT WHOM THE FATHER WILL SEND IN MY NAME, WILL INSTRUCT YOU IN EVERYTHING, AND REMIND YOU OF ALL THAT I TOLD YOU." (JOHN 14:26)

FIRST DAY   **Reread last week's readings.**

1.   What was a helpful or new thought from the readings or from the homily you heard on Sunday?

2.   From what you learned, what personal application did you choose to apply to your life this week?

SECOND DAY   **READ ISAIAH 60:1-6**   **FIRST READING**

("But upon you the Lord shines.")

1.   To what are the Israelites being called, whose light has come, and what shines upon the Israelites? Isaiah 60:1

2.   How did the glory of the Lord appear in the following scriptures?
      Exodus 16:7, 10
      Exodus 24:16, 17
      Leviticus 9:6, 23, 24
      Ezekiel 3:12-13
      Luke 2:9

Personal – In your life, in what way has "the glory of the Lord" appeared to you?

3.   What covers the earth and the unbelievers? Isaiah 60:2

4.   Upon whom does the Lord shine, and what appears over them? Isaiah 60:2

5.   Fill in the blank: Nations shall walk by your _____ and kings by your shining radiance. Isaiah 60:3

6.   Who is the light? John 8:12

7.   Why must we raise our eyes, and who comes to the light? Isaiah 60:4

8.   Who shall be radiant, whose heart shall overflow, and what will happen to the sea and the nations? Isaiah 60:5

9.   What will the camels do, and from where will they come? Isaiah 60:6

10.   What shall they bear, and what will they be proclaiming? Isaiah 60:6

Personal - In what way is the light of Christ shining through you in your family, your work, and your environment? Are people drawn to you because they see that light within you?

THIRD DAY	READ EPHESIANS 3:2-3, 5-6	SECOND READING

("In Christ Jesus the Gentiles are now co-heirs with the Jews.")

1.   Who heard of the ministry which God gave Paul, and for whose regard? Ephesians 3:2, Ephesians 2:11

2.   What was revealed? Ephesians 3:3

3.   What was unknown to men in former ages? Ephesians 3:4-5

4.   Who has revealed this mystery, and to whom was this mystery revealed? Ephesians 3:5

5.   Read the following scriptures: John 14:26, Acts 11:12, 1 Corinthians 2:13

Personal - Do you listen each day for the Holy Spirit's instructions for you? What has he taught you as you have been reading his word? Remember to pray before you read God's word, asking the Holy Spirit to teach you and give you wisdom, knowledge, and obedience to follow his plan for your life.

6.   Who were some of the holy apostles and prophets, and by whom were they sent? Isaiah 1:1, Jeremiah 1:1, John 1:35-50, Romans 1:1

7.   What is the mystery revealed? Ephesians 3:6-8

8.   How do the Gentiles and the Jews become co-heirs? Ephesians 3:6

9.   Whom has God commissioned to preach the Gospel? Ephesians 3:6 Matthew 28:18-20

Personal - In what way have you ever felt called to teach or share God's Word with others? A good beginning is to share with your spouse, children or a close friend how the Lord has touched you in his Word or from the homily on Sunday.

FOURTH DAY	READ MATTHEW 2:1-12	GOSPEL

("They prostrated themselves and did him homage.")

1.   Where was Jesus born, who was king at that time, and who arrived from the east? Matthew 2:1

2.   Read the following scriptures: Daniel 2:27 and Daniel 4:4. According to these verses, are those who read the stars able to know God's plan for their lives?

3.   Who is the only sign we follow? Isaiah 7:14 Luke 11:30

4.   For whom were the astrologers searching, and what did they observe? Matthew 2:2

5.   How did King Herod react, and who reacted along with him? Matthew 2:3

6.   Whom did King Herod summon, and what did he inquire of them? Matthew 2:4

7.   What did the chief priest and scribes tell Herod, and to what prophet were they referring? Matthew 2:5, Micah 1:1 5:1

8.   What is the ruler to do? Matthew 2:6

9.   Read the following and write out your favorite verse: John 10:11, John 10:14, John 10:16, Acts 20:28, 1 Peter 2:25, 1 Peter 5:3-4, Revelation 7:17

Personal - Share the scripture you chose and tell how it has affected your life.

10.   What did King Herod find out from the astrologers? Matthew 2:7

11.   Where did he send them, and what were his instructions to them? Matthew 2:8

12.   What was the astrologer's reaction to the star as they followed it? Matthew 2:10

Personal - Have you had any insight to God's light in his Word? What is your reaction to this?

13.   When the astrologers found the child with his mother, Mary, what did they do? Is this in fulfillment of the Old Testament prophesy? Matthew 2:11, Isaiah 60:5-6

Personal - Have you bowed before the Lord? How have you prostrated yourself in homage before our Holy God? In his presence in the Eucharist, have you knelt to do him homage, or do you do it just out of habit? Reflect on this.

FIFTH DAY   **READ PSALM 72:1-13**

("For he shall rescue the poor man when he cries out.")

Read and meditate on Psalm 72:1-13.

What is the Lord saying to you personally through the Psalm?

How can you apply this to your daily spiritual life?

SIXTH DAY   **READ ALL THE COMMENTARY**

ISAIAH 60:1-6

This week's reading from Isaiah comes from a section sometimes called Third Isaiah (Chapters 55-66), and is generally considered to be written by an unknown poet. The time of this passage is about 535 B.C. and it prophesies the role of the temple and offers to open its doors to all other nations. The invitation was given to the whole world to join the ranks of Israel as the Lord's chosen people.

Isaiah is calling on the people to rise up in the splendor and radiance of the Lord (verse 1). He tells them that the glory of the Lord shines in them and through them (verse 3). He urges them to be confident in that love and they will become leaders of all nations and many from all nations will be drawn to them (verses 4-5).

Today we are being called to rise up and become symbols of light and hope. We are called to be a light to a world that is covered with much darkness. We can be a light to the world only as long as we walk in the light of Christ. Each one of us is called by the Psalmist (Psalm 119:105) to be a light unto each other's path. We are being called today, as in the time of Isaiah, to let the glory of God's light shine through all of us.

EPHESIANS 3:2-3,5-6

Paul wrote this letter while in prison awaiting trial before Nero. He reflects on his mission to the Gentiles (those who do not believe in the Jewish faith), and he speaks about his own conversion as being a great mystery of Christ.

Paul was on a journey to Damascus to persecute disciples of the Lord when suddenly a light flashed around him that seemed to come from heaven. He was challenged by the Lord to stop persecuting him and to come follow him. Paul did and his whole life changed. He uses that conversion experience to bring others to the Lord (Acts 9:3-9). He claimed his place as an apostle because he was an eyewitness to the Lord during his "metanoia" or conversion experience.

Paul gained a deeper understanding of God's plan of salvation through Christ. He reveals to us in this letter that into his life had come the great secret of God. That secret was that the love and mercy and grace of God were meant not for the Jews alone, but for all mankind. When Paul met Christ on the road to Damascus there was a sudden flash of revelation that affected his whole life. That "metanoia" is open to all of us, and we are being called to bring to the world that same message. It was to the Gentiles that God sent Paul, to open their eyes that they might turn from darkness to light. We hear Paul stating very boldly that God's love and mercy are given to all, Jews and Gentiles alike.

MATTHEW 2:1-12

We celebrate the feast of Epiphany, which means the visitation of the seekers or as they are often called, the Magi, and Christ's manifestation of his glory to them. It was in Bethlehem, a little town six miles south of Jerusalem, that Jesus was born.

The name Bethlehem means "house of bread," and the manger in which Jesus slept was used to feed the animals. It is significant that Jesus was born in a place called "house of bread," as he chose to feed us with his Word and in his presence in the Eucharist. He calls himself "Living Bread," in John 6:35-66, and we share his living bread in our liturgies in accordance with scripture (Luke 22:14-20), in churches throughout the world.

Bethlehem was where Jacob buried Rachel (Genesis 48:7) and it was there that Ruth married Boaz (Ruth 4:13). This city was the home of David (1 Sam. 16:1, 17:12, 20:6) and it was in Bethlehem that the Jews expected God's Anointed One to come into the world (Micah 5:1-2). When Jesus was born, there came to Bethlehem seekers from the east to do him homage. The Magi were holy and wise men and were skilled in philosophy, medicine, natural sciences, soothsaying, and interpretation of dreams. Many later became members of a tribe of pagan priests in Persia and functioned much like the Levite priests in Israel.

About the same time that Jesus was born, the Roman poet, Virgil, was praising through his writings and poems the "savior of the world," the emperor, Augustus Caesar of Rome. So it was to a waiting world that Jesus came and the astrologers from lands far away gathered at his cradle. It was the first sign and symbol of the world's conquest by Jesus Christ.

Today many of the learned men and women are coming to praise the King of Kings, Jesus; but many are not. What about you? Is Jesus your King and are you bringing him your presence as a gift? We need to reflect on the gift given to all who believe in the Christ Child of Bethlehem. The gift is being co-heirs of his kingdom, members of the one body and sharers of the promise. Have we made someone feel like an unwanted stranger? Have we dared label anyone a foreigner, alien, outsider, or pagan? Have we welcomed all to our "manger scene?" Is the light in our hearts drawing others to him, as the star did in Bethlehem? The manifestation of the star's brilliance spoke to the Magi of the entry of a King into the world. The glory of God's love for all is called to be manifested in us through the power of the Holy Spirit and in the saving name of Jesus Christ.

Application

Isaiah urges us to look at the glory of God being unfolded before us, and calls upon the people to rise up from the shackles of captivity. In Ephesians Paul describes God's secret plan, and in Matthew we see the wise men overjoyed at the results of following the star.

This week, like the wise men or Magi, let us bring Jesus our gift. Yours might be a gift of joy or love, peace or patience, etc. Then you need to share this gift with someone in your family or work place. The wise men came in humility and left encouraged and full of hope. We can expect no less, when we bring Jesus our gift.

BAPTISM OF THE LORD - CYCLE A

BEFORE YOU BEGIN

Pray and ask God to speak to you through His Holy Spirit. "THE PARACLETE, THE HOLY SPIRIT WHOM THE FATHER WILL SEND IN MY NAME, WILL INSTRUCT YOU IN EVERYTHING, AND REMIND YOU OF ALL THAT I TOLD YOU." (JOHN 14:26)

FIRST DAY   **Reread last week's readings.**

1.   What was a helpful or new thought from the readings or from the homily you heard on Sunday?

2.   From what you learned, what personal application did you choose to apply to your life this week?

SECOND DAY   **READ ISAIAH 42:1-4, 6-7**   **FIRST READING**

("Here is my servant whom I uphold,")

1.   Fill in the blanks in the following scripture:
"Here is my _____ whom I uphold, my
_____ with whom I am pleased, upon whom I have put my
_____ ; he shall bring forth _____ to the
nations." Isaiah 42:1

2.   To whom do the following scriptures refer?
Luke 1:38, 48 _____, John 12:26 _____,
Acts 3:13 _____, Acts 4:29-30 _____.

Personal – Do you see yourself as a servant of the Lord Jesus Christ in your home or at work? Share how you are a servant of him.

3.   Who are the chosen ones? Read the following scriptures:

1 Chronicles 16:13 _____, Tobit 13:11 _____,
Psalm 89:3-4 _____, Psalm 106:23 _____,
Ephesians 1:3-5 _____.

Personal – Do you feel you are among the chosen ones of God?

4.   In the following scriptures, who are receiving the Spirit or have the Spirit of God working through them?

2 Samuel 23:1-2 _____, Matthew 3:16 _____,
John 20:19-22 _____, Acts 8:14-19 _____.

Personal – Do you have the power of the Holy Spirit working in your life? If not, read Matthew 7:7-8 and see what you have to do to receive this power.

5.   In the following scriptures, who brings forth justice to the nations?

Deuteronomy 10:17-18 _____,
Psalm 9:8-9 _____, Acts 17:31 _____.

6.   In what way was this prophecy in Isaiah 42:1-4 fulfilled? Matthew 12:16-21

7.   Whom has God grasped by the hand, formed, and set as a covenant of the people? Isaiah 42:6

8.   Whom has he made a light to the nations, and what are we to do? Isaiah 42:6-7

Personal – In what way are you a light to others? Do those in your family, your work, and your environment see the love of Christ shining out of you? If you are yielding to the Spirit of God dwelling in you, others will see the light.

THIRD DAY   **READ ACTS 10:34-38**   **SECOND READING**

("I begin to see how true it is that God shows no partiality.")

1.   Who was addressing the people, and what did he say? Acts 10:34

2.   In the following scriptures, what does God's Word say about showing partiality?
Leviticus 19:15 _____,
2 Chronicles 19:7 _____, Wisdom 6:7 _____.

3.   What must we do to become acceptable to God? Acts 10:35

4.   What does it mean to fear God? Daniel 6:27, Isaiah 8:13, Malachi 2:5

5.   Through whom is the Good News proclaimed, and who is the Lord of all? Acts 10:36

6.   What was reported all over Judea about Jesus, and where did it begin? Acts 10:37-38

7.   What was the baptism John preached? Matthew 3:11, Acts 19:4

8.   Who anointed Jesus, and with what? Acts 10:38

9.   Did God intend for us to be anointed with the Holy Spirit? John 14:14-17

10. What is one of the functions of the Holy Spirit? John 14:25-26

11. What did Jesus go about doing, and who was with him? Acts 10:38

Personal – When you receive the Holy Spirit, do you also receive the power to go about doing good works and healing as Jesus did? Is this evident in your life?

FOURTH DAY	READ MATTHEW 3:13-17	GOSPEL

("…he saw the Spirit of God descending like a dove coming upon him.")

1. From where was Jesus coming, and where did he appear before John? Locate this on your bible map Matthew 3:13

2. Who was John? Luke 1:13-17

3. What was Jesus' purpose in coming to John at the Jordan? Matthew 3:13

4. What did John try to do, and why did he protest? Matthew 3:14

5. What was Jesus' answer? Matthew 3:15

Personal – Do you see Jesus as being obedient to his Father in coming to John to be baptized? How are you obedient to the Father in your walk with him?

6. What did John do? Was this a sign of obedience? Matthew 3:15

7. After Jesus was baptized, what happened? Matthew 3:16-17, Mark 1:10-11

8. Read and write out the following: Matthew 17:5

9. In the last two answers, Jesus is referred to by God the Father as his Beloved. What do the following scriptures say?

    Romans 11:28

    1 Thessalonians 1:4

    1 John 3:2

    Colossians 3:12

Personal – How do you see yourself as beloved of God? Reflect on this.

FIFTH DAY   **READ PSALM 29:1-4, 9-10**

("Give to the Lord the glory due his name;")

Read and meditate on Psalm 29:1-4, 9-10.

What is the Lord saying to you personally through the Psalm?

How can you apply this to your life?

SIXTH DAY   **READ ALL OF THE COMMENTARY**

ISAIAH 42:1-4, 6-7

This week's reading from Isaiah comes from a section sometimes called Second Isaiah (Chapters 40-55) and is generally considered to have been written by an unknown poet who prophesied near the end of the Babylonian exile. In 587 B.C. the city of Jerusalem fell, the walls and palaces were destroyed and the sacred temple burned. King Zedikiah and the rest of the population were marched to Babylon in chains.

From these chapters come the great Messianic oracles known as the Song of the Servant. In each song a different viewpoint of the mysterious "servant" is given. The destiny of suffering and glorification is fulfilled in the passion and glorification of Jesus Christ.

Isaiah is calling upon a figure who represents Israel and yet still addresses her. The "servant" is both a single individual and a nation as a collective individual. He talks about the qualities of the past, and he makes his "servant" very much a key figure of the future.

Isaiah points out that the servant's role is not limited to Israel, but would become universal. He saw his people in chains and exited to Babylonia, which was one thousand miles away from Judah. The need for a messiah was of great importance, and the hope of being restored to their lost homeland was in great danger of being completely demolished. The "servant" is being described as different from other leaders, not relying on military might nor upon treaties with other nations. He will not be a victorious warrior nor king, nor like other prophets shouting out their warnings. What the servant is will speak much louder than his words. The servant will be empowered by the same "Spirit" that rushed upon David when he was anointed king by Samuel (1 Sam. 16:13). Isaiah exhorts the people to look to the servant as God's chosen one.

ACTS 10:34-38

In this passage, Peter is preaching to the crowd that God shows absolutely no partiality. We see this truth being reaffirmed constantly in the Old Testament. The Lord shows no partiality, nor does he fear the famous or powerful (Lev. 19:15 and Wis. 6:7). God will have no part of activity like that. Peter challenges his listeners to fear the Lord and act upright, which means to be in reverence and awe of the Lord and to follow his commandments. We are told that fear of the Lord is to hate evil (Prov. 8:13).

Peter tells the crowd that God has sent to all the people of Israel a Messiah, in whom he baptizes people in the power of the Holy Spirit. He preached that Jesus is Lord of all, a message that still is being presented today to a waiting, hungry world. The Good News began when John baptized people in the name of repentance. Jesus was baptized by God in the power of the Holy Spirit.

We have been anointed with the same power and Spirit as Jesus. Jesus went forth doing good works and healing the sick. Peter's message is very much alive today. We see in our newspapers and television how bribes, fear of the powerful, and partiality to favored people can be very destructive to our society. We are called to go forth in the power of the same Spirit and do good works and heal the sick in the name of Jesus (Acts 1:8). Jesus wants us to carry on through Word and sacrament (Baptism and Confirmation), and to be witnesses to the world that he is alive here and now.

MATTHEW 3:13-17

Today's Gospel tells us about the beginning of Jesus' Messianic mission. This meant that the whole human race would become eligible to be called sons and daughters of God and heirs of heaven. Jesus would accomplish this with his final act of self-humiliation of being obedient as a slave even to the death on a cross.

Jesus insisted on being baptized by John even though he knew the rite was only for sinners. John had been telling the people that someone greater than himself was coming and they needed to repent and prepare to meet their Messiah. John did not feel qualified to baptize Jesus there at the Jordan River. In fact, he wanted Jesus to baptize him. Jesus was not baptized for repentance because he had never sinned. Jesus was baptized because he was confessing the sin of the nation. He was taking on the sins of the whole world and he paid the ransom in full on Calvary. He was officially beginning his public ministry. He was identifying with the common people, not with the critical Pharisees or the elite and wealthy Sadducees who were there only to watch. He was portraying his coming ministry of death and resurrection. God voiced his approval of his Son as the perfect person who did not need baptism for sin, but accepted baptism in obedient service to the Father.

You might put yourself in John's shoes as you imagine that your work is going well and people are beginning to really notice you and follow you. You know that your time of preparing is about done and now that Jesus has arrived, the real test of your integrity is about to begin. These questions which were John's questions are still our questions. Can we, like John, put our egos and profitable work aside in order to point others to Jesus? Are we willing to lose our status so that everyone will benefit? Baptism means to die and then to rise. We can only rise with Christ when we are willing to die with Christ. As you die to yourself, the power of the Holy Spirit will give you the strength to live for others in Christ.

Application

The first reading tells us that God's chosen people are called to be servants. The second reading reveals people of the Holy Spirit as people of power. The Gospel shows us that Jesus identifies with the common man through baptism.

This week, check out your own ego and see if you draw attention to yourself, or do you do things that are good to enable others to grow? Remember, as you lead others to Christ through humility, that people are looking for someone to give them security in an insecure world. Your role is to point them to Christ and to show that he is the one they seek.

SECOND SUNDAY IN ORDINARY TIME – CYCLE A

BEFORE YOU BEGIN

Pray and ask God to speak to you through His Holy Spirit. "THE PARACLETE, THE HOLY SPIRIT WHOM THE FATHER WILL SEND IN MY NAME, WILL INSTRUCT YOU IN EVERYTHING, AND REMIND YOU OF ALL THAT I TOLD YOU." (JOHN 14:26)

FIRST DAY   **Reread last week's readings.**

1.   What was a helpful or new thought from the readings or from the homily you heard on Sunday?

2.   From what you learned, what personal application did you choose to apply to your life this week?

SECOND DAY   **READ ISAIAH 49:3, 5-6**   **FIRST READING**

("My God is now my strength.")

1.   Who is the Lord's servant? To whom is the Lord speaking and what does he show through them? Isaiah 49:3

2.   Who is being referred to as "Israel" in the following scriptures?
Genesis 35:9-11
Exodus 4:21-22
Exodus 5:1

Personal – Do you see yourself with the name "Israel?" Reread Isaiah 49:3 and put Jesus' name in place of Israel and then put your name in that place. Meditate on this.

3.   Who has spoken? Isaiah 49:5

4.   Where did he form Jesus and as what did he form him? Isaiah 49:5, Psalm 139:13

5.   Who would be brought back to the Lord and who would be gathered to him? Isaiah 49:5

6.   What is Jesus made in the sight of the Lord? Isaiah 49:5

7.   Who is Jesus' strength? Isaiah 49:5

8.   What did God make Jesus to the nations and where will his salvation reach? Isaiah 49:6

9.   What did Jesus say and what will happen to those who follow him? John 8:12

Personal – In question 4, 6, and 7 above, put your name along the side of Jesus' name and reread the question and answer.

THIRD DAY   **READ 1 CORINTHIANS 1:1-3**   **SECOND READING**

("To you who have been consecrated in Christ Jesus and called to be a holy people.")

1.   By whom was Paul called and what was he called to be? 1 Corinthians 1:1

2.   To whom did Paul and Sosthenes send greetings? 1 Corinthians 1:2

Personal – Do you see "the church of God" as a building in which you worship God, or do you see "the church of God" made up of yourself and others who believe in God?

3.   Read the following and tell to whom it refers as the church:
Acts 9:31
Acts 20:28
Ephesians 5:23

4.   Where was "the church of God" located in this particular greeting by Paul and Sosthenes? 1 Cor 1:2 whether you can locate this on your bible map

5.   How do we become consecrated in Christ Jesus? John 17:17-19

6.   What kind of people are we called to be? 1 Cor 1:2

7.   What happens when we call on the name of the Lord Jesus Christ? Romans 10:13

8.   What comes from God our Father and the Lord Jesus Christ? 1 Cor 1:3

9.   How do you receive grace? 2 Peter 1:2, 2 Timothy 1:9

Personal – How do you see yourself as one called by God to be holy, and consecrated by him daily? How do you spend time alone with the Lord, talking with him, sharing your fears and anxieties as well as your joys and peaceful times? Take at least ten minutes each day this week without any distractions and talk to him, your Lord.

FOURTH DAY   **READ JOHN 1:29-34**   **GOSPEL**

("It is he who is to baptize with the Holy Spirit.")

1.   When John caught sight of Jesus coming toward him, what did he exclaim? John 1:29

2.   Read Exodus 12:1-13 concentrating on verses 3, 6, 12 and 13. What was done to atone for the sin of idolatry (Exodus 12:12), or worshipping false gods?

3. Why is Jesus referred to as "the Lamb of God?" Isaiah 53:7, 8 and 12

4. What is the sin of the world? Exodus 12:12

5. What did John say and into what position did he put Jesus? John 1:30

6. In John's statement, "After me is to come a man who ranks ahead of me because he was before me;" would this indicate that Jesus was born before him? Luke 1:34–36

Personal - In your own words, write out what this passage means to you. John 1:30

7. What was John's reason for baptizing? John 1:31

8. What was John's testimony? John 1:32, Isaiah 11:2, Matthew 3:16, Mark 1:10 and Luke 3:21-22

9. When we receive the Spirit of God, what else do we receive? Isaiah 11:2

10. John says he did not recognize Jesus. Who told him who Jesus was? John 1:33

11. When did God reveal to him what he was to do and where did he reveal this to him? Luke 3:2

12. What did God reveal to John? What did John see for himself and to what did he testify? John 1:33–34

Personal - How has God revealed to you that Jesus is the Chosen One? Do you feel you are one of God's chosen ones? Take time this week to reflect on the way God has chosen you and for what purpose.

FIFTH DAY   **READ PSALM 40:2, 4, 7-10**

("To do your will, O my God, is my delight.")

Read and meditate on Psalm 40:2, 4, 7-10.

What is the Lord saying to you personally through the Psalm?

How can you apply this to your life?

SIXTH DAY   **READ ALL OF THE COMMENTARY**

ISAIAH 49:3, 5-6

The prophet speaks of a mysterious figure known as the servant of the Lord. Christians have recognized Jesus in this description. Today the servant speaks of his mission. The servant reveals his mission as a mission of comfort, compassion, and restoration. He is to make Israel a light to all the nations and that light shall be seen unto the ends of the earth. This was a time of joy because the captives were being brought back to Israel and the hand of the Lord, the Holy One of Israel had created it (Isaiah 41:20).

The communities were still very poor and labored under many difficulties and affliction; so this message of comfort was well received. Isaiah tells us in these verses that the servant is clearly identified with the entire nation. Isaiah shows us how the servant, by suffering through the miseries of being exiled from their homeland and still being faithful to God, is identified with the people of Israel as their ideal representative (verse 3). Upon returning to their homeland the exiles find that rebuilding the temple was not enough. Instead, a call to holiness and worship of the one true God was needed to bring a sense of fullness to the people. The servant will be a healing visible light to all of Israel and all the other nations, Jew or Gentile.

1 CORINTHIANS 1:1-3

Paul begins his letter in the ordinary style of the day, the first century equivalent of "Dear Corinthians." However, his conventional greeting includes a reminder that they are part of the Lord's plan for the world.

In the first three verses of this letter the name of Jesus Christ appears no fewer than four times. This was going to be a difficult letter, because it was going to deal with a difficult situation. Paul's first and only thought was that of Jesus Christ.

Sometimes the church, or even ourselves, try to deal with a difficult situation by means of a book of laws and in the spirit of human justice. Often we try to call on our own mental powers. Paul did none of these things. To his trying situation he brought in Jesus Christ, and it was in the light of the cross and the love of Christ that he dealt with it.

Paul speaks of the church of God at Corinth. It was not the church of Corinth; it was the church of God. We might do well to imitate Paul in this respect and become more aware of the reality which unites us, and become less aware of the local differences which divide us.

Paul tells us something about the individual Christian. 1. He is consecrated in Christ. To be consecrated to Christ is to be one for whom Jesus died, and to know and to live out that reality. 2. We are called to be God's dedicated people. The word "Hagios" means to be holy or saintly. If a person has been "called" by God, he must show that he is fit in life and in character for that holy service. The Christian is called into a community whose boundaries include heaven and earth. We are all called to be "Hagios" (saints).
JOHN 1:29-34

Once again the fourth Gospel tells us that John is paying homage to Jesus. He calls him the title which has become an integral part of our liturgy, "The Lamb of God."

John may have been thinking of the Passover lamb because he was the son of a priest and he would know all the rituals of the temple and its sacrifices. The Passover feast was not very far away (John 2:13). The blood of the slain lamb protected the people in the homes of the Israelites on the night they left Egypt (Exodus 12:1-13). The blood of the Passover lamb delivered the Israelites in Egypt from death. Jesus was considered to be the one true sacrifice who can deliver us from death. Paul, too, thought of Jesus as the Passover Lamb (1 Cor. 5:7) in that there is a deliverance only Jesus Christ can win for us.

Two great pictures of the lamb are presented in the Prophets. Isaiah has the great picture of the one who was brought "like a lamb to the slaughter" (Isaiah 53:7). Jeremiah writes, "But I was like a gentle lamb led to the slaughter" (Jeremiah 11:19). Isaiah 53 later became to the church one of the most precious forecasters in all the Old Testament. There is sheer wonder in the phrase "The Lamb of God." John used this phrase twenty-nine times in Revelation, and it has become one of the most precious titles of Christ. This title sums up the love, sacrifice, suffering, and triumph of Jesus Christ.

Something happened at Jesus' baptism that convinced John that Jesus was indeed the Son of God. In Palestine, the dove was a sacred bird and it was not hunted or eaten. The dove also symbolizes Israel, God's people formed by the Holy Spirit. The creative Spirit of God was moving across the face of the waters (Genesis 1:2)). The rabbis said that the Spirit of God moved and fluttered like a dove. The picture of the dove was one that Jesus knew and loved. The Spirit was power, power like a mighty rushing wind. The Spirit was God; the coming of the Spirit into a man's life was the coming of God.

Baptism means to dip or to submerge. It can be used for clothes being dipped into dye. John's baptism meant cleansing. It meant a man was being washed from impurities that clung to him. Jesus' Baptism was a Baptism of the Spirit, and it meant his life was strengthened with power. The church has included the same Baptism that Jesus experienced in the practice of our faith. We, too, are the beloved of our heavenly Father and his favor rests on us.

Application

The first reading tells us about a servant whose mission is to make Israel a light to all the nations. The second reading shows us that Paul responded to his trying situation in the light of the cross, and with the love of Christ. The Gospel reveals to us that Jesus is the true "Lamb of God."

John the Baptist's job was to point people to Jesus. Our job is to point them to Christ and show that it is he whom they seek. This week, lead someone to Christ by intercessory prayer, introduce them to this bible study or bring someone to your church. Try to be specific and gentle.

THIRD SUNDAY IN ORDINARY TIME – CYCLE A

BEFORE YOU BEGIN

Pray and ask God to speak to you through His Holy Spirit. "THE PARACLETE, THE HOLY SPIRIT WHOM THE FATHER WILL SEND IN MY NAME, WILL INSTRUCT YOU IN EVERYTHING, AND REMIND YOU OF ALL THAT I TOLD YOU." (JOHN 14:26)

FIRST DAY	**Reread last week's readings.**

1. What was a helpful or new thought from the readings or from the homily you heard on Sunday?

2. From what you learned, what personal application did you choose to apply to your life this week?

SECOND DAY	**READ ISAIAH 8:23-9:3**	**FIRST READING**

("The people who walked in darkness have seen a great light.")

1. What lands has he degraded? See if you can locate this on your bible map
Isaiah 8:23

2. What happened in the end, what land has he glorified, and what shall be taken away? Isaiah 8:23

3. What happened to the people who walked in darkness? Isaiah 9:1

4. Who brightens the darkness about us? 2 Samuel 22:29

5. What must we do to come out of the darkness and into the light, according to the following scriptures:

   Isaiah 58:10

   John 8:12

   Acts 26:18

   Romans 13:12-14.

Personal - How have you come out of the darkness into the light? 1 Peter 2:9 states, "You, however, are a chosen race, a royal priesthood, a holy nation, a people he claims for his own to proclaim the glorious works of the one who called you from darkness into his marvelous light." Meditate on this.

6.   What has he brought them or what is the result of walking in the light? Isaiah 9:2

7.   How did the following experience this abundant joy and in whom did they find this joy?

      David (Psalm 16:7-11)

      Mary (Luke 1:46-47)

      John the Baptist (John 3:29-30)

      Paul (Philippians 1:18)

8.   What had burdened them? Isaiah 9:3

9.   What does Jesus tell us about his yoke? Matt 11:28-30

Personal - In what way have you found life become heavy and burdensome? Write out the above verse and meditate on it.

10.   What got smashed and what comparison is made here? Isaiah 9:3, Exodus 18:1

THIRD DAY   **READ 1 CORINTHIANS 1:10-13, 17**   **SECOND READING**

(In the name of Our Lord Jesus Christ agree in what you say.")

1.   Who is being appealed to, by whom, and in whose name? 1 Corinthians 1:1, 10

2.   What is Paul begging them to do? 1 Corinthians 1:10

3.   How are we united with Christ? Romans 6:1-5

4.   What unites us in mind in the following scriptures? 1 Corinthians 5:4, Philippians 2:2-4, Colossians 2:2

5.   What was Paul informed about and by whom? 1 Cor 1:11

6.   List the four men the people were quarreling over, and tell who they were.
     1 Corinthians 1:12

     1. _____ John 1:36, 41

     2. _____ John 1:42

     3. _____ Acts 18:24-25

     4. _____ 1 Corinthians 1:1

7.   What was Paul's response to what they were quarreling about? 1 Corinthians 1:13

8.   What does God's Word tell us about quarreling? Romans 13:12-13

Personal – How do you prevent yourself from quarreling with others over God's Word? By studying his Word, you will find yourself quarreling less and standing more on the truths of his Word.

9.   Who sent Paul and what did he send him to do? 1 Corinthians 1:17

10. How is he not to preach the Gospel? 1 Cor 1:17, 1 Corinthians 2:4

11. What would happen to the cross if Paul spoke with "worldly wisdom? "
     1 Corinthians 1:17

Personal – When you speak about God to your family, friends, work acquaintances, what do you talk about? Does it end up in quarreling and arguing or do you do as Paul did in 1 Cor. 2:1-5? Reflect on this.

FOURTH DAY   **READ MATTHEW 4:12-23**   **GOSPEL**

("Repent, the kingdom of God is close at hand.")

1.   What did Jesus hear and what did he do? Matthew 4:12

2.   Where did he go when he heard the news about John? Matthew 4:13

3.   What was his reason for going there? Matthew 4:14

4.   What did Jesus begin to proclaim from that time on? Matthew 4:17

5.   What was John's message in preparing for Jesus' coming? Matthew 3:2

6.   What did Jesus say is at hand? Matthew 4:17, Luke 17:20-21

Personal – What does it mean to you to reform your life? What do you think "The kingdom of heaven is at hand" means? Do you have areas in your life that need changing? Sit before your heavenly Father and talk to him about this.

7. Where was Jesus walking and what was he watching? Matthew 4:18

8. What did he say to the two brothers? Matthew 4:19

9. What did God say through the prophet Jeremiah? Jeremiah 16:16

Personal - What must we do to become fishers of men? Fill in the blanks: _____ _____ _____ and I will make you fishers of men. Matthew 4:19

10. What was Peter and Andrew's response to Jesus' invitation and did they stop to think about it? Matthew 4:20

11. As Jesus walked along, what did he notice? Matthew 4:21

12. What were the two brothers doing and who was with them?

13. Fill in the blanks. Matthew 4:21-22.
He _____ them, and _____ they abandoned their boat and _____ to _____ him.

14. Where did Jesus tour and what did he do in their synagogues? Matthew 4:23

15. There were three things that Jesus did according to Matthew 4:23. What were they?

Personal - In your prayer time alone with Jesus, ask him to teach you his truths through his Word. Ask him to help you understand the good news of the kingdom and ask him for the gift of healing so that those in your family, your friends and your work acquaintances may come to better know him. Share this with someone.

FIFTH DAY   **READ PSALM 27:1, 4, 13-14**

("The Lord is my light and my salvation.")

Read and meditate on Psalm 27:1, 4, 13-14.

What is the Lord saying to you personally through the Psalm?

How can you apply this to your life?

SIXTH DAY   **READ ALL OF THE COMMENTARY**

ISAIAH 8:23-9:3

This passage begins with the results of Israel being invaded by Assyria and ends with Isaiah's prophecy about the coming Messiah. Isaiah was given a prophecy by the Lord that Israel and Syria, both very strong enemies of Judah, would fall to the Assyrians. Judah rejected this warning and experienced God's wrath and punishment. Isaiah was even considered a traitor because he told the people to trust only in God, not some powerful conquering nation to the north. He even predicted the fall of Judah and watched the nation plunge into darkness and fear.

The people refused to consult God about their future and even began to blame God for their trials. Today many people still blame God for their problems of health, marriage, work, etc. We need to ask ourselves why do some act like the people in scripture (Is. 8:16-21) and try to pass the blame off onto others. The darkness that the people were thrust into does not mean death necessarily, it may mean despair, trouble, anguish, defeat, rejection. Isaiah tells us in his prophecy (9:1-6) that a Messiah is coming and despair, sorrow and trouble will come to an end.

The people in those times probably felt very much as most of us do when we are going through trials, and that is, will it ever end? We can say just what it says in Psalm 23, "Yeah, though I walk through the valley of the shadow of death, thou art with me, thy rod and thy staff, they comfort me." The Lord never promised us there would be no troubles, but he did promise that he would be right there to go through them with us, and lead us to safety.

We need to be like that today and we must follow him if we are to be led safely through the times of tribulation and trial. God promises a light to all those who live in the valley of the shadow of death and the light's name is Jesus.

I CORINTHIANS 1:10-13, 17

We see in today's passage that Paul is not only an evangelist who preached God's Word and helped form Christian community, but he also kept a life-time interest in their spiritual welfare. He begins by appealing to them as brothers in the Lord. We need to ask ourselves when we come up against quarreling or bickering, do we appeal to the one who has hurt us in the name of the Lord? We are to love our neighbor as ourself (Mt. 22:37) and that means to care about one another and to be ready to forgive one another in the name of the Lord.

Human nature is still the same today in that people are still fighting over who is the most important, or who deserves the most recognition. It had only been a few years since Jesus' crucifixion, and factions and divisions were already forming in the new expanding church leaders. Personal pride was entering into their desire to follow Christ on the road to heaven. The pride and ambition shown in today's message not only inflicts damage on that community but it has given ground to long-standing division in the Christian church even today.

The divisions in the church are a scandal to the followers of Christ and a tremendous obstacle to the conversion of unbelievers, which is the result of the actions of proud and arrogant men. We cannot call ourselves humble when we forget, by our actions, that Christ died for us all and that Christ is not and will not be divided. We are all being called to live out the life of Christ who, because of our baptism, now lives within us. In our prayers, we can ask God to give us the grace to come together in his saving name and bring his love to our neighbor which can result in the work of reunion between God and all of his children. God will surely hear and respond to the call that comes from his humble children.

MATTHEW 4:12-23

When Jesus heard that John had been arrested, he left Judah and returned home to Nazareth, his hometown. He didn't stay long because of opposition and apathy of the local hometown people. He began his preaching ministry by going from one small town to another. He left Nazareth and headed for Capernaum which was to become his home base during his ministry in Galilee. Capernaum was a very busy city and Jesus' message would be heard by many people. He also would be able to have more resources and support for his ministry. Isaiah's prophecy (9:1-2) was fulfilled in that Jesus was the light to the land of Zebulun and Naphtali, the region of Galilee in which Capernaum was located.

Matthew uses the phrase "kingdom of heaven" out of respect to the Jews because in reverence they did not pronounce God's name. Jesus probably meant the kingdom of heaven is near because when Jesus is in a man's heart, the kingdom of God is definitely near. We need to know that we do not have to go out and search the wide world over to find God. He is right here within, and all we need to do is call out his name, confess with our lips and believe in our heart (Romans 10:10-17). Jesus began his ministry where John the Baptist left off, and the message is the same today, "Turn from sin and turn to God." When we become followers of Christ, we turn away from our self-centeredness and self-control.

Jesus called the brothers to come follow him and become fishers of men. He is calling us to do the same things. Are you going to fish or cut bait? These men probably had already heard about Jesus through his preaching in the area but after personally experiencing his love, and hearing his call, they immediately responded to the invitation.

Jesus is teaching, preaching, and healing today as much as he was in today's Gospel. He is teaching us how to bring others to him and be saved. He is preaching the Good News through his people today, like you and me. He certainly is healing people today, physically, emotionally, and spiritually. Jesus preached the Good News to everyone who wanted to hear it. The Good News is that God became man, that God is with us in the Holy Spirit, and that he cares very much for us. Rejoice and be glad that there is no sin or problem too great or too small for him to handle. Today, as in the days of Isaiah, Jesus the Messiah is a "Light to the Land."

Application

The first reading calls the Messiah to be "A light to the Land" to bring his people out of darkness. Paul tells us in the second reading that pride and ambition have caused great obstacles in the church. In the Gospel, we hear the kingdom of heaven is near because Jesus becomes present in our hearts when he died on the cross so that we might have eternal life.

This week, be a light to your family by being extra caring and compassionate. It could be volunteering to baby sit, wash the family car, do laundry, visit a sick relative or someone else you know that has no one else to care for them.

FOURTH SUNDAY IN ORDINARY TIME – CYCLE A

BEFORE YOU BEGIN

Pray and ask God to speak to you through His Holy Spirit. "THE PARACLETE, THE HOLY SPIRIT WHOM THE FATHER WILL SEND IN MY NAME, WILL INSTRUCT YOU IN EVERYTHING, AND REMIND YOU OF ALL THAT I TOLD YOU." (JOHN 14:26)

FIRST DAY   **Reread last week's readings.**

    1.   What was a helpful or new thought from the readings or from the homily you heard on Sunday?

    2.   From what you learned, what personal application did you choose to apply to your life this week?

SECOND DAY   **READ ZEPHANIAH 2:3, 3:12-13**   **FIRST READING**

("Seek the Lord all you humble of the Lord.")

    1.   Who must seek the Lord? Zephaniah 2:3

    2.   What happens to those who humble themselves?

        2 Chronicles 7:14
        Job 22:29
        Psalm 25:9
        Proverbs 3:34
        Proverbs 11:2
        Sirach 3:18
        1 Peter 5:5

    3.   What happens to those who do not humble themselves?

        2 Chronicles 33:23, 24
        Sirach 10:15
        Isaiah 13:11
        Daniel 4:34

    4.   What does it mean to humble yourself?

        Ezra 8:21
        Sirach 2:17
        Sirach 18:20
        Philippians 2:3-5

    5.   What happens to God through those that are humble? Sirach 3:19

6.   From whom do we learn to become humble? Matthew 11:25, 29

7.   How should Christians act toward one another? 1 Peter 3:8

Personal – Read Philippians 2:3, 4. Put your name in the following first and third blank spaces, and insert the name of a person you have the most trouble getting along with, in the second and fourth blank spaces:

(1) _____, never act out of rivalry or conceit; rather think humbly of
(2) _____ as superior to (3) _____, looking to
(4) _____ interest rather than to my own.

8.   What three things must they seek? Zephaniah 2:3

9.   What may happen to these people on the day of the Lord's anger? Zep 2:3. Also see Psalm 2:11, on how not to be affected by God's anger

10.   What will he leave in your midst and in what shall they take refuge? Zephaniah 3:12

11.   What three things shall they not do, and what shall they do? Zep 3:13

Personal – Are you one of God's remnants? Do others see you as one of his remnants? What can you do to better glorify God? Meditate on this.

THIRD DAY   **READ 1 CORINTHIANS 1:26-31**   **SECOND READING**

("If anyone wants to boast, let him boast about the Lord.")

1.   Who are among those called, and what are they to consider? 1 Corinthians 1:26

2.   What are these brothers not considered? 1 Corinthians 1:26

Personal – Who do you consider the well-born today? Who are the influential?

3.   Who did God choose to shame the wise, and who did God single out of this world to do what? 1 Corinthians 1:27

4.   How does the world see these people, and what was God's reason for choosing the low born? 1 Corinthians 1:27-29

5.   Who has God chosen according to James 2:5?

6.   Who has given us life in Christ Jesus? 1 Corinthians 1:30

7.   Was this new life in Christ Jesus accomplished by anything we have done? Ephesians 2:8-9

8. Fill in the following blanks: He has made him our _____ and also our _____, our _____ and our _____ (1 Corinthians 1:30)

9. Who gives wisdom, what is wisdom, and to whom does God give wisdom? 1 Kings 5:9, Ephesians 1:9, Job 28:28, Psalm 19:8

10. As Jesus grew in size and strength with what was he filled? Luke 2:40

11. With what does righteousness begin and end, and how will we receive justice? Romans 1:17, Luke 18:7

12. What leads us to righteousness, and what must we do with our bodies to sanctify them? Romans 6:16–19

13. How have we been sanctified? Hebrews 10:10

14. How have we been redeemed? Ephesians 1:7

15. How did we deserve to be justified by the gift of God through the redemption of Christ? Romans 3:24

Personal – At times, how do you find yourself boasting about your accomplishments? Think about this today, and when you begin to do this, discipline your mind to think on what Jesus has done for you in that situation.

FOURTH DAY   **READ MATTHEW 5:1-12**   **GOSPEL**

("Happy are the poor in spirit.")

1. When Jesus went up on the mountainside and sat down, who gathered around him? Matthew 5:1

2. What did Jesus begin to do, and where did Jesus do his teaching?

    Matthew 5:1-2
    Mark 1:21
    Mark 4:1
    Luke 5:3

Personal – How and where do you teach about God's ways? How can you follow Jesus' example to teach whenever a need arises? In what way have you learned about how Jesus acted in certain situations to be able to share that with your spouse, your children, your friends, and those with whom you work?

3. Who did Jesus tell his disciples would teach them when he was not there? Luke 12:12

4. Whose is the kingdom of God? Matthew 5:3; Luke 6:20

5.   Who shall be consoled? Matt 5:4; Luke 6:21; Psalm 126:5

6.   Who shall inherit the land? Matt 5:5; Psalm 37:11; Proverbs 2:21

7.   What will happen to those who hunger and thirst for holiness? Matt 5:6,
      Luke 6:21, Proverbs 21:21

8.   Mercy shall be whose, and who shall see God? Matt 5:7-8

9.   Who shall be called sons of God, and to whom does the reign of God belong?
      Matthew 5:9-10, 1 Peter 2:20

10.   Whose reward is great in heaven? Matthew 5:12

11.   When being persecuted, how should we act? Whom did they persecute before us
      and in what way? Matt 5:12, James 1:2, 2 Chronicles 36:16

FIFTH DAY   **READ PSALM 146:6-10**

("The Lord sets captives free.")

Read and meditate on Psalm 146:6–10.

What is the Lord saying to you personally through the Psalm?

How can you apply this to your life?

SIXTH DAY   **READ ALL OF THE COMMENTARY**

ZEPHANIAH 2:3, 3:12-13

The "day of Yahweh" was coming, the day when God would punish all disobedient nations. Judah, because of her pride and rebelliousness, was very much included. A small remnant of God's people would survive the day of wrath if they became obedient to God's commands. This same warning is issued for our benefit today. The chosen people (the Israelites) did not really believe this prophecy and their nation was subjected to incredible violence. We are that remnant today and we are called more than ever to bring his Word to those around us. Many people today are still waiting for a Messiah who will bring them recognition, wealth and power.

When Jesus finally came they were not ready for him and resented him. They condemned him to death on the cross. That cross became the banner around which the few faithful Jews and Gentiles (remnant) rallied. His kingdom on earth spread and in just 30 years after his death, Christianity was known and practiced in the entire civilized world.

Today the world is turning more and more into a pagan world, and the warnings of Zephaniah are ringing in our ears. God is opposed to the proud and arrogant of every generation. He will always bless and protect the poor and the humble because they believe in him. Self-reliance and arrogance found no place in

God's kingdom then and neither will it find any place in God's kingdom today. Zephaniah shows us that only when we faithfully follow and obey God's Word can we really ever be truly happy.

The Good Shepherd looks over his flock and provides them with the protection that they need. They know they can lie down in safety and rest in peace because he is always present among them. We need not fear any man or nation because Jesus tells us that through him, all things are possible (Philippians 4:13).

1 CORINTHIANS 1:26-31

Paul tells us how fortunate we are to have a God who loves us so much that he chose to become just like us in every way but sin. He tells us that God calls us to be one of his children, not because of what we have done or what we may own or even how smart we may be. In fact, God has made salvation available to all, especially the lowly and humble. All anyone needs is faith in order to be saved. Salvation comes from believing that Jesus Christ died so that all of our sins would be washed away by his blood. Jesus' death allowed us to become holy and spotless before God. We are justified in faith by what Jesus did on that cross, not by anything we ever did. This is tremendously Good News for us, especially those of us who are struggling in our own lives through sickness, poverty, tyranny or being from the wrong side of town. It's incredible to realize that Jesus came to earth to die for all men and women, rich or poor, weak or strong, young or old.

Not everyone accepted Jesus and the result is that many are searching in the wrong direction for the peace that surpasses all understanding (Philippians 4:7). Faith is a response to the power and presence of the living God in our lives. Salvation is free, but it is not inherited. Each one of us has to personally accept the invitation from Christ. Paul's words are great comfort and hope to the people in our world today. Much of the world is suffering through famine, tyranny, and lack of respect for human dignity. Jesus is present among all of us and he seeks out the oppressed and offers them full partnership in his kingdom in heaven and encourages all of us to bring that kingdom into reality here on earth now.

MATTHEW 5:1-12

Jesus gave this sermon on a hillside near Capernaum, and it is believed that this "Sermon on the Mount" probably lasted several days. Jesus broke through the traditional view of the law and talked about the attitudes of men. He stressed that it is as important to be, as to do. We might even call them "The Be-Attitudes" of Christianity. Tremendous crowds were following Jesus, he was the talk of everyone. He preached with such simpleness and yet with much authority.

The disciples were Jesus' closest companions, and all of this attention certainly must have made them feel important, popular and maybe even prideful. Being with Jesus gave them plenty of notoriety, as well as being faith healers of a sort. Jesus warned them about the temptations they would face as his associates, and some think his sermon on the mount may have been directed to his disciples, as well as everyone else in the crowd.

We hear a lot of comments today that if you follow Jesus' teaching, you will be successful, healthy, wealthy and wise. Jesus really tells us to expect not fame or fortune; but to expect mourning, hunger, and persecution. Jesus tells us not to look for our reward in this life. We will be rewarded but not necessarily here on earth. The beatitudes are a standard of conduct for all Christian believers. There is a strong contrast in values. The kingdom values deal with eternal life and worldly values deal with what is temporary. They contrast the superficial faith of the Pharisees with the real faith Jesus wants.

Today we are faced with the same challenge. We need to really take a look at our values and see if they are worldly values or kingdom values. The beatitudes cannot be a multiple choice, pick what you want and leave the rest. To be a real follower of Christ these have to be your be-attitudes.

Applications

The first reading talks about a day of warm healing for the humble and a day of wrath for the proud. The second reading shows us how God has chosen ordinary people to be eligible for salvation. In the Gospel, we hear the attitudes of Christ are to be our attitudes.

This week, let us reach out and give comfort to someone in our family. It might be nothing more than a letter of sympathy or a get well card. It could also be visiting someone who has lost a loved one and who is lonely.

FIFTH SUNDAY IN ORDINARY TIME – CYCLE A

BEFORE YOU BEGIN

Pray and ask God to speak to you through His Holy Spirit. "THE PARACLETE, THE HOLY SPIRIT WHOM THE FATHER WILL SEND IN MY NAME, WILL INSTRUCT YOU IN EVERYTHING, AND REMIND YOU OF ALL THAT I TOLD YOU." (JOHN 14:26)

FIRST DAY   **Reread last week's readings.**

1. What was a helpful or new thought from the readings or from the homily you heard on Sunday?

2. From what you learned, what personal application did you choose to apply to your life this week?

SECOND DAY   **READ ISAIAH 58:7-10**   **FIRST READING**

("Then light shall rise for you in the darkness.")

1. With whom do we share our bread, and how do we help the homeless? Isaiah 58:7

2. Whom do we clothe when we see them and on whom are we not to turn our back? Isaiah 58:7

Personal– In your enthusiasm to obey God and feed the hungry, clothe the naked, etc., have you ever neglected those in your home, your spouse, your children, your relatives, your close friends, your neighbors or those with whom you work? Reread verse 7 again.

3. What shall happen to us if we do these things? Isaiah 58:8, Ezekiel 18:7, 9

4. What shall happen to our wound, and what shall go before us? Isaiah 58:8

5. What shall be our rear guard and what will happen when we call the Lord? Isaiah 58:8-9

6. When we cry for help, what will he say? Isaiah 58:9

7. What three things must we remove from our midst? Isaiah 58:9

8. What does God's Word tell us about the following?

OPPRESSION	MALICIOUS SPEECH	ACCUSATIONS
Psalm 119:134	Proverbs 2:12	Prov. 10:18
Proverbs 21:7	Proverbs 4:24	Mark 15:3-5
Ecclesiastes 7:7	Sirach 27:6	
Sirach 10:7	Matthew 22:15	
Isaiah 33:15-16	John 8:43-44	
Ezekiel 45:9		

9.   If we bestow our bread on the hungry and satisfy the afflicted, what will rise for us in the darkness, and what will happen to the gloom? Isaiah 58:10

10.   How do we satisfy the afflicted? Luke 9:1-6

Personal– How have you removed oppression, false accusations, and malicious speech from your midst? In what way have you fed the hungry, given shelter to the homeless, or clothed the naked this past week? How have you been able to do this without neglecting your family?

THIRD DAY   **READ 1 CORINTHIANS 2:1-5**   **SECOND READING**

("Your faith rest not on the wisdom of men but on the power of God.")

1.   Who was speaking and to whom was he speaking in 1 Cor. 2:1? 1 Corinthians 1:1

2.   What did he come proclaiming? 1 Corinthians 2:1

3.   What was God's testimony? 1 Corinthians 2:2, 1 John 5:6-12

4.   Did Paul speak of anything else besides Jesus crucified? 1 Corinthians 2:2

5.   How did Paul come among them? 1 Corinthians 2:3

6.   Who helps us in our weakness? Romans 8:26

Personal– Have you ever experienced this weakness and fear that Paul did among people? Have you ever experienced this in your own home, around your relatives, friends, etc.? Spend an extra five minutes a day, this week, alone with the Lord dwelling on the presence of his Holy Spirit within you.

7.   What did the Lord tell Paul about his weakness? 2 Corinthians 12:9

8.   Compare weakness with the power of God using Paul's statements in 2 Corinthians 13:3-9.

9.   What two things have none of the persuasive force of "wise" argumentation, but had the convincing power of the Spirit? 1 Corinthians 2:4

10.   God sends messages to us in many ways. Read the following, and see if you can pick out who was being used as a messenger.
      Genesis 16:7-12
      Genesis 21:17
      Malachi 2:7
      Matthew 11:10, 11
      Acts 10:3

Personal– Have you been able to recognize God's messages to you? Meditate on the way God speaks to you directly and through others and whether or not you are really listening. Share with someone.

FOURTH DAY   READ MATTHEW 5:13-16   GOSPEL

("You are the light of the world.")

1.   Who is the salt of the earth? What do you do with salt if it goes flat, and can you restore its flavor? Matt 5:13; Luke 14:34-35

2.   Read the following and tell how salt was used.
     Leviticus 2:13
     Mark 9:49-50
     Colossians 4:6

Personal- The partaking in common of salt by those seated together at table was an ancient symbol of friendship and alliance. When you are seated at your table and pass the salt, is it always in friendship or is your salt beginning to go flat in your home or at your table? Is the seasoning coming from you that of love and friendship? Reflect on this. Ask the Lord to season you with his love.

3.   Who is the light of the world, and what cannot be hidden? Matthew 5:14

4.   What do we NOT do with a lamp we light, and what do we DO with it?
     Matthew 5:15

5.   In what way must our light shine before men, and what will they see in us?
     Matthew 5:16

6.   What did Jesus say about being good, and whom do we praise for his goodness?
     Luke 18:19, Tobit 13:10

7.   Who is good? Psalm 25:8

8.   Where does a man produce good? Matt 12:34-35, Luke 6:45

9.   With what are we to be filled? Romans 15:14

10. What will people do when they see goodness in the acts we perform?
     Matthew 5:16

11. What does God's Word say about giving praise to our Father, and who were the people involved?

     Exodus 15:1, 2   Mark 2:12
     2 Samuel 22:50, 51   Luke 4:14-15
     Ezra 10:10, 11   Acts 3:9
     Daniel 2:19, 23   Acts 13:46-48
     Daniel 4:34   Hebrews 13:12-15
     Matthew 11:25   Rev 4:8-11

Personal- How do you take the time each day to praise God for what he is doing in your life? Take time to praise him for giving you a new life in him, for his promises to you in his word, for your faith, for direction and guidance. Praise him for his goodness that is becoming visible to others in your actions as you yield to his Holy Spirit.

FIFTH DAY   **READ PSALM 112:4-9**

("The Lord dawns through the darkness, light for the upright.")

Read and meditate on Psalm 112:4-9.

What is the Lord saying to you personally through the Psalm?

How can you apply this to your life?

SIXTH DAY   **READ ALL OF THE COMMENTARY**

ISAIAH 58:7-10

Faith is a living response to the presence and power of God in our lives. Faith without good works is dead and useless (James 2:17). We are being told in today's reading that we cannot be saved by works, no matter how good they may be, without faith in God. We are also told that fasting can be very beneficial, both physically and spiritually, but at best the only one who benefits is you. Our response to the presence of God in our lives is what produces really effective good works. Our response to the presence of God and his power affects others, and that is what God wants from us. He wants us to make a difference in the lives of the hungry, the oppressed, the homeless, and to protect the lives of the unborn.

We do not do good things to become good; we do good things because of the goodness that is within all men of faith. That goodness is the presence and power of God, whom we know as the Holy Spirit. Our response in faith unleashes the power of God to heal a sick and wounded world. Pleasing God is not done by what we eat or do not eat; rather it is by bringing charity, justice, and generosity to the downtrodden.

We glorify God most when we can help his broken, bruised, abandoned, hungry, homeless, and aborted children into healthy loved human beings. Faith is our response to God's presence and power in our own life, and we find this revealed to us in his Holy Word and the teachings of his beloved church. He is the water that prevents men from dying of thirst.

1 CORINTHIANS 2:1-5

It is very important that we realize that Paul, was a brilliant scholar. He once used his verbal skills very well in convicting many Christians of being heretics. Paul explains very clearly in today's reading that he speaks only of the crucified Christ. We can do today what Paul was doing then, and that is keeping our Gospel message simple and basic. Our power is in the Holy Spirit, not in any gift of public speaking.

Paul is saying that while study and preparation for proclaiming God's Word are necessary, preparation must be tied into and be dependent on the Holy Spirit. Paul's own background of scripture study and preparation for preaching allowed him to lean entirely on God and still be responsive to the needs of the believers. Paul goes to great lengths to tell us that his preaching is very plain, and that Jesus is much more comfortable in the house of a plain and simple person than living in luxury with one who is proclaiming God's law and exacting its complete obedience from the people. We need to reflect on how we come across to other people when we are professing our faith. Do people see in us a weakness and trembling that is overcome because of our own personal love of Jesus? Jesus tells us that his grace is enough for us; we do not have to worry about our credentials.

God calls us to be faithful, not successful. People who are hurting will respond to a message of hope, love, and forgiveness that is immersed in the convicting power of the Holy Spirit. We are God's messengers today, and we are called to respond to him. Today's reading clearly tells us that we do not have to depend on our talents to proclaim the Gospel message. What we do need is to proclaim that Jesus is Lord and, like Paul, preach only the crucified Christ. Repentance is still man's best bet to live an abundant life (John 10:10).

MATTHEW 5:13-16

Matthew is so down to earth in this particular writing. Most of us have experienced, at one time or another, the addition of salt on a delicious salad or even on a sizzling piece of meat. Paul shows us that, like salt, Christians are called to be of a special flavor. Old salt that loses its flavor is thrown out. Salt is not called to blend in, but to be distinctive in flavor. As Christians, we are not called to blend into the rest of the world; we are called to be distinctively different.

We are worthless if people cannot see a difference in the way we live our lives. Seasoning is made to bring out the best in foods, and Christians are called to bring out the best in people. We need only to picture a great city on a hill where we can see the lights ahead for many miles. When we are living by faith and not by sight, our lives glow like tremendous lights to others. That light that is shining in a Christian is the light of Jesus Christ. That is the light that led men out of the darkness of sin.

We are the only ones who can dim that light, and many of us do it by being quiet when we should speak out, as in the abortion issue. Another way is going along with the crowd. Then there is sin that dims our light tremendously. Many of us let our light grow dim because we do not share our light with others. We are called by our very faith in God, to be a beacon of truth and to let our light shine forth in this darkened world of pain and sin.

Jesus tells us to be a favorable difference in our community and to let his Light shine in us. He is the light that guides the prostitute, the alcoholic, the drug addict, the adulterer, the thief, the liar, and all those who stagger around in the darkness of despair, out of the darkness. He welcomes and leads them back home to his church of love and forgiveness.

Application

In the first reading we see that faith is the living response to the power and presence of God in our lives. The second reading shows us that salvation is available to all, even the most ordinary of men. The Gospel calls us to be a light that leads people out of the darkness of sin.

This week, let us respond to God's call and be a light to our family and friends by showing them the way to Jesus! Try to attend daily Mass and read scripture every day this week. Spend a certain amount of time each day in prayer. Spend some time with each family member and try to do something positive for him/her. You can be the flavor and light if you just respond to God's power within you.

SIXTH SUNDAY IN ORDINARY TIME – CYCLE A

BEFORE YOU BEGIN

Pray and ask God to speak to you through His Holy Spirit. "THE PARACLETE, THE HOLY SPIRIT WHOM THE FATHER WILL SEND IN MY NAME, WILL INSTRUCT YOU IN EVERYTHING, AND REMIND YOU OF ALL THAT I TOLD YOU." (JOHN 14:26)

FIRST DAY   **Reread last week's readings.**

1.   What was a helpful or new thought from the readings or from the homily you heard on Sunday?

2.   From what you learned, what personal application did you choose to apply to your life this week?

SECOND DAY   **READ SIRACH 15:15-20**   **FIRST READING**

("To whatever you choose stretch forth your hand.")

1.   Fill in the following blanks:
     _____ you _____ you can keep the com-
     mandments; it is _____ to do _____
     _____. Sirach 15:15

2.   What is set before you _____, and what must you stretch forth? Sirach 15:16

3.   What is before man, and what will be given him? Sirach 15:17

4.   What three things must we do to choose life? Deuteronomy 30:20

     1.

     2.

     3.

5.   What happens to those who choose life? Deuteronomy 30:19-20

6.   Who shows us the way we must choose? Psalm 25:12

7.   What is immense, and in what is the Lord mighty? Sirach 15:18

8.   What do the eyes of God see and what does he understand? Sirach 15:19

9.   What does God command man NOT to do, and what specific sin does Sirach 15:20 tell you, for which God does not give you strength?

Personal – Do you ever feel you do not have a choice in certain matters? Read Sirach 15:14–15. Have you ever lied and blamed it on your background or someone else or even said, "The devil made me do it?" Meditate on this passage of scripture and confess any past sins of lying.

THIRD DAY	**READ 1 CORINTHIANS 2:6-10**	**SECOND READING**

("Yet God has revealed this Wisdom to us through the Spirit.")

1. What is it that is expressed among the spiritually mature? 1 Corinthians 2:6

2. Is it a wisdom of this age? 1 Corinthians 2:6

3. Who are passing away? 1 Corinthians 2:6

4. What is it we utter? 1 Corinthians 2:7

5. To whom has he revealed this wisdom?

   Psalm 19:8
   Luke 7:35
   James 1:5

6. Why did God plan his wisdom before all ages? 1 Cor. 2:7

7. Did the rulers of this age know the mystery? 1 Cor. 2:8

8. What would they not have done if they had known God's wisdom? 1 Corinthians 2:8

9. What is written of this wisdom? 1 Corinthians 2:9

10. Through whom has God revealed this wisdom? 1 Cor. 2:10

11. What does the Spirit do? 1 Corinthians 2:10

Personal – How do you anticipate the exciting things God has planned for you each day? How do you show your love for God, other than sitting alone with him and talking to him?

FOURTH DAY	**READ MATTHEW 5:17-37**	**GOSPEL**

("Whoever fulfills and teaches these commands shall be great in the kingdom of God.")

1. What did Jesus say he did not come to do, and what did he say he came to do? Matthew 5:17

2. How did he fulfill the law, and of what did he assure them? Romans 3:21-31, Matthew 5:18

3. What will the person who breaks these commands, and teaches others to do so, be called in the kingdom of God? What will the person who fulfills these commands and teaches these commands be in the kingdom of God? Matthew 5:19

Personal– What makes you to be considered great in the kingdom of God? In what way do others see you walking by faith? How are you teaching your spouse, children, friends, and family, etc., to walk by faith?

4. What must surpass the scribes and Pharisees, and what will happen to those whose holiness does not surpass that of the scribes and Pharisees? Matthew 5:20

5. What was the commandment imposed on our forefathers? Matthew 5:21

6. What three things does Jesus say to us in Matthew 5:22; and by becoming angry, by using abusive language, and by being contemptuous toward our brother, what do we risk? Matthew 5:22

7. If you bring your gift to the altar and there recall that your brother has something against you, what must you do? Matthew 5:24

8. What does Jesus say about time, what will your opponent do if you lose time in going to him, and what is Jesus' warning? Matthew 5:25-26

Personal– Have you ever been angry, used abusive language, and been contemptuous to those in your family? Did you settle the matter right away or did you let it continue for days? You have the choice; think about it.

9. What commandment is he talking about in Matthew 5:27, and what does Jesus say about it? Matthew 5:28

10. What must we throw away in order not to destroy the whole body? Matthew 5:29-30

11. What does Jesus say about divorce, and what was the commandment imposed on our forefathers? Matthew 5:31-33

12. What did Jesus say about this, and what are heaven, earth, and Jerusalem? Matthew 5:34-35

13. By what else must we not swear? Matthew 5:36

14. What should we say when we mean yes and what should we say when we mean no. Whom does it come from when we say anything beyond that? Matthew 5:37

Personal– We know when we should say yes and when we should say no by God's Holy Word. The answers on how to live your life are all written in his Word, the Bible. How much time do you spend each day praying and reading God's Word? Pray and ask God to reveal his truth to you through the Bible.

FIFTH DAY   **READ PSALM 119:1-2,4-5,17-18,33-34**

("Give me discernment that I may observe your law and keep it with all my heart.")

Read and meditate on Psalm 119:1-2, 4-5, 17-18, 33-34.

What is the Lord saying to you personally through the Psalm?

How can you apply this to your life?

SIXTH DAY   **READ ALL OF THE COMMENTARY**

SIRACH 15:15-20

Sirach is one of the Wisdom books of the Old Testament. It is a very earthy and plain book that deals with morality and the true religious philosophy of life. The practicality of this book has much wisdom even for the people of today. The gift of free will comes from God and it is a precious gift. We know that we can serve God by keeping his commandments, or to reject his authority and, in turn, reject him.

God loves us so much that he will not take away that gift of free will from us; because, if he did, we would be like the dumb beasts in the jungle. Today's message is telling us that we can keep God's commandments, and we know that because he tells us he will always be there (John 15:7). We can choose evil but we cannot say we could not help ourselves because we would be trying to say that we did not have a choice. We may fool our friends, family, or even society with this false line of defense; but our all-wise, all-loving, and all-knowing God cannot be deceived.

We are compelled to always remember that our God is a God of love, and our religion is a religion of love, not fear. We do good things because we choose not to offend our beloved God who loves us even when we make bad choices. Love is a decision and when we do not have a choice to decide, it is no longer love that motivates us.

Christians are motivated by the knowledge that God has chosen to love us first, and that he never stops loving us. We may favorably reflect on this incredible kind of benevolent love that he has for us and choose to respond to his love with our "yes" to his Holy Word. You may have some terrible pages in your book of life, but you have the option to choose and to tear these pages out by coming back to God in the Sacrament of Reconciliation. We choose to come back into the safe and loving arms of a forgiving Father, called "Abba," when we turn to him and ask for his pardon.

1 CORINTHIANS 2:6-10

Paul was very emphatic that the Christian faith that the converted Corinthians had received was a gift from God. He stressed that they were converted from paganism not by any great skill of preaching or earthy philosophy, but by God. The mental outlook of the majority of today's society is very similar to that of St. Paul's time. Today, much is made of the earthly wisdom of our secular and religious leaders.

The philosophy of today is not centered on the cross of Calvary; on the contrary, it is concentrated on the centers of learning and trade. The big business tycoons of today are modern counterparts of the Roman slave-drivers. Today, in many parts of the world, the destiny of the poor is in the hands of those who are very wealthy. The things of God are openly denied and ridiculed. The power of money and guns seems to drown out the cry of the poor. Jesus called out to us and said, "What you do to the least of my brothers, you do unto me." (Matthew 25:31-46)

We see the desire of choice becoming a choice of death for the unwanted unborn of our land. We have become so advanced in our technology that segregation and suppression of our weaker brothers and sisters are lost in the frenzy to have more of everything. This is a direct result of our ignoring the only true wisdom of life. God's wisdom has been revealed in his incarnation; the modern man still thinks that his true happiness is centered here on earth. Man thinks that because he only has a few years here on earth, he has to go for the "gusto." We can only be brought back to reality by a return to recognizing God's plan for us.

The time we have here on earth is our journey to heaven. The more we reach out and help our fellow-travelers on this journey, the smoother will be our own trip. We must keep our path marked out by our heavenly Father, and we must practice brotherly love along the way. The majesty of what God has in store for those who love him is beyond our wildest dreams.

MATTHEW 5:17-37

Christ is not calling for the removal of the Ten Commandments. He is telling his followers that their attitude must be righteous and more spiritual than that of the scribes and Pharisees. The moral value of any legal observance comes from the inferiority of the attitudes of those who observe and keep the law. Our compliance with the law does not honor God alone. Our attitude of love, reverence, and obedience to do his will is what honors God. This is the core of the law of Christianity. The old law of Moses is not abolished; it is deepened and given new meaning. To avoid murdering someone, or even injuring someone, is not enough; rather, we are called to help and prevent injury to anyone who is in distress wherever and whenever we can. To be someone who doesn't commit adultery is not enough; we are called as Christians to respect and esteem purity. This includes not only purity in actions but also purity in thoughts.

Today, we hear a variety of ways to prevent infectious diseases, such as gonorrhea, syphilis, or AIDS. Why do we hear so little of purity, chastity, and Christian morality? We must be truthful people, not only to ourselves, but first to God (John 8:32). God's laws were given to help people love God with all their hearts and minds (Deuteronomy 6:5). God's law is a law of love, and love is a decision that begins with the mind. By Jesus' time the religious leaders turned the law into a confusing mass of rules. Jesus spoke out against the abuses and excesses to which the law had been subjected. The Pharisees were content to obey the law outwardly and would not allow it to change their hearts. Jesus was saying that the quality of our hearts had to be greater than that of the Pharisees.

Today, we only have to look around to see the outward forms of piety being practiced, such as going to Mass, reciting the daily devotions, and seeing clergy praying the Office. This kind of obedience, while it is good, is not enough if there is no "metonoia" (a change of heart). Do people see us as the fruit of the Spirit because we keep the laws of God? If not, why not? We need to really listen as Jesus talks to us in this passage. He says that we will be held accountable for everything we do, everything we do not do, and every one of our thoughts.

Jesus is our source and our supply when we are being attacked by wrongful thoughts (Philippians 4:19). We can strike back against Satan by filling our minds with thoughts that are pure, good, and honorable (Philippians 4:8). Jesus tells us to be truthful and speak with veracity, and our need for promises and oaths will be reduced tremendously.

Application

The first reading tells us that we have a "free will" and that we can make a choice. The second reading tells us that this gift of a "free will" is available to everyone. The gift of faith is open to all men, rich or poor, schooled or unschooled, sick or healthy. The Gospel tells us that the spirit or the intent of the law is what gives it power and success. A change of heart is what makes a law a proven value.

This week, let us show by our actions that a change of heart is taking place inside of us! Parents, this week, do not allow in your home any diversion, such as TV or video, that Jesus could not sit and watch, too. Children, do not talk or listen to any conversations in school or at work that Jesus could not listen to or talk about. **All Adults** – let whatever comes out of your mouth be words that will change other people's thoughts to thinking about Jesus Christ.

SEVENTH SUNDAY IN ORDINARY TIME - CYCLE A

BEFORE YOU BEGIN

Pray and ask God to speak to you through His Holy Spirit. "THE PARACLETE, THE HOLY SPIRIT WHOM THE FATHER WILL SEND IN MY NAME, WILL INSTRUCT YOU IN EVERYTHING, AND REMIND YOU OF ALL THAT I TOLD YOU." (JOHN 14:26)

FIRST DAY   **Reread last week's readings.**

1.   What was a helpful or new thought from the readings or from the homily you heard on Sunday?

2.   From what you learned, what personal application did you choose to apply to your life this week?

SECOND DAY   **READ LEVITICUS 19:1-2, 17-18**   **FIRST READING**

("Be holy, for I, the Lord your God, am holy.")

1.   To whom was the Lord speaking? Leviticus 19:1

2.   To whom did the Lord tell him to speak, and what did he tell him to say? Leviticus 19:2

3.   Who makes us holy and how do we become holy? Exodus 31:13, Ephesians 5:25-26, 1 Corinthians 3:17

4.   What must we do to become holy? Leviticus 20:7

5.   What is with his holy ones? Wisdom 3:9

6.   Who are the holy people? Isaiah 62:12

7.   What shall you not do, and what may you have to do? Leviticus 19:17

8.   What does Prov. 9:8 say will happen to us when we reprove an arrogant man and a wise man?

9.   What must we not incur because of our brother? Leviticus 19:17

10.   What must we not do against our fellow countrymen, and what command is given in Leviticus 19:18?

Personal – Are you loving your spouse, children, relatives, friends, and neighbor as yourself? In what way is the love of your neighbor evident? Share with someone if you wish.

11.   Who does God say he is? Leviticus 19:18

Personal – Who do you say God is? In what way is he your Lord? Your friend? Your ruler? Your Lord of all? Meditate on this.

THIRD DAY   **READ 1 CORINTHIANS 3:16-23**   **SECOND READING**

("You are the temple of God.")

1.   What is it of which you may not be aware? 1 Cor. 3:16, 1 Corinthians 6:19

2.   How do we know this? 2 Corinthians 6:16

3.   What will happen to anyone who destroys God's temple? 1 Corinthians 3:17

4.   What is the temple of God and who is that temple? 1 Corinthians 3:17

5.   How can we delude ourselves? 1 Corinthians 3:18

6.   What should you become if you think you are wise in a worldly way?
      1 Corinthians 3:18

7.   What is absurdity with God? 1 Corinthians 3:19

8.   What does scripture say about the worldly wise? 1 Corinthians 3:19-20, Job 5:13

9.   What must we not let happen and what is ours? 1 Corinthians 3:21-22

10.   To whom do you belong? 1 Corinthians 3:23

11.   How do we know this? 1 Corinthians 6:20

12.   To whom does Christ belong? 1 Corinthians 3:23

Personal – If you have been purchased by the Blood of Christ and you belong to him, in what way does your life reflect him in his Spirit dwelling within you to everyone you meet? This will be evident by the love they see in you. Reflect on this.

FOURTH DAY   **READ MATTHEW 5:38-48**   **GOSPEL**

("Offer no resistance to injury.")

1.   In Verse 38 of Matthew 5, who was speaking and what did he say that they had
      heard? Matthew 4:17 5:38

2.   What does he say to us, and when a person strikes us on the right cheek, what
      should we do? Matthew 5:39

3. What should we do if someone wants to go to the law over our shirt, and should anyone press us into service for one mile, what should we do? Matthew 5:40-41

4. What should we do with the man who begs from us, and what does Jesus tell us not to do? Matthew 5:42

5. What has God given us?
    Mark 3:28
    John 5:21
    John 13:34

6. What is the other commandment that he said we have heard and what is his commandment to us? Matthew 5:43-44

7. What will this prove, on whom does he make the sun to rise, and on whom does he cause the rain to fall? Matthew 5:45

8. If we love those who love us, is there any merit in that, and who does even that much? Matthew 5:46

9. If we greet our brothers only, what is praiseworthy about that, and who does as much? Matthew 5:47

10. In a word, what must we be made, just as your heavenly Father is? Matthew 5:48

Personal – In your life, how are you being made perfect, like your Heavenly Father, as you obey his command to love since you have been studying and have been obedient to his Word? Read John 14:21 to see the correlation between love, commandments, and obedience. Share with someone on how this has affected your life.

FIFTH DAY   **READ PSALM 103:1-13**

("He redeems your life from destruction.")

Read and meditate on Psalm 103:1-13.

What is the Lord saying to you personally through the Psalm?

How can you apply this to your life?

SIXTH DAY   **READ ALL OF THE COMMENTARY**

LEVITICUS 19:1-2, 17-18

This book, "Leviticus," acquires its name from dealing with matters concerned with laws centered around the worship of God. The worship of God was conducted by the tribe of Levi, and the end result was this book. Today's reading is taken from a body of laws commonly called the Laws of Holiness. Holiness is the key theme of Leviticus, and the word "holy" appears more often in Leviticus than in any other book of the Bible. Israel was called to be totally consecrated to God. God reminded the people of Israel that he was "holy" and wanted them to be "holy" also, just like he was.

The same call is being made to us today, and that is to be holy like our God is holy. The holiness that is being called for must be expressed in every aspect of our lives. The holiness that our loving God is calling for must be visible in the way we treat our neighbors and, of course, the question always is, "Who is my neighbor?" Our neighbor is anyone who is in distress anywhere and needs our help.

Today's reading calls for all of us to put aside our grudges and become people who forgive and forget. We are called to reason with our offending neighbor and try to bring him back to true brotherly fellowship in the Lord. The natural man wants to repay the offender back in full. The spiritual man who knows and loves God, must also be holy himself.

God's call for us to be holy and to imitate HIM is not really a command; it is more like advice given by a very loving Father.

1 CORINTHIANS 3:16-23

Paul is telling the people of Corinth, and the people living at the present time, that their bodies are temples of the Holy Spirit, and our church is the house of God. He goes on to say that our temples are not to be defiled. Satan has taken direct aim at the bodies of many Christians, and their temples have become defiled with alcohol, drugs, cigarette smoking, and sexual immorality. Our church is not to be spoiled by divisions within it through bickering, pettiness, jealousy, slandering, and false teachings, as its members come together to worship God.

Paul is telling the people that they have to choose between worldly wisdom or heavenly wisdom. Worldly wisdom that holds us back from God is no wisdom at all. Paul is telling us that some of the leaders of the community were caught up in pride and worldly wisdom, and the result was they valued their message more than its content.

Today, we can see a great deal of worldly wisdom being exercised in our nations and even in some areas of our church. Scripture tells us that God knows beyond any question how the human mind reasons and how foolish and desperate it is (1 Cor. 20). Paul closed by telling us that, as believers, all is for us and we belong to Christ.

To a believer in Christ, life and death become our servants. We know life's true purpose; but to the non-believers, only the latest trend in behavior is all they have. Non-believers are like victims of life who are swept along by its current and wonder if there is a meaning to it. For Christians, death holds no terrors because Christ conquered them all. Because of Jesus, you and I will live forever.

MATTHEW 5:38-48

Today's Gospel reveals the core of the Christian life and the conduct which should separate Christians from all others. Jesus begins by citing the oldest law in the world - an eye for an eye, and a tooth for a tooth. That was known as the "Lex Talionis" law and it came out of the Code of Hammorabi, who reigned in Babylon about 1700 years before Christ.

The law clearly stated that the injury a victim suffers shall be duplicated and suffered by the person who committed the crime. We find in today's reading the Mosaic law "an eye for an eye and a tooth for tooth" (Exodus 21:24) a subtle change.

This law was the beginning of mercy because it deliberately limited vengeance. Jesus completely moved away from that law because retaliation or "getting even," no matter how controlled or restricted, has no place in the life of his followers.

Jesus establishes a spirit of non-resentment and abolishes the concept of even limited vengeance. Today, Jesus is calling us to hear his message that in order to be one of his followers, we have to learn to resent no insult and to seek no vengeance. We are to be like Jesus, and forget what it is to be insulted, and not to respond with vengeance but with love. Jesus never insisted to stand on his rights. In fact, he did not consider himself as having any legal rights at all (Philippians 2:3-4).

The Christian who really follows Christ does not think of his rights, but of his duties. He does not think of his privileges; instead, he thinks of his responsibilities. Jesus strikes at the core of our belief by showing that our actions really demonstrate what we believe. Do you show disgust when someone requests that you do a menial task? Do you feel insulted when you do a good job and no one recognizes what you did? Do you work with some inefficient workers? Do you work with an ungracious helper?

Jesus calls us to respond only with love and he tells us that he will give us all that we need when we are tempted to respond otherwise (1 Cor. 10:13). Jesus' response, in today's reading, is that whatever we do to the least of his brothers and sisters, we do unto him (Matthew 25:31-46).

Application

The first reading is a call to holiness, and the second reading calls us to remember that we are temples of the Holy Spirit. The Gospel reveals that Christians do not have to "get even." Let us, this week, show that our call to holiness is being answered with a "yes" by attending Mass as often as we can and to be modest in the way we dress and in the way we talk.

We can respond to the person who irritates us with Christian love instead of pagan retaliation. Let us be kind and gentle to everyone we meet and, individually, be prepared for some "neat" miracles to happen!

EIGHTH SUNDAY IN ORDINARY TIME - CYCLE A

BEFORE YOU BEGIN

Pray and ask God to speak to you through His Holy Spirit. "THE PARACLETE, THE HOLY SPIRIT WHOM THE FATHER WILL SEND IN MY NAME, WILL INSTRUCT YOU IN EVERYTHING, AND REMIND YOU OF ALL THAT I TOLD YOU." (JOHN 14:26)

FIRST DAY   **Reread last week's readings.**

1.   What was a helpful or new thought from the readings or from the homily you heard on Sunday?

2.   From what you learned, what personal application did you choose to apply to your life this week?

SECOND DAY   **READ ISAIAH 49:14-15**   **FIRST READING**

("I will never forget you.")

1.   Who was speaking in verse 14 of Isaiah 49?

2.   Where or who is Zion?
        1 Kings 8:1
        Psalm 132:13–14
        Isaiah 46:13
        1 Peter 2:4–8

3.   What did Zion say? Isaiah 49:14

Personal– Have you ever felt, as the people of God, forsaken and forgotten by God? Do you give in to discouragement or do you seek the face of God by quietly talking to him? Tell him how you feel.

4.   Was there a time Jesus felt forsaken by God? Where did this happen, and what did Jesus say? Mark 15:34

5.   What is the question asked in verse 15 of Isaiah 49?

6.   What promise does the Lord give us that he will never do? Isaiah 49:15, Isaiah 44:21

7.   What are we in the eyes of God? Isaiah 43:4

8.   How does God feel about us? Isaiah 43:4

THIRD DAY	READ 1 CORINTHIANS 4:1-5	SECOND READING

("The first requirement of an administrator is that he prove trustworthy.")

1. How should men regard us? 1 Corinthians 4:1

2. What are the mysteries of God? Judges 13:19

3. Who reveals these mysteries? Daniel 2:28

4. What is the first requirement of an administrator? 1 Corinthians 4:2

5. How do we prove to be trustworthy? Exodus 18:21, John 4:50

6. What matters little to Paul? 1 Corinthians 4:3

7. Does he have anything on his conscience? 1 Corinthians 4:4

8. Does that mean he is declaring himself innocent? 1 Corinthians 4:14

9. Who does he say is the one to pass judgment on him? 1 Corinthians 4:4

10. What does Paul tell the people to avoid doing before the time of the Lord's return? 1 Corinthians 4:5

11. What two things will the Lord do? 1 Corinthians 4:5

    1.

    2.

12. What will happen at that time? 1 Corinthians 4:5

Personal - Do you have a clear conscience before God and man? If not, repent of whatever is bothering you. Do you declare yourself innocent? Do you pass judgment on yourself? Who is the one to pass judgment on you? Reflect on this.

FOURTH DAY	READ MATTHEW 6:24-34	GOSPEL

("You cannot give yourself to God and money.")

1. What can no man do and what are the two things we cannot serve together? Matthew 6:24

2. What is the root of all evil? 1 Timothy 6:10

3. What is the warning given in Matthew, what is more important than food, and what is more valuable than clothes? Matthew 6:25

4.   In Matthew 6:26, at what does he tell us to look, what do the birds do for their food, and who feeds them?

5.   What is the question he asks in Matthew 6:26?

Personal - Refer back to Isaiah 43:4 to see how important you are to the Lord. Do you look at yourself as Jesus does? How do you look at yourself? Reflect on this.

6.   Read Matthew 6:27-28 about worrying. What does God's Word say about worrying, and what about the wild flowers?

7.   Who was not in all his splendor arrayed like the flowers of the fields, and what happens to the grass of the fields? Matthew 6:29-30

8.   About what three necessities should we NOT worry? Matthew 6:31

        1.

        2.

        3.

9.   Who is always running after these things, and who knows all that we need? Matthew 6:32

10.   What two things are we to seek first? Matthew 6:33

        1.

        2.

11.   What will be given us if we do the above, and what does Jesus say about tomorrow and today? Matthew 33-34

Personal - Do you spend too much of your time worrying about the roof over your head, the food on your table, and the clothes on your back? Take one day this week and make yourself aware of how much time you spend doing this. Bring this before your heavenly Father.

FIFTH DAY   **READ PSALM 62:2-3, 6-9**

("Only in God is my soul at rest.")

Read and meditate on Psalm 62:2-3, 6-9.

What is the Lord saying to you personally through the Psalm?

How can you apply this to your life?

SIXTH DAY **READ ALL OF THE COMMENTARY**

ISAIAH 49:14-15

The people of Israel thought that God had deserted and forgotten them while they were in captivity in Babylon. Today's passage points out that God is like a loving Father who would never leave his child under any condition. God is telling us that he has each one of our names stamped on the palms of his hands. The people realized that their own sinfulness had brought about much of their captivity.

The Israelites saw that God would not tolerate or condone sin. They felt that God had punished them for their turning away from him. Today sin separates us from God, just as it did in the time of Isaiah; and it brings much pain and suffering to many innocent people. We need to confess our sins and repent and enjoy the forgiveness and love of our God who reigns over all the earth. Isaiah draws upon the sacredness of a mother's love, devotion, perseverance, and courage in relating her to the love God has for us. He did not forget his people; He delivered them from slavery in the Exodus, using Moses as his instrument of justice. He knows every one of us personally and he died on the cross so that each one of us would experience his love and saving grace.

When we experience loneliness, abandonment, doubt, confusion, rejection, or even despair, we must ask ourselves whether we have turned away from his loving arms. No hurt or problem that we have is too big for him to heal or solve. He will never walk away and leave us orphans. He will take us to his bosom and love us back into his kingdom of justice.

1 CORINTHIANS 4:1-5

Paul calls out the Christian leaders of the day to lead by being servants. A servant does what his master tells him to do, and he does not check to see whether the crowd agrees with his master or not. The people in Paul's day wanted to be leaders and they wanted recognition, fame, respect, and power. We today are being called to be servants of God, and we are called to obey his commandments and abide in him (John 15:7). Abide means to live in, to take up residence. This means we have to be completely available to be obedient to our Lord Jesus' call.

God speaks to us every day through his Holy Word, his Sacraments, and his people through the teachings of the Church. Only God knows a person's heart and he alone has the right to judge someone. Paul warns the Christians that they are called, not to be judges but, to be servants. This warning applies to us in this day and year. There are many who condemn others because of their race, or belief or the color of their skin.

A servant is called to be of service to another, to be helpful, courteous, honest and responsible. A servant never judges; he only serves, and in Christianity a real servant is a real leader in the eyes of Jesus Christ. We are called to celebrate our being saved by Jesus Christ by serving others so that they may also find Jesus who is salvation, and who is the servant of servants.

MATTHEW 6:24-34

Jesus really gets into the people's mind and hearts when he talks about God and money. He tells them that they can have only one master and that master has to be God. He tells them to seek him and his kingdom first and all else will be added (Matthew 6:33). Today in many societies the desire to make money, have money, and spend money is so strong that people will lie, cheat, steal, and even kill to get their share of the money. The incredible truth is that, after spending most of their life serving the god of money, they die and leave every single penny to someone else. We come into this world with nothing and we leave it with nothing. Jesus is not saying that money is evil or that people who have money are evil. He is saying that the love of money is evil. We are to love people, not things. Money is a thing that is to be used. We use things, not people.

We need to reflect about our own use of time, talent, and wealth. Where and whatever we spend most of our time, is where our heart is. Jesus calls us to look at our spiritual values and our earthly values and make sure that our spiritual values get our top priority. We are called to use our wealth to help the least of our brothers (Matthew 25:31-46). We are called not to let our wealth use us and possess us.

Someday, when we stand before God on judgment day, we will be called to answer some very hard questions. The main questions asked of us will not be: How rich were you? How big was your house? How long was your car? What college did you attend? The real questions will be DID you love me by loving your brothers and sisters? DID you clothe my nakedness? DID you feed my hungry? DID you give shelter to my homeless? DID you visit my sick in hospitals? DID you visit my people in prisons? DID you seek my kingship first? The answer can be a resounding YES if we put Jesus Christ, our Lord and Savior, first in our priority of values right now. Let him be the one who is the Lord of our lives right now and you will live forever.

Application

The first reading tells us that God has each one of our names stamped on his hand. The second reading reveals that Christians are called to be leaders by being servants. The Gospel tells us that we can only have one master and that master has to be God.

This week, let us show that God is our master. Sacrifice a time of pleasure or entertainment and take that money that you would normally spend and give it to the poor. You might want to give it to some charity in your church or maybe even take someone whom you know out to lunch or dinner. The person whom you are helping is Jesus: do you believe that?

NINTH SUNDAY OF ORDINARY TIME – CYCLE A

BEFORE YOU BEGIN

Pray and ask God to speak to you through His Holy Spirit. "THE PARACLETE, THE HOLY SPIRIT WHOM THE FATHER WILL SEND IN MY NAME, WILL INSTRUCT YOU IN EVERYTHING, AND REMIND YOU OF ALL THAT I TOLD YOU." (JOHN 14:26)

FIRST DAY   **Reread last week's readings.**

1.   What was a helpful or new thought from the readings or from the homily you heard on Sunday?

2.   From what you learned, what personal application did you choose to apply to your life this week?

SECOND DAY   **READ DEUTERONOMY 11:18, 26-28**   **FIRST READING**

("Therefore, take these words of mine into your heart and soul.")

1.   What did Moses tell the people to do with the words he said? Deuteronomy 11:18

2.   What is to be on the people's lips and for what reason? Exodus 13:9

3.   On what is man to live? Matthew 4:4

4.   What does Moses set before the people this day? Deuteronomy 11:26

5.   Who shall receive a blessing from the Lord? Psalm 24:4-5

6.   Why will some be cursed? Malachi 2:2

7.   Why is a blessing given? Deuteronomy 11:27

8.   How are we to love the Lord and what are we to do with these words? Deuteronomy 6:4-6

9.   What will happen to the people if they follow other gods they have not known? Deuteronomy 11:28

10.   What did Jesus say will happen to us if we obey his commandments? John 15:10

Personal – In what way is the Word of God a sign from you that others recognize? How do your family and friends see his Word written in you?

THIRD DAY   **READ ROMANS 3:21-25, 28**   **SECOND READING**

("For we consider that a person is justified by faith apart from works of the law.")

1. How has the righteousness of God been manifested and by whom was it testified? Romans 3:21

2. To what did the law and the prophets testify? Romans 3:21-22

3. What is the name given Jesus by the prophet Jeremiah? Jeremiah 23:5-6

4. Who is the one who will live in faith? Romans 1:17

5. To those who pursue righteousness by good works, what does Jesus become? Romans 9:30-33, Galatians 2:16

6. Who have sinned and are deprived of the glory of God? Romans 3:23

7. How are we justified? Romans 3:24

8. For what was Jesus handed over and for what was he raised? Romans 4:24-25

9. For what did God set Jesus forth and what did it prove? Romans 3:25

10. By what is a person justified and with whom does he have peace? Romans 3:28, Romans 5:1

Personal - How do you see yourself justified by faith and not by the works you do? What has your faith in God done for you?

FOURTH DAY   **READ MATTHEW 7:21-27**   **GOSPEL**

*("Everyone who listens to these words of mine and acts on them
will be like a wise man who built his house on rock.")*

1. Who will enter the kingdom of heaven? Matthew 7:21

2. What did the virgins say to the bridegroom, and what did he say to them? Matthew 25:11-12

3. Who is brother, sister, and mother to Jesus? Matthew 12:50

4. What will many say to the Lord and what will his answer be? Matthew 7:22-23

5. What is faith without works? James 2:14-17

6. What will everyone be like who listens to God's words and acts on them? Matthew 7:24

7. Who will be blessed in what he does? James 1:25

8. Who is the rock? Isaiah 26:4

9. When you set your house on rock and the rains, winds, and buffeting come, what will happen? Matthew 7:25

10. What will happen to the man who listens to God's Word and does not act on it? Matthew 7:26-27

Personal – What do you need to do in your home, work, school, or neighborhood to act upon what you have learned from God's Word today? What happens to you when the storms hit you like financial disaster, or your health goes bad, or you are rejected in any way? Do you collapse, or do you stand firm?

FIFTH DAY   **READ PSALM 31:2-4, 17, 25**

("For your name's sake you will lead and guide me.")

Read and meditate on Psalm 31:2-4, 17, 25.

What is the Lord saying to you personally through the Psalm?

How can you apply this to your life?

SIXTH DAY   **READ ALL OF THE COMMENTARY**

DEUTERONOMY 11:18, 26-28

A strong call is being made to bring God's Holy Word into the hearts and minds of the Jewish people. The reminders that were put on the wrists and on the foreheads of the people were very visible, and they served as a deterrent to doing things against God's commandments. Storing God's Word in our heart and minds is a powerful deterrent to sin, and this alone should make us want to memorize scripture. But memorization alone will not keep us from sin, because we must also put God's Word to work in our lives.

Christians do not need visible reminders placed on their bodies to remember God's Holy Word. The world will be able to see what they believe by the way Christians love one another (John 13:34).

You might well remember that for some people the only bible that they will ever read will be you. In today's passage, we see many people choosing curses over blessings. It is amazing that people actually choose a curse of rebellion over a blessing of peace. God's Holy Word shows us that obedience brings love and blessings. Rebellion, on the other hand, brings on the curse of punishment, fear, and judgment.

We have the same fundamental choice today. We can live for ourselves or live in service to God. To choose our own way is to travel on a dead-end road, but to choose God's way is to receive eternal life (John 5:24).

ROMANS 3:21-25, 28

Did you know that God loves you and has a wonderful plan for your life? He loves you so much that he gave his only begotten Son so that anyone who believes in him should not perish but have eternal life (John 3:16). His plan for you is that he came that you might have life and might have it abundantly (John 10:10). Why then is it that most people are not experiencing the abundant life? Because man is sinful and separated from God; man, therefore, cannot know and experience God's love and plan for his life (Romans 3:23).

In today's reading Paul now gives us some wonderful news. We can be declared "not guilty" by trusting Jesus Christ to take away our sins. Trusting means putting our confidence in him to forgive our sins. We have a tremendous blessing in the Sacrament of Reconciliation. We need to reflect, repent, confess, and be forgiven of our sins; and when we do that, the Holy Spirit empowers us to live the way Jesus wants us to live.

Jesus Christ is God's only provision for man's sin. Through him we can know and experience God's love and plan for our lives. This is God's solution, and it is available to all of us regardless of our background or past behavior. When God forgives our sins, our record is wiped clean. From his viewpoint it is as though we have never sinned.

MATTHEW 7:21-27

Matthew is telling the people in today's Gospel that not everybody who talks about heaven belongs to God's kingdom. Jesus is more concerned with our "walk" than our "talk." He wants us to do what is right, not just say what is right. Today we have many people say they are against abortion but they do not do anything to stop it. What we do cannot be separated from what we believe.

Jesus warned against religiosity and it was clear that only a personal relationship with him and obedience to his Father's will is what will matter. Many people think that if they are good and sound religious, and keep busy with many activities within the church, they will be rewarded with eternal life. In reality, a living faith in Jesus Christ - one demonstrated in love for God and neighbor - is what will count at the judgment. The judgment is the final day of reckoning when God will settle all accounts, judging sin and rewarding faith authenticated in love.

He talks about a house in today's reading, but you can call that house your life and you will not withstand the storms of life if you do not have a strong practicing faith in Jesus Christ. For a strong practicing faith in Jesus Christ you need to be in daily prayer, receiving the sacraments, studying scripture, and growing and learning in the fellowship of the Catholic Church.

Application

The first reading tells us that what you see is not always what you get. The second reading reveals that Jesus Christ is God's only provision for man's sin. The Gospel shows us that a house built on rock will stand but a house built on sand will wash away.

This week, let God's love for you and his plan for you be experienced by you. Take stock of what you say about God, your church, and your faith. Now compare what you say with what you do about your God, your church, and your faith. Do you live what you profess to believe? Ask the members of your family to honestly describe you. Does their description of you match your description of yourself? Begin first in prayer and let your prayer life be the foundation of your action. For one to be holy, one has to be balanced in body, mind, and spirit.

FIRST SUNDAY OF LENT - CYCLE A

BEFORE YOU BEGIN

Pray and ask God to speak to you through His Holy Spirit. "THE PARACLETE, THE HOLY SPIRIT WHOM THE FATHER WILL SEND IN MY NAME, WILL INSTRUCT YOU IN EVERYTHING, AND REMIND YOU OF ALL THAT I TOLD YOU." (JOHN 14:26)

FIRST DAY   **Reread last week's readings.**

1.   What was a helpful or new thought from the readings or from the homily you heard on Sunday?

2.   From what you learned, what personal application did you choose to apply to your life this week?

SECOND DAY   **READ GENESIS 2:7-9, 3:1-7**   **FIRST READING**

("Creation of our first parents, and sin.")

1.   Out of what did the Lord God form man? Genesis 2:7; Sirach 33:10; Isaiah 64:7

2.   What did he blow into his nostrils and what did man become? Genesis 2:7

3.   What did the Lord God plant, where did he plant it, and whom did he place there? Genesis 2:8

4.   What did the Lord make out of the ground? Genesis 2:9

5.   Fill in the following blanks: Out of the ground the Lord God made
_____ _____ grow that were delightful to
_____ at and good for _____, with the
_____ _____ _____ in the
middle of the garden and the _____ of the
_____ of _____ and _____.
Genesis 2:9

Personal – How do you see yourself being molded by Jesus each day? Have you offered yourself to God and allowed him to shape you in his own image, or have you offered yourself to those around you and allowed them to shape you into the world's image? Meditate on this.

6.   Who is the most cunning of all the animals that the Lord God has made and to whom did the serpent ask the question, and what was the woman's answer to the question? Genesis 3:1-3

7.   What did God say would happen to them if they ate from the tree in the middle of the garden? Genesis 2:17, 3:3

8. What did the serpent say to the woman? Genesis 2:17, 3:4-5

9. Compare the three things the woman saw in Genesis 3:6 with the three things the world has to offer in 1 John 2:16.

GENESIS 3:6 1	**JOHN 2:16**
1.	
2.	
3.	

10. What did she do, who was with her, and what happened when they ate the fruit? Genesis 3:6-7

THIRD DAY   **READ ROMANS 5:12-19**   **SECOND READING**

("The results of the gift, Jesus Christ, outweigh one man's sin.")

1. How did sin enter the world and what went with sin? Romans 5:12

2. To whom did death come and what was in the world before the law? Romans 5:12-13

3. What reigned from Adam to Moses and even over those who had not sinned yet? Romans 5:14

4. What is the gift not like and what overflowed for the many? Romans 5:15

5. To whom is grace given? Ephesians 6:24, Psalm 84:12, Romans 11:5

6. How does God's grace work in us and what is God's gift to us? Ephesians 2:8, Acts 2:38 and 1 Peter 2:19

7. What is entirely different from the sin committed by the one man? Romans 5:16

8. What happened in the first case and what happened in the second case? Romans 5:16

9. If death began to reign through one man because of his offense, what will those receive through the one man, Jesus Christ? Romans 5:17

10. Compare the following and fill in the blanks: Romans 5:18-19

a single offense   a single righteous act

_____   _____

one man's disobedience   one man's obedience

_____   _____

Personal – How are you walking in obedience to God's Word? Do you know it enough to distinguish whether you are or are not walking in obedience? In what way is his grace sufficient for you? Think about this.

FOURTH DAY   **READ MATTHEW 4:1-11**   **GOSPEL**

("Like Adam and Eve, Jesus was tempted, but did not sin.")

1. What happened just before Jesus was led into the desert? Matthew 4:2, Matthew 3:13

2. Who led Jesus into the desert and by whom was he tested? Matthew 4:1

3. How long did he fast and what was his physical condition after he fasted? Matthew 4:2

4. What is the devil called and what did he say to him? Matthew 4:3

5. What was Jesus' reply and how did he say this man was not to live? Matthew 4:4

6. What are some other ways besides hunger by which the devil can tempt us? Ephesians 4:26, 27 James 4:6-7, 1 Peter 5:8

7. What did the devil do next and what did the devil say to Jesus? Matthew 4:5-6

8. What did the devil quote in Matthew 4:6, and where did the quote come from? Psalm 91:11

9. What did Jesus answer him and on what did Jesus again rely? Matthew 4:7, Deuteronomy 6:6

10. What did the devil then do, what did the devil promise Jesus, and what would he have to do in order to receive this promise? Matthew 4:8-9

11. What did Jesus say to him, what did the devil do, and who came and waited on Jesus? Matthew 4:11

Personal – If, when being tempted by the devil, Jesus responded with "Scripture has it," should we not also respond to temptation with "Scripture has it?" How has the study of God's Word helped you resist temptation and make Satan flee? Use God's Word and concentrate on areas in which you are weak and are tempted. If you cannot think of a scripture in that particular area, remember to ask the Holy Spirit to reveal one to you.

FIFTH DAY   **READ PSALM 51:3-6, 12-14, 17**

("In the greatness of your compassion, wipe out my offense.")

Read and meditate on Psalm 51:3-6, 12-14, 17.

What is the Lord saying to you personally through the Psalm?

How can you apply this to your life?

GENESIS 2:7-9; 3:1-7

We see in this passage the tremendous gift that comes from God, and that, of course, is life. The body is lifeless until God breathes life into it. Our bodies return to dust when God removes his life-giving breath from us. It is incredibly important that we see that man's life and worth come from the breath of God. This passage clearly shows us our need for God. We need only to look around and see how temporary our achievements are. We find that God is the only permanent value in our lives. Because of him, you and I can face tomorrow without any need to fear.

God has given us a miraculous gift called life and we need to value it as much as he does. We do this by valuing the lives of others and protecting the sanctity of human life wherever we may go. God showed us how special we were by placing Adam and Eve in a beautiful and safe garden of plants and trees.

We need to confront the age-old question, why would God place a tree in the garden and then forbid Adam to eat from it? God, of course, wanted Adam to obey him, but he also gave him the freedom to choose. Today, God gives us that choice, and many times, like Adam, we make a wrong choice. These wrong choices that we make today can cause us and others great pain and irritation. They also can help us to learn and grow and make better choices in the future. Adam was given a choice, because he would have been a prisoner forced to obey if he couldn't say "no". We see Satan disguised as a serpent trying to tempt Eve.

Satan is still trying to tempt everyone away from God even as you read this commentary. Satan failed and he was crushed by God (Gen. 3:14). Adam and Eve learned that since God is holy and hates sin, he must punish sinners. Why does Satan tempt us? Temptation is Satan's invitation to give in to his kind of life and give up on God's kind of life. Satan tempted Eve and was successful in getting her to sin, and ever since that time he's been busy getting people to sin.

We can resist temptation by praying for the strength to resist. We can run away or remove ourselves from situations that cause the temptation (bad movies, dirty jokes, bad companions, etc.). Finally, we can say no when confronted with what we know is wrong. Satan tries to show Eve that sin is lovely, and today, we see that same philosophy in our movies and TV shows at home. People usually choose wrong things because they have been convinced that these things are good. Be prepared to resist the attractive temptations that may come your way.

ROMANS 5:12-19

"It isn't fair." That is the cry of many who refuse to be declared guilty of something Adam did thousands of years ago. Many people feel it is not right or fair for God to lay his judgment on us today for what Adam did so long ago. Yet each one of us confirms our identification with Adam by our sins. We are made of the same stuff, quick to rebel, quick to make judgments on others. We are all sinners who fall short of the glory of God (Romans 3:23) and what we really need is not fairness, rather it is mercy.

Paul tells the people that keeping the law does not bring salvation. He goes on to tell them that the law helps people to see their sinfulness. The law points out our sin and places the responsibility for it squarely on our shoulders. The law does not save us from the results of sin; only the healing power of Jesus Christ can save us.

We must turn to Jesus in order to be saved. Adam has brought to all of us the results of his sin, inherited guilt, the tendency to sin, and God's punishment. Because of Jesus' dying for us on the cross even while we were yet sinners (Romans 5:8), we can still trade judgment for forgiveness. Jesus has offered us the chance to be born into his spiritual family, the family that begins with forgiveness and leads to eternal life.

We have an incredible opportunity to make a choice. If we do nothing we have death through Adam. If, on the other hand, we decide to come to God through faith, we will have life through Christ. Think about this question very seriously. To which family line do you now belong?

MATTHEW 4:1-11

Matthew shows us, in this passage, the humanness of Jesus and his being tempted while being very vulnerable and hungry in the desert. This experience allowed Jesus to reaffirm God's plan for his own ministry. This temptation of Jesus is very important for us because it showed that even Jesus had to face temptation, and we should expect no less than this, too.

Jesus did not give in to his temptation, and we can do the same through faith and obedience to Our Lord Jesus Christ. A person has not shown true obedience if he has never had the opportunity to be disobedient. We need to realize that we too will be tested and we should be alert and ready for it. We are not being tempted by Christ because he does not try to drag us down. We are being tempted by Satan, and only through faith in Jesus can we resist and make the devil flee.

It is important for us to remember our convictions are only as good as they are under pressure. Testing is a time that we experience as we react to the temptation. We need to remember that temptation itself is not a sin. We sin when we give in and disobey God. We see in this passage that Satan's temptations focused on four crucial areas in our lives: physical desires, possessions, power, and pride. These temptations are very much in activities against the people of today as well as they were for Jesus.

Jesus resisted Satan because he knew scripture and he called on it and obeyed it. We are told that God's Word is a weapon, like a hammer that smashes rocks (Jeremiah 23:29). Knowing scriptures is important in resisting Satan's attacks, but we must obey God's Word as well. We might well remember that Satan knew scripture too, but he chose to disobey God's Holy Word. Satan used scripture to try to convince Jesus to sin, and today, sometimes a friend will try to convince you with a scripture that seems to support his viewpoint. Pray, read, and study God's Word daily and you will be ready when Satan tries to trap you into giving in to temptation.

Application

The first reading shows us that distortion of the Word is dangerous. In the second reading we clearly see that the gift of Jesus' death on the cross totally wipes out the results of Adam's sin. The Gospel reveals that knowing God's Word, while important, is not enough to resist temptation. We must act on God's Word to really be free of the temptation.

This week, let us look for a scripture that fits a particular temptation that we come up against. An example is that we should never go to bed while angry at someone, such as a spouse, father, mother, brother, sister, etc. We should act upon the scripture, Ephesians 4:26, which says, "Don't let the sun go down with you still angry, get over it quickly." We do that by confessing our sin and asking that person to forgive us. That is a great way to resist Satan and make him flee.

SECOND SUNDAY OF LENT – CYCLE A

BEFORE YOU BEGIN

Pray and ask God to speak to you through His Holy Spirit. "THE PARACLETE, THE HOLY SPIRIT WHOM THE FATHER WILL SEND IN MY NAME, WILL INSTRUCT YOU IN EVERYTHING, AND REMIND YOU OF ALL THAT I TOLD YOU." (JOHN 14:26)

FIRST DAY   **Reread last week's readings.**

1.   What was a helpful or new thought from the readings or from the homily you heard on Sunday?

2.   From what you learned, what personal application did you choose to apply to your life this week?

SECOND DAY   **READ GENESIS 12:1-4**   **FIRST READING**

("The call of Abraham, the father of God's people.")

1.   Who was the Lord God talking to in Genesis 12:1?

2.   Where did the Lord tell him to go? Genesis 12:1

3.   What four things did the Lord say he would do for Abram? Genesis 12:2-3

    1.

    2.

    3.

    4.

4.   What will God do to those who bless Abram? Genesis 12:3

Personal – The dictionary defines the word bless as: l. to make holy, hallow, 2. to ask divine favor for, 3. to wish well to, 4. to make happy or prosperous, 5. to guard, preserve. In what way have you felt blest by the Lord? In what way have you made it a practice to bless your spouse, your children, relatives or friends?

5.   What will God do to those who curse Abram? Genesis 12:3

6.   Who shall find blessing in Abram? Genesis 12:3

7.   What did Abram do, and who went with him? Genesis 12:4

8.   Who was Lot? Genesis 11:31

9.   How old was Abram when he left Haran, land of his kinsfolk? Genesis 12:4

10.   What other name was given to Abram by the Lord and what did the Lord make him? Genesis 17:5

Personal – In what way do you recognize the voice of the Lord when he is speaking to you, and do you obey that voice as Abram did? How do you think you can discern whether God is or is not speaking to you? Share with someone.

THIRD DAY   **READ 2 TIMOTHY 1:8-10**   **SECOND READING**

("God has saved us and called us to be holy.")

1.   Who is speaking in verse 8 of 2 Timothy 1 and to whom is he speaking?
2 Timothy 1:1-2

2.   Of what are we **not** to be ashamed?
2 Timothy 1:8
Sirach 4:26
Sirach 51:29
Romans 1:16
1 Peter 4:16

3.   What will happen if we are ashamed of Jesus and his doctrine? Luke 9:26

4.   From where does our strength come? 2 Timothy 1:8

5.   What must we bear? 2 Timothy 1:8

6.   Who can we take as models in suffering hardship and patience? James 5:10

7.   What has God done for us, and to what kind of life has he called us?
2 Timothy 1:9

8.   Have we been saved by anything we have done? 2 Timothy 1:9

9.   How has God saved us? 2 Timothy 1:9-10, Titus 3:5

10.   How did he rob death of its power? 2 Timothy 1:10, Romans 6:9-10

Personal – What is the testimony to our Lord you have to share? Do you have a personal testimony of how God has worked in your life? Have you shared this with your spouse, children, family, friends, or work acquaintances? Pray and ask God to reveal to you your own personal testimony this week.

FOURTH DAY   **READ MATTHEW 17:1-9**   **GOSPEL**

("His face became as dazzling as the sun, his clothes as radiant as light.")

1.   Who did Jesus take up on a high mountain and what happened to Jesus?
     Matthew 17:1-2

2.   Who suddenly appeared there and what did Peter then say? Matthew 17:3-4

3.   As Peter was speaking, what overshadowed them and what came out of the cloud?
     Matthew 17:5

4.   What prevents us from listening to the Lord?
     Exodus 7:13
     Deuteronomy 1:43
     Deuteronomy 21:18
     Acts 28:27
     Hebrews 12:25

Personal – In what way have you been able to tune your mind into hearing what God is saying to you through prayer and his Word? Meditate on this.

5.   How did God the Father address Jesus in Matthew 17:5? Matthew 3:17

6.   What happened to Peter, James, and John when they heard the voice from the cloud and with what were they overcome? Matthew 17:6

7.   What did Jesus do and what did he say? Matthew 17:7

8.   In the following scriptures, what happened to those on whom Jesus laid his hand?
     Matt 8:3, 14-15, Matt 9:23-25

9.   What does 1 John 4:16-18 say is the relationship of God, love, and fear?

10. What did God say to Abram about fear in Genesis 15:1?

11. To whom did Jesus say "Do not be afraid? " Matthew 28:1, 8-10 Mark 6:45, 49-50, Luke 5:10

12. When Peter, James and John looked up, whom did they see and as they were coming down the mountain side, what was Jesus' command to them?
     Matthew 17:8-9

Personal – In what way have you felt Jesus' healing touch upon you? Have you laid your hand on those in your family who may be sick? If a friend or a family member is afraid, lay your hand on them and reassure them of God's presence.

FIFTH DAY   **READ PSALM 33:4-5, 18-20, 22**

("For upright is the Word of the Lord.")

Read and meditate on Psalm 33:4-5, 18-20, 22.

What is the Lord saying to you personally through out Psalm?

How can you apply this to your life?

SIXTH DAY   **READ ALL OF THE COMMENTARY**

GENESIS 12:1-4

It is very significant and quite proper that the passage of Abram should lead us into the second Sunday of Lent. Abram was a pagan living in an idol-worshipping country. He was about 75 years old and enjoyed a reputation as a successful man of the community. Abram had experienced a personal conversion and was convinced that God alone was the true God. First came the call to Abram and then came the "Great Commission" to "go forth and make disciples of all nations" (Matthew 28:19).

God's mercy and love for us are the first lesson this call of Abram teaches us. Through Abram God began the preparations that would lead to the coming of Jesus Christ, our Lord and Savior, who would reopen heaven's gates for us. Only a God of love and mercy could have persevered in the face of such a stubborn people. We, too, are to extend God's love to all nations, not just our own. Through Abram's family, Jesus was born to save all humanity. Through Jesus all people and all nations can have a personal relationship with God and the blessings will continue even unto today, beyond measure.

God's promise to make Abram great was tied to a promise of obedience by Abram. This meant leaving the comfort and safety of his home and friends and traveling to a new and strange land. Abram obeyed, walking away from all of his possessions, for God promised him even greater things. We are called, like Abram, to be chosen people.

When we make our conversion, as Abram did, and experience God personally, we will also be called to go forth in his name. God may be trying to lead you to a place of holiness and of greater service to his people. Don't let the comfort and security of what you have achieved, allow you to miss out on God's plan. God's plan for Israel is the same as it is for you and me. Jesus said, "I have come to give you, not just life, but life in its fullness." (John 10:10).

God planned to develop a nation of people he would call his own. Through the death and resurrection of Jesus Christ, you and I have the privilege of being called sons and daughters of God. God calls today and we are to listen and respond by accepting him personally, and then to go forth and tell others what we have experienced. This is called evangelizing or witnessing. We are called to make disciples of all nations (Matthew 28:19).

2 TIMOTHY 1:8-10

Paul, in prison writes this letter to Timothy in hopes of encouraging him to persevere in his ministry. There was much persecution going on in the Christian communities, Paul was concerned because of

Timothy's youth and the amount of opposition to him as a leader. Paul was urging him to be bold. Oh, how much boldness is needed by our Christian leaders today.

We see boldness everywhere in secular world leaders and not enough belief in the religious leaders. Paul tells Timothy, what everyone of us should never forget, that suffering will come to those who live out the Gospel message. In fact, Paul was jailed for preaching the Gospel (Hebrews 13:23). Paul promised Timothy that God would give him strength and that he would be ready when it was his turn to suffer.

We too must be ready and we too will be given strength by Jesus (1 Corinthians 10:13). Today, the threat of ridicule, rejection, being politically defeated, and, in some places in the world, being assassinated is the price for standing up for Christ. When we stand up for Christ in spite of the persecution, we are living out the Gospel message of God who loves us, chose us and sent Jesus to die for us. We die for Christ by dying to ourselves and when we call on the power of the Holy Spirit to defend us. We can stand up for Christ and endure peer pressure by walking away from pornography, refusing to go to R-rated movies, and not buying the videos that portray women as sexual play-toys.

Persecution is active today in many ways, and we must remember that we do not deserve to be saved, but God offers us salvation anyway. All we have to do is believe and respond with obedience to him. We must never forget that evil will succeed only when righteous people do nothing.

MATTHEW 17:1-9

The Transfiguration was a special revelation of Jesus' divinity to three of his disciples. God affirmed everything that Jesus had done and was about to do in the near future. The presence of Moses and Elijah with Jesus confirmed his mission of salvation. Moses represented the law. He is the central figure in the Pentateuch (first five books of the Bible), and he predicted the coming of a great Prophet (Deut. 18:15-19).

Elijah represents the prophets who foretold the coming of the Messiah (Malachi 4:5-6). Jesus is the fulfillment of both the law and the prophets. God's voice at the Transfiguration gave authority to Jesus' words. Peter wanted them all to stay and offered to build a place for all three. He wanted to act, but it was a time to pray and worship.

We must remember that before anything is acted upon, we must first pray and give worship to God. Peter did not realize that Christ was not to be compared to anyone, especially on any mountain top. Today much of the world looks at Jesus Christ as being a good leader, a good influence or a great prophet. The fact is, he is more than that, he is the Son of God. When you understand this incredible truth, the only appropriate response is worship.

We need to know about Christ in order to obey him completely. We must pray, read scripture, study scripture, share scripture and then live the scripture. Jesus told the disciples not to tell what they had seen until after his resurrection. He said this because he knew that they did not fully understand who he was, or what his mission was all about. They knew he was the Messiah, but they had much more to learn about him through his death and resurrection. The disciples were amazed at the radiance of Jesus' face and they were transfigured themselves.

The incredible reality of who Jesus really was hit them full force. When a person meets Jesus and accepts him personally, a great transfiguration takes place. The amazement and radiance of Jesus is imprinted on the person's heart. The change or "metonoia" brings about a radiance that glows from within the person. Jesus wants you to be transfigured and he wants your heart to shine like the sun and be dazzling bright, just like his.

Application

The first reading brings the power of God's love and mercy to those who respond to his promise. The second reading calls on us to bear our burden of hardships and know that Christ will give us the needed strength. The Gospel reading shows that Jesus wants us to be changed and he wants us to give him glory by our response to him.

This week, let us be very sensitive Christians as we relate to our families, jobs, and community. Let us show by example how we can bear up under hardship, for example: being sick and trying to be cheerful, or being tired and trying to respond to another's needs. Let the change within us be a sign to others that we act out what we say and what we believe. You and your family will be transfigured and others will be drawn to your radiance and they will know that the Holy Spirit dwells within you.

THIRD SUNDAY OF LENT - CYCLE A

BEFORE YOU BEGIN

Pray and ask God to speak to you through His Holy Spirit. "THE PARACLETE, THE HOLY SPIRIT WHOM THE FATHER WILL SEND IN MY NAME, WILL INSTRUCT YOU IN EVERYTHING, AND REMIND YOU OF ALL THAT I TOLD YOU." (JOHN 14:26)

FIRST DAY   **Reread last week's readings.**

1.   What was a helpful or new thought from the readings or from the homily you heard on Sunday?

2.   From what you learned, what personal application did you choose to apply to your life this week?

SECOND DAY   **READ EXODUS 17:3-7**   **FIRST READING**

("God satisfies the thirst of the Israelites whose hearts had become hardened and rebellious.")

1.   What made the people grumble against Moses, and what did they say to him? Exodus 17:3

2.   To whom did Moses cry out, and what did he say? Exodus 17:4

3.   Where did the Lord tell Moses to go, whom was he to have with him, and what was he to have in his hand as he went? Exodus 17:5

4.   What happened when Moses outstretched the staff at the river? Exodus 14:15-16, 21-22

5.   Where did the Lord say he would be? Exodus 17:6

6.   What did he tell him to do to the rock, and what would happen? Exodus 17:6

7.   What was Moses' response? Exodus 17:6

8.   What was the place called where this happened, and why was it called this? Exodus 17:7

9.   Before Moses outstretched the staff over the Red Sea, how were the Israelites acting? Exodus 14:11

10.   What did they say to test the Lord? Exodus 17:7

Personal - When the Israelites were thirsty they complained and went to Moses. Moses went to the Lord. Do you complain and grumble to others about your own situation, or do you humbly go to God with your request? Do you see yourself complaining and grumbling because you are thirsty? Examine your conscience each day before the Lord. Ask the Holy Spirit to reveal to you your thirst.

THIRD DAY   **READ ROMANS 5:1-2, 5-8**   **SECOND READING**

("Through his Spirit has his grace been poured into our hearts.")

1. How have we been justified? Romans 5:1 , Romans 3:28

2. In whom is our faith? Galatians 2:16 , Romans 5:9

3. If we have been justified by faith, what are we with God through our Lord Jesus Christ? Romans 5:1

4. Through whom do we gain access by faith to the grace in which we now stand? Romans 5:1-2

5. About what can we boast? Romans 5:2

6. In what is our hope? Acts 23:6

7. In whom can we find hope? Matthew 12:21

8. How will this hope leave us? Romans 5:5

9. What has been poured out in our hearts, and how has this been done? Romans 5:5

10. Fill in the following blanks: At the _____ _____ when we were still _____ Christ died for us _____. Romans 5:6

11. What is a rare thing? Romans 5:7

12. How did God prove his love for us? Romans 5:8, 1 John 4:10

Personal– In what way have you accepted the love of God for you personally through the death of his Son Jesus? Ask the Holy Spirit to reveal to you the great love of the Father for you by sacrificing his beloved Son Jesus at Calvary.

FOURTH DAY   **READ JOHN 4:5-42**   **GOSPEL**

("The water that I shall give will turn into a spring of eternal life.")

1. Where did Jesus' journey bring him; and what were the Samaritans like, according to the following verses: 2 Kings 17:24-29, Jeremiah 23:13; Matthew 10:5 and Luke 9:52-53

2.   What was the plot of land that Jesus entered and what did Jesus do when he got to Jacob's well? Why did he do it and what time was it? John 4:5-6

3.   When the Samaritan woman came to draw water, for what did Jesus ask her? John 4:7

4.   What three points did the woman bring out and what are we to recall? John 4:9

     1.

     2.

     3.

5.   What was the woman's response to Jesus' reply? What did Jesus say would happen to those who drink the water from the well? John 4:10-13

6.   What did he say would happen to the person who drinks the water he has to give and what was the woman's response? John 4:14-15

7.   After she asked him for this water, what did Jesus tell her to do and what did he exclaim to her and what did she say he was? John 4:16-19

8.   Where did she say her ancestors worshiped, where did she claim was the place where they say they ought to worship and where did Jesus say they would worship, and why? John 4:20-22

9.   What two ways will authentic worshipers worship, and what is God? John 4:23-24

Personal - Where is your place of worship? Do you spend time each day worshiping God as Spirit and Truth? Do you understand not what you worship, but whom you worship, and why you worship him? Close your eyes and ask the Holy Spirit to teach you how to worship him as Spirit and Truth.

10.   What did the woman say about the Messiah and who did Jesus say he was? John 4:25-26

11.   What was the disciples' reaction on their return? When the woman then left her water jar and went into the town, what did she say to the people? John 4:27-29

12.   Meanwhile the disciples were urging him to eat something. What did he tell them, what was their reaction and what did Jesus tell them was his food? John 4:31-34

13.   Jesus tells them to listen to him, open your eyes and see, the reaper already collects his wages and gathers a yield, for what reason? John 4:35-38

14.   Many believe in him because of what occurrence and when he stayed with the Samaritans for two days, what brought many more to come to the faith? John 4:39-41

15.   What did they tell the woman? John 4:42

Personal - Are people coming to believe in the Lord through your word of testimony? If not, what do you personally need to do? See John 4:34.

FIFTH DAY   **READ PSALM 95:1-2, 6-9**

(*"O, that today you would hear his voice."*)

Read and meditate on Psalm 95:1-2, 6-9.

What is the Lord saying to you personally through the Psalm?

How can you apply this to your life?

SIXTH DAY   **READ ALL OF THE COMMENTARY**

EXODUS 17:3-7

The Israelites, or as we have called them, the chosen people of God, were suffering under slavery and were in danger of being completely destroyed by their Egyptian captors. God chose for them a miracle, and a man would lead them in this miracle, and his name was Moses. God set them free from the Egyptians by parting the Red Sea, and Moses led them toward the promised land of Canaan. The human condition produced a series of rebellious murmuring, as they soon forgot what God had done for them. They began to complain that the difficulties of the journey were too hard to bear. They complained so much that they accused God of leading them out to the desert and leaving them to die. Moses asked God again for another miracle, and God in his mercy and love, agreed, and water came gushing forth from a rock.

Many people today are like those who were on that journey. They desire freedom, but they do not want to pay the price for it. The place where Moses drew the water from the rock is called Massah and Meribah, which means testing place. The people with Moses cried out, "Is the Lord amongst us or not?" We need to trust the Lord, not test him, because he never goes back on a promise. Like the people in the desert, many people today wonder whether God has deserted them in their hour of trial.

All the past favors, all the good times are forgotten because at the beginning their level of sincerity with God was not very high. As we begin to murmur in protest and feel abandoned or rejected we need to remember that our God is a God of love, joy, mercy, gentleness, and healing. He has promised to take us, not just to Canaan, but rather to heaven, and he will.

ROMANS 5:1-2, 5-8

As we read this passage we need to keep in mind that the Christian reality of life has two sides. One side is that we are complete in Christ (our acceptance with him is secure). On the other side, we are growing in Christ (we are becoming more and more like him). We feel both the presence of Christ and the pressure of sin. We enjoy the peace that comes from being made right with God, but we still face the daily problems that make us grow.

We need to remember these two sides in our Christian advancement and then we will not be discouraged as we face temptations and problems. Paul tells us that as believers we now stand in a place that could never be achieved by our own merits. God not only declares us not guilty, but, in fact he has drawn us closer to him. Instead of being his enemies, we have, in the response of our faith, become his own children.

Paul tells us in scripture that faith, hope and charity are at the heart of the Christian life (1 Corinthians 13). Our relationship with God begins with faith. This helps us to believe that we are delivered from our past. Hope gives promise of the future, and charity or God's love fills our lives and gives us the ability to reach out to others. The amazing part of this passage is that while we were still sinners God allowed his only begotten Son to die for all of us.

Let that sink in... Christ died for us, not because we were good enough, but because he loved us so much. He knows what is going on inside of you. He knows the problems that you are having with your own personality and yes, he died for you, especially for you. We need to remember that whenever we feel uncertain about God's love for us, he loved us even before we decided to turn to him. The Father loved us so much that he sent his Son down to die for us and his Holy Spirit gives us the power to repent, believe and rejoice.

JOHN 4:4-42

Jesus had left Jerusalem because opposition was rising against him from the Pharisees. They resented his popularity as well as his message, which challenged much of their legalistic teachings. Jesus traveled north toward the region of Galilee and it was here that he met the woman at Jacob's well in Samaria. Samaritans were the object of tremendous racial abuse by the Jews, because when the Assyrians conquered Samaria, many of them intermarried with their conquerors.

The intermarriage resulted in a mixed race, impure in the opinion of the Jews, who lived in Judah, the southern kingdom. The Jews hated these people because they felt the Samaritans had betrayed their people and nation. Jesus was not compelled to live by such cultural restrictions and so he was not afraid to travel directly through Samaria. Jesus spotted the woman at about mid-day. The woman probably came at that time to avoid meeting people because of her reputation.

Jesus knew that in the hot, blazing sun this woman needed a message about fresh and pure water that would quench her spiritual thirst forever. The woman was a Samaritan, had a bad reputation and was in a public place. No respectable Jewish man would talk to a woman like this under any circumstance, **but JESUS did**. Jesus's message is the Good News and it is a message of hope. Jesus' message is for every person, regardless of his or her race, social position, or age.

Jesus crossed all economic, social and racial barriers by dying on the cross for each and every one of us. We, who call ourselves Christians, must be prepared to do no less than he did. Jesus knew who the Samaritan woman was, and what she was, and he made sure that she knew it. He made sure that she knew he saw her as a child of God and told her that he was the only well that would never run dry. She knew he was different, because he did not ridicule her, and he did not try to preach the law to her. He did not even attempt to tell her that she was a sinner. He did not have to; she knew that he was offering her life, not death. She ran and told the community, not a bit worried about what they would think. She told them that he revealed everything about her, and the towns people came running to see this "Messiah."

We need to reflect on what the Samaritan woman did when she left the well. She went forth to proclaim the Good News. The nourishment about which Jesus was speaking did not just include prayer, bible study, attending church or receiving sacraments. We also are nourished by doing God's will and helping to bring his work of salvation to completion. We are nourished not only by what we take in, but also by what we give out for God. The woman at the well did not make excuses that her family was not ready to believe. Take a look around and, like the woman at the well, you will find plenty of people ready to hear and listen to God's Holy Word. Tell them.

Application

The first reading tells us that even today, many people desire freedom, but do not want to pay the price for it. The second reading shows us that faith, hope, and charity are at the heart of Christian love. The Gospel reveals that Jesus will quench our spiritual thirst and that because of him we will never need to thirst again.

Jesus showed us that our looks and our reputations do not always tell others who and what we really are. This week look around at your family, friends, co-workers, church, and community. Pick out one person whom you think is a problem, and for a whole week, talk respectfully to them. Do not ignore them, but visit them in a hospital, prison or at home. We can make all the men and women of Jacob's well feel loved if we follow Jesus' example this entire week.

FOURTH SUNDAY OF LENT - CYCLE A

BEFORE YOU BEGIN

Pray and ask God to speak to you through His Holy Spirit. "THE PARACLETE, THE HOLY SPIRIT WHOM THE FATHER WILL SEND IN MY NAME, WILL INSTRUCT YOU IN EVERYTHING, AND REMIND YOU OF ALL THAT I TOLD YOU." (JOHN 14:26)

FIRST DAY   **Reread last week's readings.**

1.   What was a helpful or new thought from the readings or from the homily you heard on Sunday?

2.   From what you learned, what personal application did you choose to apply to your life this week?

SECOND DAY   **READ 1 SAMUEL 16:1, 6-7, 10-13**   **FIRST READING**

("In the presence of the Lord God they anointed David king of Israel.")

1.   To whom did the Lord speak and who was Samuel? 1 Samuel 16:1, 1 Samuel 1:19-22

2.   Whom did the Lord say he has rejected as king of Israel, where was the Lord sending Samuel, and who has been chosen and from whom has he been chosen? 1 Samuel 16:1

3.   When they came, Samuel looked at whom, and what were his thoughts and who was Eliab? 1 Samuel 16:6, 1 Samuel 17:13

4.   What did the Lord say to Samuel; according to what does man see things and into what does God look? 1 Samuel 16:7

5.   How many sons did Jesse present to Samuel, and how many did he have? 1 Samuel 16:10, 1 Samuel 17:12

6.   What did Samuel tell Jesse about the seven sons; what did Samuel ask Jesse, and what did he reply? 1 Samuel 16:10-11

7.   What was the youngest son doing when Jesse sent for him? 1 Samuel 16:11

8.   When Jesse sent for him and he came, what was his appearance, and what did the Lord say? 1 Samuel 16:12

9.   What did Samuel do? 1 Samuel 16:13

10. When he was anointed with the oil, what rushed upon him? 1 Sam 16:13

Personal – Have you been anointed by the Lord for a special task? At baptism the Spirit came upon you. How have you released the Spirit within you?

| THIRD DAY | READ EPHESIANS 5:8-14 | SECOND READING |

("Rise from the dead and Christ will shine on you.")

1.   What are we in the Lord, and how must we live? Ephesians 5:8

2.   What does light produce? Ephesians 5:9

3.   Fill in the following blanks: "Be _____ in your _____ of what _____ the Lord." Eph. 5:10

4.   In what must we not take part, and what must we do with them? Ephesians 5:11

5.   What happens when we mention the things people do in secret? Ephesians 5:12

6.   What happens to such deeds that are condemned? Eph 5:13

7.   That is why we read what? Ephesians 5:14, Isaiah 60:1

Personal – We are commanded not to take part in vain deeds done in secret. Examine your conscience. Are you holding on to anything done in secret that was not right? Ask the Holy Spirit to reveal this and to bring it into the light. Remember, we are called to live as children of the light.

| FOURTH DAY | READ JOHN 9:1-41 | GOSPEL |

("The blind man went off and washed himself and came away with his sight restored.")

1.   As Jesus walked along, what did he see and what did the disciples ask him? John 9:1-2

2.   Jesus replied that it was neither the man's sin nor the parents sin that caused the man to be born blind; rather for what purpose and what did he refer to himself? John 9:3-5

3.   What did Jesus do, what did he tell the man to do, and what was the result? John 9:6-7

Personal– When the Lord speaks to you and tells you to do something, are you always obedient, even if it doesn't seem practical to you? Think about this.

4.   What did the neighbors and the people who had been accustomed to seeing him beg begin to ask, what was the confusion among them, and what did the man say? John 9:8-9

5. As the people questioned the man born blind, what did he answer, what did they do next, and when did this occur? John 12-14

6. What was the confusion between them; when the Pharisees addressed the blind man, what did they ask him and what did he answer? John 9:15-17

7. What did the Jews refuse to believe, and whom did they summon? John 9:18

8. What did the Jews ask the man's parents, what was their response, and why were they afraid of the Jews? John 9:19-22

9. The second time the Jews summoned the man who had been born blind, what did they say to him; what was his answer, and whose disciples did they say they were? John 9:24-30

10. To whom did they say God listens? John 9:31

11. What was unheard of and what was their doubt? John 9:32-33

12. Of what did they accuse the man who had been born blind, and what did they do to him; and when Jesus heard of his expulsion, what did he do, and ask? John 9:34-35

13. What was his answer; what did Jesus say to him, what was the man's answer, and what did he do? John 9:36-38

14. What did Jesus say; how did the Pharisees react to this and what was Jesus' reply? John 9:39-41

Personal – In what way have your eyes been opened to your personal knowledge of Jesus as the Son of the living God? In what way have you bowed down and worshiped and praised God for his great gift to you? Take time to thank and worship him right now where you are.

FIFTH DAY   **READ PSALM 23:1-6**

("The Lord is my shepherd; I shall not want.")

Read and meditate on Psalm 23:1-6.

What is the Lord saying to you personally through the Psalm?

How can you apply this to your life?

SIXTH DAY   **READ ALL OF THE COMMENTARY**

1 SAMUEL 16:1, 6-7, 10-13

The Lord said to Samuel, "Do not look on his appearance or the height of his stature. The Lord sees not as man sees; man looks on outward appearances, but the Lord looks at the heart." (1 Samuel 16:7). Saul was a tall and handsome king, and Samuel may have been looking for someone who looked impressive. But God warned Samuel against judging by appearance.

How many times today do we judge others by the way they look? How many people have been refused work or shelter just because they look different? The difference might be in their manner of dress or even the color of their skin. The Lord tells Samuel that God judges by character, not appearance.

God sees others with the heart, not the eyes. He knows what is going on inside, therefore, only he can accurately judge people. We spend a tremendous amount of time maintaining our outward appearance. We should do even more to develop our inner character. We can do this by spending more time alone with the Lord, praying and meditating with him.

We can improve our inner character by reading, studying and living out God's holy Word. Everyone can see your face, but only you and God know what your heart really looks like. What is the more attractive part of you? It is good for us to reflect that Saul was the first king of Israel, and he was very popular (1030 B.C.); but he offended God and the kingship was taken from him and his descendants. Samuel chose a very simple shepherd boy to become Israel's next king. He anointed David with olive oil. The anointing signified that they were God's representatives now invested with a sacred character. They became "God's Anointed" and were respected by all. The choice of David, the least likely of Jesse's sons, is a strong lesson of humility for us and helps us see our own limitations.

EPHESIANS 5:8-14

Today's passage is calling us, not only to be called children of the light, but to live as children of the light. The light of Christ that shines in us will be that light which leads others out of their own darkness into a world of light. The way we live is a direct statement of what it is we believe. The morality of a Christian's life needs to be reflective of God's love and mercy. Jesus called on us to be more than he called on us to do in the Sermon on the Mount (Matthew 5:1-12).

Your example of what a Christian is will not make someone who is in the darkness even more desolate. Instead, it will be the encouragement that they need to come forth into the healing light of Christ. God is calling for his Christian warriors to do more than to avoid evil pleasures. He is calling them to rebuke and even expose them. Too many times our silence in the middle of a dirty joke, obscene movie, or gutter talk is a sign of approval.

God wants us to take a stand for what is right. You are called to lovingly speak out for what is true and right. Today, many of the evils, such as x-rated movies, pornography, free sex, drug abuse and the break-down of morality, have taken place because of the attitude: "Let them do their thing as long as it does not affect me." This attitude has poisoned many countries, and the result has been anarchy, violence, and the banishment of God. Jesus tells us that he is the light of the world and if we follow him, we will not be stumbling in the darkness (John 8:12).

We need to reflect on today's passage. Paul wrote this to a group of people living in a very worldly place. He knew that many were being tempted to return to their old lifestyle of sin. His message to them is crystal clear to us, that only by living as children of the Light can we really ever be set totally free (John 8:32).

JOHN 9:1-41

This Gospel story really brings home that "Jesus is the Light of the world." The Pharisees were opposed to Jesus from the very beginning of his public life. He preached love, mercy and forgiveness; he even ate with the publicans and other sinners considered outcast of society. He was becoming extremely popular because he was not a legalist; rather, he was a compassionate lover of people, and the oppressed and broken recognized this and flocked to him. They could see this because they were looking at his heart. They were not blinded like the Pharisees. The Pharisees looked first at the law and then at the power and wealth of the person. They were "legally blind" in the area of love, compassion and justice.

Today's Gospel reading is a story of faith, love, pride and prejudice. The blind man was born blind, and he didn't know how or why he was healed, but he knew he could now see. He believed in the man who gave him sight, and he shared his new faith in him.

Jesus' love was so strong that even though he knew the opposition was waiting to trap him, the desire to make men free was stronger. Jesus not only gave him bodily light (eyesight), but he also gave him the Light of Faith. The Pharisees tried so hard to discredit Jesus and then the man. Their pride and total lack of humility led them to their prejudicial attitude by attributing the miracle to Satan. The Pharisees even went so far as to excommunicate the man from the community.

The question we need to respond to today is: Do we still refuse to see the truths of God's revelation brought to its fullness in the teachings of Jesus Christ? Are we still blinded by pride and prejudices of culture and habit? Christ is "the Light of the world" to whom the Pharisees and their followers and many people of today shut their eyes. You are being called to be the world's light, a city glowing in the night for all to see.

Don't hide your light! Let it shine for all; let your good deeds glow for all to see, so that they will praise your heavenly Father (Matthew 5:14-16). Remember, it is far better to shine a light than to curse the darkness.

Application

The readings today really bring out the power of God's chosen and our response. We see that in the first reading. Paul tells us that we are called to be the Light of the world. We see in the Gospel that many followed a blindness far darker than physical loss of eyesight. Jesus shows us that he heals and makes us lights in a world of darkness.

This week, speak out when you know what is being said is untrue. Don't go along with the crowd. Be yourself. Don't let foul talk, sinful actions or lying, dim your light. Respond to the needs of others. Be a beacon of truth, don't shut your light off from the rest of the world.

FIFTH SUNDAY OF LENT - CYCLE A

BEFORE YOU BEGIN

Pray and ask God to speak to you through His Holy Spirit. "THE PARACLETE, THE HOLY SPIRIT WHOM THE FATHER WILL SEND IN MY NAME, WILL INSTRUCT YOU IN EVERYTHING, AND REMIND YOU OF ALL THAT I TOLD YOU." (JOHN 14:26)

FIRST DAY   **Reread last week's readings.**

1. What was a helpful or new thought from the readings or from the homily you heard on Sunday?

2. From what you learned, what personal application did you choose to apply to your life this week?

SECOND DAY   **READ EZEKIEL 37:12-14**   **FIRST READING**

("I shall put my Spirit in you and you will live.")

1. Who is Ezekiel? Ezekiel 1:1-3

2. Who is speaking, to whom is he speaking, and how is this done? Ezekiel 37:12

3. How is prophesy put forth? 2 Peter 1:21

4. What did the Lord say to the people? Ezekiel 37:12

5. By his doing this, what will the people know? Ez 37:13

6. What will he put in them and why? Ez 37:14

7. Where will he settle them? Ez 37:14

8. In what two ways does the Lord show them that he is the Lord? Ez 37:12, 14

9. What does the Lord say about what he promises? Ez 37:14

10. What are some of the promises of God?
    Matthew 10:42
    Luke 24:49
    Acts 1:4-5
    1 Corinthians 10:13
    2 Peter 3:13
    1 John 2:25

Personal – How do you stand on the promises of God? In what way do you believe God will do what he says he will do for you in his Word? God is faithful and promises you life to the fullest. How do the promises of God penetrate your whole being? Allow his Spirit which he has given you to comfort and guide you in all you do.

THIRD DAY	READ ROMANS 8:8-11	SECOND READING

("If the Spirit of him who raised Jesus from the dead is living in you, then he will give life to your mortal bodies.")

1. What happens to those who are in the flesh? Romans 8:8

2. What does Jesus say in John 6:63 about the flesh?

3. Whose Spirit dwells in us? Romans 8:9

4. Who are those who do not belong to Christ? Romans 8:9

5. How do we know we belong to God? 1 John 4:2, 15

6. If Christ is in us, what happens to the body? Romans 8:10

7. What does the spirit do, and for what reason? Romans 8:10

8. Those who belong to Christ Jesus have done what with the flesh? Galatians 5:24

9. If the Spirit of him who raised Jesus from the dead dwells in us, what will happen to our mortal bodies and who will do this? Romans 8:11

10. How will this be done? Romans 8:11

Personal – How much time do you spend praising and thanking the Lord for dying for you so you could have life? How often do you recognize the power of his Spirit in your life? What does your family see in you? Ask someone in your family or a friend to evaluate how often they see the fruits of the Spirit manifested through you. Galatians 5:20. The fruits of the Spirit are love, joy, peace, patience, kindness, goodness, faithfulness, gentleness, and self-control.

FOURTH DAY	READ JOHN 11:1-45	GOSPEL

("I am the Resurrection and the Life.")

1. What was a certain man's name who was sick, what were the names of his two sisters, and what had the one sister done with the Lord? John 11:1, 2; John 12:3

2. What did the sisters inform Jesus, what was his response and even though Jesus loved Martha, her sister and Lazarus very much, what did he do? John 11:3-6

3. What did he finally say to his disciples, what was their protest and what did Jesus answer them? John 11:7-10

4. After he uttered these words, what did he add, what was the disciples response, what was Jesus talking about, and what did the disciples think? John 11:11-13

5. What did Jesus say plainly about Lazarus, why was Jesus glad he was not there when he died, and when Jesus said "Let us go to him," what did Thomas say? John 11:14-16

Personal – How have you experienced fear of others—especially rejection—for following what you know God has called you to do or say? How have you been willing and obedient in following through? Have you been willing, as Thomas was, to die in order to stand with Jesus? How have you experienced rejection from your spouse, children, friends, work acquaintances, etc., because you have stood firm on God's promises? Read Romans 8:35-39 for reassurance.

6. Who went to meet Jesus when she heard he was coming; who stayed home, and what did Martha say to Jesus? John 11:20-21

7. Of what was Martha even now sure; what did Jesus say to her, and what was her response? John 11:22-24

8. Who did Jesus tell her was the resurrection and the life, what did he say would happen to those who believe in him, and what will **never** happen to those who believe in him? John 11:25-26

9. What was Jesus question to Martha, and what was her response. After she said this, she went back and called her sister Mary. What did she whisper to her, and what did she call him? John 11:26-29

10. What did the Jews do when they saw Mary get up quickly? How did Jesus feel when Mary fell at his feet and was weeping, what did he ask them, and what did they say? John 11:31-34

11. What did Jesus begin to do, and what was the reaction of the Jews to this? John 11:35-36

12. What did Jesus say, what did Martha say to him, and what did he say to her? John 11:39-40

13. Where did Jesus look when they took the stone away, and whom did he thank for having heard him, and of what was he always sure and why? John 11:41-42

14. After he said this to the Father, what did he say loudly and how did the dead man come out? What did Jesus say to the crowd, and what did this cause many of the Jews to do? John 11:43-45

Personal – When you pray, in what way do you thank the Father, as Jesus did, for answering your prayer even if you have not yet seen the results? When you pray to the Father in the name of Jesus this week, practice thanking him for always hearing your prayer.

FIFTH DAY   **READ PSALM 130:1-8**

("I trust in the Lord; my soul trusts in his Word.")

Read and meditate on Psalm 130:1-8.

What is the Lord saying to you personally through the Psalm?

How can you apply this to your life?

SIXTH DAY   **READ ALL OF THE COMMENTARY**

EZEKIEL 37:12-14

This passage reveals the vision Ezekiel had of a valley filled with dried up bones or skeletons. The bones represented the Jews in captivity — scattered and dead. Ezekiel probably felt as though he was speaking to the dead as he preached to the exiles, because they rarely ever responded to his message. But these bones responded, and just as God brought life into these bones, he would breathe life again into his spiritually dead people. This passage is a tremendous message of hope for us today.

How many times have you been in a church and felt as if you were in the valley of dry bones that Ezekiel talked about? The dry bones represented the people's spiritually dead condition. Your church may seem like a heap of dried bones to you, spiritually dead and with no vitality. God promised Ezekiel that he was going to restore his nation and any church regardless of how dry or dead it appeared to be.

Don't give up on your church. Don't leave it, rather pray for renewal, for God can and will restore it to life. The Lord tells Ezekiel that he will put his Holy Spirit into his people and his nation will again come alive (Ezekiel 37:14). The Lord promises you and me that very same miracle. The hope and prayer of every church should be that God will put his Spirit into it (37:14).

God is at work right now calling his people back to him, bringing New Life to dead churches through prayer, bible studies, evangelization, and the receiving of the sacraments. There is a call out to the church and it's a call to holiness, and agents of holiness are clergy who assist the people. "I will replace the flesh and muscles on you and cover you with skin. I will put breath into you and you shall live and know that I am the Lord."

Come back and celebrate with us, we no longer are the valley of dry bones. We are the temples of the Holy Spirit. We bring to our churches the Spirit of the living God. Come back and let him breathe his Holy Spirit and you will come alive, too.

ROMANS 8:8-11

The theme of this passage is like that of the first reading and of the Gospel. It is the theme of resurrection, and it tells us that before we were saved by Christ's death on the cross, we were slaves to our sinful nature. But now we can choose to live for Christ because we are people of the Spirit, not of the flesh. The penalty of sin and its power over our lives died with Christ on the cross. This is an incredible assurance that our lives are secure in that we belong to Jesus Christ. This frees us to be completely obedient to his will and enjoy an unbroken fellowship with the Lord. This living in the spirit will affect all of our activities. It will touch our work, our worship, our role as a married spouse, our role as a parent, even our role as a child. You will have a stronger hunger and desire to spend more quiet time with the Lord in prayer and Bible study. You will have a whole new outlook in your caring for others. Today many people wonder whether they really are Christians.

A Christian is anyone who has the Spirit of God living in him. People will see a difference in the way you live and act (Galatians 5:22-23). You will learn how to pray (Romans) and you will be able to deal with the situations in your life with greater wisdom (Romans 8:28). You will receive power to do God's will from the Holy Spirit (Acts 1:8). You will be a tremendous partner in the building up of God's church (Ephesians 4:12-13).

Today there is no condemnation for those who belong to Jesus Christ. The power of the Holy Spirit is ours through the justification of Jesus Christ. This means because of what Jesus did for us, we are entitled to complete access to his Holy Spirit, his Father and, of course, we become heirs to the Kingdom of Heaven. You are a child of the Spirit! Rejoice and be glad!

JOHN 11:1-45

Jesus had been preaching in the small towns and villages beyond the Jordan, when he received the news of Lazarus' sickness. He knew that he would find Lazarus dead when he arrived in Bethany, but he also knew that he was going to perform a great miracle. The village of Bethany was just a little east of Jerusalem on the way to Jericho. The two sisters thought that they had a right to expect help from the Lord. They stepped forward and claimed that help.

We need to realize that a claim upon the power of Christ is the right of every one of his children. Once we have been redeemed by him, we belong to him. The contrast between the two women was very noticeable. Martha was the doer and Mary was the people person. Martha was irritated because Mary was not doing her kind of work. There was a definite clash between drudgery and devotion. Martha was looking more at things instead of person. She was looking at the tasks of the house and all the chores instead of remembering that she was part of a greater partnership of love.

That day her devotion turned into drudgery and Jesus admonished her for overlooking his wants. He wanted her receptivity, her presence, and companionship, but she had other ideas about his wants. So she cleaned and cooked, while Mary listened and conversed with Jesus. He told this to Martha, and he is telling you this very same message today.

Do you place your attention on things instead of people? Do you worry more about what your home looks like when a friend stops by to say hello? Are you afraid to tell a friend about how unhappy you are with your job? Do your children seem like they are drifting away from their faith or family? Jesus shows us tremendous insight in Mary's ability to talk, listen and wait on the Lord. We need to do this more often. We need to wait on the Lord. He will come to us in many different places and in many different ways. He told the women that he is the resurrection and the life, and we are not to worry.

Is he the resurrection of your life? Martha was an activist and Mary was a contemplative and they both were loved by Jesus. The activist pushes on to new frontiers and the contemplative waits and prays for God's guidance and direction first. We need them both and Jesus looks to us to be bold and yet prudent in our walk to the kingdom. The Lord knew what he was doing in Lazarus' life and he knows what he is doing in ours. Listen to him – Listen to him – Listen to him!

Application

The theme is resurrection and the first reading shows the dry bones coming back to life and forming a new army of the Lord. The second reading tells us that if the Holy Spirit dwells within us we will then be controlled by the Spirit and not by the flesh and we will receive our reward in Heaven. The Gospel tells us that we need to put our attention upon Jesus and not on the temporary things of the world such as health, youth or power.

This week, listen to someone in your home and try to meet one of their needs: such as someone desiring to be understood, a car to be washed, a room cleaned, a child to be cared for, or lead someone in prayer.

PASSION (PALM) SUNDAY – CYCLE A

BEFORE YOU BEGIN

Pray and ask God to speak to you through His Holy Spirit. "THE PARACLETE, THE HOLY SPIRIT WHOM THE FATHER WILL SEND IN MY NAME, WILL INSTRUCT YOU IN EVERYTHING, AND REMIND YOU OF ALL THAT I TOLD YOU." (JOHN 14:26)

FIRST DAY   **Reread last week's readings.**

1.   What was a helpful or new thought from the readings or from the homily you heard on Sunday?

2.   From what you learned, what personal application did you choose to apply to your life this week?

SECOND DAY   **READ ISAIAH 50:4-7**   **FIRST READING**

("The Lord God is my help, therefore I am not disgraced.")

1.   Where did the well-trained tongue come from, to whom has he given it and for what reason has he been given a well-trained tongue? Isaiah 50:4

2.   When and what does he open, that we may hear? Isaiah 50:4

3.   What has he **not** done? Isaiah 50:5

4.   What happens to those that rebel? 1 Samuel 12:15

5.   What did the servant do to those who beat him and plucked his beard? Isaiah 50:6

6.   From what did he not shield his face? Isaiah 50:6, Matthew 26:67 and 27:30

7.   Who is the servant's help and how has he set his face? Isaiah 50:7

8.   What does the servant know? Isaiah 50:7

Personal – When do you hear the Lord speaking to you? What is he saying to you? In what way, by using a well-trained tongue, do you rouse the weary in your own household? Pray and ask the Lord to reveal to you how you can train your tongue.

THIRD DAY   **READ PHILIPPIANS 2:6-11**   **SECOND READING**

("Jesus Christ is Lord.")

1.   What must be your attitude? Philippians 2:5

2. Of who was he in the form? Philippians 2:6

3. Who is Christ? John 1:1, 14

4. What was something at which he did not grasp? Phil. 2:6

5. Rather, of what did he become empty, and why? Phil. 2:7 2 Corinthians 8:9

6. What form did he take and in whose likeness was he born, and of what was he known to be? Philippians 2:7

7. What two things did he do in verse 8 of Philippians 2?

8. For what reason did he do the above two things? Hebrews 2:14-17

9. Because he humbled himself and accepted death on the cross, what two things did God do for him? Philippians 2:9

10. What must **every** knee do, in the heavens, on the earth, and under the earth, at the name of Jesus and what must **every** tongue proclaim? Philippians 2:10-11

11. What does this tell you beyond a doubt? Acts 2:36

12. For whose glory is this proclaimed (Phil. 2:11) and what will happen to you if you confess with your lips that Jesus is Lord and believe in your heart that God raised him from the dead? Romans 10:9

13. Who gives you the power to say "Jesus is Lord?" 1 Cor. 12:3

Personal – In what way is your attitude that of Christ? In what way have you humbled yourself? What cross have you obediently accepted? Read Mark 8:34 and meditate on this.

FOURTH DAY   **READ MATTHEW 26:14-27:66**   **GOSPEL**

*("For this is my blood, the blood of the covenant, to be poured
out in behalf of many for the forgiveness of sins.")*

1. Who went to the chief priest, what did he ask them and what were they willing to pay him to betray and hand Jesus over to them? Matthew 26:14-16

2. What was paid to the owner for a gored slave? Ex 21:32

3. What did the disciples ask Jesus on the first day of the feast of the unleavened bread and what did he say to them? Matthew 26:17-18

4. What did Jesus call himself and who prepared the passover supper? Matt 26:18-19

5. When it grew dark and in the course of the meal what did Jesus say to his disciples, how did they feel, and what was their response? Matthew 26: 20-25

6. During the meal, what did Jesus do and say about the bread? Matthew 26:26

7. What did he do with the cup, who did he say must drink from it, for what reason and what did they do after this was said? Matthew 26:27-30

8. From what did Jesus quote, what did he say to them, and what was Peter's response and all the other disciples? Matthew 26:31-35, Zechariah 13:7

Personal – In what way have you drunk from the cup of Jesus' blood? Hebrews 9:22 says "According to the law almost everything is purified by blood, and without the shedding of blood there is no forgiveness." Reflect on this.

9. Where did Jesus go with his disciples and what did he say to them? Matthew 26:36

10. Who did he take with him, what did he do and who did he address? Matthew 26:37-39

11. What did Jesus pray to his Father, how many times did he say this to him and what were the disciples doing? Matt 26:39-46

12. While Jesus was still speaking, who arrived, who sent them, and how did his betrayer signal them? Matthew 26:47-48

13. How was this fulfilled, what did Peter do, and what did Jesus say about this? Matthew 26:49-56

14. After they apprehended Jesus, where did they take him; where was Peter, and what were the chief priests trying to obtain? Matthew 26:57-60

15. When two came forward, what did they declare; what was the high priest's reaction, how did Jesus act, and what was the verdict? Matthew 26:61-66

16. What did they do to Jesus? Matthew 26:67-68

17. Where was Peter, what did he do, how many times did he do this and what did he do on hearing a cock crow? Matthew 26:69-75

Personal – How do you act when things get tough in your home or work environment? Do you keep your eyes on Jesus and stand firm with him or do you keep your eyes on your circumstances?

18. What happened at daybreak, what was the fate of Jesus' betrayer and what happened to the thirty pieces of silver for which Judas betrayed him? Matthew 27:1-10

19. When Jesus was arraigned before the procurator, what was said and what was his reaction? Matthew 27:11-14

20. What were they accustomed to doing on this occasion of a festival, who was Barabbas, what did Pilate say to them, and what did Pilate's wife say? Matthew 27:15-19

21. What was the chief priest doing, what was the result and why did Pilate wash his hands? Matthew 27:20-26

22. Who sentenced Jesus to death? Matthew 27:2, 26

23. What did they do next and of what was Jesus' crown made? Matthew 27:27-31

24. On their way out, who did they meet, what did he do, where did they arrive, and what did they try to give him to drink? Matthew 27:32-34

25. When they crucified him, what did they do with his clothes, what did they put above his head, who was on each side of him and what were the people doing? Matthew 27:35-44

26. Where was Jesus when people cried out, "He saved others but he cannot save himself?" Matthew 27:40-42

27. While Jesus hung on the cross what was over all the land? Matthew 27:45

28. Complete Jesus' words from the cross – "My God, My God _____" Matthew 27:46

29. When Jesus said these words, what did some of the bystanders say? Matthew 27:47

30. What happened to the curtain in the sanctuary, the earth, and the bodies of the saints? Matthew 27:51-53

31. What was the reaction of the centurion and his men and who looked on from a distance? Matthew 27:54-56

32. Who was another of Jesus' disciples, what did he do and what sealed the mouth of Jesus' grave? Matthew 27:57-61

33. What happened the next day, what did Pilate tell them, and what did they fix on the stone? Matthew 27:62-66

Personal – In what way has the shedding of Jesus' blood affected your life? This week, in preparation for Easter, reflect on the cleansing blood of Jesus in your life.

FIFTH DAY   **READ PSALM 22:8-9, 17-20, 23-24**

("They have pierced my hands and my feet.")

Read and meditate on Psalm 22:8-9, 17-20, 23-24.

What is the Lord saying to you personally through the Psalm?

How can you apply this to your life?

SIXTH DAY   **READ ALL OF THE COMMENTARY**

ISAIAH 50:4-7

The source of strength and courage for all suffering, trial and tribulations is the suffering and death of our divine Lord Jesus Christ. We need to hold fast to him when the world closes in with its assault, rejection and abandonment. He not only traveled this same road before the saints of old, but he travels it today, constantly waiting to be with us in our suffering. His suffering and death opened the road to heaven for all of us, even though many refuse the gift. He gave up everything for us, and he gave us love, trust, hope, respect, eternal life. In return he was spat upon, ridiculed, beaten, jeered, scourged and mocked. He finally was executed on Calvary by being nailed to a cross between two criminals.

This is a day of reflection. We are about to enter holy week. Let us not forget the actions and words of Isaiah's suffering servant. We need to reflect how fast the crowd changed from adoring him to rejecting him. He took up his cross for us; I need to remember that I, too, am called to carry my cross for others as Christ did. Sometimes we think our cross is too heavy, or that it is unfair to carry such a heavy cross. How heavy is your cross compared to Christ's? How is your Calvary compared to Jesus' Calvary?

PHILIPPIANS 2:6-11

Paul tells us that our attitudes should be like that of Jesus Christ (Phil. 2:5). He describes putting on the attitude of a servant rather than that of a king. Jesus though being God, did not demand his rights and privileges of royalty. He deliberately set them all aside and took on the role of a servant. There lies the incredible formula of a successful leader.

Jesus, a true leader serves all of us. He showed us that putting others first and being humble was the only way a person can become a real leader. The sheep followed the shepherd because they trusted him. People will follow a leader if they know that he has their welfare at heart. Jesus showed us everything of God's character in human terms. He was obedient even unto death, and the type of death the Father chose for him was extremely painful.

Jesus is the perfect role model for us today. How many times do we demand our rights when we feel we are being treated less than fairly? The name of Jesus should bring to every Christian the name of a person who willingly died so that all could be free. He died for us knowing very well that we are sinners (Romans 5:8). Jesus voluntarily laid aside his divine rights, privileges, and position out of love for his Father. We, too, are called to lay aside our rights and privileges for our oppressed brothers and sisters in the Holy Name of Jesus.

MATTHEW 26:14-27:66

The coming of the Messiah was a dream that the Jews envisioned for many, many centuries. They visioned the Messiah as one who would deliver the Jews from the tyranny of the pagan government that was ruling at the time. Judas wasn't any different when he saw that possibility grow during the ministry of Jesus. The major difference, in what Judas hoped for and what was really happening, was that Jesus did not intend to bring a new and more powerful government to the people.

Judas expected to be on the inside of something really big. Jesus' kingdom was not of this world. He only promised eternal life to all those who believe in him. He said he was the way, the truth and the life (John 14:1-6). Judas finally realized that Jesus' kingdom was not physical or political, but spiritual.

Many people today are being told that if they accept Jesus they will become handsome, beautiful, prosperous and healthy. That is not what Jesus promised. He told us that we have to pick up our cross and carry it daily. He told us that we would be persecuted in his name. He told us not to be concerned about what we wear and what we eat. He told us that if we are to rise with him we need to die with him also.

We are called to die to ourselves. We are called to put him on the throne of our lives. This is difficult to accept, because all honor and glory belongs to him and not to us. We can only do this when we are obedient to his Holy Word. The people shouted death, death, death to our Lord Jesus at the meeting of the Sanhedrin. Jesus was convicted of committing the sin of blasphemy, a crime punishable by death. They not only rejected his claim but even crucified him on Calvary. You need to decide today, whether Jesus' Words are blasphemy, or truth. The result of your decision is eternal.

Application

The first reading showed us that suffering can lead to obedience. The second reading shows that humility is the cornerstone of leadership. And the Gospel tells us that suffering for something that you didn't do and showing humility in your actions calls for a spirituality that only Jesus can give.

This week, look around and see if you can be helpful and set an example of Christ to someone who is suffering. This could be your spouse, your children or someone at work.

EASTER SUNDAY - CYCLE A

BEFORE YOU BEGIN

Pray and ask God to speak to you through His Holy Spirit. "THE PARACLETE, THE HOLY SPIRIT WHOM THE FATHER WILL SEND IN MY NAME, WILL INSTRUCT YOU IN EVERYTHING, AND REMIND YOU OF ALL THAT I TOLD YOU." (JOHN 14:26)

FIRST DAY   **Reread last week's readings.**

1.   What was a helpful or new thought from the readings or from the homily you heard on Sunday?

2.   From what you learned, what personal application did you choose to apply to your life this week?

SECOND DAY   **READ ACTS 10:34, 37-43**   **FIRST READING**

("We have eaten and drunk with him after his resurrection from the dead.")

1.   Whom was Peter addressing? Acts 10:24-28

2.   What did he say to them? Acts 10:34-35

3.   How does Deuteronomy 10:17 describe God, and what does it say he does **not** do? 2 Chronicles 19:7

4.   For what reason does God have no favorites? Job 34:19, Wisdom 6:7

Personal – In what way do you show partiality with your children, your friends, and your co-workers? Spend time alone with the Lord, repent of this, and ask the Lord to help you look at others through his eyes.

5.   What was reported all over Judea about Jesus of Nazareth? Where did it begin, and with what? Acts 10:37-38

6.   Who anointed Jesus and who anointed Paul, Silvanus, and Timothy? Acts 10:38, 2 Corinthians 1:21-22

7.   What two things did Jesus go about doing and who was with him? Acts 10:38

8.   To what are they witnesses, what did they finally do to him, and what did God do? Acts 10:39-40

9.   What did God grant, and by whom? Acts 10:40-41

10.   Who are the chosen and for what purpose are they chosen? Ephesians 1:13

11. What did he commission us to do? Acts 10:42

12. Whom has he sent to preach to the people? Mark 3:14, 2 Corinthians 4:1-2

13. Who are his disciples today? John 8:31, John 13:35

14. To what are we to bear witness and to what do all the prophets testify?
Acts 10:42-43

Personal – What results and power do you see in your everyday life from your anointing with the Holy Spirit? Does your family see good works and healing taking place from your touch? Reflect on this.

THIRD DAY   **READ COLOSSIANS 3:1-4**   **SECOND READING**

("Be intent on things above rather than things of earth.")

1. With whom have we been raised up, and on what should we set our heart?
Colossians 3:1

2. Where is Christ seated? Colossians 3:1

3. Who raised us up and gave us a place in the heavens? Ephesians 2:4-6

4. On what are we to be intent and why? Colossians 3:2-3

5. What are things that are rooted in earth? Col 3:5, 8-9

6. How do we become intent on things above? Col 3:10

7. Where is our life hidden now? Colossians 3:3

8. Who is Christ to us? Colossians 3:4

9. When Christ appears, what will happen to us and in what way? Colossians 3:4

Personal – As you have died with Christ to your old desires and to things rooted in this earth, do your family, friends, and work acquaintances see you as a reflection of Christ? On a sheet of paper, name some of the characteristics of Christ in one column and in another column list your characteristics through a 24-hour day and compare the two columns.

FOURTH DAY   **READ JOHN 20:1-9**   **GOSPEL**

("He saw and believed.")

1. Who came to the tomb, what time was it, and what day was it? John 20:1

2. Where was Mary Magdalene as Jesus hung on the cross? John 19:25

3. What did Jesus drive out of Mary? Mark 16:9

4. What did Mary see when she arrived at the tomb? John 20:1

5. To whom did she run, and what did she say to them? John 20:2

6. What did Peter and the other disciple do? John 20:3

7. Who reached the tomb first, and how did they get there? John 20:4

Personal – In what way do you see yourself running to see Jesus? Are you persevering in running the race? On whom are you keeping your eyes fixed? Do your family and friends see you as someone with eyes looking up or cast down? Read Hebrews 12:1-2.

8. What did the disciple do when he got to the tomb and what did he see lying on the ground? John 20:5

9. What did Peter do when he got there? What did he observe on the ground, and what did he notice about the cloth which had covered Jesus' head? John 20:6-7

10. What did the disciple who had arrived first do, and what was his reaction to this? John 20:8

11. What does it take to believe? John 1:12

12. What will you receive by believing in the name of Jesus? John 3:36

13. After Jesus rose from the dead, what did the disciples come to understand and believe? John 2:22

14. When did they understand and believe? Luke 24:30-32

15. What does Jesus say about those who believe and have not seen? John 20:29

Personal – How have you seen a change take place in your life through reading the scriptures? Have you come to believe in the spoken Word of Jesus through the scriptures? Remember, John tells us Jesus is the Word made flesh. Pray and ask God to fill you with an understanding of the Word through his gift of the Holy Spirit that you received from him.

FIFTH DAY   **READ PSALM 118:1-2, 16-17, 22-23**

("The right hand of the Lord has struck with power.")

Read and meditate on Psalm 118:1-2, 16-17, 22-23.

What is the Lord saying to you personally through the Psalm?

How can you apply this to your life?

SIXTH DAY   READ ALL OF THE COMMENTARY

ACTS 10:34, 37-43

Alleluia is a Hebrew word that means "praise ye the Lord." On this great day of Easter Sunday we give thanks, gratitude and our complete joy in the form of praise to our Lord Jesus Christ. This passage strongly shows that the resurrection is the basic doctrine and proof of the truth of the Christian faith. We are told in scripture that if Christ has not risen, then our preaching is in vain, and our faith is worthless also (1 Cor. 15:14).

There are many today who disregard the physical resurrection and say that it is no big deal. They say that it is the spiritual resurrection that really matters. St. Paul says just the opposite. Jesus rose from the dead, and then he was seen by witnesses who had not only spoken with him, but had actually eaten with him. The Apostles were devastated on Friday night after the crucifixion. They remained locked in the upper room, fearful of what the Roman soldiers were going to do next. They were even too afraid to do any wishful thinking about their beloved master Jesus. They were hard to convince even when it happened.

We need to reflect on this passage. Have we seen him, have we talked with him, have we eaten with him? He is alive today, and like the Apostle Peter, we too are called to evangelize and teach about Jesus. We are called to fellowship with others who believe that he is risen and that he lives today. We need to discover through Christ something significant about each other, both believers and non-believers. He has risen for the whole world - Alleluia - Alleluia!

COLOSSIANS 3:1-4

In this passage, Paul begins by bringing us into the core meaning of our baptism. In the early days of the church, baptism was by total immersion. When you heard the story of Christ and you were ready to believe in the one true God, the Father, the Son, and the Holy Spirit, you were then immersed in water. You were cleansed from your sins and worldliness. Immersion was a symbol of being drowned or buried with Christ. This signified that the new Christian has died to all earthly attachments and desires. He was raised out of the water or the tomb to be with the risen Christ. Paul said, "If you have been raised with Christ, seek the things that are above." This means that we must mean what we say and do.

We have been raised with Christ and we no longer need to dwell on things of the earth. This does not mean we can walk away from responsibilities. It does not mean just being obedient to parents and to society. It does not mean just having to work to support ourselves or our families. It means that our earthly possessions must not dominate our life.

We are called to love people, not things, money, power, status, etc. Our lives need to show that what we did at baptism has life-long meaning. What we do is far more effective on others than what we say. We were created for unending happiness in heaven and this happiness is now within our grasp, thanks to the death and resurrection of Jesus Christ. We are helped in our daily living by God's holy grace. Remember, God wants us to go to heaven and he has an Easter resurrection planned for all of us.

JOHN 20:1-9

The divine plan of God for all people was accomplished through the death and resurrection of Jesus Christ. All would now be eligible to be called sons and daughters of God because of Jesus Christ's perfect act of obedience. Because of him, we will one day, like Christ, rise from the grave in our glorified bodies.

The resurrection is the basis of the new Christian faith. Had it not happened, Christianity would never have started. There would have been no Easter Sunday. Peter would have returned with his companions to their fishing nets and boats, and Jesus Christ would have been forgotten after a few short years.

Mary Magdalene's discovery of an empty tomb brought shock and fear. She ran to Peter and told him that she thought someone had stolen the body of Jesus. Peter had to see for himself and check out the facts.

We might take notice how the clothes were folded after they discovered Jesus' body was gone. They would not have been arranged that way if there had been a robbery. The disciples were completely surprised when they found the empty tomb. It was only then that they remembered that Jesus had said that he would rise again.

Many people today do not believe in Jesus because they say the "facts" do not check out. We can only accept the fact of the resurrection when we have first personally encountered Jesus Christ. The understanding of the resurrection takes on a special meaning as we commit our lives to Jesus and his presence remains with us.

Jesus' resurrection is the key to our Christian faith because death, as we know it, is not the end. Jesus' bodily resurrection shows us that he is ruler of God's kingdom. Because of his promise, we who die to ourselves with him, will rise from the dead with him. Because of him, you and I can face tomorrow without fear. Because of him, we have his Holy Spirit living within us and protecting us against all evil (1 John 4:4). Because of him, we can witness to the whole world that if they believe in Jesus Christ, they may also receive eternal happiness. Because of him, all mankind can really be free and live forever.

Alleluia - he is Risen - Alleluia - he is alive.

Application

Jesus' death brought us freedom from sin and death. We are now called to free others from sin and death here on earth. Some of us can do that by our professions as medical people, legal people, politicians, educators, business people, parents, and children.

This week, free someone in your family, home, or work from a chore that you know they don't like. Let them see that joy in someone who really knows that he is free. Then each day have your family gather together to pray that all may become free from sin through Jesus Christ. Because of him, you are free. Let freedom ring throughout this land.

SECOND SUNDAY OF EASTER – CYCLE A

BEFORE YOU BEGIN

Pray and ask God to speak to you through His Holy Spirit. "THE PARACLETE, THE HOLY SPIRIT WHOM THE FATHER WILL SEND IN MY NAME, WILL INSTRUCT YOU IN EVERYTHING, AND REMIND YOU OF ALL THAT I TOLD YOU." (JOHN 14:26)

FIRST DAY **Reread last week's readings.**

1. What was a helpful or new thought from the readings or from the homily you heard on Sunday?

2. From what you learned, what personal application did you choose to apply to your life this week?

SECOND DAY **READ ACTS 2:42-47** **FIRST READING**

("The early Christians live a life of prayer and share all things in common.")

1. Those who were baptized were devoted to what four aspects of Christian living? Acts 2:42

   1. _____ 3. _____

   2. _____ 4. _____

2. Why did a reverent "fear" overtake them? Acts 2:43

3. What did it mean to live in common? Acts 2:44-45

4. How were goods and property divided? Acts 2:45

5. In the earliest times, where did the Jewish Christians continue to go daily to pray and hear the Word of God? Acts 2:46

6. Where did these Christians break bread and celebrate the Eucharist? Acts 2:46

7. What was the condition of their hearts as they took their meals in common? Acts 2:46

8. What two things were happening as they took their meals in common? Acts 2:47

9. What was added, day by day, and by whom? Acts 2:47

Personal - How have I been living out God's presence in my life? Do I think of salvation as something very individual and private, or how does my view compare to this picture of the early church? How do I share my goods and feel about the lifestyle described here?

THIRD DAY   **READ 1 PETER 1:3-9**   **SECOND READING**

("The people celebrate God's gift of grace to the Gentiles.")

1. Who is to be praised, and for what reason? 1 Peter 1:3

2. What does this birth give, and from what does it draw its life? 1 Peter 1:3

3. On what is our hope fixed? 1 Timothy 4:10

4. In the end, what three things last? 1 Cor 13:13

5. What is incapable of fading or being defiled, where is it kept, and how is it guarded? 1 Peter 1:4-5

6. What three things does this new truth give, and when will this be revealed? 1 Peter 1:3-5

7. For what is there cause, what may you have to do, and for what reason? 1 Peter 1:6-7

8. Why do you rejoice with inexpressible joy touched with glory? 1 Peter 1:8

9. What is faith's goal? 1 Peter 1:9

Personal – In what way have I been tested in my faith? How did my faith grow as a result?

FOURTH DAY   **READ JOHN 20:19-31**   **GOSPEL**

("Jesus appears to the disciples in the room.")

1. Why had the disciples locked the door where they were staying? John 20:19

2. What was Jesus' greeting as he stood before the disciples? John 20:19 Compare it to his greeting in John 14:27

3. What did Jesus show the disciples, and what was their reaction? John 20:20

4. At the apostles' sight of him, what did Jesus say again; whom did he say sent him and, in turn, is sending them? John 20:21

5. Jesus "breathed on them and said: 'Receive the _____ _____'. " John 20:22

6. After receiving the Holy Spirit, what authority did the disciples have regarding sin? John 20:23. What did Jesus say about forgiving sins? Luke 17:3-4

Personal – How does the life of Christ penetrate my daily life and actions? Does his greeting, "Peace be with you," fill me with joy and peace or other emotions? Just as Jesus has sent his disciples out to the world, so also he sends me. By my baptism, I have received the Holy Spirit. How do I live out this commission in my everyday life?

7. Who was absent when Jesus came to the disciples, and what did they tell Him they had seen? What was his response? John 20:24-25

8.   A week later, Jesus again came to them in the room. What was Jesus' greeting to the disciples? John 20:26

9.   How did Jesus challenge Thomas to believe, and what was Thomas' response? (Write it out.) John 20:27-28

10.   Jesus blest Thomas because he _____ and _____, and Jesus blessed all those "who have not _____ and have _____." How does this help to strengthen my faith? John 20:29

11.   How do these signs affect our faith? John 20:30-31

Personal – Just as Thomas came to believe through seeing and touching, how does Jesus invite me to faith in my life through sight and touch? When have I passed from fear or sadness to joy "at the sight of the Lord?"

FIFTH DAY   **READ PSALM 118:2-4, 13-15, 22-24**

("My strength and my courage is the Lord, and he has been my Savior.")

Read and meditate on Psalm 118:2-4, 13-15, 22-24.

What is the Lord saying to you personally through the Psalm?

How can you apply this to your life?

SIXTH DAY   **READ ALL OF THE COMMENTARY**

ACTS 2:42-47

This passage reveals a tremendous sense of love and commitment to one another. The Apostles gave their teachings about the life and events of Jesus Christ with a high degree of enthusiasm and authority. An apostle meant one who was an eyewitness to the ministry, passion, death, and resurrection of the Lord.

The fellowship between the followers and new converts was warm, strong, and incredibly joyful. The poor and needy were taken care of physically as well as in prayer. The hungry were being fed, the homeless were being sheltered, the naked were being clothed, and the lonely were being loved and affirmed. They ministered to outcasts in prisons or leper colonies.

There were many signs of God's healing presence in the community. The bond between them was shared through their giving up of their personal pleasures in order that the community might be saved.

The core of this healing action by the community was Faith in the Lord Jesus Christ, not through their own individual talent. Today, we need to remember that all we have that is good comes from our loving God. The people attended the temple and broke bread together in their homes.

Today, we are called to church to "celebrate." We are celebrating the incredible victory that Jesus won for us by dying and rising for us. We share in the "Bread of Life" or "Eucharist." At this celebration, we become nourished with the presence of Jesus Christ in the Eucharist. We are then called to go out from the Church and "Eucharist" with all that we come into contact. We do this because he is wherever we are. (1 John 4:4).

1 PETER 1:3-9

Today, St. Peter's words remind us, once again, what that unique event, "the Resurrection," means to us, and to the Christian Faith that we profess. The first converts to Christianity had grasped the truth of sharing eternal life with the Father because of what Jesus had done for all mankind. These people were in much pain, in much sorrow, and with no hope for their future. They grasped this truth about the Lord with a hunger and a thirst, and they rejoiced in it. We, too, have grasped this truth. We, too, know that through the Incarnation, death, and resurrection of Christ, we also have been made heirs to the kingdom of our heavenly Father.

We need to reflect now and ask ourselves why so many people do not let this consoling Christian conviction govern and regulate their lives and actions. Our technology today is so sophisticated that it prevents many from thinking about the real and permanent Lawmaker. God is the Creator of all, and he has planned and is in control of all of our futures.

Many of us are so busy using and enjoying the earthly gifts of God that we forget and, in many cases, ignore the greatest gift of all – the one that will last forever – Eternal Life. St. Peter tells us that our Faith is more precious than gold and, like gold, it will be purified and tested under the fire of adversity. We are called "Easter people" because he is risen and lives within us. We are alive in Christ, and our Eternal Life with him begins today. Rejoice and be glad. He is alive and well within you, so you may be well, too.

JOHN 20:19-31

The disciples were meeting behind locked doors because they were terribly frightened that the soldiers were going to come and arrest them and, possibly, even put them to death. Fear for themselves and their families was deep in their hearts when Jesus appeared to them. In their fear, loneliness, rejection, and failure, Jesus makes the incredible statement, "Peace be unto you!" He showed them his wounds but most of all, he let them know that he was still among them. They were overcome with tremendous joy. Today, millions of people are behind locked doors; many are in prisons or hospitals and many are trapped behind the locked door of a closed, broken mind. Jesus' message to us today, regardless of where we are or what we are going through, is to remember that he is always with us.

Jesus identified himself with his Father, and told the disciples by whose authority he did his work. Now he passed the job on to his disciples to spread the "Good News" around the world. God has chosen you to do that today, and your authority comes from him. Jesus has shown us by his words and actions how to accomplish the "Great Commission." As the Father has sent Jesus, he now sends you with the protection and power of his Holy Spirit. He gives you that power by breathing upon you. There is life in the breath of God, and through the breath of Jesus, God directed eternal spiritual life. With this inbreathing came the power to do God's will on earth. Jesus told them their mission, and it is the same mission that we must undertake. Tell the people about the "Good News" that Jesus has forgiven their sins. We do not have that power to forgive, but Jesus does. People of today cannot receive the message of forgiveness until they receive the one who forgives; his name is Jesus.

Application

The first reading tells us that community is love in action. The second reading tells us that hope is eternal. The Gospel tells us to go out and spread the "Good News."

This week, let us go forth and spread the Good News by our words and actions. Bring a Bible Study to someone who is confined to a home, hospital, or prison. Take a Scripture this week, such as love is kind (1 Corinthians 13:4), and practice it in your family, job, or school. Jesus' message to the world is, "Peace be with you," and he wants it to begin with you first.

THIRD SUNDAY OF EASTER – CYCLE A

BEFORE YOU BEGIN

Pray and ask God to speak to you through His Holy Spirit. "THE PARACLETE, THE HOLY SPIRIT WHOM THE FATHER WILL SEND IN MY NAME, WILL INSTRUCT YOU IN EVERYTHING, AND REMIND YOU OF ALL THAT I TOLD YOU." (JOHN 14:26)

FIRST DAY   Reread last week's readings.

1.   What was a helpful or new thought from the readings or from the homily you heard on Sunday?

2.   From what you learned, what personal application did you choose to apply to your life this week?

SECOND DAY   READ ACTS 2:14, 22-28   FIRST READING

("It was impossible for him to be held by the power of Hades.")

1.   What did Peter do with the Eleven? Acts 2:14

2.   Whom did he address, and what did he tell them to do? Acts 2:11, 14

3.   What did Jesus tell the disciples to do if the people would not listen to them? Matthew 10:14

4.   Who sent Jesus, what were Jesus' credentials, and what did God do with these credentials? Acts 2:22

5.   Why was he delivered up, and whom did they make use of to crucify and kill Jesus? Acts 2:23

6.   Of what did God free him, what did he do with him, and what was impossible? Acts 2:24

7.   What did Jesus say of God about all things that are impossible? Matthew 19:26

8.   What did David say? Acts 2:25

9.   What will his heart be, and what will his tongue and body do? Acts 2:26

10.   In verse 27 of Acts 2, of what is David assured?

11.   What has the Lord shown us, and with what will he fill us in his presence? Acts 2:28

Personal – God's set purpose was for Jesus to die so you could have life. Do you know what God's plan is for your life? In John 10:10, it says God's plan for you is that you may have life and have it to its fullness. In what way are you living the full life?

THIRD DAY	READ 1 PETER 1:17-21	SECOND READING

("The ransom that was paid to free you was the blood of the lamb Jesus Christ.")

1.   In what way do you call upon the Father, and how does he judge each one? 1 Peter 1:17

2.   If this is so, how should we conduct ourselves? 1 Peter 1:17

3.   How must we worship God? Hebrews 12:28

4.   In what way must we obey our human masters? Ephesians 6:5

5.   What are we to realize concerning from what we were **delivered?** Who ransomed this futile way of life for us and our fathers? How is it not handed on to us? 1 Peter 1:18

6.   What is Christ's blood beyond? 1 Peter 1:19

7.   By what have we been delivered and purified? 1 Peter 18-19

8.   When was the blood of the spotless lamb chosen, and when is it revealed? 1 Peter 1:20

9.   It is through whom that we are believers in God? 1 Peter 1:19, 21

10.   What did God do for Jesus? In what is our faith and hope centered? 1 Peter 1:21

Personal – In what way have you allowed what your parents may have said or done, to control your life? Are you carrying around any old garbage? Through the blood of Jesus we have been delivered from the power of sin. We recognize him in the breaking of the bread, him whom God raised from the dead and who now sits at the right hand of God forever.

Think about this and confess any unforgiveness toward anyone in your past, and let the blood of Jesus wash you clean and deliver you from any futile way of thinking. Be washed by the blood of the lamb. You have been delivered.

FOURTH DAY	READ LUKE 24:13-35	GOSPEL

("They had recognized him in the breaking of the bread.")

1.   What day were two of them making their way to a village named Emmaus, and how far was this village from Jerusalem? Luke 24:1, 13

2.   What were they doing? Who approached them and started to walk with them? Did they recognize him? Luke 24:14-16

3.   What did Jesus say to them? How did they react to this question? What did Cleopas ask Jesus? Luke 24:17-18

4.   Jesus asked them, "What things?" and they proceeded to explain to him the events of the past few days. They called Jesus a prophet who was powerful in what two things and in whose eyes? Luke 24:19

5.   Who delivered him up to be condemned to death and crucified? Luke 24:20

6.   For what were they hoping? Luke 24:21

Personal – In what way have you been personally set free by the coming of the Messiah? How do others see you? Do they look at you as a slave to bad habits or someone set free by the death and resurrection of Jesus?

7.   What was the astonishing news brought to them by some women? Luke 24:22-24

8.   What did Jesus say to them? And beginning with whom, what did Jesus interpret in regard to himself Luke 24:25-27

9.   By now, where were they located, and how did Jesus act? Luke 24:28

10.   What did they say to him, and what did Jesus do? Luke 24:29

11.   When Jesus sat with them to eat, what four things did he do with the bread? With that, what was their reaction, and what happened to Jesus? Luke 24:30-31

12.   What did they say happened to them as Jesus talked to them on the road and explained the Scriptures? Luke 24:32

13.   Who does it say explains scripture to us? Luke 24:27, 32

14.   Where did they go immediately, and whom did they find there? With what were they greeted, and what did they recount? Luke 24:33-35

Personal – How do you feel when you read scripture? Who explains it to you, and what is your reaction? Read Luke 2:26 and Luke 12:12.

FIFTH DAY   **READ PSALM 16:1-2, 5, 7-11**

("You will show me the path of life.")

Read and meditate on Psalm 16:1-2, 5, 7-11.

What is the Lord saying to you personally through the Psalm?

How can you apply this to your life?

ACTS 2:14, 22-28

This passage tells us that God has called each one of us by name. God has a plan for each one of us, and we are called to respond to his plan to save his people which was fulfilled in the birth, death and resurrection of Jesus Christ. God has called you and told you that if you believe in his Son, Jesus Christ, you will have eternal life (John 3:16). God's plan is that not only do we have life, but that we have life to its fullest. God's plan is not to make us rich, but to make us whole. He wants us to be healthy, physically, emotionally, and spiritually (John 10:10). The one provision that brings people out of the darkness of bondage and back into the light of freedom is Jesus Christ.

Peter was telling the crowd that the death of Jesus was part of God's plan. He tells them that even David knew that the Lord would deliver him up to the Heavenly Kingdom of God. You need to know God's plan for your life, and you need to respond to his call. God has disclosed that he loved you so much that he sent his only Begotten Son Jesus to die for you. If you believe that Jesus paid the ransom in blood, then you will live forever with God. Today you must decide whether God is telling the truth or whether this is just some story to make you feel good.

Your response to his call will dramatically change your life. You will begin to follow his plan for you, and forever your life will continue on in glory within his presence. Your response to his call will be how you live and how much you love yourself and others. God loves you to the extent that he died for you, so that you could forever live with him.

1 PETER 1:17-21

In this passage the people were called to revere a loving God and were reminded that they were not to be treated like slaves of a ruthless master. They are, in fact, the adopted children of the most High God. We do not need to assume that being special, such as being the children of God, takes away the freedom to do whatever we desire. We really need to become, not spoiled children, but grateful children of a heavenly Father who loves and forgives us. A terrible crime was committed against God, and only God's Son could free us from the heavy bondage that was left upon us. God paid a heavy ransom for our sins and it was paid with the precious blood of his Son Jesus, so that we could become his adopted children.

This passage reveals that both the law and the coming of Christ were part of God's eternal ongoing plan (Rom. 8:29). We see in God's action a love that is real. A real love is sacrifice, forgiveness, patience, and kindness. Giving up of one's own self means to put the needs of another first. Jesus manifested what is real in life, and because of this, he showed us how to love, so we can love others as he has loved us (John 15:12). You need to remember that everything in this life, possessions, accomplishments, and people, will some day be all gone. The only thing in life that is permanent is God's will, his word, and his works. We can only put our faith and hope in God because it is he who has raised Christ from the dead. In Christ's name everything we do, everything we say, and everything we hope to become really is what we could call a life of freedom.

LUKE 24:13-35

The two disciples in today's story missed the significance of what happened at the empty tomb, because they were too wrapped up in their own hurt and disappointment. They didn't even recognize Jesus when he walked beside them and joined them in their conversation. To make matters worse, they actually walked the wrong way, away from the fellowship of their fellow believers in Jerusalem.

Many times people in their hurt or grief turn away from the support of loved ones and withdraw into a corner of silence by themselves. We need to realize that it is only when we are looking for Jesus in our midst that we will experience the power and help he can bring us.

The disciples could not understand how Jesus could be so uninformed about what had happened. They saw that Jesus was very much aware of what was going on as he explained the role of God among his people. The disciples were looking for a triumphant Messiah who would break the rule of Rome. Jesus tells them about a Savior who changes the hearts of people, not their hold on power. The disciples began to see that this was no ordinary man who they met "by accident." Their hearts began to burn like fire, and they could not get enough of his teaching.

Do our hearts burn like fire over him? Do we hunger and thirst to know him more intimately than we do? Do we really understand that the death and resurrection of Jesus Christ is our only hope of Salvation? These disciples did not understand this at first despite the witness of the women and the biblical prophecies of that incredible event.

Today, after 2000 years, the resurrection of Jesus Christ is still a surprise to many people. Today, many people still refuse to believe that it took the living, breathing Jesus to come in to their midst and to break bread with them before they believed. Today for many people, it takes the fellowship and presence of living, breathing Christians to show these same people that Jesus is alive and in our midst.

Application

The first reading tells us that God knows each one of us by name. In the second reading, we are being called to show reverence to our God. The Gospel tells us not to get wrapped up in our own problems, but to be open and seek others and their problems so that they, too, can see and hear God all around them.

This week, let us reach out to someone who is hurting in our family, school, work or community. Let us call on that person and show our concern by our presence. It may be nothing more than a telephone call or a short visit to just say "Hello." Remember, the greatest gift we give to others is our presence. It is in our presence that they will see God in their midst.

FOURTH SUNDAY OF EASTER - CYCLE A

BEFORE YOU BEGIN

Pray and ask God to speak to you through His Holy Spirit. "THE PARACLETE, THE HOLY SPIRIT WHOM THE FATHER WILL SEND IN MY NAME, WILL INSTRUCT YOU IN EVERYTHING, AND REMIND YOU OF ALL THAT I TOLD YOU." (JOHN 14:26)

FIRST DAY   **Reread last week's readings.**

1.   What was a helpful or new thought from the readings or from the homily you heard on Sunday?

2.   From what you learned, what personal application did you choose to apply to your life this week?

SECOND DAY   **READ ACTS 2:14, 36-41**   **FIRST READING**

("It was to you and your children that the promise was made.")

1.   Who was Peter addressing, who stood up with him, and what was he telling them to do? Acts 2:14

2.   What did he want them to know beyond a doubt? Acts 2:36

3.   What does Scripture say will happen to us if we believe that God made Jesus both Lord and Messiah? Romans 10:9

4.   What happened when they heard this, and what did they ask Peter and the other disciples? Acts 2:37

5.   What did Peter say we must do in order to receive the Holy Spirit? Acts 2:38
      Acts 16:31

6.   Who first received the promised Holy Spirit? Acts 2:32-33

7.   To whom was this promise made? Acts 2:39

8.   From what did Peter keep urging them to save themselves? Acts 2:40

9.   What happened to those who accepted his message and how many were added that day? Acts 2:41

Personal – In what way have you accepted the message that it was to you **and** your children that the promise was made? In what way has this sign of hope for your family been reflected in your attitude?

THIRD DAY   **READ 1 PETER 2:20-25**   **SECOND READING**

("He did no wrong; no deceit was found in his mouth.")

1. If you put up with suffering for doing what is right, what is this in God's eyes?
   1 Peter 2:20

2. What do the following Scriptures say about suffering:

   Isaiah 53:11?
   Philippians 1:29
   1 Peter 4:16
   Mark 8:31

3. To what is it we are called, and whose footsteps do we follow as our example?
   1 Peter 2:20-21

4. What did Christ not do, and what was not found in his mouth? 1 Peter 2:22

5. When he was insulted, what did he not do, and when he was made to suffer, with
   what did he not return? 1 Peter 2:23, Isaiah 53:7

6. Instead, to whom was he delivered, and how does he judge? 1 Peter 2:23

7. When did Jesus deliver himself up? Luke 23:44-46

8. How did he bring our sins to the cross, and for what reason? 1 Peter 2:24

9. How have we been healed? 1 Peter 2:24

10. What were we doing at one time, and now to whom have we returned?
    1 Peter 2:25

11. Who is our shepherd, and what does he do for us? Read and meditate on
    Psalm 23

Personal – In what way have you brought your sins to the cross and let go of them? How have you been healed? Jesus brought us freedom. Are you still holding on to old sins, or have you allowed him to set you free? Meditate on this passage of Scripture (1 Peter 2:20-25).

FOURTH DAY   **READ JOHN 10:1-10**   **GOSPEL**

("I came that they might have life.")

1. Who is speaking, and to whom is he speaking? John 10:6, John 10:19

2. What is a man who does not enter the sheepfold through the gate but climbs in
   some other way, and what is the one who enters through the gate? John 10:1-2

3. What does the keeper do, what do the sheep hear, how does he call his own, and what does he do with them? John 10:3

4. Where does he walk when he has brought out all that are his, what do the sheep do, and for what reason? John 10:4

5. Who will they not follow and for what reason? John 10:5

6. Did the listeners grasp what Jesus was trying to tell them, who did Jesus say he was, and what were all who came before him? John 10:6-8

7. What did Jesus say he was again, what will happen to those who enter through him, and what will they find? John 10:9

8. What does the thief do, and why did Jesus come? John 10:10, John 1:4

9. How are we to live our life and what are we to receive? John 10:10, Romans 5:17

10. What must we do to have eternal life? John 3:16

Personal – When you lose the peace of Jesus and feel as though you are being destroyed by things going on around you, how do you handle it? Where do you go to receive the fullness of life?

FIFTH DAY   **READ PSALM 23:1-6**

("He guides me in right paths for his name's sake.")

Read and meditate on Psalm 23:1-6.

What is the Lord saying to you personally through the Psalm?

How can you apply this to your life?

SIXTH DAY   **READ ALL OF THE COMMENTARY**

ACTS 2:14, 36-41

In this passage we hear Peter boldly tell the crowd that they should listen to him because the Old Testament prophecies had been entirely fulfilled in Jesus. He told them that Jesus is the Messiah (Acts 2:25-36) and the risen Christ could dramatically change their lives. This is a new Peter, humble but bold and the power of the Holy Spirit flowed through him like a mighty river.

This was the same Peter who had denied he had ever known Jesus, regardless of being one of the disciples. But the Lord forgave and restored him after his denial. We see the transformation take place as Peter becomes a powerful and dynamic speaker. What an incredible sense of mercy has God. He watched as Peter denied him and then listened as he confessed and repented with great passion.

Where are you at the present time in your life? Have you ever felt as if you have made such bad mistakes that God could never forgive you and use you? That is what Satan wants you to believe, but don't buy it. It is a lie, and Satan is the father of lies (John 8:44). God will forgive us of anything if we turn to him with a sincere and contrite heart (Psalm 51). His love is a love that has no limit. Tell him your terrible mistake and repent, and let him take care of your fears.

Remember, true love drives out fear, because fear has to do with punishment (1 John 4:18), while a relationship of love denotes a right relationship with God, therefore, there is no reason for punishment. God promises to forgive and he never falls back on his word. Allow him to forgive and use you effectively to serve him by bringing others into his healing light. Try to be quiet and listen to him telling you how much he loves you (Psalm 46:10).

1 PETER 2:20-25

Peter really brings home a painful truth in many of our lives and that is to endure unjust suffering. We only need to look around our world and see millions of people starving and struggling just to survive. We see tyrants tearing their nations apart and putting people through all kinds of unjust suffering.

Today's message is a call to patience, loyalty and forgiveness. Just look and see the suffering that is experienced by the spouse of an unfaithful partner. Many people live in a marriage where the spouse is oppressive, and verbally, physically, and sexually abusive. Much suffering is endured because of the power of God's Holy Spirit.

Many adults have been physically or sexually abused as children, and the long-term suffering is still going on internally. Only the healing love of Jesus Christ who was the victim of unjust suffering can bring patience, forgiveness or love to someone who has suffered unjustly. Because we know that Christ did not do any wrong and suffered through his torture and death on the cross, we too, can try to follow his example.

Parents have been known to be ridiculed, mocked and disgraced by their children and are, therefore, called as Christians to be Christ-like examples of patience, forgiveness and love to them. You and I are not capable of this type of power. We can forgive others only when we realize that we ourselves are forgiven and loved completely by Jesus Christ. Suffering becomes bearable only when Christ is the bearer of the pain.

We call on him and he hears us and he responds to us. He never abandons us or leaves us alone. We must be ready to follow Jesus, regardless of where the road may lead. Suffering will be thrust upon many of us, but we must respond only to Jesus' call.

JOHN 10:1-10

John tells us of the love and dedication of a good and faithful shepherd. We clearly see that this is a story about someone protecting his flock even at the risk of losing his life. No hired hand would do this, only a total commitment of love is enough to fend off the wolves and other dangers to the flock. The sheep know their shepherd by the sound of his voice. They follow him wherever he goes. They eat wherever they are directed, and drink at the spot that is prepared for them. They safely rest at night in their sheepfold, and feel secure at the sound of his voice.

We are told in Scripture, "The Lord is my shepherd and I shall not want." The Lord Jesus knows each and everyone of us by name and he provides us with food for our bodies and food for our spirit (Eucharist and his Holy Word). He tells us to be aware of those who want to steal our hearts and destroy our lives through sin. He tells us that he is "the way, the truth and the life." (John 14:6) Look at that Scripture closely and see how it states that he is THE way, not a way, but THE way.

John ends this passage by giving us the answer to God's plan for all of us. We know that millions of people know about Jesus Christ and that he has a plan for us, and that is to live a life in all its fullness. Really, to be holy, one has to be WHOLE. We need to be physically and spiritually in tune with Christ. Our bodies are called to be temples of the Holy Spirit (1 Cor. 3:16). We are called to put on the mind of Christ (Phil. 2:1-4) and be filled with the Spirit (Eph. 5:18). When we do this we can personally say with the Psalmist, "The Lord is my Shepherd and I shall not want."

Application

The first reading deals with the virtue of hope. There is hope that we can all change for the better. The second reading helps us to see the power in redemptive suffering. It is a visual sign of Jesus Christ as he, too, once suffered for us. The Gospel brings home the message that he knows us personally, and he can identify us even by our own names.

Let us, this week, look at the suffering that is going on in our own families. We know who needs to be consoled. We know who is in danger of physical harm. We need to protect others from being exposed to unjust suffering. If you know someone who is being abused, report it at once to the proper authorities. The Lord wants us to be whole and healed. He wants us to draw upon Him for strength to endure the unjust suffering.

FIFTH SUNDAY OF EASTER – CYCLE A

BEFORE YOU BEGIN

Pray and ask God to speak to you through His Holy Spirit. "THE PARACLETE, THE HOLY SPIRIT WHOM THE FATHER WILL SEND IN MY NAME, WILL INSTRUCT YOU IN EVERYTHING, AND REMIND YOU OF ALL THAT I TOLD YOU." (JOHN 14:26)

FIRST DAY   **Reread last week's readings.**

1.   What was a helpful or new thought from the readings or from the homily you heard on Sunday?

2.   From what you learned, what personal application did you choose to apply to your life this week?

SECOND DAY   **READ ACTS 6:1-7**   **FIRST READING**

("The Word of God continued to spread.")

1.   About what were those who spoke Greek complaining? Acts 6:1

2.   What makes for pure worship? James 1:27

3.   Whom did the twelve assemble, and what did they tell them it was not right for them to neglect? Acts 6:2

4.   For what did the disciples tell them to look, and what are these men to be like? Acts 6:3

5.   By words being taught by the Spirit, what does this enable us to do? 1 Cor 2:13

6.   On what two things would this permit the disciples to concentrate? Acts 6:4

7.   By this proposal being unanimously accepted by the community, whom did they select? Acts 6:5

8.   With what was Stephen filled? Acts 6:5

9.   What two things did the disciples do to them when they were presented? Acts 6:6

10.   What happened at the same time the word of God spread? Acts 6:7

11.   Who were among those who embraced the faith? Acts 6:7

Personal – How have you responded in your role of leadership as clergyman, parent, teacher, etc.? How have you shown that you are deeply spiritual and prudent in your home and work or community?

| THIRD DAY | READ 1 PETER 2:4-9 | SECOND READING |

("Those who stumble and fall are the disbelievers in God's word;")

1. To whom are you to come, what kind of a stone is he, by whom was he rejected, and by whom is he approved and precious? 1 Peter 2:4, Acts 4:11

2. What are we, how have we been built, and into what have we been built? 1 Peter 2:5

3. What are we offering, to whom have they been acceptable, and whom is it through? 1 Peter 2:5

4. What does Scripture say is being laid in Zion, and what kind of stone? 1 Peter 2:6, Isaiah 28:16, Romans 9:33

5. What will happen to him who puts his faith in the corner-stone (Jesus)? 1 Peter 2:6

6. To whom is the stone of value? 1 Peter 2:7

7. What is the stone for those who have no faith? 1 Peter 2:7-8

8. Who are those who stumble and fall? 1 Peter 2:8

9. Who are we, and what does he claim for his own? 1 Peter 2:9

10. From what did the one call you? 1 Peter 2:9

Personal – In what way do those around you see in whom you put your faith? In what way do your actions reflect what you believe to your spouse, children, family, friends, co-workers, etc.

| FOURTH DAY | READ JOHN 14:1-12 | GOSPEL |

("I am the way, the truth, and the life.")

1. What are we not to do, and in whom are we to have our faith? John 14:1

2. Where are there many dwelling places, and what did Jesus say he was going to do? John 14:2

Personal – How do you picture heaven, and what will it be like? Whom do you think you will see there?

3. What does Jesus repeat in verse 3 of John 14, what does he say he will come back to do, and for what reason, and what does he say you know? John 14:3-4

4. What did Thomas say to Jesus, and what are the three things that Jesus says he is, and how do you come to the Father? John 14:5-6

5.   From where does salvation come, and what assures us entrance into the sanctuary? Acts 4:11-12, Hebrews 10:19-20

6.   Who does Jesus say he is? John 6:35, John 10:9

7.   To whom do we have access through Jesus? Eph 2:13, 18

8.   If we really knew Jesus, who else would you know, and what does Jesus say from this point on? John 14:7

9.   What does Philip say to Jesus and what was his response? John 14:8-9

10.   What question does Jesus ask them, what does he say about the words he speaks, where does the Father live, and for what reason? John 14:10

11.   What is Jesus asking us to believe, and what does he do to help us believe? John 14:11

12.   What will the person who has faith do and why? John 14:12

13.   What is the work of God? John 6:29

Personal – How has Jesus been the way, the truth, and the life in your life? How have others seen the way, the truth, and the life of Jesus in you?

FIFTH DAY   **READ PSALM 33:1-2, 4-5, 18-19**

("Prepare your words and you will be listened to.")

Read and meditate on Psalm 33:1-2, 4-5, 18-19.

What is the Lord saying to you personally through the Psalm?

How can you apply this to your life?

SIXTH DAY   **READ ALL OF THE COMMENTARY**

ACTS 6:1-7

The Greek-speaking Jews were probably from other lands and they complained that their widows were being treated unfairly. This discrimination was probably compounded by a language barrier. The apostles put seven Greek-speaking, respectable men in charge of the food and shelter program. This allowed the apostles to keep the focus of their ministry on teaching and preaching the Good News about Jesus.

We may wish that we could belong to a church like the early church with all its miracles, sharing, and joy of being part of a community, but they had just as many problems as we do today. No church will ever be perfect until Christ and his church are united at his second coming. All churches are struggling in their growth and if your church's shortcomings distress you, ask yourself; would a perfect church let me be a member?

We need to remember that we are all called to be faithful, not successful. We can all pitch in to make our own particular church a vibrant, living, healthy community of God by focusing on the teaching and the preaching of the Good News of Jesus Christ.

We might ask, "What is the Good News?" The Good News is a message of hope - a hope that the oppressed will be free, the sick will be healed, the lame will walk, the blind will see, the naked will be clothed and the homeless will be sheltered.

We can bring this Good News to everyone we meet because within us is the power of the Holy Spirit (1 John 4:4), and it is important for us to realize that we are called to live our lives for others, not for ourselves. We are called to die to ourselves and love others just as Jesus has done.

The early church is still here today and it is being guided by the same Holy Spirit. You need to pray, and let your God-given abilities become revealed to you, and then seek others in your community to help.

1 PETER 2:4-9

Peter is giving the new Christians a reminder that they are called to be holy, and this will be revealed by the way they witness to others. Christians must be the living material from which the new temple of God is formed. The temple of Jerusalem was built out of ordinary dead stones, but we, because of Jesus Christ, have become living temples of God (1 Cor. 3:16).
John tells us in Scripture that he is our vine and we are his branches and, without the vine, the branches cannot bear any fruit (John 15:5). In the temple of Jerusalem they sacrificed animals and offered fruits of the field to God.

Now, you and I, because of Christ, through Christ, and in Christ, will offer ourselves and our sacrifice of praise to Christ. As temples of God we will perform good works, and the Eucharist will be a daily way of life for us. Jesus is our cornerstone, and upon that stone he has built a human temple of living saints. We do good things, not to become good or to earn a reward. We do good things because of the goodness that is within us. That goodness is the presence of the Holy Spirit which empowers us to reach out and bring our brothers and sisters out of the darkness and into the light. Much of the world today is in darkness because people have not experienced being personally loved by Christ. You are called to bring that light to them. I pray that you will start within your own family, your priestly family.

JOHN 14:1-12

Jesus tells us that if we really believe in him, there is no uncertainty about death and to what it leads. He tells us that heaven is as positive as our trust and faith in him. He has prepared the way; that is certain.

The only uncertainty is our willingness to believe that he has prepared eternal life for us. We do not have to fear death for ourselves or our loved ones. We know that he has prepared a place for us and when it is ready he will come and take us home to our Father's mansion. This is the incredible promise that Jesus has made to all who believe in him.

We see Jesus describing the way to find God, and it is only through him that we can reach the Father. He states, I am THE way because he is both God and man. By uniting our lives with his, we become united with God. Trust in Jesus and he will personally take us to the Father. Some people think that saying Jesus is the only way to the Father is too narrow. His way is wide enough for the whole world, if the world chooses to accept it. Have you really chosen to accept him as the way, the truth and the life?

We must remember that Jesus was the visible image of the invisible God. As the way, he leads us to the Father. As the truth, he is the reality of all God's promises. As the life, he joins his divine life to ours, both now and eternally.

Jesus Christ, being divine, was the only person who was ever born to die for us. Because of him, you and I will never die; believing in him, we will live forever with him in his Father's mansion (John 3:16). The question that Philip asked, "Who is the Father; show us," is answered by Jesus at that time and is being answered by him today.

Be still and listen to God speaking to you (Psalm 46:10) and you will hear him say, I love you, even when you were a sinner, I still decided to die for you (Rom. 5:8) because I simply love you. He is the way, the truth and the life. Let your life show others that this is true.

Application

The first reading tells us that we are to be servants of the Lord. The second reading calls us to be holy people, a people who care about others. In our Gospel, we are shown that only through Jesus can we be with the Father.

Let us, this week, practice this by being a servant to someone who is causing us some difficulty. Do not let the person know that you are making a special effort to serve him. Let your holiness be grounded in service and prayer this week. A suggested way might be to offer to help a family member with household chores or to help a co-worker with some of his work.

SIXTH SUNDAY OF EASTER – CYCLE A

BEFORE YOU BEGIN

Pray and ask God to speak to you through His Holy Spirit. "THE PARACLETE, THE HOLY SPIRIT WHOM THE FATHER WILL SEND IN MY NAME, WILL INSTRUCT YOU IN EVERYTHING, AND REMIND YOU OF ALL THAT I TOLD YOU." (JOHN 14:26)

FIRST DAY   **Reread last week's readings.**

1.   What was a helpful or new thought from the readings or from the homily you heard on Sunday?

2.   From what you learned, what personal application did you choose to apply to your life this week?

SECOND DAY   **READ ACTS 8:5-8, 14-17**   **FIRST READING**

("Samaria had accepted the Word of God.")

1.   Where did Philip go, and what did he proclaim? Acts 8:5

2.   Who was Philip? Acts 6:5, Acts 21:8

3.   What did the crowds do who heard Philip, and what did they see? Acts 8:6

4.   What happened to the unclean spirits, and what happened to the paralytic or cripples? Acts 8:7

5.   What rose to fever pitch in that town? Acts 8:8

Personal – In what way do you see family or friends being healed by your words or touch?

6.   What had Samaria accepted, and what two men did the apostles send to them? Acts 8:14

7.   What does the Word of God judge? Hebrews 4:12

8.   What did Peter and John do, and what did they pray that they might receive? Acts 8:15

9.   Why had the Holy Spirit not yet come down on them? Acts 8:16

10.   What happened when the pair laid hands on them? Acts 8:17

11.   How did the apostles receive the Holy Spirit? John 20:22

Personal – What signs do your family, friends and work acquaintances see performed by you through the power of the Holy Spirit that you have received by way of your baptism and confirmation and belief through the Word of God?

THIRD DAY **READ 1 PETER 3:15-18** **SECOND READING**

("The reason why Christ died for sins,... was that he might lead you to God.")

1. Where are we to venerate the Lord? 1 Peter 3:15

2. Upon what does God look, and of what is he the tester? uke 16:15, 1 Thess 2:4

3. If anyone asks us the reason for this hope, what should we be ready to do, and how are we to do it? 1 Peter 3:15-16

4. Whenever we are defamed by those who libel our way of life in Christ, what are we to do, and what will happen to them? l Peter 3:16

5. If it is God's will that we suffer, for what is it better to suffer? 1 Peter 3:17

6. Whose footsteps do we follow in suffering? 1 Peter 2:21

7. How many times did Christ die for sins and for whom, also the just man? 1 Peter 3:18

8. For what reason did Christ die? 1 Peter 3:18

9. In what existence was Christ put to death, and in what realm was he given life? 1 Peter 3:18

10. What came before life in the Spirit? 1 Peter 3:18

11. How did God prove his love for us? Romans 5:8

Personal – In what way have you responded to others when they ask you why you are so hopeful? Do others see you as a hope-filled person? Ask those closest to you if they see this hope in you and, if not, reread and pray over 1 Peter 3:18 and Romans 5:8-9.

FOURTH DAY **READ JOHN 14:15-21**

GOSPEL

("He who loves me will be loved by my Father.")

1. Who is speaking in John 14:15-21? John 14:9

2. What two things must we do in order to receive the Paraclete (the Holy Spirit)? John 14:14-16

3. For whom will Jesus ask the Father, will he always be with us, what is another name for the Paraclete, and how does the world see him? John 14:15-17

4. How do we recognize him, and to what will he guide? John 14:17, John 16:13

5. What does the truth do to us? John 8:31-32

6. What does Jesus tell his disciples he will not do, and what does he say he will do? John 14:18

7.   Who will see him no more, and who will see him as one who has what? John 14:19

8.   Where is Jesus, and where are we? John 14:20

9.   Who is the man who loves Jesus, and how does he conduct himself? John 14:21, 1 John 2:5-6

10. Who will love him who loves Jesus? John 14:21, John 16:27

11. What will Jesus reveal to him? John 14:21

Personal - What are the ways that Jesus has revealed himself to you at home, at school, at work, or at church?

FIFTH DAY   **READ PSALM 66:1-7, 16, 20**

("…sing praise to the glory of his name;")

Read and meditate on Psalm 66:1-7, 16, 20.

What is the Lord saying to you personally through the Psalm?

How can you apply this to your life?

SIXTH DAY   **READ ALL OF THE COMMENTARY**

ACTS 8:5-8, 14-17

Philip went to Samaria, a country of people who were regarded with condescension by the Israelites because they did not follow the law of Moses. It is incredible that he had chosen to go to an unwelcome city to bring the healing power of the Lord. The healings were many, and a sense of joy spread throughout the city. When the apostles heard of what happened, they followed and baptized many in the name of the Lord and consequently many received the Holy Spirit.

Jesus told his apostles to go forth and be witnesses in all areas even to the ends of the earth (Acts 1:8). The new faith was officially formed when Stephen was killed and this began the rejection of the new faith (Acts 8;1). We ask, what does baptism bring to us today? Baptism brings us into a new beginning, a new family (God's family). It is a cleansing of old ways and the beginning of a new way (Jesus' way). The Holy Spirit releases his full range of power through you in Confirmation (Acts l:8). The great tragedy of our times is that so many Christians today do not even know that within them they have the greatest power in all the world (1 John 4:4).

Do we really believe that the Holy Spirit dwells within each one of us who believes that Jesus Christ is Lord? The way we live our life is a visible proof of what we really believe. If the Holy Spirit does not seem to be present in your life, seek him out through Scripture and prayer. The Holy Spirit gives us the power to resist the devil and causes him to flee (James 4:7). Much of the world today is hostile to Jesus Christ, but because of his Holy Spirit, we are called to be victorious disciples and baptize all the nations of the earth (Matt 28:19). With God's help, we will.

1 PETER 3:15-18

Faith, to many people, is a personal and private matter that we try to keep to ourselves. Yet, probably the best kept secret is the revelation that Jesus Christ is the Lord and Savior of the whole world. We do not have to be boisterous or objectionable in sharing our faith, but we should not hide it under a bushel basket (Matthew 5:15) or keep it from being seen like a city on a hill (Matthew 5:14).

When asked about our lifestyle, we should always try to answer gently and respectfully in compliance to our faith. Is your faith in Christ readily observable by others? I don't mean, by what you do, I mean by who you are. Are you prepared to tell others what Jesus Christ has done in your life? Are you prepared to suffer for Christ, such as losing your job, going to prison, opposing abortion or even being assassinated because you have convinced others that you are a Christian? If you were arrested today for being a Christian, would there be enough evidence to convict you? Let your lifestyle be so much in accord with what Jesus teaches that their accusations will be empty and only embarrass them. Your conduct as a follower of Christ must be above criticism. We are called to be his messengers and, like Jesus, we can expect suffering along the way.

JOHN 14:15-21

Jesus had promised to leave his Holy Spirit with his followers and they were somewhat confused, and wondered how he could leave them and still be with them. In the form of human flesh, Jesus was available only to those who were where he was, but now he is available wherever we are through his Holy Spirit. his Spirit resides in our temple (body - 1 Cor. 3:16) and he is always prepared to use his presence to help his people. The Holy Spirit is the very presence of God within us and all believers.

He promised that his Father would give us another comforter and that he would never leave us. Do you really believe the presence of God exists within you? Jesus stated that he does live within us and that he will never leave the heart of one who believes in Him. The comforter is a combination of comfort and counsel. The Holy Spirit is a powerful person who is working for us and with us. We have to know that the Holy Spirit is the Spirit of truth (14:17), and is our teacher. We must remember that he will show us what to do and what to say when we are in a crisis. All of our intelligence and human wisdom are weak and insignificant compared to his wisdom. We must never seduce ourselves or others into thinking that the Holy Spirit is not our teacher or that he will ever leave us.

He is our Spirit of truth. He will give us the courage to speak when it is easier to be silent. He will be within us and comfort us when all others will mock us, abandon us, or even kill us. But, we are not to be pitied; rather, we are to be ecstatic with joy because Jesus has chosen us to be his ambassadors. This means we have the incredible privilege of being messengers of the Good News and, with the Holy Spirit who resides within us, we are far more than conquerors.

Application

The first reading reveals to us that the gift of healing can be present through just an ordinary touch of the hand on someone who is suffering. The second reading reveals the depth of our faith by our response. The Gospel tells us of the promise of Jesus to leave his Holy Spirit with us and empower us with his love.

This week, look at the members in your family and respond to their needs and hurts by affirming them with a helping hand, possibly with the chores, or with the washing of a car, or simply sitting and listening to a loved one share his needs. Take a leap in faith and allow the Holy Spirit to give you boldness this week and be a loving servant to your family, friends and community.

SEVENTH SUNDAY OF EASTER – CYCLE A

BEFORE YOU BEGIN

Pray and ask God to speak to you through His Holy Spirit. "THE PARACLETE, THE HOLY SPIRIT WHOM THE FATHER WILL SEND IN MY NAME, WILL INSTRUCT YOU IN EVERYTHING, AND REMIND YOU OF ALL THAT I TOLD YOU." (JOHN 14:26)

FIRST DAY   **Reread last week's readings.**

1.   What was a helpful or new thought from the readings or from the homily you heard on Sunday?

2.   From what you learned, what personal application did you choose to apply to your life this week?

SECOND DAY   **READ ACTS 1:12-14**   **FIRST READING**

("Together they devoted themselves to constant prayer.")

1.   Where is the mount called Olivet and what had previously occurred there? Acts 1:1-2, 12

2.   Entering the city, who went to the upstairs room where they were staying? Acts 1:13

3.   To what did they devote themselves? Acts 1:14

4.   What do the following scriptures say about prayer?

     Mark 11:24
     Philippians 4:6-7
     Colossians 4:2
     1 Timothy 2:8
     1 Timothy 4:4-5

Personal – In what ways do you come together to pray with others, how do you pray, and for what do you pray?

5.   Who were in the company of the disciples? Acts 1:14

6.   When was there another occasion that women were present? Luke 8:1-3

7.   What did Jesus say about his mother and brothers in Luke 8:19-21?

8.   What does not exist among us and for what reason? Galatians 3:24-28

Personal – In what ways have you prayed with Mary, the mother of God, this week? How often do you pray with the men, women and children who are closest to you?

THIRD DAY   **READ 1 PETER 4:13-16**   **SECOND READING**

("When his glory is revealed, you will rejoice exultantly.")

1. In what are you to rejoice? 1 Peter 4:13

2. How can you share in Christ's sufferings? 2 Timothy 2:11

3. To what do our sufferings or afflictions lead? Romans 5:3-5

4. How do we become glorified with Jesus? Romans 8:17, John 12:23-24

5. What will you do when his glory is revealed? 1 Peter 4:13

6. What are we when we are insulted for Christ's sake and who in his glory has come to rest on us? 1 Peter 4:14

7. What will be present in us when the Spirit rests on us? Isaiah 11:2

8. What reasons must we see to that none of us suffer? 1 Peter 4:15

9. If anyone suffers for being a Christian, what must he not be, rather, what should he do? 1 Peter 4:16

Personal - In what way have you died to your way of doing things in order to bear the name Christian? What does that name mean to you? How have you suffered because of the name, and what has been your attitude?

FOURTH DAY   **READ JOHN 17:1-11**   **GOSPEL**

("I revealed your name to those whom you gave me out of the world.")

1. What reassuring words had Jesus spoken? John 16:33

2. Where did Jesus look and what did he say? John 17:1

3. What has been given Jesus over all mankind, and what may he do? John 17:2

4. What is eternal life? John 17:3, 1 John 5:20

5. What did Jesus do on earth and how did he do it? John 17:4

6. Where does the Father give Jesus glory and when did he have this glory? John 17:5

7. What did he make known and what did those given him keep? John 17:6

8. What do they realize, what was entrusted to them, and what did they have to do? John 17:7-8

9. How is it known to them that Jesus came from the Father and what did they have to do? John 17:8

10. For whom does he pray? John 17:9

11.   How has he been glorified? John 17:10

12.   Where does he say he will no longer be, what does he ask the Father to do, and how is he to do it so that they may be one even as the Father and Son are one? John 17:11

Personal – In what way have you made Jesus' name known to those he has given to you? List the ways you have come to know Jesus. How has he revealed the way, the truth and the life to you? Meditate on this and share with someone.

FIFTH DAY   **READ PSALM 27:1, 4, 7-8**

("...your presence, O Lord, I seek.")

Read and meditate on Psalm 27:1, 4, 7-8.

What is the Lord saying to you personally through the Psalm?

How can you apply this to your life?

SIXTH DAY   **READ ALL OF THE COMMENTARY**

ACTS 1:12-14

The central theme from today's passage is the absolute need for prayer. In today's world, the strongest area in our lives must be our prayer time with Jesus Christ. We have seen all through the New Testament that Jesus went off and prayed alone to his Father before he did anything. We are called to do no less than he. Jesus told them not to leave the upper room until his Spirit returned to them. They prepared for the coming event that would change the face of the entire known world in about 25 years by spending the next ten days in solemn prayer.

This time of preparation which we would call a retreat is a time of waiting, praying, and expecting the Holy Spirit's power and guidance. A difficult decision, or a very hard task should never be attempted without praying first to the Holy Spirit. We need to take the apostles' example and not rush in and hope everything turns out all right. We need to ask ourselves, how often do we stop and pray before we do anything or even say anything.

These apostles had been with Jesus for three years and had seen many miracles, and yet, they knew that they lacked something. Jesus did not want them to go into the world unprepared. He does not want us to go unprepared either. He has given us his Holy Spirit who will never leave us. His power will be what we will use to resist Satan and make Satan flee (James 4:7).

1 PETER 4:13-16

There is much talk in the Christian world today that if you follow Christ, you will be happy and live a prosperous life. Some people are drawn to the Christian faith thinking it is like an insurance policy. Many people think if they attend services every week, receive all the sacraments and are obedient to the church, they will make it to heaven without too much pain.

Jesus tells us that he does not have a place to lay his head, never mind being successful in the world. In today's message, Peter is telling the new converts that we will be with Christ in heaven, if we carry the crosses he sends us. This is not a theology of works, this is a covenant of love. Our love for him will be what holds us up when we are persecuted for being a Christian.

Living the Christian life is not the product of mere men, it is the product of human nature raised to a higher plane by Divine Grace. The channels by which we receive his Divine Grace are sacraments, prayer and sacred scripture. We really can not say that being a Christian is too severe, because when we see how our baptism has made us brothers and sisters of Christ and has prepared us for the other sacraments, then we know that nothing can separate us from the love of God. No persecution, no trial and conviction, not even death itself will separate us from the love of God (Romans 8:31-39).

To experience suffering because we are Christian is a cause for tremendous joy. It means that we belong to Christ, not the world. I must say that we have to pray and discern that the suffering that we are going through is because we are doing God's will and not our will. We must all remember our time here on earth is but a moment in eternity, but the time that we will spend with Christ in heaven will be eternal, and that is "Good News."

JOHN 17:1-11

This passage from the Gospel of John is a prayer of Jesus. We can see that the world is a battle ground and the forces under Satan's power are driven by bitterness and hatred for Jesus and all of his followers. We must never forget that we are locked in spiritual warfare and that we, by ourselves, are no match for Satan. We are called to put on our spiritual armor (Eph. 6:10-18) and be ready.

Again we see Jesus going to his Father in prayer. He prayed to the Father to protect his followers and that protection extends today to you and me. We respond to that protection through our prayer life, our scripture study, and our receiving of the sacraments. He will make us holy and unite us in his truth if we abide in him and keep his commandments (John 15:7).

Jesus is telling us that eternal life is entering into a personal relationship with God in Jesus Christ. We see Jesus asking the Father to restore him to his original place now that his time on earth is coming very quickly to an end. We need to realize that Jesus' resurrection and ascension were proof that this prayer was indeed answered in full. Jesus said that his disciples are his glory and that, of course, means us who have decided to follow Jesus.

What a tremendous blessing that Jesus can find glory in our lives. It is a tremendous sign of encouragement to all of us. If you have slipped or even walked away from Christ, now is the time to come back to him. His prayer to the Father was for all of his brothers and sisters. He wants all of us to have eternal life. His real and full glory is sharing with all of us who believe in him, the reality of seeing and giving praise and glory to his heavenly Father. We must remember, Jesus said, "I have not lost any whom you have given me." So come on back; "Abba" is waiting.

Application

The first reading tells us the first Christian community devoted themselves to prayer. The second reading tells us that those who suffer because of righteousness are very much blessed. The Gospel reveals that everything that was of the Father was also of Jesus at his hour of glory.

This week, let the presence of God fill you in your home, work, and school area. Let the power of prayer transform your attitude and your conduct this week. Make a commitment to yourself to begin each morning in a quiet time alone with the Lord. In the middle of your day take a few minutes again to spend a quiet time with the Lord in prayer. Before you go to sleep review your day with the Lord, and go to sleep with him on your mind.

PENTECOST – CYCLE A

BEFORE YOU BEGIN

Pray and ask God to speak to you through His Holy Spirit. "THE PARACLETE, THE HOLY SPIRIT WHOM THE FATHER WILL SEND IN MY NAME, WILL INSTRUCT YOU IN EVERYTHING, AND REMIND YOU OF ALL THAT I TOLD YOU." (JOHN 14:26)

FIRST DAY   **Reread last week's readings.**

1. What was a helpful or new thought from the readings or from the homily you heard on Sunday?

2. From what you learned, what personal application did you choose to apply to your life this week?

SECOND DAY   **READ ACTS 2:1-11**   **FIRST READING**

("All were filled with the Holy Spirit.")

1. What day had come, and where were the disciples gathered? Acts 2:1

2. How many days after the Passover was Pentecost celebrated, and what are other names for it? Leviticus 23:15-16, Exodus 23:16, Numbers 28:26

3. What suddenly happened from up in the sky, and where was it heard? Acts 2:2

4. Read the following scripture, and tell what the Spirit gives to a person? Ezekiel 37:9, 14

5. What appeared, and what did it do? Acts 2:3

6. What was Jesus' promise just before he ascended to heaven? Acts 1:5, 8

7. With what were all filled, and how did they express themselves? Acts 2:4

8. What did the Spirit prompt them to do? Acts 2:4, Acts 4:31

9. Who was staying in Jerusalem at the time, and what did they hear? Acts 2:5-6

10. About what were they confused? Acts 2:6

11. What was their reaction? What did they ask, and about what were they so amazed? Acts 2:7-11

Personal – How can your family or friends identify the Spirit of God's presence in you? What comes forth from your mouth, and what do you need to do so people will be astonished by your words?

THIRD DAY **READ 1 CORINTHIANS 12:3-7, 12-13** **SECOND READING**

("No one can say "Jesus is Lord," except in the Holy Spirit.")

1. What is Paul telling the brothers that you cannot do in the Spirit of God, and what can be said only in the Holy Spirit? 1 Corinthians 12:3

2. What is there different, but with the same Spirit? 1 Corinthians 12:4

3. There are different ministries and works but the same God who accomplishes what? 1 Corinthians 12:5-6

4. To each person the manifestation of the Spirit is given for what reason? 1 Corinthians 12:7

5. In what gifts should you try to be rich? 1 Corinthians 14:12

6. Fill in the following blanks: The body is _____ and has _____ members, but all the members, _____ though they are, are _____ body; and so it is with Christ. 1 Corinthians 12:12

7. In the one Spirit, who were baptized into the one body? 1 Corinthians 12:13

8. What have all of us been given to drink? 1 Corinthians 12:13

9. Into whom have we been baptized? Galatians 3:27

10. When were we chosen and sealed with the Holy Spirit? Ephesians 1:13

Personal – From the above scriptures, how can you identify the **manifestation** of the Spirit in your life, and in those you come in contact with? Reread 1 Corinthians 12:3, and take note of what comes forth from your mouth this week.

FOURTH DAY **READ JOHN 20:19-23** **GOSPEL**

("Receive the Holy Spirit.")

1. Why did the disciples lock the doors of the place where they were? John 20:19

2. Who came and stood before them, and what did he say to them? John 20:19

3. When he had said this, what did he show them? John 20:20

4. What did the disciples do at the sight of the Lord? John 20:20

Personal – In what way has our Lord appeared to you when you have been gathered with others praying, and what has been your response?

5. What did Jesus say again, and what is his gift to you? John 20:21, John 14:27

6. Whom has the Father sent, and who sends us? John 20:21

7. What did Jesus do to the disciples, and what did they receive? John 20:22

8. How did the Lord God form man, and how did he give him life? Genesis 2:7

9. If we forgive other's sin, what happens to them, and if we hold them bound, what happens? John 20:23

10. What did Jesus say to the Father while on the cross, and whom should we imitate? Luke 23:34

Personal – How do others see in you, spiritually and physically, the breath of his life? How do others see you living out your sign of baptism through repentance, which means change? How do others see you as you practice forgiveness of others, and ask others to forgive you? How often do you feel the need for the Sacrament of Reconciliation, and why?

FIFTH DAY   **READ PSALM 104:1, 24, 29-31, 34**

("When you send forth your Spirit, they are created.")

Read and meditate on Psalm 104:1, 24, 29-31, 34

What is the Lord saying to you personally through the Psalm?

How can you apply this to your life?

SIXTH DAY   **READ ALL OF THE COMMENTARY**

ACTS 2:1-11

In today's readings we celebrate the Feast of "Pentecost," which means fifty (50). This was a feast that was celebrated about fifty days after Passover and was a feast of thanksgiving for the harvest. The first fruits of the crop were offered to God that day. All Jewish men were expected to come to the temple for the feast. The city was usually full to overflowing, and it was fitting that this day was chosen as the day the Holy Spirit descended on the Apostles.

Today is, in reality, the birthday of the church, and the Christian religion was to be a church for the whole world. The old law was given by God to Moses for the Jews only. The new law, given by Christ and confirmed by the power of the Holy Spirit, was for all peoples. That means you, and that means today, right where you are. The very fact that you are reading this Bible Study is proof that the power of the Holy Spirit is drawing you near to him.

Let today be the day that you fall upon your knees and invite Jesus Christ to come into your heart and become the Lord of your life. Take a few moments and confess to the Lord all that is twisted within you, and then ask him to let his Holy Spirit fill you with the power and peace that surpasses all understanding. The celebration of Pentecost is for us as well as it was for the Jews in today's passage. Let the power of the Holy Spirit flow through you, and you will enjoy that same gift that the Apostles had, the gift of speaking in tongues.

The signs and wonders of that incredible day brought huge crowds of Jews to the place where the Apostles were staying. This was the day chosen for the Apostles to go forward and make disciples of all nations. We are called also to go forward and make disciples of all nations (Matthew 28:19). Let us remember, after the Jews celebrated the Feast of the Passover (Moses leading his people to freedom), they celebrated the Feast of Weeks and the Feast of Harvests which were celebrated on the same day and were later called Pentecost. It was one of three major feasts of the year (Leviticus 23:16), a feast of thanksgiving for the harvested crops. The Holy Spirit came fifty days after the resurrection and Peter's speech resulted in a harvest of new believers.

The Lord needs some good laborers to work in the vineyard. Are you ready to join the workers?

1 CORINTHIANS 12:3-7, 12-13

In this passage, we see that the gifts of the Holy Spirit were given for the good of the whole community to help build up the body of Christ. We should not refuse to use the gifts of the Holy Spirit nor claim them as our own. Paul clearly warns against listening to false teachers, and he shows us how to check out their credentials. We are to find out what they teach about Christ.

We see people today who mock Jesus Christ, not only with their words, but in the way they live. We see people using their gifts to split communities apart, and then trying to tell us that they are only doing God's will. Anyone can claim to speak for God, and we need only to look at some of the leaders in some countries, and we can see a lot of false messiahs running around. God has given us many different gifts, but we must remember, they all come from the same Spirit, and they are to be used to help the community or church. They will know we are Christians by the way we love and help one another.

Paul compares the body of Christ to a human body. Each part is an individual, and has a specific job to do. In their differences, all of the parts must work together for the good of the whole body. Jesus Christ is the head, and the rest of us make up the body of Christ. It is very important that we are not too proud of our abilities, and we must not compare ourselves with one another. We are called to use our different gifts together, to spread the "Good News" to a world that is filled with "bad news." The church, which is the people who believe that "Jesus is Lord," must be united in its belief in Christ. It must not let its leaders or members use any gifts to cause divisions or strife.

Faith in Christ is the core of Christian unity. We are one body, with one spirit, united in Christ with the Father through the power of the Holy Spirit. When we were baptized into the Christian Faith, the Holy Spirit took up residence in us and we became the temple of the Holy Spirit (1 Corinthians 3:16). You, by your baptism, have been born into God's family, and our common goal is faith in our Lord and Savior, Jesus Christ.

JOHN 20:19-23

Today's Gospel passage reveals to us the incredible gift of the Holy Spirit being given publicly to the disciples of Jesus by Jesus himself. This is a tremendous feast day in the church. We look back, and we see that Advent was a time to prepare for the Incarnation of God (God becoming man). Christmas was the happening of this great Incarnation act. We then moved into Lent and began to prepare ourselves for the sufferings endured by Christ on our behalf during his holy week. We celebrated victory in Jesus' triumph over death which guaranteed our union with him in heaven.

Today, we celebrate in Pentecost the Holy Spirit coming to abide within his church. This means abiding in you, me, and all believers of the Lord Jesus Christ. The Holy Spirit gives the power to preserve, to teach, to explain, and to spread the Gospel of "Good News," which is a message of hope and love for everyone in the world.

This Holy Spirit who came upon the disciples and all of the people in the upper room is the same Spirit who wants to abide in us. We can let him come into our heart right now by getting down on our knees and confessing our sins to the Lord. Invite him to come and take up residence in your temple, and let him take control of your life. His power will flow through you, and your life will never be the same again. His peace will be your peace, and it will be a peace that surpasses all understanding (Philippians 4:7).

The power from the Holy Spirit helps all of us live a life of holiness and wholeness. We need to always remember that God's plan for each one of us is to live a life that is abundant and full (John 10:10). The Holy Spirit gives us the power, in the name of Jesus, to bind Satan and his cohorts, and in his name, to loosen the Spirit of the Lord Jesus to heal, to restore and, to forgive. We can release others from the bondage of sin by our compassion and forgiveness. We are more than conquerors; we are children of the Living God and we are called to set the captives free and give sight to the blind. We do that by forgiving them, and loving them through the power of the Holy Spirit, and in the mighty name of Jesus Christ, our Lord and Savior. Pentecost – the harvest is now, the Kingdom of God is at hand, come and be fishers of men. I pray that the Holy Spirit today will fill you with his love and power, and fill all of us with gratitude for all that God has done for us.

Application

The first reading tells us that we celebrate the birthday of the church when we celebrate "Pentecost." The second reading reveals that the gifts of the Holy Spirit are to be used to uplift the community. The Gospel reveals to us that the Holy Spirit gives us power in the name of Jesus. This power is a healing power.

Let us take a long look at our gifts, and then share them with others this week. You might visit someone who is sick, or visit someone in jail. You might write a letter to someone who is lonely, or cook someone a special meal. Do something beautiful for God this week, and keep on giving your gift away. God will never let you be without a gift – try it, you'll like it.

TRINITY SUNDAY - CYCLE A

BEFORE YOU BEGIN

Pray and ask God to speak to you through His Holy Spirit. "THE PARACLETE, THE HOLY SPIRIT WHOM THE FATHER WILL SEND IN MY NAME, WILL INSTRUCT YOU IN EVERYTHING, AND REMIND YOU OF ALL THAT I TOLD YOU." (JOHN 14:26)

FIRST DAY   **Reread last week's readings.**

1.   What was a helpful or new thought from the readings or from the homily you heard on Sunday?

2.   From what you learned, what personal application did you choose to apply to your life this week?

SECOND DAY   **READ EXODUS 34:4-6, 8-9**   **FIRST READING**

("The Lord, the Lord, a merciful and gracious God...")

1.   What did the Lord say to Moses and who inscribed the tablets? Exodus 24:12, Exodus 31:18

2.   Why did Moses go to Mount Sinai? Exodus 34:4

3.   What happened to the stone tablets? Exodus 32:19

4.   What did Moses cut, where did he go, and who commanded it? Exodus 34:4

5.   Having come down in a cloud, who stood with Moses, and what did he proclaim? Exodus 34:5

6.   What did the Lord do, and what did he cry out? Ex 34:6

7.   In what is the Lord slow, and in what is he rich? Exodus 34:6

8.   What did Moses do? Exodus 34:8

9.   What does Psalm 95:6 say we should do, and what has the Lord done?

10.   What did Moses ask the Lord to do, and what did he say about the people? Exodus 34:9

11.   What did Moses ask the Lord to pardon and receive? Ex. 34:9

Personal – In what way have you revealed your slowness to anger to those around you? How can you improve in this area?

| THIRD DAY | READ 2 CORINTHIANS 13:11-13 | SECOND READING |

("Mend your ways. Encourage one another.")

1. Who is writing and to whom is he writing? 2 Corinthians 1:1

2. As he says good-bye, what two things does he tell them to do and how are they to live? 2 Corinthians 13:11

3. Where will be the God of love and peace? 2 Corinthians 13:11

4. How are we to greet one another and what do all the holy ones do? 2 Corinthians 13:12

5. What is of the Lord Jesus Christ? 2 Corinthians 13:13

6. As a child, what was upon Jesus as he grew in size and stature? Luke 2:40

7. What is of God? 2 Corinthians 13:13

8. What is God and how do we abide in God? 1 John 4:16

9. What is of the Holy Spirit? 2 Corinthians 13:13

10. To what have we been called with the Son? 1 Corinthians 1:9

Personal – In what way do you have fellowship with the Holy Spirit? How do you see the grace of Jesus Christ and the love of God within you? How do you see Jesus in those around you?

| FOURTH DAY | READ JOHN 3:16-18 | GOSPEL |

("…whoever believes in him may not die.")

1. Whom did God love, and whom did he give? John 3:16

2. What happens to those who believe in him, and what will they have? John 3:16

3. How is God's love revealed to us? 1 John 4:9

4. What did God send the Son into the world **not** to do? John 3:17

5. Through him (the Son) what would happen to the world? John 3:17

6. Read the following Scriptures and write next to each one what it says about being saved.
   a. Acts 2:21
   b. Acts 4:12
   c. Acts 15:11
   d. Romans 10:9
   e. Titus 3:4-5

7. What happens to whomever believes in Jesus? John 3:18

8. What happens to those who do not believe in him? John 3:18

9.   Who has no condemnation? Romans 8:1

10.   What did Jesus come to do and what condemns a person? John 12:47–48

Personal – In what way have you experienced the love of the Father through Jesus' death on the cross? In what way do you share this love the Father has for you with your family, friends, business acquaintances, school friends, etc. on a daily basis? Is there a balance with word and deed?

FIFTH DAY   **READ DANIEL 3:52–56**

("and blessed is your holy and glorious name.")

Read and meditate on Daniel 3:52–56.

What is the Lord saying to you personally through the Psalm?

How can you apply this to your life?

SIXTH DAY   **READ ALL OF THE COMMENTARY**

EXODUS 24:4-6, 8-9

Today, we celebrate the feast of the Holy Trinity, and in this passage we see God making a covenant with the Israelites. He declared them as his chosen people through whom he would eventually send his Divine Son and to whom he would give his Holy Spirit. In this way all mankind had the possibility and the means of reaching their permanent home with him. His plan for them would be complete for all eternity.

To explain this mystery is impossible, and, yet, it is very simple. God loved us so much that he sent his only begotten Son to die for us, and he left his Holy Spirit to empower our lives. In stages, a woman marries and becomes a wife, then a mother, and later, a grandmother. While God does not go through stages, the woman who is wife, mother, and grandmother in some ways reflects the Trinity. She never stops being a woman through these different phases of her life. We might ask what part becomes a wife? What part becomes a mother? She is totally woman in all three ways, while she is several persons in the one person of being a woman.

God is God, and he told Moses, "I am who am." The covenant made on Mount Sinai by God with Moses was the preparation for God to become Incarnate (God became man) and then to forever reside by his Holy Spirit with us. This has been a mystery that one day God will reveal to us in Heaven where we will see him face to face. The Israelites were stubborn, sinful people and did not deserve another chance, but Moses pleaded for them and God forgave and promised them that a Messiah would emerge from them and bring salvation to the whole world.

Today there are many stubborn, cruel and violent people who walk in darkness. The Messiah has come, and he died and rose from the dead for all who believe in him. We have within us a Holy Spirit that is far greater than the one who leads the world (1 John 4:4). We must never forget that we are the chosen children of God in the name of the Father, in the name of the Son, and in the name of the Holy Spirit. Amen.

2 CORINTHIANS 13:11-13

Paul's last words in this passage apply to us in today's world. He tells us to be happy by growing in Christ. We are called to mend our ways; in other words, to repent and to change. We can live in peace with one another when we follow the teachings of the Prince of Peace, Jesus Christ. We are called to greet each other with a holy sign of Christ's blessings. We only have to look around to see the discord in our families, communities, and countries throughout the world. We may ask, "Where is the strife and jealousy originating?"

Paul is telling us that all discord comes when we try to be in control of others and play God with other people's lives and their nations. In order to live in peace with one another, we must be at peace with ourselves. Jesus told us that he would leave his Holy Spirit and he would never leave us.

Paul closes this passage with words of encouragement and cheer for all. He tells us how the Blessed Trinity is always active and present in our lives. He says, "May God's love and the Holy Spirit's friendship be yours." He also calls upon the grace of our Lord Jesus Christ and says that Jesus' grace will always be available to us.

Paul is once again calling upon God to bless, direct, and protect his people through the power of the Holy Spirit in the name above all names, Jesus Christ. You are called to bring God's blessing upon yourself and your family. This will help you live in peace and harmony with all people.

JOHN 3:16-18

If we had only one passage in the Bible to read, I believe this would be the choice of many people: "For God so loved the world that he gave his only Son that whoever believes in him should not perish, but have eternal life." Do you really believe this? God is saying that he loves us so much that he let his only begotten Son Jesus die for us, so that we could live forever with him in heaven. God did this for us knowing well that we would be sinners, and yet, he is still loving us very much.

Scripture tells us that, "Eye has not seen, ear has not heard, nor has it so much as dawned on men, what God has prepared for those who love him." (1 Cor. 2:9) We cannot even image that kind of love, nevertheless, it is true. We only have to believe in Jesus Christ. When we believe, our lives change and this change is noticed by others. We become vulnerable, lovable, gentle, kind and trustworthy.

God knows where we have been and what we have done and he still offers us the incredible gift of eternal life and a peace that surpasses all understanding (Phil. 4:7). Memorize this verse (John 3:16) and put your name in place of the word "world" and "whoever" and see how personal is this promise.

We have to remember that true love is not static or self-centered; it reaches out and draws in others. God has set the pattern of true love in this passage, the basis of all love relationships. If we love someone considerably, we are willing to pay dearly for that person's responsive love. Jesus Christ paid the ultimate price for love with his life. God paid for our love with his Son's life. Jesus accepted the punishment, paid for our sins, and then offered us the new and eternal life he bought for us with his blood. When you and I share the Gospel message, our love must be like his. We must be willing to give up our comfort, and maybe our lives, so that others might join us in receiving this incredible gift of God's love.

Application

The first reading reveals that God is present to us in himself, his Son, and his Holy Spirit - a true Blessed Trinity. The second reading tells us that to grow in Christ will bring a happy, positive response, and that is what we really need in today's world. The Gospel tells us that God loved us so greatly that he gave us his begotten Son, so that we could live forever.

This week, let us call on the power of the Holy Spirit and be positive in our words and actions to the members of our family and those whom we meet at work and at school. Let us try to give up our comfort to bring someone to Christ this week, or to read Scripture to someone or encourage someone to read a bible. Remember - make a friend, be a friend, and bring that friend to Christ.

THE BODY AND BLOOD OF CHRIST - CYCLE A

BEFORE YOU BEGIN

Pray and ask God to speak to you through His Holy Spirit. "THE PARACLETE, THE HOLY SPIRIT WHOM THE FATHER WILL SEND IN MY NAME, WILL INSTRUCT YOU IN EVERYTHING, AND REMIND YOU OF ALL THAT I TOLD YOU." (JOHN 14:26)

FIRST DAY **Reread last week's readings.**

1. What was a helpful or new thought from the readings or from the homily you heard on Sunday?

2. From what you learned, what personal application did you choose to apply to your life this week?

SECOND DAY **READ DEUTERONOMY 8:2-3, 14-16** **FIRST READING**

("Not by bread alone does man live, but by every Word that comes forth from the mouth of the Lord.")

1. Who is speaking, and whose words is he announcing? Deuteronomy 5:1-5

2. What is he asking the Israelites to remember? Deuteronomy 8:2

3. What two things does the Holy One of Israel, the Lord, our God, do for us? Isaiah 48:17

4. Why did affliction come upon the Israelites? Deuteronomy 8:2

5. With what did the Lord let them be afflicted? With what did he feed them, and for what reason? Deuteronomy 8:3

6. How many days was Jesus tempted in the desert by Satan? What was one of the temptations, and what was Jesus' answer? Luke 4:2-4

7. Of what is he telling them to be careful after they have their fill? Deuteronomy 8:14

8. What did the Lord do for the Israelites? Deuteronomy 8:15-16

9. What do affliction and testing make us in the end? Deuteronomy 8:16

10. When under trial or affliction, what are we to do? Romans 12:12

Personal – In what way is there a balance in your life between the food you eat and obedience to the Word of God? In what way are you taking in the Word? Are you eating what is good for you in bread and Word? Is Eucharist part of your daily nourishment?

What Kind of Physical Food
4 Basics   **Junk Food**

How Often
Attitude

Listening and Obeying the Word
God's Word   **Man's Word**

How Often
Attitude

When Receiving Eucharist
Repentant Heart   **Hard Heart**

How Often
Attitude

THIRD DAY   **READ 1 CORINTHIANS 10:16-17**   **SECOND READING**

("We all partake of the one loaf.")

1. Who wrote this letter and to whom was he writing? 1 Corinthians 1:1-2

2. What are the two questions he asks them in 1 Cor. 10:16?

3. What did Jesus do with the bread and what did he say it was? Matthew 26:26

4. What did he do with the cup, and what did he say it was? Matthew 26:27-28

5. In what do we share or participate? 1 Corinthians 10:16

6. Because the loaf of bread is one, we, many though we are, are what, and for what reason? 1 Corinthians 10:17

7. In whom are we one body? Romans 12:5

8. Just as there is one body, there is also one what, and what is given you by your call? Ephesians 4:4

Personal – In what way do you share in the body and blood of Jesus with your family and friends? Is there a oneness and unity among those with whom you associate? Read the rest of 1 Corinthians 10. Examine your conscience to see whether you have been worshiping the One, True God.

FOURTH DAY   **READ JOHN 6:51-58**   **GOSPEL**

("If anyone eats this bread, he shall live forever.")

1.   Who is speaking? Who did he say he was, and from where has he come down? John 6:43, 51

2.   What did he say would happen to those who eat this bread? John 6:51

3.   What did he say the bread he will give is, and for the **life** of whom? John 6:51

4.   How did the Jews react to this, and what did they ask? John 6:52

5.   Jesus assured them that if they did not eat the flesh of the Son of Man and drink his blood, they would have no what? John 6:53

6.   What happens to him who feeds on his flesh and drinks his blood? John 6:54

7.   What does Jesus say his flesh and blood are? John 6:55

8.   The man who remains in Jesus, and Jesus in him, does what? John 6:56

9.   What does the Father have? Whom did he send, and what does he who was sent have because of him? John 6:57

10.   What will the man who feeds on Jesus have because of him? John 6:57

11.   Where did this bread come from, and what is it unlike? John 6:58

12.   How long will the man live who lives on this bread? John 6:58

Personal – How has the eating of Jesus' flesh, and drinking of his blood, which is the Eucharist, shown others that he is truly present in you?

FIFTH DAY   **READ PSALM 147:12-15, 19-20**

("...swiftly runs his Word.")

Read and meditate on Psalm 147:12-15, 19-20.

What is the Lord saying to you personally through the Psalm?

How can you apply this to your life?

SIXTH DAY   **READ ALL OF THE COMMENTARY**

DEUTERONOMY 8:2-3, 14-16

Today's passage reveals what it really means to live the "real life." You have to ask yourself a very difficult question: "How do you find "real life?" Today, many people think it comes when you eat the right foods, or drink the light and tasty drinks. Some go to extreme measures to make sure they dress well so that they may look good. Others spend enormous amounts of time trying to build up their bodies in order to look more attractive, younger or stronger. An incredible number of people think the "real life" is to obtain an education so they can earn a fortune and live wherever they choose and do whatever they decide. Today, we call this "living the good life," and for many, the way others must live does not enter into their concern. But these desires leave us empty because they satisfy only our appetites, not our deepest longings.

Moses tells us that real life comes from total commitment to God. It requires sacrifice, discipline, and plain hard work. Many people today are looking for the quick fix whether it be for a diet, an education, marriage, or work. Only as our relationship with God deepens will our character and strength develop. The long-term rewards for obeying God are greater than anything the world has to offer. The bread God gave Moses was a special kind of Bread, and it came from heaven.

God showed what was coming in the form of another special kind of bread at the Last Supper. Jesus gave us himself in the taking and eating of his Body and Blood. He said, "This is my Body, take and eat. This is my Blood, take it and drink." We call this "Eucharist," which we receive at Mass. We become "Eucharisted" when we eat his body and drink his blood. We might ask, "How do we Eucharist others?" You can Eucharist others by giving of yourself in many ways. You Eucharist others when you give them a smile, a hug, a kiss, a loving pat on the shoulder when they are emotionally in pain, a cup of coffee, a glass of cold water, and a few moments of your time to listen. There are many ways to give yourself away to others, and be Eucharisting every one you meet. "Eucharist" is at its best when we joyfully give it away. When we say "amen" at communion time, we are saying "Yes, I am the body of Christ." That is why we are called to go out and Eucharist his people.

1 CORINTHIANS 10:16-17

Paul tells us that we have unity with God when we ask God to bless the wine and bread that is offered, he accepts it, and blesses it through the presence of his Son, Jesus. The ideal of experiencing unity with God through eating a sacrifice was strong in the old days of Judaism, and in the early days of Christianity.

In the Old Testament days, when a Jew offered a sacrifice, he ate part of that sacrifice (Deut. 12:17, 18). Christians then, and today, participate in Christ's once-and-for-all sacrifice when they eat the bread and drink the wine that is changed into his body and blood. This unity that we call the body of Christ is shared by all who eat and drink of the body and blood of Christ. We call this Communion, which means the believers share in the benefits of the same source (body and blood of Christ). When we all eat from the same loaf, then we are blessed with the gift of unity.

We may ask, "What does it mean to eat the body of Christ, and to share in his glory?" We are asked to reflect to the age-old question, "Is this an act of faith that we believe in, or is it some great story that we are expected to believe?" Communion is com-union which means with or union with Christ. Are you in communion with Christ and his family? When we say we share the blessings of Christ's blood, are we saying that his blessings are only for the spiritually clean, and that his blood covers only the righteous with glory? We need to reflect on our attitude as we come to the table of the Lord. Do we really believe that the bread and wine of our sacrifice has been transformed into the body and blood of Jesus Christ. The way we live out our lives will be our greatest testimony to what we say we profess and believe. His "Yes" is our whole healing presence of himself in the Holy Eucharist.

JOHN 6:51-58

This passage challenges us to reflect on Jesus being the "bread of life." Many people today ask, "How can Jesus give us his flesh as bread to eat?" To eat his living bread means to unite ourselves with Jesus Christ. Jesus tells the people that their fathers in the wilderness ate the bread that came from the skies, and gave them life for a time, but they eventually died. The bread that Jesus gives is eternal life to anyone who partakes of it.

We are united with Christ when we believe in his death and resurrection, and depend on his teaching for guidance, and trust in the Holy Spirit for power. The people of Jesus' day were shocked just to imagine drinking his blood and eating his flesh. They probably thought this was very cannibalistic. The Jewish law forbade drinking blood (Lev. 17:10-11), and they could not tolerate such a statement. Jesus was saying that his life had to become their life.

Today, the celebration is called the Eucharist which means thanksgiving or giving thanks in unity that Christ died for all mankind. Paul calls it the Lord's Supper (1 Corinthians 11:23), and he tells us that Jesus taught us about his Last Supper on the night of the Passover (Luke 22:13-20). We need to remember that just as Passover celebrated deliverance from slavery in Egypt, so the Lord's supper or communion as most of us know it, celebrates deliverance from sin by Christ's death. We need to really remember that Jesus is present to us in the bread and wine, and when we eat his body and drink his blood, we are proclaiming to the world that he will be within us, and bless us until he comes again. This is the tremendous benefit of the new covenant that allows us personally to approach God and communicate with him.

Eating the Sacred Body and drinking the Sacred Blood makes us "Amen" people. That is, we are saying "Amen or yes, I believe it, and I will live it out" when the celebrant hands the consecrated bread and wine to us and says "Body of Christ, Blood of Christ." Our "Amen" is a yes, not only present in bread and wine, but also to his total presence in ourselves and others as we consume it. We are then called in unity to go forth and present the power and presence of that Eucharist to others by giving it away through our love and service. "They will know we are Christians by our love" is more than just a saying.

Application

The first reading tells us that real life comes from total commitment to God. The second reading shows us that "communion" is com-union which means with or in union with Christ. The Gospel tells us that "communion," or Eucharist, means giving thanks, in unity that Christ died for all mankind.

The body and blood of Christ is given to us in Holy Communion. Let us, this week, show others that he lives within us by the way we act in love, kindness and gentleness. Let others see that this bread of life is a food that nurtures the heart, the mind, the body and the spirit. Your taking time to be compassionate, caring, and loving will be a sign to others that this is much more than a symbol.

Show those around you how you bring Eucharist to them. You can Eucharist people with a caring touch, a little note of affirmation, a cup of tea, a shoulder to cry on, a back that needs rubbing. Eucharist is what we call the Body and Blood of Christ. We can receive Eucharist in church and then go out and Eucharist every person with whom we come in contract.

TENTH SUNDAY IN ORDINARY TIME – CYCLE A

BEFORE YOU BEGIN

Pray and ask God to speak to you through His Holy Spirit. "THE PARACLETE, THE HOLY SPIRIT WHOM THE FATHER WILL SEND IN MY NAME, WILL INSTRUCT YOU IN EVERYTHING, AND REMIND YOU OF ALL THAT I TOLD YOU." (JOHN 14:26)

FIRST DAY   **Reread last week's readings.**

1. What was a helpful or new thought from the readings or from the homily you heard on Sunday?

2. From what you learned, what personal application did you choose to apply to your life this week?

SECOND DAY   **READ HOSEA 6:3-6**   **FIRST READING**

("For it is love that I desire, not sacrifice, and knowledge of God…")

1. From what are we to strive, what is certain, and how will he come to us? Hosea 6:3

2. How do we get to know the Father? John 8:19

3. What is asked about Ephraim and Judah, and like what is their piety or love? Hosea 6:4

4. What stands out at the restoration of the people? Hosea 7:1

5. By whom were the people torn to pieces or slaughtered, and how was this done? Hosea 6:5

6. What did the Lord say he would do through the prophet Jeremiah? Jeremiah 1:9-10

7. What does the Word of God do? Hebrews 4:12

8. What two things does God desire? Hosea 6:6

9. In what two things does Samuel say the Lord delights? 1 Samuel 15:22

10. What is worth more than all burnt offerings and sacrifices? Mark 12:33

11. To what are our ears to be open? Psalm 40:7-9

Personal - In what way have you loved those around you today and what have you learned from God today?

THIRD DAY	READ ROMANS 4:18-25	SECOND READING

("He did not doubt God's promise in unbelief.")

1. What did Abraham believe hoping against hope? Romans 4:18

2. When the Word of the Lord came to Abraham, what did the Lord tell him to do, what did he say to him, and as what was it credited to him? Genesis 15:5-6

3. Even though Paul considered his body dead, in what did he not weaken? Romans 4:19

4. What did Abraham think about the one who made the promise? Hebrews 11:11

5. What did Abraham not do, by what was he empowered, and what did he give to God? Romans 4:20

6. Of what was Abraham fully convinced, and as what was it credited to him? Romans 4:21-22

7. What is possible for God? Matthew 19:26

8. What did Abraham do that was credited to him as righteousness? Romans 4:3

9. To whom is it credited as righteousness, and for what reason? Romans 4:23-25

10. In whom are your faith and hope, and through whom is it? 1 Peter 1:19-21

Personal – In the areas of trials in your life, such as, bad health, a child going astray, a marriage, difficulty, etc. what promise of God do you believe in?

FOURTH DAY	READ MATTHEW 9:9-13	GOSPEL

("Those who are well do not need a physician, but the sick do.")

1. Whom did Jesus see sitting at the customs post, what did he say to him, and what did the man do? Matthew 9:9

2. What did Jesus tell his disciples? Matthew 16:24

3. What must the one who serves Jesus do? John 12:26

4. What was Matthew's work? Matthew 10:3

5. Who was with Jesus and his disciples at table in Matthew's house? Matthew 9:10

6. What did the Pharisees say to the disciples? Matt 9:11

7. What did the people grumble about when Jesus went to stay at the house of Zacchaeus? Luke 19:7

8. When Jesus heard the Pharisees, what did he say? Matthew 9:12

9. What did Jesus tell the Pharisees to go and learn, who did he not come to call, and for whom did he come? Matthew 9:13

10. What would we not do if we knew what "I desire mercy, not sacrifice," meant? Matthew 12:7

11. What did Jesus come to do? Luke 19:10

12. What did Paul say about Jesus, and what did he say about himself? 1 Timothy 1:15

Personal - How have you, in your sinfulness (sickness), reached out to Jesus and begun to follow him?

FIFTH DAY   **READ PSALM 50:1,8, 12-15**

("Offer to God praise as your sacrifice...")

Read and meditate on Psalm 50:1, 8, 12-15.

What is the Lord saying to you personally through the Psalm?

How can you apply this to your life?

SIXTH DAY   **READ ALL OF THE COMMENTARY**

HOSEA 6:3-6

Today's passage is about the Jewish people who do not show genuine repentance. They did not understand the depth of their sins and did not turn away from idols or pledge to make any change. In fact, they really did not have any regret for their sins. They thought God's displeasure and wrath would be light and last only a few days. They never dreamed that their nation would actually be taken into exile. The nation of Israel was interested in God only for the material benefits he provided. They did not value the eternal benefits that come from being obedient to him and worshipping him.

You might want to consider your attitude about God and faith at this time. Have you ever tried to hide from God behind an easy act of repentance? With what type of "sacrifice" or burnt offerings have you tried to please God? Some people try going to church, giving a large amount in the collection plate, praying more, fasting, and even putting on potluck meals for the poor in the community. Have you become frustrated when these actions or sacrifices did not seem to work? What do you do then, and how has your attitude been during these good acts of service?

God answered his people. He told them that their love had to be more than a cloud of mist that easily evaporates. He is telling all of us that we should profess our loyalty and love to him, then back it up with our words and actions. Religious rituals can help people understand God and even help develop their relationship with him, but only if this ritual is carried out with an attitude of love and obedience to God. God didn't want their rituals; he wanted their hearts. Today, more than ever, he wants our love and our mercy shown to others far more than any kind of sacrifice we could present to him.

ROMANS 4:18:25

The power in today's reading is that God can bring life out of death. Abraham was blessed by his tremendous faith in God. He never doubted that God would fulfill his promise of making him a "father of all nations." His life was marked with sins and failures as well as wisdom and goodness; but he consistently trusted God. His whole life was an example of faith in action. The promise was that Abram would be the father of many nations and the whole world would be blessed by him.

Abraham and Sarah became parents when they both were very old. If Abraham had looked only at his own resources for subduing a nation, he would have given up in despair. But Abraham, in all of his maturity, in all of his wisdom, and in all of his obedience looked to God and obeyed him and waited for God to fulfill his Word to him. This promise was also fulfilled in Jesus Christ. When we believe, an exchange takes place. We give Jesus our sins and he gives us his goodness and forgiveness (2 Corinthians 5:21).

We can do nothing to earn the incredible gift of faith. We see in today's reading that only through Christ can we receive his goodness. This is a tremendous bargain for us, but many still choose to pass it up to continue enjoying their sin. Remember, faith is the living response to the power and presence of God in our life right now.

MATTHEW 9:9-13

Today's Gospel is a powerful invitation to all of us to come and be Jesus' disciples. Matthew was a Roman-appointed tax collector, who made commissions on the taxes he collected. Tax collectors were hated by the Jews because of their reputation for cheating and their support of Rome. Matthew responded to Jesus' call immediately, and he left a lucrative but sordid career.

When God calls us to follow or obey him, do we respond with as much enthusiasm as Matthew? Sometime the decision to follow Christ is very painful, and we must decide to leave behind those things that separate us from Christ. Jesus hurt his reputation by visiting Matthew, because people knew that Matthew cheated them, but Jesus found and changed even him. We don't need to be afraid to reach out to those who are different, because God's message can change anyone. The Pharisees were more concerned with the outward sign of being "holy" or "religious" than they were about the interior of Jesus' heart.

We must remember, Christianity is not a popularity contest, and like Christ, we must be very concerned for all people, including the sinful and hurting ones. We are to follow Jesus' example and share who we are and what we have with the poor, the lonely, and the outcast, not just the beautiful, good, talented, and popular. Jesus calls out through the ages for our mercy, not only our justice. We can say to all he is our need and our source and our supply to everything.

Application

The first reading tells us that God is not fooled by external signs of repentance. The second reading shows that God can bring life out of death. Jesus' death gave life to the world. The Gospel reveals to us that God is calling out to all of us to be merciful to one another.

This week show your family and friends the new you. Let this new you be a person who extends mercy to others, not justice. Don't let others see you as authoritative and righteous. You can bring life out of death in your marriage, family or work by simply believing that God's promise is for you and that it is being fulfilled now. Abraham and Sarah in nothing more than faith allowed their tired, old, and "dead" bodies to be the source of new life. You can bring new life to others by believing that you are being called, just like Matthew was. You are a new creation and the old is gone. Say yes, like Matthew did, and become a disciple of Christ and a bearer of "Good News."

ELEVENTH SUNDAY IN ORDINARY TIME – CYCLE A

BEFORE YOU BEGIN

Pray and ask God to speak to you through His Holy Spirit. "THE PARACLETE, THE HOLY SPIRIT WHOM THE FATHER WILL SEND IN MY NAME, WILL INSTRUCT YOU IN EVERYTHING, AND REMIND YOU OF ALL THAT I TOLD YOU." (JOHN 14:26)

FIRST DAY   **Reread last week's readings.**

1. What was a helpful or new thought from the readings or from the homily you heard on Sunday?

2. From what you learned, what personal application did you choose to apply to your life this week?

SECOND DAY   **READ EXODUS 19:2-6**   **FIRST READING**

("You shall be to me a kingdom of priests, a holy nation.")

1. Where did the Israelites camp, who went up the mountain to God, and who spoke to him? Exodus 19:2-3

2. Where did Jesus go to pray? Matthew 14:23

3. What did the people do while Moses approached the cloud where God was? Exodus 20:21

4. What did God tell Moses to tell the Israelites? Ex 19:4

5. What does an eagle do to its young, and what has the Lord done for his people? Deuteronomy 32:11

6. What does the Lord say you must do if you want to be his special possession, dearer to him than all other people? Exodus 19:5, Deuteronomy 26:18

7. What belongs to the Lord? Exodus 19:5, 1 Corinthians 10:26

8. What was Moses to tell the Israelites? Exodus 19:6

9. Why are we "a chosen race, a royal priesthood, a holy nation, a people of his own?" 1 Peter 2:9

10. To what did Jesus choose us before the foundation of the world? Ephesians 1:4

Personal – In what way do you feel you are a special possession of God? What makes you holy in his sight and the sight of your family and friends?

| THIRD DAY | READ ROMANS 5:6-11 | SECOND READING |

("But God proves his love for us in that while we were still sinners Christ died for us.")

1. When did Christ die for the ungodly? Romans 5:6, Galatians 4:4

2. What is difficult to do and how does God prove his love for us? Romans 5:7-8

3. What did God do for us and for what reason? John 3:16

4. What did Jesus do for us, and what does this say about love? 1 John 4:10, 19

5. From what sins were we set free? Romans 3:25

6. How have we been justified, and from what are we saved? Romans 5:9

7. Against what is the wrath of God being revealed from heaven? Romans 1:18

8. How were we reconciled to God while we were enemies, and once reconciled how will we be saved? Romans 5:10

9. Of what has God given us the ministry? 2 Cor 5:18

10. Of what do we boast, and what do we have through him? Romans 5:11

Personal – How have you experienced God's love and forgiveness in your life? How have you died to yourself, your way of doing things, in order to be reconciled with someone who may have hurt you?

| FOURTH DAY | READ MATTHEW 9:36-10:8 | GOSPEL |

("The harvest is abundant but the laborers are few.")

1. Why was Jesus' heart moved with pity? Matthew 9:36

2. What did Jesus say to his disciples about the harvest, and what were they to ask the master of the harvest? Matthew 9:37

3. What did Jesus say for us to look up and see? John 4:35

Personal – In what way have you gone out and tried to bring someone back to church?

4. Over what did Jesus give his disciples authority, and what would they be able to do with diseases and illness? Matthew 10:1

5. What were the names of the twelve apostles? Matthew 10:2-4

6. Who was Judas, and what had to be fulfilled? Acts 1:16

7. Who did Jesus send out, and where did he instruct them not to go? Matthew 10:5

8. Where did Jesus tell the twelve to go? Matthew 10:6

9. What proclamation were the disciples to make? Matthew 10:7

10.   What did John the Baptist and Jesus both preach? Matthew 3:2 , Matthew 4:17

11.   What were the disciples to do, how did they receive, and how were they to give? Matthew 10:8

Personal – What have you received without cost in your life and what have you given away without charging for it?

FIFTH DAY   **READ PSALM 100:1-3, 5**

("…He made us, his we are; his people, the flock he tends.")

Read and meditate on Psalm 100:1-3, 5.

What is the Lord saying to you personally through the Psalm?

How can you apply this to your life?

SIXTH DAY   **READ ALL OF THE COMMENTARY**

EXODUS 19:2-6

Mount Sinai is one of the most sacred locations in the history of Israel. On this mountain Moses met God as a burning bush, God made his covenant with Israel, and Elijah heard God in "the sound of a gentle whisper." This is where God's people learned the potential blessings of obedience and the tragic consequences of disobedience. God was ready to tell the Israelites why he had rescued them from slavery. He tells them of how he wanted Israel to become a holy people, a nation of priests in which anyone could approach God freely. These priests were to represent what the entire nation should be like. Though all of the men from the Tribe of Levi were dedicated to the service of God, only Aaron's descendants were allowed to be priests. This distinction allowed them to perform sacrifices at their worship services. The priests had to make sure they were cleansed and rededicated to God before they could help the people follow the path of righteousness. As part of their dedication rite, blood was placed on the priests to let them know that the entire person was set apart for service to God. This ritual was to show that holiness came from God and not from the role of being a priest.

God's plan was soon corrupted. God then established the Levites as priests. All the people were not chosen or selected to be priests, but all the people were to hold the priestly vision in their hearts and actions. However, with the coming of Christ, God extended his plan to all believers. We are to become holy, a priestly people, a changed people filled with God.

Today, there is a strong and urgent need for a holy and changed people. God wanted to have a special nation on earth, to represent his ways and to be a saving presence in the world. Pray that your nation, your community, your family and you will be "filled with God." Pray, especially, that your spiritual leaders will remember that their holiness comes from God and not their social standing.

ROMANS 5:6-11

In today's reading, we discover that we are helpless because we cannot do anything on our own to save ourselves. Someone had to come and rescue us. God controls all history in his time and in accordance with his will, and we were rescued through the death on the cross by our Lord and Savior, Jesus Christ.

Now, we are at peace with God, which differs from mere peaceful feelings of security and confidence. Peace with God means being one with him, being reconciled with him. Peace with God is possible only because Jesus paid the price for our sins with his death on that cross at Calvary. He died for us while we were still sinners. God sent Jesus to die for us, not because we were deserving, but because he loved us. He loved the lovable; he loved the unlovable. He would have died on that cross if you were the only person in the world, because he loved you before you ever converted to him.

His love is that same love that gives us the power to resist Satan every day. The power that saved Christ from the dead is the power that lives in us at the present time. The Father's love that allowed his Son to die for our sins is the same love that sends the Holy Spirit to live in us. Be assured, you have a reserve of power and love to call on each day to help you meet every challenge or trial. As surely as you can pray for forgiveness, so also, you can pray expectantly for God's power and love as necessary.

MATTHEW 9:36-10:8

Jesus requires workers who know how to deal with the problems of people. We can comfort others and guide them on how to live, because we have been helped in our problems, because we know that he is the source and supplier of all our needs (Phil. 4-19). In today's Gospel we see the tremendous need for laborers to be in God's field to harvest his crop. The harvest is for men and women's souls and we are the laborers. Jesus looked at the crowds following him and referred to them as a field ripe for harvest.

Today, there are many people who will give their lives to Christ if someone will show them the way. That someone can be you, so be prepared for God to use you. Jesus called his disciples and, as of now, he is calling you. He didn't force them into his group but he did ask for volunteers. Being called by Christ means to be chosen to serve Christ in a special way.

Jesus asked his disciples to go only to the Jews, because they were chosen to tell those remaining in the world about God's saving power. Jewish disciples preached the "Good News" all over the Roman Empire and soon Gentiles poured into the church. Today, the Good News is that the kingdom is still near. Jesus, the Messiah, has already begun his kingdom on earth in the hearts of his followers.

Jesus called people from all walks of life - fishermen, political activists, tax collectors, rich, poor, and educated. Today many people discriminate as to who qualifies to follow Christ. God can use anyone, regardless of how insignificant he feels. He uses ordinary people to do his extraordinary work.

Application

The first reading tells us that obedience leads to blessings and disobedience leads to loneliness and frustration. The second reading tells us that Jesus loves us so much, he died for all, even the ones who could care less about him. The Gospel reveals to us that people are ripe for the harvest, but more laborers are necessary to lead and to show them the way.

This week, let your actions reveal to your family that you are a person who wants the very best for them. Let them know what is obedience and humility by your actions. Give your family the gift of your service.

Since you have received the gift of joy and other gifts, give them away freely. Give them a gift of your joy. Make an attempt to read to a small child. Take an elderly person to lunch, and share your faith and your love for the Lord with someone. Your ability to freely give will inspire someone to freely follow Christ.

TWELFTH SUNDAY IN ORDINARY TIME - CYCLE A

BEFORE YOU BEGIN

Pray and ask God to speak to you through His Holy Spirit. "THE PARACLETE, THE HOLY SPIRIT WHOM THE FATHER WILL SEND IN MY NAME, WILL INSTRUCT YOU IN EVERYTHING, AND REMIND YOU OF ALL THAT I TOLD YOU." (JOHN 14:26)

FIRST DAY   **Reread last week's readings.**

1.   What was a helpful or new thought from the readings or from the homily you heard on Sunday?

2.   From what you learned, what personal application did you choose to apply to your life this week?

SECOND DAY   **READ JEREMIAH 20:10-13**   **FIRST READING**

("For he has rescued the life of the poor from the power of the wicked.")

1.   What does Jeremiah hear, and for what are those who were his friends on the watch? Jeremiah 20:10

2.   What will a false friend do? Sirach 37:4

3.   What will a friend do who is a friend when it suits him, and with whom are we to be on guard? Sirach 6:8-13

4.   Who is with Jeremiah, and what will happen to his persecutors? Jeremiah 20:11

5.   What did the Lord say to Jeremiah? Jeremiah 1:8, Jeremiah 15:20

6.   From what are malicious persecutors far? Psalm 119:150

7.   What does the Lord test and probe, and what does Jeremiah ask to witness? Jeremiah 20:12

8.   Why does the Lord probe the mind and test the heart? Jeremiah 17:10

9.   To whom should we sing and praise, and whom has he rescued? Jeremiah 20:13

10.   Why do we thank and praise the Lord? Psalm 109:30-31

Personal - How has the Lord rescued you from someone you thought was a friend? In what way do you sing his praises for what he has done for you?

THIRD DAY	READ ROMANS 5:12-15	SECOND READING

("But the gift is not like the transgression.")

1. What entered the world through one man, what came to all, and what have all done? Romans 5:12

2. Through what did death enter the world, and who experiences it? Wisdom 2:24

3. What does envy and anger do? Sirach 30:24

4. Where was sin up to the time of the law, and when is sin not accounted? Romans 5:13

5. What does the law produce, and where is there no violation? Romans 4:15

6. What reigned from Adam to Moses, who dies even though they did not sin, and what was Adam? Romans 5:14

7. What happened in Adam, and what happened in Christ? 1 Corinthians 15:22

Personal – How has sin and death affected your life?

8. What is the gift not like? Romans 5:15

9. What overflowed for the many? Romans 5:15

10. How do we believe we have been saved? Acts 15:11

Personal – How has the grace of God affected your life? What does grace mean to you? From you, what is the result it has on others?

FOURTH DAY	READ MATTHEW 10:26-33	GOSPEL

("And do not be afraid of those who kill the body but cannot kill the soul.")

1. What are we not to be, and what is concealed that will be revealed? Matthew 10:26

2. What Jesus speaks to us in the darkness, where are we to speak it? What we hear whispered, where are we to proclaim it? Matthew 10:27

Personal – When the Lord speaks to you in your quiet prayer time, how do you make it known to others?

3. What will happen to the person who does not speak? Psalm 32:3

4. Of whom are we not to be afraid, and who are we to fear? Matthew 10:28

5. With what are we not to make alliance, with whom are we to make alliance, and who are we to fear and be in awe? Isaiah 8:12-13

6. What does not fall to the ground without the Father's knowledge? Matthew 10:29

7.   What is even counted, and why should we not be afraid? Matthew 10:30-31

8.   What will happen to us because of Jesus, what will not be   destroyed, and what will secure our life? Luke 21:17-19

9.   What are we not to fear? Isaiah 51:7

10. Who will be acknowledged before our heavenly Father, and who will be denied before him? Matthew 10:32-33

11. What will happen to whomever is ashamed of Jesus and his words, in this faithless and sinful generation? Mark 8:38

Personal – In what ways have you acknowledged Jesus and his words to your family, friends, school friends and co-workers?

FIFTH DAY   **READ PSALM 69:8-10, 14, 17, 33-35**

("For the Lord hears the poor,")

Read and meditate on Psalm 69:8-10, 14, 17, 33-35.

What is the Lord saying to you personally through the Psalm?

How can you apply this to your life?

SIXTH DAY   **READ ALL OF THE COMMENTARY**

JEREMIAH 20:10-13

Jeremiah goes straight from the Hinnom Valley to the temple, and with his message challenged the people's social and moral behavior. He was not afraid to give unpopular criticism. The people could either obey or silence him, and they chose the latter. Their false prophets told them what they wanted to hear. The priest in charge called Pashur, heard Jeremiah's words and because of his guilt forced him into the wooden stocks. With his hands and feet made fast in the wooden stocks, and being ridiculed in front of the entire community, Jeremiah pours out his heart to God. Yet, even this did not stop him from making God's Word known.

Jeremiah's role as a prophet put him under terrific pressure. He has faithfully proclaimed God's Word and has received nothing in return, only persecution and sorrow. He tried to withhold God's word, but it became like a fire in his bones.

Today, there are many places where people need to be challenged about their moral behavior. The Jeremiahs of today are being ridiculed and silenced, and the false prophets "tickle their ears" with stories of how wonderful they are. When you feel like you are at the end of your rope, remember, there is never an end to hope. You will feel "the fire in your bones," and you will feel compelled to share it with others, whatever the situation.

ROMANS 5:12-15

The question, "How can we be declared guilty for something Adam did thousands of years ago?" rages on. There are many who feel it is not right for God to judge us for Adam's sin. Yet, each one of us identifies with Adam by our own sins. We are made of the same "high-fluting," rebellious, exaggerating attitude and prejudices. We are judged for the sins we commit, because we are sinners. It is not fairness that we need, it is mercy.

Paul tells us once again that keeping the law does not bring salvation. Death is the result of Adam's sin and for the sins we all commit. The Law was added to help people see their sinfulness and to show them the seriousness of their offense and to drive them to God for mercy and pardon. This was true in Moses' day, and it is still true today. Sin is a profound rupture between who we are and who we were created to be. The Law points out our sin and places the responsibility on our shoulders, but the Law offers no remedy for it.

In many nations, prisons are overflowing because accountability calls for discipline, and discipline calls for a commitment to an idea. When we are convicted of sin, the only way to heal is through Jesus Christ. Remember, only the truth can really set us free (John 8:32) and the truth is our Lord and Savior Jesus Christ.

MATTHEW 10:26-33

Today's Gospel reveals to us the cost of following Jesus Christ. Jesus helped his disciples prepare for the rejection many of them would experience by being Christian. Being God's person will usually create reactions from others who are resisting him. The disciples experienced hardships not only from without (government, courts, etc.), but also from friends and family.

Living for God often brings on trials and tribulations, but with it comes the opportunity to tell the Good News of Salvation. We can always be confident because Jesus has "overcome the world" (John 16:33), and it is very crucial for us to remember that those who "endure to the end" will be saved (10:22).

You are of incredible worth to God, and you are never lost from his sight or touch. You never are to fear personal threats or difficult trials because they can not shake God's love and Spirit from you. God placed a tremendous value on each one of us, and he lets us have the choice and the chance to say "No, Lord." The closer you get to God, the more the world will reject and abuse us. They hated Christ and rejected Him; would we expect anything less? Those who stand up for Christ in spite of their troubles truly will have lasting value and will receive the acknowledgement of God and God's love will sustain them through any kind of trial.

Application

The first reading tells us that God's Word is like a hammer that smashes away at the rocks of obstacles. The second reading tells us that death is the result of Adam's sin, and life is the result of Christ's sacrifice on the Cross. The Gospel reveals fear as useless, and we must trust in God.

This week, ask yourself what you are doing to be a witness to your faith. How have you responded to the scourge of abortion in your community? See if you can help with letter writing, picketing, protesting, praying and voting on moral issues concerning abortion. You will be ridiculed and attacked, socially, emotionally, spiritually, and maybe even physically for your loyalty and belief.

This week, become a disciple of Christ and let the Spirit within you be a reminder that the spirit of the world has been defeated.

THIRTEENTH SUNDAY IN ORDINARY TIME - CYCLE A

BEFORE YOU BEGIN

Pray and ask God to speak to you through His Holy Spirit. "THE PARACLETE, THE HOLY SPIRIT WHOM THE FATHER WILL SEND IN MY NAME, WILL INSTRUCT YOU IN EVERYTHING, AND REMIND YOU OF ALL THAT I TOLD YOU." (JOHN 14:26)

FIRST DAY   **Reread last week's readings.**

1. What was a helpful or new thought from the readings or from the homily you heard on Sunday?

2. From what you learned, what personal application did you choose to apply to your life this week?

SECOND DAY   **READ 2 KINGS 4:8-11, 14-16**   **FIRST READING**

("I know that he is a holy man of God.")

1. Who came to Shunem, and who urged him to dine with her? 2 Kings 4:8

2. How often did he dine with the woman? 2 Kings 4:8

3. Whom did Elisha succeed, and what was to rest on him? 2 Kings 2:9-15

4. What did the Shunammite woman call Elisha? 2 Kings 4:9

5. What does he who welcomes a prophet or a holy man receive? Matthew 10:41-42

6. In what should we be generous? Romans 12:13

7. What did the woman arrange for Elisha? 2 Kings 4:10

8. What did Elisha do sometime later? 2 Kings 4:11

9. What did Elisha ask his servant Gehazi, and what did he say? 2 Kings 4:14

10. Elisha told his servant to call the woman, and as she stood at the door, what did he promise her? 2 Kings 4:15-16

11. What did she say, and what did she call Elisha? 2 Kings 4:16

Personal – What is your attitude when a priest comes to your home? What is your attitude toward what he says to you? In what way do you show hospitality to God's chosen ones?

THIRD DAY	READ ROMANS 6:3-4, 8-11	SECOND READING

("His death was death to sin, once for all;")

1. We who have been baptized into Jesus Christ, into what have we also been baptized? Romans 6:3

2. With whom have all who have been baptized into Christ clothed themselves? Gal 3:27

3. In baptism we were not only buried with him but also raised to life with Him because of what? Col 2:12

4. Just as Christ was raised from the dead by the glory of the Father, what might we live? Romans 6:4

5. What do we believe if we have died with Christ? Romans 6:8

6. What will Christ, once raised from the dead, never do again? Romans 6:9

7. What was the last enemy to be destroyed? 1 Corinthians 15:26

8. For what was Christ's death and for whom is his life? Romans 6:10

9. For whom did he die? Romans 6:10

10. In the same way, to what must we consider ourselves dead? Romans 6:11

11. For whom and in whom are we alive? Romans 6:11

Personal – In what way have you died to sin in your life? In what way are you living a life for God?

FOURTH DAY	READ MATTHEW 10:37-42	GOSPEL

("He who welcomes me, welcomes him who sent me.")

1. Who is speaking in verses 37–42 of Matthew, and to whom is he speaking? Matthew 10:5 , Matthew 11:1

2. What did Jesus say about those who love father or mother, son or daughter more than him? Matthew 10:37

3. If a man wishes to come after Jesus, what three things must He do? Matthew 16:24

4. He who will not take up what and come after him is not worthy of whom? Matthew 10:38

5. To what does he who seeks only himself bring himself, and how does a person discover who he is? Matthew 10:39, Mark 8:35

6. Whom does he welcome who welcomes us, and he who welcomes him also welcomes whom? Matthew 10:40

7. What does he receive who welcomes a prophet because he bears the name of prophet? Matthew 10:41

8. What does he receive who welcomes a holy man because he is known as a holy man? Matthew 10:41

9. What does Jesus promise us, and what does he call a disciple? Matthew 10:42

10. What will happen to any man who gives a drink of water to you because you belong to Christ? Mark 9:41

Personal – What is the cross that you have taken up in order to follow Christ? In what ways do you die to yourself on a daily basis in your home, at work, or at school? In what way are you supportive to your brothers and sisters in the Lord who are following Jesus?

FIFTH DAY   **READ PSALM 89:2-3, 16-19**

("The favors of the Lord I will sing forever.")

Read and meditate on Psalm 89:2-3, 16-19.

What is the Lord saying to you personally through the Psalm?

How can you apply this to your life?

SIXTH DAY   **READ ALL OF THE COMMENTARY**

2 KINGS 4:8-11, 14-16

This passage reveals to us the need to show hospitality and respect to God's chosen ones, his clergy. When a priest or deacon comes into your home, is your attitude loving, caring, and reverent? The Scriptures tell us that he who received the king's messenger will, in reality, be receiving the king himself (Matt. 10:40-42). The Jews always felt that to receive a person's messenger was the same as to receive the person himself. To welcome with love the messenger of our Lord Jesus was the same as to welcome Jesus himself.

The Shunemite woman knew that Elisha was a prophet and a special messenger of God and she trusted him with great respect. He promised her a gift of a son and she received this miracle of God from the prophet she respected so much.

Today there is a great amount of disrespect shown toward the clergy of Christian denominations. Many people fail to look at whom these people represent. There are failures among the clergy who fall into sin, but they still have been called to represent the Lord. David was terribly mistreated by Saul the King, but David never harmed a hair on Saul's head. David respected the office of what Saul represented. God rewarded David for this compassion, respect, and obedience. God called David a "man after my own heart."

Look at the clergy in your parish and see where you can help them, encourage them, but most of all, love them. You can love your clergy by praying for them daily and by inviting them to your home to share your lifestyle and hospitality. Elisha was amazed at the Shunemite woman's hospitality, and today, our clergy need that hospitality and acceptance very much. Jesus said, "What you do to the least of my brethren, you do unto me." (Matt 25:31-46). This verse also applied to those who had given up the comfort of a loving family and the security of a permanent home and community and have gone out to serve a hostile world. How we treat our clergy is very well indeed how we treat Our Lord, Jesus. Remember, they are messengers of the King.

ROMANS 6:3-4, 8-11

The power of sin is broken through the death and resurrection of Jesus Christ. His death shattered the power of our sinful nature. Our old sin-loving nature was buried with Jesus by baptism when he died for our sins. Through baptism, we share his new life, and we shall rise as he did. Baptism means to sink, submerge, and to drown. We die to our old sinful nature and we emerge or rise in baptism with the Risen Christ. We have invited Christ to take up residence in us. He, in turn, welcomes us into his Holy Family of Christianity. He is present in his Heavenly Father and the Holy Spirit. Through baptism we become sons and daughters of God the Father and enjoy the power of the Holy Spirit and live and love others in the name of Jesus Christ.

In the church of Paul's time, immersion was the usual form of baptism. This means that new Christians were completely buried in water. This symbolized the death and burial of the old way of life, followed by resurrection to life with Christ. It is very important to realize why baptism is so important to being a Christian. We are cleansed of sin and clothed in the power of the Holy Spirit. This is the power that we use to resist the devil and make him flee from us (James 4:7). We now have the incredible power to choose life over death because we have the presence of the Holy Spirit within us. We know that the Spirit within us is far more powerful than he that is in the world (1 John 4:4). Because of our baptism we have become adopted sons and daughters of the King. Jesus tells us that he has prepared a place in his Father's house for each one of us (John 14:1-6). This passage gives us tremendous comfort and assurances as believers in Jesus Christ. Because of Jesus, we never need to fear death or wonder where we will go when we die (John 3:16).

MATTHEW 10:37-42

Today's Gospel message tells us that a Christian commitment may separate friends and loved ones. Jesus showed that his presence demands a decision. This was true in Jesus' time, and it is especially true in today's world. Two things are happening today. Either the world is changing you or you are changing the world. A decision for Christ is a decision to make the world a better place to live.

As we take up our cross and follow Jesus, an inevitable conflict will follow. Our different values, morals, goals, and purposes will set us apart from others. Today's message is that God should be our first priority, not friends or even family. God has called all of us to a higher mission than to find comfort in this life. To take up our cross and follow Jesus we must lay down other cares and priorities. We need to be totally committed to God (Matt. 10:39) and willing to face anything, even suffering and death, for the sake of Christ. We can see around us that the more people love this life's rewards (leisure, power, popularity), the more they discover how empty they are.

Mother Teresa has a saying, "Unless life is lived for others, it is not worthwhile." We can tell how much we love God by how well we treat others. God notices every good deed we do or don't do, as if he were the one receiving it. We cannot all be prophets and proclaim the Word of God, but he who gives God's messenger the simple gift of hospitality will receive no less a reward than the prophet himself. We must remember that even the prophet must get his breakfast and attend to his clothes. We must never forget to love, honor, and thank those who have the often thankless task of making a home, cooking meals, washing clothes, shopping for household items, and caring for children. It is God's greatest task, and they will be far more likely to receive the prophet's rewards than those whose days are filled with committees and comfortable homes.

Application

The first reading teaches us to honor and respect the clergy. The second reading shows us that the power of sin is broken through baptism. The Gospel tells us that our first priority is loving God.

Let this week be a week of loving God by loving others. Husbands, take your wife out to dinner or some where to relax and enjoy. Husbands, watch the children so Mom can take a few hours to relax and pamper herself. Wives, take time to be present to your husband alone. Children, help your parents by cleaning up after yourself and do some errands for Mom. Parents, take time to play with your children and each other. Families, pray every day to God in thanksgiving and invite your priests or deacon to your home to pray and relax with you.

FOURTEENTH SUNDAY IN ORDINARY TIME – CYCLE A

BEFORE YOU BEGIN

Pray and ask God to speak to you through His Holy Spirit. "THE PARACLETE, THE HOLY SPIRIT WHOM THE FATHER WILL SEND IN MY NAME, WILL INSTRUCT YOU IN EVERYTHING, AND REMIND YOU OF ALL THAT I TOLD YOU." (JOHN 14:26)

FIRST DAY **Reread last week's readings.**

1.   What was a helpful or new thought from the readings or from the homily you heard on Sunday?

2.   From what you learned, what personal application did you choose to apply to your life this week?

SECOND DAY **READ ZECHARIAH 9:9-10** **FIRST READING**

("…he shall proclaim peace to the nations.")

1.   Who is to rejoice heartily and shout for joy? Zechariah 9:9

2.   Who is to come to you, and what is he? Zechariah 9:9

3.   How is he to come, and on what is he riding? Zechariah 9:9

4.   Whom did Jesus send, with what instructions, and what was this to fulfill? Matthew 21:1-5

5.   What shall he banish from Ephraim and Jerusalem? Zechariah 9:10

6.   What will happen to the warrior's bow? Zechariah 9:10

7.   How does the Lord, their God, **not** save Judah? Hosea 1:7

8.   What does he proclaim to the nations? Zechariah 9:10

9.   Where shall be his dominion? Zechariah 9:10

10.   In whom do we find peace? John 16:31-33

Personal - What message do you proclaim to your family, friends, or work acquaintances, and how do you proclaim it? How can you develop a peaceful atmosphere in your home?

| THIRD DAY | READ ROMANS 8:9, 11-13 | SECOND READING |

("If anyone does not have the Spirit of Christ, he does not belong to Christ.")

1. In what are we not, in what are we, and who dwells in us? Romans 8:9

2. What have those who belong to Christ done? Gal 5:24

3. Toward what is the tendency of the flesh, but toward what is that of the Spirit? Romans 8:6

4. What must we put to death? Colossians 3:5

5. What are the fruits of the Spirit? Galatians 5:22-23

6. Who belongs to Christ? Romans 8:9

7. What will happen to our mortal bodies if the Spirit of him who raised Jesus from the dead dwells in us, and how will he do it? Romans 8:11

8. To what are we not debtors, so that we should live according to it? Romans 8:12

9. What are all called who are led by the Spirit of God? Romans 8:14

Personal - In what way are you living your new life in Christ on a daily basis? How do you know personally whether you are being led by the Spirit of God or by your own flesh?

| FOURTH DAY | READ MATTHEW 11:25-30 | GOSPEL |

("Take my yoke upon your shoulders and learn from me.")

1. To whom was Jesus speaking, and what does he offer him? Matthew 11:25

2. Fill in the following blanks: ... for what you have hidden from the _____ and the _____, you have revealed to the merest _____. Matthew 11:25

3. Whom did the Lord choose, and for what reason? 1 Corinthians 1:26-29

4. To whom is Jesus talking, and what has been given over to Jesus by the Father? Matthew 11:26-27

5. Who knows the Son and who knows the Father? Matthew 11:27

6. Whom does the Father love and what has he given him? John 3:35

7. To whom does Jesus say to come when we are weary and find life burdensome, and what will he do? Matthew 11:28

8.   What will flow from him who comes to Jesus? John 7:37-39

9.   What are we to cast upon Jesus, what will he do, and who will he not permit to be disturbed? Psalm 55:23

10.   What are we to take upon our shoulders, and what are we to do? Matthew 11:29

11.   What two things does he say he is, and what will our soul find? Matthew 11:29

12.   How does Jesus describe his yoke and his burden? Matthew 11:30

Personal – What do you do and where do you go when the problems of everyday life are too much for you? How are you being weighted down by the burdens of life? How can you take your load off your back and put Jesus' yoke there? What is Jesus' yoke and burden to you?

FIFTH DAY   **READ PSALM 145:1-2, 8-11, 13-14**

("The Lord is faithful in all his words.")

Read and meditate on Psalm 145:1-2, 8-11, 13-14.

What is the Lord saying to you personally through the Psalm?

How can you apply this to your life?

SIXTH DAY   **READ ALL OF THE COMMENTARY**

ZECHARIAH 9:9-10

Zechariah was a prophet to the remnant of the Jews who returned from Babylon after 70 years of captivity. The Jews, once a powerful nation as God had planned them to be, were now a pitiful and insignificant group of left overs, dwelling in their promised land only because of the courtesy of a foreign ruler. Zechariah tried to tell the people that it would not always be so. He told them that one day the Messiah would come and God's chosen people would once again be a light to all nations.

Zechariah foretells the character of Jesus more than any other prophet except Isaiah. He shows us how Christ entered into Jerusalem on the back of a donkey. This triumphant entry of Jesus riding into Jerusalem is predicted here 500 years before it happened (Matt. 21:1-11). He has described this king as a servant king rather than a warrior king. He goes on to describe a peace that will come over the land and nations shall live together in harmony. Zechariah talks now about a king who will rule sea to sea and from the rivers to the ends of the earth. This sounds like the second coming of Christ when all the nations of the earth will be subjected to Jesus Christ.

We are told in Scripture that every knee will bow to Christ and every tongue confess him as Lord (Phil. 2:9,10). We need to reflect on this prophecy that was fulfilled in this reading and be expectant that the prophecy of the Lord's second coming will also be realized. We are all to be ready for his return; for, remember, he IS coming.

ROMANS 8:9, 11-13

Paul defines very clearly in this passage what being a Christian is. Have you ever wondered what would happen if you were arrested and charged with being a Christian? Would the authorities have enough evidence to convict you? Have you been challenged to witness to your faith? Paul tells us that a Christian is anyone who has the Spirit of God living in him. Many people think that when the Holy Spirit comes upon us, a magical wondrous feeling takes place. We can know that the Holy Spirit resides in us simply because Jesus promised he would (John 14:16).

We are a Christian if we believe that Jesus Christ is our Lord and Savior, and we give him permission to be in control of our lives. A Christian who receives the Holy Spirit is a temple of the Living God (1 Cor. 3:16). When the Holy Spirit is active within us, we will experience that his power is greater than any power in this world (1 John 4:4). We will receive power (Acts 1:8) and through it we will resist the devil and he will be forced to flee (James 4:7). The Holy Spirit helps us to act as Jesus directs us to act (Rom. 8:5). Here we are told that those who follow the Holy Spirit find themselves doing things that please the Lord.

Jesus has broken the power that Satan has had on our life. We do not have to be in bondage anymore, and we do not have to blame our parents or our background as a child for the hurt that we are experiencing now. There is no condemnation in Jesus Christ (Rom. 8:1), and that means that what we were or did yesterday does not have to be what we are or do today.

Today, right now, wherever you are, take a few minutes and ask the Lord to forgive you of your sins. Tell him that you are tired of living a life of pain and emptiness. Then ask him to heal the hurts that have come from specific people in your life. You will be empowered to serve God and do his will (Acts 1:8) and you will become part of God's plan to build up his church (Eph. 4:12-13), which is made up of people like you and me.

MATTHEW 11:25-30

"Come to me and I will give you rest." You might ask, "rest from what?" We all are working beneath a yoke as we go through life. Some people are unevenly yoked in marriage and the result is bitterness and resentment, followed many times by divorce. Jesus calls us to wear his yoke and not to worry because he will make sure it fits perfectly. A yoke is a heavy wooden harness that fits onto one or more oxen. When an ox wears a yoke, it means that the animal is going to have a long day of hard work.

Jesus mentions a "heavy yoke" and that could mean the burden of sin, the burden of the law, or the excessive demands of the Pharisaic leaders. It could mean government oppression, like the pressure being put upon those who protest abortion. It could also be just weariness in the search for God.

Jesus frees people from all these heavy burdens. The rest that Jesus promises is peace with God, not the end of the effort of living out our life. Jesus mentions two kinds of people in his prayer. He mentions the wise, who are smug and secure in the safety behind following all of the laws and being in the right places and with the right people. He also calls those who are humble, trusting and open to change, to be "children" or child-like in their faith. We are called to be open, trusting and honest, like a child, when we are praying to God. He wants us to be happy and well.

Remember – His plan for us is clearly stated in scripture, "My purpose is to give you life in all of its fullness" (John 10:10). His yoke fits us perfectly. Let us put it on and joyfully join him in the vineyard of life.

Application

The first reading tells us that the gift of prophecy was used for the coming of Jesus' triumphant entry into Jerusalem. The second reading tells us what a Christian is and how to live a Christian life. The Gospel shows us how to lighten the burdens of life by inviting Jesus to carry our burdens and how we can let go of them.

This week, show your Christianity by helping to lighten someone else's burden. Take time to be available and present to your family. Respond gently and with love to a need of someone in your life. It can be very simple, such as, taking to church a family member, friend or someone you know that is alone. Maybe you can visit or write to someone in prison. Jesus often lightens someone else's burdens through one of us. He has your yoke and it will fit you perfectly. His love for others can be seen through your love.

FIFTEENTH SUNDAY IN ORDINARY TIME – CYCLE A

BEFORE YOU BEGIN

Pray and ask God to speak to you through His Holy Spirit. "THE PARACLETE, THE HOLY SPIRIT WHOM THE FATHER WILL SEND IN MY NAME, WILL INSTRUCT YOU IN EVERYTHING, AND REMIND YOU OF ALL THAT I TOLD YOU." (JOHN 14:26)

FIRST DAY	**Reread last week's readings.**	

1. What was a helpful or new thought from the readings or from the homily you heard on Sunday?

2. From what you learned, what personal application did you choose to apply to your life this week?

SECOND DAY	**READ ISAIAH 55:10-11**	**FIRST READING**

("It shall not return to me void, but shall do my will.")

1. What comes down from the heavens and what does it do to the earth? Isaiah 55:10

2. What does it give to one who sows and one who eats and what shall go forth from the Lord's mouth? Isaiah 55:11

3. How shall it not return to the Lord, what shall the Word do, and what shall it achieve? Isaiah 55:11

4. To what is the earth to hearken, and what is instructed? Deuteronomy 32:1-2

5. Who is the word? John 1:1, 14

6. How long will the Word stand? Isaiah 40:8

7. To whom do we turn to be safe, and what does he utter? Isaiah 45:22-23

8. What does God's Word do for us? Hebrews 4:12

9. Of whom does the Lord confirm the words, and how does he carry out his plan? Isaiah 44:26

10. What does the Lord say about whatever he speaks? Ezekiel 12:25

Personal – In what way have you been a messenger of God's Word to your family and friends? What results have you seen take place in yourself and those you contact as you have been reading and studying God's Word.

THIRD DAY **READ ROMANS 8:18-23** **SECOND READING**

("I consider the sufferings of the present to be as nothing compared with the glory to be revealed in us.")

1. With what is the suffering of the present nothing by comparison? Romans 8:18

2. What will we do when his glory is revealed? 1 Peter 4:13

3. What does the whole created world eagerly await? Romans 8:19

4. To what was creation made subject, and by whose accord? Romans 8:20

5. From what will the world be freed, and in what will it share? Romans 8:21

6. What do we await? 2 Peter 3:12-13, Rev 21:1

7. What do we know all creating has done? Romans 8:22

8. Why are we weighted down? 2 Corinthians 5:1-5

9. Although we have the Spirit as first fruits, what do we await? Romans 8:23

10. For what do we hope, and how do we yield to it? Galatians 5:5

11. What will he do to our bodies, how will he do it, and for what reason? Philippians 3:21

Personal – In what do you place your hope? In what ways are you suffering, and how is your body groaning inwardly?

FOURTH DAY **READ MATTHEW 13:1-23** **GOSPEL**

("To you has been given a knowledge of the mysteries of the reign of God,....")

1. As Jesus sat by the lake shore, who gathered around him? Where did he go, and what did he do at length? Matthew 13:1-3

2. Part of what the farmer sowed landed in four different areas. Where were these, and what happened to the seed? Matthew 13:4-9

3. What is everyone to heed and what did the disciples ask Jesus? Matthew 13:9-10

4. What have they been given that others have not been given and what will happen to the man who has and the man who has not? Matthew 13:11-12

5. Why did Jesus say he uses parables when he speaks? Matthew 13:13

6. What is fulfilled in them? Fill in the blanks:
    "Listen as _____ _____, you shall not under-
    stand; look intently as _____ _____, you shall
    not see." Matthew 13:14

7. How are the people's hearts? What have they done with their ears and their eyes?
    Otherwise, what might happen with their ears, eyes, and hearts? Matthew 13:15

8. What would happen if they would turn back to the Lord? Matthew 13:15

9. What are those who see and hear? Who longed to see and hear what we see and
    hear, but did not? Matt 13:16-17

10. What is the seed along the path and from where does the evil one steal it?
    Matthew 13:19

11. What is the seed that fell on patches of rock and what causes this person to falter?
    Matthew 13:20-21

12. What is the seed that was sown among briers, what two things choke it, and what
    does it produce? Matthew 13:22

13. What is the seed that was sown on good soil and what does this person yield?
    Matthew 13:23

Personal – When you hear the message of God and do not understand it, what do you do? When you hear the message, but have no roots, how can you develop roots? What do you do when anxiety and money come before your thoughts of Jesus and the well being of others?
What changes can you make in your life right now?

FIFTH DAY   **READ PSALM 65:10-14**

("You have visited the land and watered it.")

Read and meditate on Psalm 65:10-14.

What is the Lord saying to you personally through the Psalm?

How can you apply this to your life?

SIXTH DAY   **READ ALL OF THE COMMENTARY**

ISAIAH 55:10-11

In this passage Isaiah shows us a tremendous example of how God's Holy Word is so dependable and long lasting. We need only look around at our world today and see what happens when rain and snow do not come upon the earth. There are droughts; then there are no crops, and the tragic result is famine. Yet, so many of us take for granted that we will never run out of water or experience a time of famine.

God's Word is like the rain that falls on a dry, parched land. It brings forth a seed of eternal truth. The bread that is harvested from the spreading of God's Holy Word is eternal bread; it is the real bread of life. God's Word does not come back empty upon us. His Word is life-giving, like the soft rain on a dry desert land. His love for us feeds our spirit; and it changes our heart and inspires us to go forth and sow his seed of love, justice, mercy, hope, and faith.

Have you ever been so hungry and thirsty that you would do anything to get food or drink? Jesus is our drink, he is our food, and he will strengthen us to go forth and strengthen the least of his brothers and sisters (Matt. 25:31-41). Take hold of his Holy Word today and water the deserts of your mind and feed the hunger in your heart. You are his chosen one, he has called you by name, and his plan for you is to live a life that is at its fullest (John 10:10). God wants his Holy Word to fill all nations and bring them peace and harmony. We are called to be his chosen messengers by bringing his Word with us wherever we go (Matt. 28:19).

ROMANS 8:18-23

Paul tells us that there is a high price to be paid for being identified with Jesus. We need only look around our planet and see the results of nations that are being attacked by godless people and godless governments. Paul tells of the suffering Christians must face.

Today we might look around and say what kind of suffering are we to endure? The horror of abortion has become so commonplace that those who speak out against it are subject to ridicule, and economic and social rejection. Today many people are going to prison for the crime of trying to save unborn babies. We have read about the Babylonian god "Mardok" where the people sacrificed their children to the "fires of Mardok." Today we see millions of children being sacrificed to the great gods of "greed and convenience." The price for practicing our faith can be very high, and it can, in some places, result in death. We must not become complacent in the comforts of our society and ignore the responsibility to live as Jesus did. We must continue serving others, giving up our own rights, and resisting the pressures to conform to the world which always exacts a price.

We are people of hope and must not become pessimistic. We await God's new order that will free the world of sin, sickness and evil. In the meantime, we can not watch, and stand by and do nothing, while they drag the defenseless innocents to their death. This passage refers particularly to abortion (Proverbs 24:11). We must remember that one day we will be resurrected with bodies, but they will be glorified bodies like the body that Christ now has in heaven (1 Cor. 15:50-56).

MATTHEW 13:1-23

Jesus used many parables when he was speaking to the crowds. A parable helps us to understand spiritual truths by using everyday objects and relationships. A parable encourages the listener to discover truth, while at the same time concealing the truth from those too stubborn or too busy to see it.

We see in today's Gospel passage that the call to listen is very strong. We are to have eyes that really see and ears that really hear what is going on. This passage encourages all to become spiritual farmers - those who preach, teach, and lead others to the Lord. The farmer sowed good seed, but not all responses were good because of the locations. Do not become discouraged if you spread your seed of the Holy Word of God and it is not properly received. We need to remember that it is the Holy Spirit who opens up the hardened hearts of people. The miracle of God's Holy Spirit will take place as he uses our words to move others to come to him. A human being can hear many types of sound, but there is a deeper and special kind of listening that results in spiritual understanding. We can be assured that if we honestly seek God's will, we will have spiritual hearing and these parables will take on dynamic new meanings for us.

Jesus did not hide the truth in parables; those who were receptive to spiritual truth understood the parables completely. To others who did not believe in God, they were only stories with various meanings. The parables allowed Jesus to give spiritual food to those who hungered for it. Today, many times, God's Word is proclaimed with little power and much confusion by messengers who refuse to be submissive to him. We who know Jesus personally are called to love others as he loves us. We are to be held accountable to the Lord if we do not follow his commands very specifically. If we reject Jesus, our hardness of heart will drive away even the little understanding we had.

The seed in today's passage is the Word of God, and we are called to sow it to all we meet. The four types of soil represent the different responses people have to God's message. Some people are hardened, some are shallow, some are very distracted by the world, and some are very receptive. How have you responded? What kind of soil are you? Remember, the Word was God, (John 1:1) and the Word became Flesh (John 1:14), and the Spirit that is in you is greater than the spirit that is in the world (1 John 4:4).

Application

The first reading tells us that God's Word is dependable, long lasting, and will not return empty. The second reading shows us that the cost of discipleship is very high. The Gospel reveals that the seed in today's passage is the Word of God and we are all called to sow it.

Let us, this week, be faithful, humble messengers of God by reading our scripture readings to someone we know. Take the day's readings and read them to a sick relative or a small child, a loved one, and especially your husband or wife. Study the readings, share what they mean to you, and LIVE THE READINGS, especially with your family. His Word will not return empty when you are being his messenger.

SIXTEENTH SUNDAY IN ORDINARY TIME – CYCLE A

BEFORE YOU BEGIN

Pray and ask God to speak to you through His Holy Spirit. "THE PARACLETE, THE HOLY SPIRIT WHOM THE FATHER WILL SEND IN MY NAME, WILL INSTRUCT YOU IN EVERYTHING, AND REMIND YOU OF ALL THAT I TOLD YOU." (JOHN 14:26)

FIRST DAY   **Reread last week's readings.**

1. What was a helpful or new thought from the readings or from the homily you heard on Sunday?

2. From what you learned, what personal application did you choose to apply to your life this week?

SECOND DAY   **READ WISDOM 12:13, 16-19**   **FIRST READING**

("For your might is the source of justice;")

1. For whom does God care and what has he not done? Wisdom 12:13

2. What does the Lord not show toward people, and how does he provide for all? Wisdom 6:7

3. What must we learn from God? Deuteronomy 32:39

4. What does it say of the Lord in Isaiah 44:6,8?

5. What is his might, and what does his mastery over all things make him? Wisdom 12:16

6. When does he show his might? Wisdom 12:17

7. What does he rebuke in those who know him? Wisdom 12:17

8. Although God is the master of might, how does he judge and govern us? Wisdom 12:18

9. What did we teach our people? Wisdom 12:19

10. What did we give our sons, and what did we permit for their sins? Wisdom 12:19

Personal – How has God shown his might to you personally and been lenient with you? Verse 19 tells us that those who are just must be kind. In what way, this past week, have you been kind to your family, friends, and those around you? In what way have you been lenient and forgiving to those around you?

THIRD DAY   **READ ROMANS 8:26-27**   **SECOND READING**

("The Spirit, too, helps us in our weakness,...")

1. What does the Spirit do? Romans 8:26

2. What do we not know how to do as we ought? Romans 8:26

3. Who intercedes for us, and how does he do it? Romans 8:26

4. For whose sake are we content with weakness, and what happens when I am powerless? 2 Cor 12:10

5. Who is at the right hand of God, and what does he do for us? Romans 8:34

6. For whom are we to intercede, and to what will this lead? 1 Timothy 2:1-2

7. What does he know who searches hearts? Romans 8:27

8. For whom does the Spirit intercede, and with whom is the Spirit in accordance? Romans 8:27

9. For what does the Son of God search, and to whom does he do this? Revelations 2:18, 23

10. What does God read? Luke 16:15

Personal – How have you interceded in prayer for those around you? Who among your family or friends is in most need of prayer right now? Take a few minutes and intercede to the Father through Jesus for them.

FOURTH DAY   **READ MATTHEW 13:24-43**   **GOSPEL**

("The reign of God is like...")

1. To what did Jesus propose the reign of God might be compared; and while everyone was asleep, who came and sowed weeds through the wheat? Matthew 13:24-25

2. What happened when the crop began to mature and yield grain, and what did the owner's slave say to him? Matthew 13:26-27

3. What did the owner recognize, and what did his slaves offer to do? Matthew 13:28

4. What did the owner say would happen if they pulled the weeds, and what did he tell his slaves to do? Matthew 13:29-30

5. In another parable Jesus proposed, to what was the reign of God compared? Matthew 13:31

6.   How big is the mustard seed, and what happens when it is full grown? Matthew 13:32

7.   Jesus offered them another image. What is the reign of God like in Matthew 13:33?

8.   How did Jesus teach the crowds, what was it to fulfill, and what was he to announce? Matthew 13:34-35, Psalm 78:2

9.   After dismissing the crowds, where did Jesus go, who went with him, and what was their request? Matthew 13:36

10. Who was the farmer sowing the good seed, what was the field, the good seed, and the weeds? Matthew 13:37-38

11. Who is the enemy who sowed them, what is the harvest, and who are the harvesters? Matthew 13:39

12. How will it be at the end of the world, whom will the Son of Man dispatch, and what will they collect from his kingdom? Matthew 13:40-41

13. What will the angels do with them, what will happen to the saints, and what should everyone heed? Matthew 13:42-43

Personal - To what are you drawing others by your actions? In what way does the evil one try to plant weeds in your family, in your work, in school, or in your neighborhood? As you are growing side by side, how do you counteract the weeds?

FIFTH DAY   **READ PSALM 86:5-6, 9-10, 15-16**

("For you, O Lord, are good and forgiving.")

Read and meditate on Psalm 86:5-6, 9-10, 15-16.

What is the Lord saying to you personally through the Psalm?

How can you apply this to your life?

SIXTH DAY   **READ ALL OF THE COMMENTARY**

WISDOM 12:13, 16-19

This passage is a powerful testimony of God's fantastic love for us and a testimony of God's continuing leniency toward his stubborn people. God shows us his power and might most visibly in the way he forgives. He shows us that the greatest force in our world is not power, not might, but love. He very clearly tells us in Deuteronomy 32:39 that he is our only God and he wants us to love and honor him first of all. He tells us that he is in control of life and death. He shows us in Isaiah 44:16 that he is the beginning and the end of all things.

Jesus fulfills this prophecy when he said, "I am the Alpha and the Omega." (Rev. 1:8). Jesus fulfilled all of these descriptions of God and his love of his people. The people rejected Jesus; in fact they killed him, because he called for a response of love. The people were expecting a great warrior-God to lead them out of poverty, slavery, and fear.

Today much of the world is in fear, and many countries are exploding with violence. Drugs, alcohol, and crime seem to be spreading throughout many cities. "Where is this wonderful God of mercy," some ask, and like the Israelites in the desert, they, too, asked, "Is he in our midst or not?" (Ex. 17:7)

Our God is a God of love, compassion, and justice. He is a God who constantly forgives and encourages us to become healed. In today's passage, we read of a God who is filled with power and yet rules with compassion and justice. Our God is a God who rules with great mercy, and that is what he seeks from you and me. He does not want our rituals or even our sacrifices.

Our God wants us to be merciful to one another, as he has been to us. We are all called to be a righteous people, a just people. To be really righteous or just, one has to be right with God first. We do that by following the words of Scripture that are in today's passage. He is our God and we believe only in him. Jesus is our beginning and end. He is mighty and just, because he is kind and gentle. We will be a mighty and just nation when we are kind and gentle to all of God's children. We must never forget that our actions tell others what kind of a God it is in whom we believe.

ROMANS 8:26-27

Today's passage brings us into a time of reflection and response to the quality of our prayer life. We need only look around our families and communities to find many hurting people. We are told to dismiss all of our anxieties and to present our needs to God in every form of prayer (Phil. 4:6-7). Jesus showed us very clearly that he was a man of deep prayer. He would rise very early in the morning, go off to some lonely place, and be completely immersed in prayer. Jesus was very obedient in his public prayer routines, but it was when he was alone with his Father, or "Abba," that he really poured out his heart.

Jesus reads people's hearts and that is what he wants to change in us. He wants to give us a heart of flesh in exchange for a heart of stone. We must remember that believers in Jesus Christ are not left to their own resources to cope with problems.

Prayer is now being recognized in the medical world as a great protector against life-threatening diseases, especially high blood pressure. We do not have to succumb to our emotions; we can pray, and let the Holy Spirit take all of our concerns. There are times when we do not know what to pray for, or how to pray the prayer that needs to be prayed. The Holy Spirit prays with and for us and God answers every time. You do not need to be afraid of coming before God with your petitions. Just ask the Holy Spirit to plead for you in harmony with God's own will.

Remember, when we bring our requests to God, trust that he will always do what is best for us, even if it does not make sense at that time (Rom. 8:28). We will find tremendous peace in letting the Holy Spirit pray in us and with us. We need to give ourselves permission to let our vocal cords make some sounds and let ourselves be led into a prayer of praise. We will then be praying in tongues, and the Holy Spirit will be talking within us and for us in Jesus' name to our heavenly Father.

MATTHEW 13:24-43

All of the parables in this Gospel passage teach us about God and his kingdom. They explain what the kingdom is really like as opposed to our expectations of it. We need to remember that the kingdom of heaven is not just some place in the sky; but rather, it is a spiritual realm in which God rules and in which we have God's eternal life. We are told that the thistles and the young blades of grass look very much the same and can not be recognized until they are grown and ready for harvest. The thistles are unbelievers and the wheat are the believers. They both must live side by side in this world.

God is like the farmer; he allows the unbelievers to remain in this world so the believers are uprooted with them. At the harvest the thistles will be uprooted and thrown away. God's harvest (judgment day) of all people is coming, and we need to make sure our faith in Jesus Christ is secure. Jesus teaches us that we are to be mild and patient even toward the evildoers, letting the weeds continue to grow until harvest time.

Jesus wants us to inspire others interiorly, not to force them exteriorly. He wants us to be encouragers, not discouragers. He wants us to change people's hearts, not just their minds. This passage talks about the mustard seed which becomes a very large bush, and we are to encourage others to let their faith grow. We are to show them how and not dominate them with our faith and our gifts. We are to let them make mistakes and urge them onward to better things. We are, in effect, like the leaven which enables the dough to rise into a loaf of bread.

The weeds that are growing in the field can be parts of our own temperament by which we dominate others. We may not be wrong, but we need to be sure we do not choke off anyone else's growth. Most of the sins of a believer are the excess use of their good qualities. Those who are good administrators easily over-administrate and suffocate the spirit of others. Those who possess control over law, like lawyers, policemen, judges and clergy, can find fault with the innocent and enable the guilty to go free. Somehow the good seed which should grow into good fruit turns into rank growth. The yeast is to raise the dough into delicious bread, and if it is misused, we are left with a hard flat cake. Our good qualities should enable others to make the best of their interior gifts.

Application

The first reading shows us that the greatest force in our world is not power, not might, but love. The second reading reveals to us that Jesus was a man of deep prayer. The Gospel tells us that Jesus wants us to inspire others interiorly, not to force them exteriorly. He wants us to be encouragers, not discouragers.

All three readings today draw much attention to our inner qualities of strength, inspiration, and ability. This week, draw out the inner qualities of someone in your family, school, or work, by encouraging them. You can do this by listening to them when they speak, and by giving them praise, not flattery, for something that they have done recently. Let them know what you like most about them. Finally, make a friend, be a friend, and bring that friend to Christ.

SEVENTEENTH SUNDAY IN ORDINARY TIME - CYCLE A

BEFORE YOU BEGIN

Pray and ask God to speak to you through His Holy Spirit. "THE PARACLETE, THE HOLY SPIRIT WHOM THE FATHER WILL SEND IN MY NAME, WILL INSTRUCT YOU IN EVERYTHING, AND REMIND YOU OF ALL THAT I TOLD YOU." (JOHN 14:26)

FIRST DAY   **Reread last week's readings.**

1.   What was a helpful or new thought from the readings or from the homily you heard on Sunday?

2.   From what you learned, what personal application did you choose to apply to your life this week?

SECOND DAY   **READ 1 KINGS 3:5, 7-12**   **FIRST READING**

("I give you a heart so wise and understanding...")

1.   Where did the Lord speak to Solomon, and what was known about that place? 1 Kings 3:4-5

2.   Who were Solomon's parents? 2 Samuel 12:24

3.   What did God say to Solomon, and where did he say it? 1 Kings 3:5

4.   Why did God show great favor to Solomon's father? 1 Kings 3:6

5.   What did Solomon say God has made him, and what did he call himself? 1 Kings 3:7

6.   Because of his age, what did he recognize about himself? 1 Kings 3:7

7.   Whom would Solomon serve, and how many were there? 1 Kings 3:8

8.   What kind of heart did Solomon ask God to give him, and what two things would this help him to do? 1 Kings 3:9

9.   How did the Lord feel about Solomon's request? 1 Kings 3:10

10.   God was pleased with Solomon because he did not ask for what three things? 1 Kings 3:11

11.   What did God say he would do? What kind of heart would Solomon have, and would there ever be anyone like him? 1 Kings 3:12

12.   What has God given us through Christ? Ephesians 1:9

13.   Where is every treasure of wisdom and knowledge hidden? Colossians 2:2-3

Personal – What have been your requests from God this past week? How have you been praying for a loved one who may have strayed from the faith? After you have done the above study, what changes can you make in your prayers (requests from God)?

THIRD DAY   **READ ROMANS 8:28-30**   **SECOND READING**

("Those he called he also justified;")

1.   What do we know God makes, and to whom does he make this happen?
      Romans 8:28

2.   For those whom God foreknew, what did he predestine them to share?
      Romans 8:29

3.   Of whom might the Son (Jesus) be the first-born? Romans 8:29

4.   Through whom has God predestined us to become his adopted sons and daughters, and when did God plan this? Ephesians 1:3-5

5.   What did God do for them? Romans 8:30

6.   What did God do to those he called and in turn glorified? Romans 8:30

7.   How does God administer everything, and how were we predestined?
      Ephesians 1:11

8.   What two things were our responses to being chosen in Jesus? Ephesians 1:13

9.   As was promised, with whom were we sealed? Ephesians 1:13

10.   How have we been justified? Romans 8:30, Ephesians 1:7, 13

Personal – What is your response to what Jesus has done for you personally? Do your actions in public show your belief? How do you act in a crisis? Is the reality of what Christ has done in your life visible to others in all circumstances? Reflect on this.

FOURTH DAY   **READ MATTHEW 13:44-52**   **GOSPEL**

("Angels will go and separate the wicked from the just.")

1.   The reign of God is like a man who finds a treasure. What does he do when he finds it? Matthew 13:44

2.   Again, like what is the kingdom of heaven? Matthew 13:45

3.   What did the merchant do when he found a really valuable pearl? Matthew 13:46

4.   What did Jesus say we would have in heaven if we sell all our possessions, and whom are we to follow? Matthew 19:21

5.   What does Paul consider a loss in the light of the surpassing knowledge of his Lord Jesus Christ, and for Jesus' sake, what has he forfeited? Philippians 3:7-8

6.   The reign of God is also like a dragnet thrown into the lake which collected all sorts of things. When the haul is brought   ashore, what is done with what is worthwhile, and what is done with what is useless? Matthew 13:47-48

7.   What will it be like at the end of the world? Matthew 13:48-49

8.   What will the angels do? Matthew 13:49-50

9.   What is the question Jesus put to his disciples, and what was their reply? Matthew 13:51

10.   By whom are we taught in order to interpret spiritual things, and whose mind do we have? 1 Cor 2:10-16

11.   What is every teacher of the law like who is learned in the reign of God? Matthew 13:52

Personal – Take an inventory of your life and reflect on the areas where you have been worthwhile or useful for God. Also, reflect where you have not been worthwhile or useful for God. How can you become more useful? A good example of usefulness for God is Mother Teresa. Pray on this.

FIFTH DAY   **READ PSALM 119:57, 72, 76-77, 127-130**

("The revelation of your words give light, giving understanding to the simple.")

Read and meditate on Psalm 119:57, 72, 76-77, 127-130.

What is the Lord saying to you personally through the Psalm?

How can you apply this to your life?

SIXTH DAY   **READ ALL OF THE COMMENTARY**

1 KINGS 3:5, 7-12

Today's passage from the book of 1 Kings, is about Solomon, the third king of Israel. He was called the wisest man who ever lived. He sealed many of his foreign agreements by marrying pagan women, and he allowed his lust for women and power to affect his loyalty to God. Solomon is an example to all of us how effective leadership can be blocked by an ineffective personal life. He was a tremendous politician, diplomat, trader, and collector of fine arts, but he was very disobedient to God in running his own household. He had it all and yet he failed to obey God, and he did not learn repentance until late in life. Today's story brings out what is really lasting in life and what is temporary. Solomon was given a chance to have anything he requested and he asked for wisdom to be a good leader of his people. God was very pleased at his request.

We need to ask ourselves: if God gave us the same chance to have anything we wished, would we have responded like Solomon? We need to ask for this same kind of wisdom. Solomon asked for wisdom to do what was expected of him, and today more than ever, we need to ask God for the wisdom to know what to do and the courage to do it. Solomon, like many of us, received great gifts; but again, like some of us, he did not apply the benefits of these gifts to all areas of his life.

You and I need to reflect on our own lives and discern how much we are living for God instead of ourselves. Solomon was wise, but he did not put that wisdom fully into action. Wisdom is both the discernment to know what is best and the strength of character to act upon that knowledge. Solomon asked for wisdom, not wealth, power or fame. God gave him all of this because of his generosity. Solomon sought only God's Kingship, not anything else, and we too must do the same and have the courage to follow his way all of our life (Matt.6:33). You can be wiser than Solomon by putting God and his work first in your life. The real wise man is the one who has put on the mind of Christ and serves others rather than rules over others (Phil. 2:2-5).

ROMANS 8:28-30

Today's reading from Paul to the Romans is one of the most powerful verses in the New Testament, and it is also one of the most misunderstood. God works out all things, not just a few isolated incidents, for our good. All that happens to many of us is not just good; sometimes bad things happen too. God is able to take them and turn them around for our long-range good. God is not working to make us happy, but to fulfill his purpose. We must recognize that this promise applies only to those who love God and are fitting into God's plans. We are called to trust in God, not in life's treasures. We are called to look for our security in heaven, not here on earth (Cor. 3:2-4). Then, and only then, can we learn to accept pain and persecution on earth, because they bring us closer to God. This sounds rather hard; but when the force of some catastrophic event slams into your life, the healing power of God's love can take you through the dark raging waters.

God does work things out for our good. Many times we do not see them at first, but time shows us how God was very much present when we thought we were all alone. God's ultimate goal is for all of us to become like Christ (1 John 3:2). God's Holy Word reveals to us that we can become the persons we were created to be. We need to remember that God's purpose was that no one should perish. We are all called to serve and to glorify God. The sovereignty of God should always be a reason for rejoicing and confidence, not of puzzlement or doubt.

Remember, if God gave his Begotten Son to die for us, he is not going to hold back the gift of salvation. If Christ gave his life for us, he is not going to turn around and condemn us. No matter what may be happening to you, just rest in his redeeming grace and he will work things out for your ultimate good, simply because he loves you.

MATTHEW 13:44-52

The kingdom of heaven is more valuable than anything else we can have, and a person must be willing to give up everything to obtain it. The kingdom of heaven is ours because of Jesus' death and resurrection. His death bought our freedom and eternal life with him forever in heaven.

We might ask, who would oppose us in our goal to obtain the kingdom of heaven. In many places the tyranny of governments strictly puts the pressure of threats and physical harm on Christians, and in many cases, subjects them to public ridicule. We need only look around and see how society treats those who object to abortion. The people who choose pro-life instead of pro-death are many times arrested and sentenced to jail (Matt. 10:18-19).

Today's Gospel passage deals with a treasure found by accident and the value was so great that everything else was sold in order to possess the great treasure. How much of your treasures are you willing to let go in order that you might possess the greatest treasure in the universe? We cannot serve God and money, power or status. We are called as Christians to go out and tell others of this priceless treasure.

We need to show others that they too may possess this treasure by giving up their temporary treasures and claiming the treasure of treasures, a personal relationship with Jesus Christ. We must never forget Jesus' words in Matthew 10:39, "If you cling to your life, you will lose it, but if you give it up for Me, you will save it." Jesus taught that the kingdom was now and he was the real treasure, not power, money, sex, or status. He tells us again today that to gain his treasure, we must let go of the earth's treasures and cling only to him. If you sometimes doubt your salvation, the forgiveness of your sins, or God's work in your life, look at the evidence in Scripture and the changes in your life. About what do you spend most of your time thinking? Remember, where your treasure is, there is your heart also (Matthew 6:21).

Application

The first reading this week shows Solomon really choosing a great treasure in asking for wisdom. In the second reading we see Paul going beyond the quick fix, and in faith proclaiming God's will for those who believe in the Lord. The Gospel brings us into touch with the what and where of our real treasure.

This week, let us use our spiritual vision and see what God wants to do with our lives. Look around and choose someone in the family, or in school or at work, and show by your action that you want to serve them and that their interest comes first. Your treasure is serving others in the name of Jesus. Serve them by doing a chore for them, helping out at home, or spending time with your family. Do not let anything interrupt.

EIGHTEENTH SUNDAY IN ORDINARY TIME – CYCLE A

BEFORE YOU BEGIN

Pray and ask God to speak to you through His Holy Spirit. "THE PARACLETE, THE HOLY SPIRIT WHOM THE FATHER WILL SEND IN MY NAME, WILL INSTRUCT YOU IN EVERYTHING, AND REMIND YOU OF ALL THAT I TOLD YOU." (JOHN 14:26)

FIRST DAY   **Reread last week's readings.**

1.   What was a helpful or new thought from the readings or from the homily you heard on Sunday?

2.   From what you learned, what personal application did you choose to apply to your life this week?

SECOND DAY   **READ ISAIAH 55:1-3**   **FIRST READING**

("Listen, that you may have life.")

1.   Who is to come to the water and who is to receive grain and eat? Isaiah 55:1

2.   Who seeks water in vain, and what will the God of Israel not do? Isaiah 41:17

3.   What does Jesus say he will give us? John 4:10

4.   What do we not have to do to drink wine and milk? Isaiah 55:1

5.   Who is the bread of life, and who will never be thirsty? John 6:35

6.   What question is asked in verse 2 of Isaiah 55?

7.   What are we to do to eat well, and in what shall we delight? Isaiah 55:2

8.   What are we to do that we may have life? Isaiah 55:3

9.   What will he renew with us? Isaiah 55:3

10.   What is the covenant or promise made to David? 2 Samuel 7:12-16

Personal – An invitation to come to him is given over and over in these passages. In what way have you come to him without feeling you have to pay in some way? In what way do you see this invitation as a free gift?

THIRD DAY   **READ ROMANS 8:35, 37-39**   **SECOND READING**

("...we are more than conquerors because of him who has loved us.")

1. Fill in the following blanks:
   What will separate us from the _____ of
   _____? _____ or _____, or
   _____, or _____, or _____,
   or _____, or the _____? Romans 8:35

2. Because of him who has loved us, what are we? Romans 8:37

3. How does God prove his love for us? Romans 5:8

4. Of what am I certain? Romans 8:38-39

5. List the ten things that cannot separate us from the love of God stated in
   Romans 8:38-39.

   1. _____   6. _____

   2. _____   7. _____

   3. _____   8. _____

   4. _____   9. _____

   5. _____   10. _____

6. In whom does the love of God come to us? Romans 8:39

7. What way are we to follow? Ephesians 5:2

8. What does 1 Cor. 13:4-8 say about love?

9. What separates us from God? Isaiah 59:2

10. What is the way we come to understand love? 1 John 3:16

Personal – In what way have you personally been a conqueror in your life? In what way are you experiencing the love of God in your life on a daily basis? Is your relationship with a family member or friend separating you from the love of God? What can you do to be reconciled with that person?

FOURTH DAY   **READ MATTHEW 14:13-21**   **GOSPEL**

("There is no need to disperse. Give them something to eat yourselves.")

1. What had Jesus heard; how and where did he go? Matthew 14:1-13

2. What did the crowds do? Matthew 14:13

3. When Jesus disembarked and saw the vast crowd, what were his feelings and what did he do? Matthew 14:14

4.   Who, also, took pity upon someone and was moved to respond? Luke 10:30-34

5.   What does Mark's Gospel say Jesus did when he saw the vast crowd? Mark 6:34

6.   As evening drew near, what did Jesus' disciples suggest he tell the crowd? Matthew 14:15

7.   Jesus responded by telling them there was no need to tell them to disperse. What did he tell the disciples to do, and what was their response? Matthew 14:16-17

8.   What did Jesus tell the disciples to do with the five loaves and two fish, and what did he order the crowd to do? Matthew 14:18-19

9.   When Jesus took the five loaves and two fish, where did he look, and what three things did he do with them? Matthew 14:19

10.   What did the disciples do, and what happened to all those present? Matthew 14:19-20

11.   How much was left over, and how many were present? Matthew 14:20-21

Personal - In what way, this past week, have you lost the benefits of having your hunger filled through Jesus by either eating out or focusing on the preparation of the physical food?

FIFTH DAY   **READ PSALM 145:8-9, 15-18**

("You open your hand and satisfy the desire of every living thing.")

Read and meditate on Psalm 145:8-9, 15-18.

What is the Lord saying to you personally through the Psalm?

How can you apply this to your life?

SIXTH DAY   **READ ALL OF THE COMMENTARY**

ISAIAH 55:1-3

This passage invites us to seek nourishment from the real source of food and water, not just a temporary source that satisfies only our bodies. Jesus tells us, as well as the woman at the well, that the water he gives us becomes a perpetual spring within us. We, then, are free from thirst forever, with eternal life (John 4:14).

There is a tremendous parallel in the functions of our spiritual and physical life. We spend money on food that lasts only a short time and meets only our physical needs. Can you imagine how people would react if there were notices in the community that all kinds of food and drink were to be given away for free? The response would be incredible and immediate. Yet that is what God is offering us right this very moment. He is offering us perpetual, living water and nourishment that will fill us spiritually. We can all receive this food for our soul, but first we must come to the Lord by responding to his call. We must listen to him, seek him out, and call upon the name of the Lord. God's salvation is freely offered, but to nourish our souls we must openly receive it.

It is very important for us to remember that we will starve spiritually without his food, as surely as we will starve physically without our daily bread. As our bodies hunger and thirst, so do our souls. The living Word, Jesus Christ, can satisfy our hungry and thirsty souls.

ROMANS 8:35, 37-39

This passage affirms our faith and hope in the Lord Jesus Christ by clearly showing us that nothing, not even death itself, can separate us from God's love. The power of the Holy Spirit frees us from falling into sin, and we know that power is at our side always. If you were standing in a courtroom and waiting for the verdict to be read, what would those words mean to you if you were on death row? We must remember that the whole world is on death row, justly condemned for repeatedly breaking God's holy law. Without Jesus Christ, we would have no hope at all. But thanks be to God, he has declared us not guilty and has offered us freedom from sin and the power to follow his will.

In the face of trouble or calamity, or when we are hunted down or devastated, the question continually arises, "Who can ever keep God's love from us?" Are our trials and tribulations a sign that he doesn't love us any more or that he even has deserted us? We need to hear, read, and believe the scriptures that tell us over and over that he will never leave us or take away his love from us. These words were written to a church that soon would undergo terrible persecution. In just a few short years, Paul's words would turn into painful realities.

Today's passage reaffirms God's incredible love for his people. Today, in many countries throughout the world, these words are a tremendous reality. We must all be ready to lose everything we own and even be ready to face death itself. Christ did that and we are called to follow his example. It is very important for us to remember that no matter where we are or what happens to us, we can never be separated from his love. When suffering comes, it will not drive us away from God. On the contrary, through the power of the Holy Spirit, it will bring us closer to God. We will be able to identify with him, and allow his love to heal us.

These verses contain one of the most comforting and healing promises in all scripture. We may have to face the hardship of persecution, illness, imprisonment, even death itself. Any one of these hardships could cause us to fear that we have been deserted by Christ. Paul tells us that nothing can separate us from God's love, because his death is proof of how much he loved us. Nothing can stop his constant presence with us. God tells us how great his love really is so that we will be totally secure in him and we will not be afraid. Because of Jesus Christ, you and I need not fear tomorrow, because we, too, can live forever.

MATTHEW 14:13-21

Galilee was a small part of the country, and there were people from many small towns who heard about Jesus and flocked to hear him speak. Jesus was filled with grief over the news about John the Baptist, his cousin, and like many of us in our time of grief, he needed to rest and be alone with his thoughts. The crowd saw where Jesus was heading and followed him by land from many villages.

Jesus sought solitude after the news of John's death. However, he did not dwell on his grief, and he returned to his ministry. He had tremendous compassion for those who came to him. He pitied them and healed their sick, even while he grieved. How many times do we feel cheated when we need to rest or just simply be alone, and the pressures of our families, jobs, or communities prevent us from being able to minister to ourselves through taking time for God in solitude and peace.

Jesus listened to the disciples complain about the crowd and tell him to send them away to the villages and feed themselves. Can you imagine over 5,000 people out in the middle of no where all of a sudden being told to go look for a place to buy food? Jesus' compassion was in full force when he told the disciples to feed the crowd. The disciples were shocked and said, "Where are we going to get the food and how are we supposed to do it?" Whenever we come up against something that appears to be "difficult to impossible," it is common to complain and predict failure. The impossible to men becomes the possible through Christ; and the 5,000 people were fed with just five loaves and two fishes. Jesus even provided enough food to have leftovers. Do you believe this story? Do you believe that with Jesus all things are possible?

Jesus made room in his busy schedule to be alone with the Father. His time of solitude was not to sulk, but to be with his Father in prayer. He knew that this time would equip him to meet the challenges and struggles of life. Jesus took the bread and fish and looked to his Father and gave thanks, and blessed the meal. He then, in confidence, broke the bread and distributed it to the people. The disciples were flabbergasted, the people were ecstatic and Jesus was thankful to his Father.

What about today? There are many people tired and in need of food, not just physical food, but spiritual food. Who is to feed them? We are, according to today's passage. We are the disciples of Jesus Christ, and by our baptism we are called to go forth and make disciples of all nations (Matthew 28:19). We are to follow Jesus' example and take time to rest in the solitude of God. We are not to dwell in grief and fall prey to self-pity over our illness, misfortune or even death of a loved one. We are to give thanks, rise up and feed our brothers and sisters with the living, healing Word of God.

Application

The first reading tells us to seek nourishment from the real source of food and water, not just temporary nourishment. The second reading tells us nothing, not even death, can separate God's love from us. The third reading shows us how God wants us to feed our brothers and sisters with his Holy Word, and not be caught up in any self-pity.

This week, try to bring the Eucharist to someone you know who is sick or shut-in. Feed your family this week by reading a scripture passage everyday at the main meal time. Make a family visit to help feed the poor at a local soup kitchen. Remember, whatever you do for the least, you do for Jesus!

NINETEENTH SUNDAY IN ORDINARY TIME – CYCLE A

BEFORE YOU BEGIN

Pray and ask God to speak to you through His Holy Spirit. "THE PARACLETE, THE HOLY SPIRIT WHOM THE FATHER WILL SEND IN MY NAME, WILL INSTRUCT YOU IN EVERYTHING, AND REMIND YOU OF ALL THAT I TOLD YOU." (JOHN 14:26)

FIRST DAY	**Reread last week's readings.**

1. What was a helpful or new thought from the readings or from the homily you heard on Sunday?

2. From what you learned, what personal application did you choose to apply to your life this week?

SECOND DAY	**READ 1 KINGS 19:9, 11-13**	**FIRST READING**

("Go outside and stand on the mountain before the Lord; the Lord will be passing by.")

1. Where was Elijah, and what came to him? 1 Kings 19:8-9

2. What did the Lord ask him? 1 Kings 19:9

Personal – When you pray, how do you communicate with God? Does he ever ask you any questions?

3. Who is another prophet who communicated with God and the glory of God was revealed to him, and where did this take place? Exodus 33:6, 18-23

4. Where did the Lord tell Elijah to go, and who did he say would be passing by? 1 Kings 19:11

5. What was hitting the mountains and crushing the rocks before the Lord, and where was the Lord not to be found? 1 Kings 19:11

6. What came after the earthquake? 1 Kings 19:12

7. What came after the fire? 1 Kings 19:12

8. What did Elijah do when he heard the tiny whispering sound? 1 Kings 19:13

9. What was the question repeated to Elijah by the Lord? 1 Kings 19:13

10. When Jesus was transfigured, where did he go, and who appeared with him? Matthew 17:1-3

11. How beautiful upon the mountains are the feet of him who brings glad tidings. What are they announcing? Isaiah 52:7

Personal – Where is the mountain of the Lord for you? In what way does God communicate with you?

THIRD DAY　　　　　　　**READ ROMANS 9:1-5**　　　　　**SECOND READING**

("I speak the truth in Christ: I do not lie.")

1. Who is speaking, what does he speak, and what does he not do? Romans 9:1 Romans 1:1

2. With whom does Paul's conscience join witness, and to what is it he bears witness? Romans 9:1-2

3. Who bears witness to what Paul does? Romans 1:9

4. What is the truth? 1 Timothy 2:4-6

5. What does Paul say he could wish for himself for the sake of his brothers, his kinsmen, the Israelites? Romans 9:3

6. What does God tell Moses when he asked God to strike him out of the book that he has written? Exodus 32:30-33

7. What seven things does he say were theirs, and who came from them? Romans 9:4-5

8. Where did the Messiah come from according to the flesh? Romans 9:5 and Romans 1:3

9. What does the term Messiah mean? John 1:41 4:25

10. Who is over all? Romans 9:5

Personal – How do you show your concern for a family member, friend, schoolmate or work acquaintance who is not following the way of the Lord? In what way do you speak the truth, as Paul did, to those around you?

FOURTH DAY　　　　　　**READ MATTHEW 14:22-33**　　　　　　**GOSPEL**

("When he had sent them away, he went upon the mountain by himself to pray.")

1. What did Jesus insist his disciples do, and what preceded this? Matthew 14:16-22

2. When Jesus had sent them away, where did he go? Matthew 14:23

3. After Jesus was baptized, what was he doing when the skies opened and the Holy Spirit descended on him? Luke 3:21-22

4. Who was with Jesus as he prayed, where did he go, and what time of day was it? Matthew 14:23

Personal – Over the next 24 hours, see how much time you spend alone with the Lord. See whether you can list how many times Jesus prayed alone in the New Testament.

5. What was happening to the boat the disciples were in, and what time was it when Jesus came walking on the water towards them? Matthew 14:24-25

6. When the disciples saw him walking on the water, how did they react? Matthew 14:26

7. What did Jesus hasten to do, and what did he say to his disciples? Matthew 14:27

8. Who spoke up? What did he say to Jesus, and what did Jesus say to him? Matthew 14:28-29

9. When Peter got out of the boat and started toward Jesus walking on the water, what did he perceive? Matthew 14:30

10. What happened to Peter when he perceived this, and to whom did he cry out? Matthew 14:30

11. Jesus **at once** stretched out his hand and caught him. What did he exclaim, and what did he ask him? Matthew 14:31

12. What happened when they climbed into the boat? What did those in the boat show him, and what did they declare? Matthew 14:32-33

Personal – What happens to you when you take your eyes off Jesus and dwell on what's going on around you? What does Jesus do when you call out to him in your distress?

FIFTH DAY   **READ PSALM 85:9-14**

("I will hear what God proclaims; the Lord-for he proclaims peace, to his people,..")

Read and meditate on Psalm 85:9-14.

What is the Lord saying to you personally through the Psalm?

How can you apply this to your life?

SIXTH DAY   **READ ALL OF THE COMMENTARY**

1 KINGS 19:9, 11-13

This passage shows us how God speaks to his people in all kinds of circumstances. Elijah had killed the false prophets and then, in fear himself, he fled from the pagan queen, Jezebel. Elijah experienced the depths of fatigue and discouragement just after his two spiritual victories, the defeat of the false prophets, and the answered prayer for rain. Many times discouragement sets in after we have had a very great spiritual experience. God let Elijah eat and rest (19:34), and then sent Elijah to the mountains to wait for him.

Elijah, like many of us do when we are under heavy pressure, began to think that he was the only one following God's work. He became frustrated and fearful and began to lose sight of what God had in store for him. God asked Elijah what he was doing there, and Elijah told him that he was in danger of losing his life for following God's orders. Then God said to Elijah, go stand before me on the mountain. Elijah then experienced terrific windstorms and even an earthquake, followed by fire, and still no sign of God. How many times do we look to see whether God is speaking to us in some spectacular way or event? The minute Elijah heard the gentle whispers in that cave, he knew that it was the voice of God.

God speaks to all of us, and the challenge for us is to be quiet and listen. He told Elijah that he wanted him to go back and continue on in his ministry, and not to be afraid of anyone. Do you feel as if no one really cares about you, or what you are doing? Are you afraid of what other people might think about you?

God will come to us just like he did to Elijah in that cave. He will speak in gentle whispers to a humbled heart, and he will change our lives. God doesn't reveal himself ordinarily in miraculous ways. To look for him in just big rallies, churches, conferences or visible leaders may be to miss him. Are you listening to God right now? Step back from the noise and activity of your life and listen to his gentle whisper. If you listen, listen real close, you will hear him say "I love you."

ROMANS 9:1-5

Paul's love and concern for his people was like that of a parent towards his or her child. Parents would do anything to prevent their children from hurting themselves, and yet the children must experience maturity and growth themselves. Paul tells them that they are fortunate to have such a loving, caring God, and it was not only foolish to ignore his teachings, it was also dangerous. Paul is willing to lose not only his life for his people, but also his salvation.

Today, as in this passage, so many Christians take their faith for granted. They assume their salvation is a non-refundable object. Today, much of the world looks at God as sort of an amusing fantasy to which only oppressed and lonely people cling. Do you have such a concern for others who do not know Christ personally? How concerned are you for those in your own family who do not know Christ personally?

The real challenge to believing Christians today is how much are we all willing to sacrifice of our time, money, energy, comfort and safety to see our loved ones come to faith in Jesus. What do you think about most of the time? Where do you spend most of your free time? Remember, our treasure is where our heart is. We are called to seek his kingship first, and then everything else will fall into line (Matthew 6:33).

A loving parent, like Paul, would gladly die for a child, but like Paul, we see that living for Christ is harder than dying for Christ. To live for Christ means to die to ourselves every day.

MATTHEW 14:22-33

The miraculous feeding of the 5,000 occurred on the shores of the Sea of Galilee near Bethsaida. Jesus then told his disciples to get into their boats and cross to the other side of the lake while he stayed to get the people started home. We then see him going up into the hills and praying far into the night.

Praying was the core of Jesus' activity. He prayed in all circumstances. He was praying even when the skies opened up and the Holy Spirit descended upon him. He often prayed alone, no distractions, just complete union with his Father. We need to look at ourselves honestly and see how much time every day we share in personal prayer with the Lord. This is a time of tremendous intimacy and a time of hope.

The sea became angry and the storm threatened to overturn the boat that carried the disciples. It was early in the morning when, through the fog and heavy seas, they saw Jesus coming toward them walking on the water. They were terrified because they didn't really recognize him and thought he was some kind of ghost or evil spirit. Jesus called out to them and Peter replies, still not sure whether it really is Christ, **"If** it really is you, tell me to come over to you walking on the water." Peter began to walk toward Jesus and then he noticed the high winds, and when he took his eye off Jesus and began to sink he screamed to the Lord, "Save me." Jesus **instantly** reached out his hand and rescued him. He looked at them and said, "Why do you always doubt me," and as they stepped into the boat the wind immediately and obediently died down.

Today's passage reveals to us how important solitude is to Jesus. He never began or ended anything without spending time alone in prayer with his Father. He was always equipped to handle anything because he was a man full of prayer. Spending time in prayer will help us meet the challenges and struggles of life. Peter sank because he took his eyes off Christ. You need to ask yourself whether you take your eyes off Christ, during a time of crisis.

Jesus is the center of all healing, and no other means can take his place. The high waves in our lives can be tension, turmoil, sickness, marital discord, and many other forms of destruction. When we keep Jesus as the Lord of our life we too will walk on water and stay above the raging seas of destruction. That really means that we will be able to walk through tough situations when we are focused on Christ, rather than the situation. We need not fear that we will sink in any kind of trouble because, just as Jesus told the men in the boat, "Do not be afraid," he tells us the same. True love drives out fear, because fear has to do with punishment (1 John 4:18). There is no condemnation in one who accepts the Lord as his or her Savior (Romans 8:1). Pray about everything, worry about nothing and the peace that surpasses all understanding will be yours (Philippians 4:6, 7).

Application

The first reading showed us the power of communication through a gentle whisper of God. The second reading dealt with the power of truth in all that we speak. The Gospel brought home the power of prayer, especially as we prepare to deal with the challenges of life.

This week, make a special effort to speak only the truth, and nothing but the truth, and speak in a clear and gentle manner to those in your family, in your work area, and in your school. His Word is truth. Take some extra time to be alone with the Lord so he can reveal to you what his truth is and how to communicate that to others. Always remember, before you speak to pray and ask the Lord to give wisdom and discernment. This sounds easy but it is not, because Satan, the father of all lies, will try to discourage you in every way he can. Remember, your actions tell others what you really believe.

TWENTIETH SUNDAY IN ORDINARY TIME - CYCLE A

BEFORE YOU BEGIN

Pray and ask God to speak to you through His Holy Spirit. "THE PARACLETE, THE HOLY SPIRIT WHOM THE FATHER WILL SEND IN MY NAME, WILL INSTRUCT YOU IN EVERYTHING, AND REMIND YOU OF ALL THAT I TOLD YOU." (JOHN 14:26)

FIRST DAY   **Reread last week's readings.**

1. What was a helpful or new thought from the readings or from the homily you heard on Sunday?

2. From what you learned, what personal application did you choose to apply to your life this week?

SECOND DAY   **READ ISAIAH 56:1, 6-7**   **FIRST READING**

("Observe what is right, do what is just;")

1. Who is speaking, what does he say to observe, and what does he say to do? Isaiah 56:1

2. Of what must you never grow weary? 2 Thessalonians 3:13

3. Whom are we to follow because all his works are right and his ways are just? Daniel 4:34

4. What does the Lord say is about to come and be revealed? Isaiah 56:1

5. What leads to justification and salvation? Romans 10:10

6. What are the foreigners doing who join themselves to the Lord? Isaiah 56:6

7. What are the foreigners doing to the name of the Lord, and what are they becoming? Isaiah 56:6

8. Whom will the Lord bring to his holy mountain, and what will he make them? Isaiah 56:6-7

9. What shall he call his house, for whom is his house, and what will be acceptable on his altar? Isaiah 56:7

10. What are we to offer continually to God, and with what kind of sacrifices is God pleased? Hebrews 13:15-16

Personal – In what way are you keeping Sunday as the Lord's Day? Are you made to feel joyful at church? Is it a house of prayer and worship for you? If you do not feel the Joy of the Lord at church, examine your conscience and see whether you have any of the following things blocking you:

- not doing what is right and just
- not ministering to the Lord (the poor)
- not loving his name
- not being his servant
- not keeping the Sabbath (Sunday) free from profanity
- not holding to his covenant.

THIRD DAY	READ ROMANS 11:13-15, 29-32	SECOND READING

("God has imprisoned all in disobedience that he might have mercy on all.")

1. Who is speaking, and to whom is he speaking? Who does he claim to be? Romans 1:1, Romans 11:13

2. In what does Paul glory, and what is he trying to do? Romans 11:13-14

3. What does the Lord say about Paul in Acts 9:15?

4. If the Jew's rejection has meant reconciliation for the world, what will their acceptance mean? Romans 11:15

5. How were we reconciled to God, and how have we been saved? Romans 5:10

6. What are God's gifts and his call? Romans 11:29

7. What does Numbers 23:19 say about God?

8. What have you received through the Jew's disobedience, and what did they also receive through this? Rom 11:30-31

9. Into what has God imprisoned all, and for what reason? Romans 11:32

10. What happens to those who conceal their sins, and what happens to those who confess and forsake them? Proverbs 28:13

11. What did God do for us in his great mercy, and from where does it draw its life? 1 Peter 1:3

Personal – How do you see yourself, as one disobedient and in need of a savior, or as someone who feels and has experienced the mercy of God through Jesus?

FOURTH DAY   READ MATTHEW 15:21-28   GOSPEL

("Woman, you have great faith? Your wish will come to pass.")

1.   To what district did Jesus withdraw? See whether you can find this on a Bible map
      Matthew 15:21

2.   Who was living in that locality, what did she cry out to Jesus, and what did Jesus
      say to her? Matthew 15:22-23

3.   When Jesus' disciples came up to him, what did they say to him? Matthew 15:23

4.   What was Jesus' reply and to whom was he referring? Matthew 15:24,
      Romans 15:8

5.   What did the woman come forward and do, what was her plea, and what was
      Jesus' answer to her? Matt 15:25-26

6.   What did the woman call Jesus, and what did she say about the dogs?
      Matthew 15:27

7.   What did Jesus say the woman had that was great, and what happened to her
      daughter? Matthew 15:28

8.   What did Jesus say about the centurion, and what happened to his servant?
      Matthew 8:10, 13

9.   What did Jesus see in the people who brought him a paralytic, and what happened
      to him? Matthew 9:2, 6-7

10.   What will happen to the person who puts his faith in Jesus? John 14:12

Personal – Examine yourself and see how much faith you have. How do you respond when a loved one gets sick? What do you ask from the Lord? Spend more time alone with the Lord this week and ask him to increase your faith. Listen to what he says and memorize Romans 10:17, "Faith, then, comes through hearing, and what is heard is the Word of Christ."

FIFTH DAY   READ PSALM 67: 2-3, 5-6, 8

("May the peoples praise you, O God,")

Read and meditate on Psalm 67: 2-3, 5-6, 8.

What is the Lord saying to you personally through the Psalm?

How can you apply this to your life?

SIXTH DAY   READ ALL OF THE COMMENTARY

ISAIAH 56: 1, 6-7

The Sabbath was the day set aside for prayer, rest, and worship. We are commanded by God to observe his Sabbath because we need to spend unhurried time in worship each week. Scripture tells us very clearly to remember the "Sabbath" as a holy day. Six days a week are for our daily duties and regular work. But the seventh day is a day of Sabbath rest before the Lord our God. On that day we are to do no work of any kind, nor shall our children or even our guests. "For in six days the Lord made the heavens, earth and sea and everything in them, and rested on the seventh day: so bless the Sabbath day and set it aside for rest." (Ex. 20:8-11)

Today there are many people who ignore this special day and treat it with little or no respect at all. Sunday in many parts of the world, is a day of sports, not a "Day of the Lord." Sunday was never intended to be a day in which you did all the odd jobs around the house that you did not have time to do during the week. We all need to ask ourselves, "Do I really give honor and glory to the Lord on Sunday, or do I just look at it as a day off from work?"

God has called us to make his house of prayer a place of holiness. He tells us that all who make his temple a house of prayer will receive his blessings. God is pleased with our sacrifice of praise, our joyfulness and our confessing with our lips that he is the Lord of our life. God shows us in this passage that if we respond to him, he will send his blessings upon us, no matter what our color, social position, work or financial situation. Remember, God's blessings are as much for us as anyone else. Remember, Sunday is a day of adoration and fellowship with the Lord.

ROMANS 11: 13-15, 29-32

We need to remember that in the days following Pentecost, the new Christian church was filled mostly with Jewish people. Because of the missionary efforts of Peter, Paul, Philip and others, Gentiles became believers. It was not very long before the Gentiles, or non-Jewish believers, became the majority in the church. This turning from the Jews toward the Gentiles did not mean that God had abandoned them; it meant that when a Jew came to Christ, there was great rejoicing, as if a dead person had come back to life.

Paul's vision was for a church in which all Jews and Christians were united in their love for God. Today our world is so much smaller and that vision is so much wider. There are many types of people in the Christian church today. We must remember that Christ redeemed the whole world by his death on the cross, and salvation is for those who accept and believe in him.

God's mercy and his love are not limited to one special elite group. Scripture shows us that the Jews would freely share the blessings with the Gentiles. God calls upon us to bless each other and "Love one another as I have loved you." (John 15:12) God's mercy is intended to fall on all of his people. In Paul's day there was tremendous brutality toward the poor, oppressed and the despised.

Today we see much mercy and compassion extended toward the homeless, the poor, those in the soup kitchen lines, and the prisons. We have a tremendous opportunity to extend the mercy and compassion of God to those who are suffering from AIDS. Brutality still exists in all segments of our society, because only by obeying the Word of God will we bring about a real permanent healing to our people.

When God's Word is on every person's tongue, and when every knee bends and everyone calls Jesus Lord, then and only then, will there really be a lasting peace in the world. All of us have experienced the mercy of God because he died for us, knowing full well that we would be sinners (Rom. 5:8). I have found in my personal life that my need for my Savior is a daily one, and it is only through daily quiet time and Scripture study I begin to feel his incredible presence.

MATTHEW 15:21-28

This Gospel passage shows us that faith is available to all people. Consider faith to be a response to the living power and presence of God in your life. The woman in today's reading had a tremendous amount of faith in Jesus. Consider that in those days even approaching the teacher was very restricted. Yet, not only is the teacher approached and even being bothered by her begging, but all this is being done by a woman. There were no equal rights for women in those days.

This woman was taking a tremendous risk for her daughter's sake. She responded to the living power and presence of Jesus in her life by insisting that he talk to her. The apostles were outraged that this woman was interrupting their schedule. The apostles did not hear the fright in her voice, and there was no compassion in their voices. We must always remember that even when we are about to do something good or even spiritual, we must always be ready to hear and respond to God's call.

Jesus was incredibly impressed with this woman's faith and he made no pretense about it. She was not a Jew and she knew that her boldness was out of order, yet she also knew that the power of life and death was standing right before her very eyes. Jesus knew that the disciples had become occupied with spiritual matters and missed the spiritual needs of this woman. He wanted them, and he wants us, to be aware of the opportunities that surround them and us today.

The woman didn't mind the use of the word dog, and her faith in Jesus led her to ask only for the crumbs beneath the table, as even that was not denied to a dog. Jesus healed the daughter because of her mother's faith. He will heal your children, too, if you really believe in him and obey his teachings.

Application

This week's first reading called for respect for the Lord's day. The second reading showed how God's mercy is open to all people, and the Gospel revealed faith as the response to the living power and presence of God in your life.

This week, do nothing on Sunday other than celebrate in church and spend time with your families. Do no work unless it is absolutely necessary. Parents, plan an activity with your children that will increase their faith. Children, this Sunday, study God's readings and share them with your parents before going to church. Single people, join a church fellowship and get into a Bible study. Learn how his Word will make every day the "Lord's Day."

TWENTY-FIRST SUNDAY IN ORDINARY TIME - CYCLE A

BEFORE YOU BEGIN

Pray and ask God to speak to you through His Holy Spirit. "THE PARACLETE, THE HOLY SPIRIT WHOM THE FATHER WILL SEND IN MY NAME, WILL INSTRUCT YOU IN EVERYTHING, AND REMIND YOU OF ALL THAT I TOLD YOU." (JOHN 14:26)

FIRST DAY   **Reread last week's readings.**

1. What was a helpful or new thought from the readings or from the homily you heard on Sunday?

2. From what you learned, what personal application did you choose to apply to your life this week?

SECOND DAY   **READ ISAIAH 22: 15, 19-23**   **FIRST READING**

("...and give over to him your authority.")

1. Who is speaking, and where does he say to go? Isaiah 22:15

2. Who is Shebna, and what does Isaiah 36:3 say about him? Isaiah 22:15

3. What happened to Shebna? Isaiah 22:16-19

4. Who does the Lord summon, and who is his father? Isaiah 22:20

5. With what does the Lord clothe and gird Eliakim, and what does he give over to him? Isaiah 22:21

6. Who has full authority over heaven and earth? Matthew 28:18

7. Who established the existing authority? Romans 13:1

8. To whom is Eliakim the father? Isaiah 22:21

9. What will the Lord place on Eliakim's shoulder, and what will happen when he opens and shuts the house of David? Isaiah 22:22

10. What did Jesus entrust to Peter, and what authority does that give him? Matthew 16:19

11. How does the Lord fix Eliakim, and where does he place him with his family? Isaiah 22:23

Personal – Where do you see yourself as far as "when you open, no one can shut; when you shut, no one can open?" How has God given you the key to forgive or hold others bound by your unforgiveness? Think about this, and ask the Holy Spirit to reveal his truth to you.

THIRD DAY	**READ ROMANS 11:33-36**	**SECOND READING**

("For from him and through him and to God are all things.")

1. Fill in the following blanks: Oh, the depth of the _____ and _____ and _____ of God? Romans 11:33

2. How is God's wisdom made known? Ephesians 3:10

3. In whom is every treasure of wisdom and knowledge hidden? Colossians 2:2-3

4. What is inscrutable and unsearchable? Romans 11:33

5. What questions are being asked in Romans 11:34 and in Wisdom 9:13?

6. How has God revealed this wisdom to us? 1 Corinthians 2:10

7. What is given to God, and for what reason is it given? Romans 11:35

8. How are all things? Romans 11:36

9. What is to him forever? Romans 11:36

10. From whom do all things come, and for whom do we live? Through whom was everything made, and through whom do we live? 1 Corinthians 8:6

11. How was everything on the earth created? Colossians 1:16

Personal – In what way do you show the Lord your love for him as the Great Creator? Take a few moments right now and praise him for the All Powerful Mighty God that he is.

FOURTH DAY	**READ MATTHEW 16:13-20**	**GOSPEL**

("Who do you say that I am?")

1. To what neighborhood has Jesus come, and what did he ask his disciples? Matthew 16:13

2. Who do the people say Jesus is? Matthew 16:14

3. Who did Herod the Tetrarch say Jesus was? Matthew 14:1-2

4. What direct question did Jesus ask his disciples? Matthew 16:15

5. Who answered Jesus, what did he call him, and who did he say was his Father? Matthew 16:16

6. What is the meaning of Messiah? John 4:25

7. What was Jesus' reply to Peter's answer, and who revealed this to Peter? Matthew 16:17

8. What did Jesus declare to Peter, what will he build on him, and what will not prevail against it? Matthew 16:18

9. What does he entrust to Peter? Matthew 16:19

10. What happens when he declares something bound on earth and loosed on earth? Matthew 16:19

11. What did Jesus tell his disciples not to do? Matthew 16:20

Personal - Who do you say Jesus is? Write out on a piece of paper who Jesus is to you?

FIFTH DAY   **READ PSALM 138: 1-3, 6, 8**

("You build up strength within me.")

Read and meditate on Psalm 138: 1-3, 6, 8.

What is the Lord saying to you personally through the Psalm?

How can you apply this to your life?

SIXTH DAY   **READ ALL OF THE COMMENTARY**

ISAIAH 22:15, 19-23

This passage is the result of Isaiah's prophecy of the destruction of Jerusalem. Isaiah warns his people against making alliances with foreigners and telling them they should trust in God alone for their future. Jerusalem was savagely attacked and its people were slaughtered. The real tragedy, in today's reading, is the people had plenty of warning and chose to trust in their own ingenuity, weapons and even their pagan neighbors. Isaiah told them that unless they repented of their evil ways, they would face God's punishment. They did not want to hear this kind of talk. They said, "Let us eat, drink and be merry for tomorrow we die."

We need to reflect on how much we depend on God to help us in our decision making. Too often we turn to things which, though good in themselves, really will not give us the help we need. We must do all the necessary work today in our homes, community, and country, but God must guide our efforts. Today, national danger should be a call to national repentance. The essence of all sin is self. We are called to root out the rebellion in our spirit before we start to clean out anyone else. We can only do that by repentance, a complete change of mind (Rom. 12:2). We need to confess with our lips and believe with our hearts that Jesus Christ is Lord (Rom. 10:10). We can only repent or change when we obey God's law and not man's law (Acts 5:29).

Today we see people giving up hope and following drugs, alcoholism and immoral sex. The world's response to hopelessness is despair and self-indulgence. The proper response is to turn to God and trust in his promise of eternal life (John 3:16).

Shebna was a high official who got above the Law of God and became a law unto himself. We see that type of individual in many nations today. Shebna was the peg that was pulled out of the wall and all his power and riches were gone. You are a good leader when you are building up others, and the source of your good leadership is Jesus Christ.

ROMANS 11:33-36

Paul tells us the greatness of our God is almost beyond description. The depth of his riches, knowledge and wisdom is far beyond the comprehension of our mind. Scripture tells us that "eye has not seen, ear has not heard, nor can man ever comprehend what God has in store for those who love him" (1 Cor. 2:9). The wisdom of God has been revealed to us by means of the Holy Spirit. The Holy Spirit is God's guarantee that he will do what he has promised. The presence of the Holy Spirit in our lives is our assurance of eternal life with all of its blessings.

The world fears power, yet we belong to the God of the universe, who raised Jesus Christ from the dead. We do not need to fear any power whether it be dictator, nation, death or Satan himself. God's incomparable power is for us who choose to believe in him. The Holy Spirit searches out and shows us all of God's deepest secrets. These secrets are contained in Jesus Christ. The secrets are his resurrection and the plan of salvation which has been revealed to those who believe that what God says is true.

Those who believe and put their faith in Jesus will know all that they need to know to be saved. To really put on the "mind of Christ" we need to realize that it means to get a true perspective of humility for ourselves. We do not need to put ourselves down, that is not true humility. We do need to see that we are sinners, saved only by God's grace. To put on the "mind of Christ" is to avoid selfishness, and the cure for selfishness is servanthood. This brings unity among believers and is a witness to unbelievers that God's power is present in this world. We must always remember that selfish ambitions destroy church unity by putting one Christian against another.

The full glory of God is manifested to us in the Incarnation of Jesus Christ. God glorified Jesus because of his obedience. God glorified him by raising him to his original position at the right hand of the Father, where he will reign forever as our Lord and judge (Phil. 2:2-4). Jesus Christ was humble and willing to give up his rights in order to obey God and serve people. Like Jesus, we must serve out of love for a God who is all-knowing, all-powerful, all-wise, and the riches of his will all be ours through the saving grace of our Lord and Savior Jesus Christ.

MATTHEW 16:13-20

Today's Gospel passage took place in territory ruled by Caesarea Philippi. The influence of Greek and Roman culture was everywhere and pagan temples and idols were extremely popular. The city was rebuilt and named after Caesar and called Caesarea.

Jesus asked the disciples, "Who do people say that I am?" They told him that many people thought he was a great prophet returned. Peter told him that he was "the Christ, the Messiah, the Son of the Living God." Jesus was pleased that Peter was not fooled by the culture or the latest fad. He knew that his Father had revealed his identity to Peter.

Jesus tells Peter that he is a stable leader, a rock, and that he will build his church on that rock. Jesus personally tells Peter that his church would stand up victorious against even the gates of hell. This is a tremendous statement made by Jesus. We have a church that was commissioned by Jesus Christ who tells the whole world that his church will never fall. He gives Peter the keys of the kingdom of heaven, which means the authority to rule in his name. He tells Peter, "Whatever you bind on earth shall be bound in heaven, and whatever you loose on earth shall be loosed in heaven." Jesus gave this authority to Peter and his successors who passed this on down until today.

A Catholic is forgiven his sins by a priest in the name of Jesus Christ. You can hold someone in bondage by not forgiving them and cutting off their supply of love. This will result in your damaging not only the other person but yourself too. You can loose the person of their bondage by your forgiveness and the result is freedom to both of you. Jesus wants all of us to be free, and he calls all of us into repentance. God has chosen each one of us to help someone find the way. Remember, to all who believe in Christ and obey his words, the kingdom doors are swung wide open.

Application

This week's first reading tells us to trust in God, not people. The second reading tells us that no one can fully understand the mind of Christ, but we can put on his mind by following his example. The Gospel shows how God built his church and gave Peter the keys of heaven to preach, teach, and rule. The church is guaranteed by Christ to never fail.

If you are holding a grudge against anyone and you are having trouble forgiving them, try the following three steps:

1.   Forgive that person for what has been done to you.

2.   Ask the Lord to forgive that person for what has been done to you.

3.   Ask the Lord to cleanse your heart of the bitterness, resentment, anger, and the unforgiveness that you have towards that person who hurt you. This will bind the spirit of anger, resentment, bitterness and unforgiveness. It will loose the spirit of forgiveness and love and set you and that person free.

TWENTY-SECOND SUNDAY IN ORDINARY TIME - CYCLE A

BEFORE YOU BEGIN

Pray and ask God to speak to you through His Holy Spirit. "THE PARACLETE, THE HOLY SPIRIT WHOM THE FATHER WILL SEND IN MY NAME, WILL INSTRUCT YOU IN EVERYTHING, AND REMIND YOU OF ALL THAT I TOLD YOU." (JOHN 14:26)

FIRST DAY   **Reread last week's readings.**

1.   What was a helpful or new thought from the readings or from the homily you heard on Sunday?

2.   From what you learned, what personal application did you choose to apply to your life this week?

SECOND DAY   **READ JEREMIAH 20:7-9**   **FIRST READING**

("But then it becomes like fire burning in my heart.")

1.   Who is speaking and to whom is he speaking? Jeremiah 20:1, 7

2.   How did the Word of the Lord come to Jeremiah, and what was his response? Jeremiah 1:4-7

3.   What did he say the Lord did to him, what happened, and why? Jeremiah 20:7

4.   What happens all the day long? Jeremiah 20:7

5.   Whenever he speaks, what is his message? Jeremiah 20:8

6.   What has the Word of the Lord brought to him? Jer 20:8

7.   What does Jeremiah say to himself? Jeremiah 20:9

8.   What happens to his heart and his bones when he does not speak out? Jeremiah 20:9

9.   Of what does Jeremiah grow weary, and what can he not endure? Jeremiah 20:9

10.   What did Paul say about preaching the Gospel? 1 Corinthians 9:16-17

Personal – In what way have you had a burning desire to teach or preach the Word of God since you have been studying his Word? Stop growing weary by holding it in, and share with those closest to you what the Lord has taught you.

THIRD DAY	**READ ROMANS 12:1-2**	**SECOND READING**

("…be transformed by the renewal of your mind,")

1. To whom is Paul speaking? Romans 1:7, Romans 12:1

2. What does he beg them to do to their bodies through the mercy of God, and how are they to do it? Romans 12:1

3. For what was Christ's death, once for all; and to what must we consider ourselves dead? Romans 6:10-11

4. For whom are we alive, and what must we not let our body do? Romans 6:11-12

5. To whom do we offer our body, and for what reason? Romans 6:13

6. To what must we not conform? Romans 12:2

7. By what must we be transformed, and for what reason? Romans 12:2

8. From where does renewal come? Titus 3:5

9. On what do we live that transforms the mind? Matthew 4:4

10. How can we judge God's will? John 12:44-48, concentrating on verse 48

Personal – Through your study of scripture, what way has God transformed your mind this week? How has that affected those around you? In what way have you worshipped God in your body? Is your body holy and acceptable for worship?

FOURTH DAY	**READ MATTHEW 16:21-27**	**GOSPEL**

(If a man wishes to come after me, he must deny his very self,…")

1. Where did Jesus say that he must go, what would happen there, and by whose hand? Matthew 16:21

2. What did Peter do and say to Jesus? Matthew 16:22

3. How did Jesus respond to Peter, whom did he say was an obstacle to him, and how did Jesus say Peter was thinking? Matthew 16:23

4. What kind of Jews are nothing other than members of Satan's assembly? Revelation 2:9

5. Whom did Jesus say a man must deny, what must he take up, and what must he begin to do? Matthew 16:24

6.   What happens to him who seeks only himself, and how do we discover who we are? Matthew 10:39

7.   What is not self-seeking? 1 Corinthians 13:5

8.   Whoever would save his life will do what, but whoever loses his life for Jesus sake will what? Matthew 16:25

9.   What two questions does Jesus ask his disciples in Matthew 16:26?

10.   When the Son of Man comes with his Father's glory accompanied by his angels, how will he repay each man? Matthew 16:27

11.   How do we follow in Jesus' footsteps? Matthew 25:31-40

Personal – Write down on a piece of paper things you have done this week that indicate a dying to self. Also, write down specific ways in which you are following Jesus. Read and meditate on Philippians 2:3-5. Give one specific way you deliberately thought of another's interest before your own interest.

FIFTH DAY   **READ PSALM 63:2-6, 8-9**

("…with lips of joy my mouth shall praise you.")

Read and meditate on Psalm 63:2-6, 8-9.

What is the Lord saying to you personally through the Psalm?

How can you apply this to your life?

SIXTH DAY   **READ ALL OF THE COMMENTARY**

JEREMIAH 20:7-9

Jeremiah was a prophet who served God for over 40 years. His message was coming to a nation that had rejected God and was sliding head long into ruin. Jeremiah was regarded as a meddler and a traitor. People, nobles and kings alternately tried to put him to death. Jeremiah had reached the point where, if he proclaimed God's word, people became angry. They did not want to hear the truth from him, because the truth would convict them of their sinfulness.

Jeremiah is considered "out of date," "not in the mainstream of today's theology," and "old fashioned." He becomes a laughing-stock of the countryside. When he would not proclaim God's Word because of the constant rejection, his whole body would constrict and his heart would become like a burning fire. He became weary of trying to hold it in and preach what the people wanted to hear. He could not do it because the call to truth was the call of God and he would not turn away from that call.

Do you speak God's holy truth when you are among your friends, or do you fall into line and speak what you think people want to hear? Jeremiah never felt he was qualified to be a prophet, and he never had a following of adoring fans. He chose to go on because his heart was burning like a fire for the Lord.

Today's passage is a tremendous message of hope to all of God's children, and that message is that God loves you. He formed you in your mother's womb, and he knows you by name (Jer. 1:4-7).
Do not let the voice of the world be your guide. Let the quiet whisper of God who spoke to Elijah in the cave be the source of your words.

People will laugh and mock us today for proclaiming God's word, but that is all right because the Lord is our shepherd and we shall not want (Psalm 23:1). A shepherd always protects his flock, and we have a shepherd who loves us so much he even died for us.

ROMANS 12:1-2

The call of God is so vibrant in the message of the New Testament. He is calling us to believe in his only begotten Son, Jesus, and if we do, we will have eternal life (John 3:16). This promise is made by God to the whole world. Yet much of the world has rejected this message which lets us live life in all of its fullness.

Why is so much of the world not living a life of fullness (John 10:10) when so many know about Jesus Christ? The answer is sin. To live abundantly we must serve the Lord, Jesus Christ. Jesus showed us how to be an example of service by dying for us on the cross. As stated in this reading from Romans, we are to "present our bodies" in voluntary surrender to the will of God. God must control the use of the whole person, and we are to present our bodies as a living and holy sacrifice.

We have been called to be temples of the Holy Spirit (1 Cor. 6:20), and we must set our sights on what is above (Col. 3:1-2). Our temple of the Holy Spirit does not include drugs, alcohol or fornication. The world laughs at the description of our being a temple of the Holy Spirit, but Jesus commands us to be filled with his Holy Spirit.

You, my Christian friends, have been transformed by the power of God and no longer conform to the agenda of the world. Because of the Holy Spirit who lives in you, you now have the power to conform to the good, acceptable and perfect will of God; and you will enjoy a life that is physically, emotionally and spiritually full. Let your mind be renewed by God's Holy Word, by spending time in quiet prayer and in fellowship with other Christians. And, finally, as the Psalmist so powerfully describes, "Be still and know that I am God." (Psalm 46:11)

MATTHEW 16:21-27

Discipleship is very costly, and yet, it is a cost that we can not afford to reject. A disciple is a learner who follows the teachings of the master. Jesus tells us that if we really wish to follow him, we are to take up our cross and carry it in his name. Jesus took up his cross and carried it to Calvary and allowed himself to be crucified for us. He dies on his cross so that you and I could have eternal life.

We are called to carry our cross daily and do the same things that Christ did. We are called to die to self and to put others before us (Phil. 2:2-4). We look around and see so much turmoil in our world, and the main reason is that many people do not want to pick up and carry their daily cross. The essence of sin is self and the only way that we break the bondage of sin is to die to self. It is in the losing of our life for Christ or in the dying to self that the saving of one's life happens. "Why are some people's crosses heavier than others?" is asked by many people. The more one dies to self on a daily basis, the lighter that cross becomes. We see people going through some horrendous events in their lives and there is a sense of inner peace and joy. This is a person who has yielded to the call of Christ and has cast all his cares upon the Lord (1 Peter 5:7).

When we yield to the power of the Holy Spirit, he will empower us to become disciples of the Lord, Jesus Christ. We can go out and make disciples of others (Matt. 28:19) only when we have learned to die to ourselves and live for Jesus Christ. To die for Christ is very noble; to live for Christ is much harder. It calls for a daily commitment. We need to remember that anything we achieve or own in this life will end when we die. When we die to ourselves and pick up our daily cross and live for others in Christ, we will live forever in victory with our Lord and Savior, Jesus Christ.

Application

The first reading shows us that perseverance is a virtue of a prophet. The second reading tells us to live the abundant life, and calls for a commitment of our mind, body and soul. This week's Gospel tells us that in order to live forever, we must die like Christ if we are to rise like Christ.

This week let us practice dying to ourselves in our family by trying to do some of the following:

Parents – set aside some time every day to share with each child and your spouse.

Children – find a time each day to serve a member of your family, such as helping a brother or sister do their chores. Help your parents around the home, or financially as they get older.

Everyone – Die to yourself in school or work by listening to others and really hearing what they have to say.

Remember, to lose our life for Christ is the best way to rise with Christ.

TWENTY-THIRD SUNDAY IN ORDINARY TIME - CYCLE A

BEFORE YOU BEGIN

Pray and ask God to speak to you through His Holy Spirit. "THE PARACLETE, THE HOLY SPIRIT WHOM THE FATHER WILL SEND IN MY NAME, WILL INSTRUCT YOU IN EVERYTHING, AND REMIND YOU OF ALL THAT I TOLD YOU." (JOHN 14:26)

FIRST DAY   **Reread last week's readings.**

1. What was a helpful or new thought from the readings or from the homily you heard on Sunday?

2. From what you learned, what personal application did you choose to apply to your life this week?

SECOND DAY   **READ EZEKIEL 33:7-9**   **FIRST READING**

("You, son of man, I have appointed watchman for the house of Israel.")

1. To whom did the Word of the Lord come, and who has been appointed watchman for the house of Israel? Ezekiel 1:3 3:17, and 33:7

2. What is Ezekiel to do for the Lord? Ezekiel 33:7

3. If the Lord tells the wicked man that he shall surely die, what was Ezekiel to do, and what will happen to the wicked man? Ezekiel 33:8

4. Who will be held responsible for the death of the wicked man? Ezekiel 33:8

5. What will happen if we do not speak out? Psalm 32:3

6. What happens to the wicked man, and how is he repaid? Isaiah 3:11

7. Who is the one who shall die? Ezekiel 18:20

8. How are we to warn the wicked man? Ezekiel 33:9

9. If he refuses to do this, what will happen to him, and what will happen to us? Ezekiel 33:9

10. What kind of a God do we have? Psalm 7:12

Personal - What do you say to those you see doing wrong within your household? What do you think will happen to you if you remain silent when you see those around you being sinful?

| THIRD DAY | READ ROMANS 13:8-10 | SECOND READING |

("You shall love your neighbor as yourself.")

1. What are we not to owe anyone, and what exception is there to this? Romans 13:8

2. What has he who loves his neighbor done? Romans 13:8

3. What is the virtue that binds all the rest together and makes them perfect? Colossians 3:14

4. What is all summed up in "You shall love your neighbor as yourself?" Romans 13:9

5. What did Jesus give us, and how are we to love one another? John 13:34

6. How are we to treat others? Matthew 7:12

7. What are we not to bear in our heart against our brother, and what are we not to take and cherish against our fellow countrymen? Leviticus 19:17-18

8. What does love never do, and what is the fulfillment of the law? Romans 13:10

9. What is love, and what does it not do? 1 Corinthians 13:4-7

10. Who is our neighbor? Luke 10:25-37, concentrating on verses 36-37

Personal – Have you seen anyone in need this week, and how did you respond to that need? In what way have you loved your neighbor? Write down a time you loved your neighbor each day this week.

| FOURTH DAY | READ MATTHEW 18:15-20 | GOSPEL |

("If your brother should commit a crime against you, go and point out his fault,")

1. If our brother should commit some wrong against us, what are we to do? Matthew 18:15

2. Who did Jesus say were brother, sister, and mother to him? Mark 3:35

3. After going to our brother who has wronged us, what have we done if he listens. If he does not listen, what should we do, and for what reason? Matthew 18:15-16

4. What is laid down in the law? John 8:17

5. If our brother ignores the others we have summoned, to whom do we refer him? Matthew 18:17

6. If the brother who committed the wrong ignores the church, how should we treat him? Matthew 18:17

7. Whom do we have no business judging, what should happen to those who bear the title "brother" and who is immoral? 1 Corinthians 5:9-13

8. Whatever we declare bound on earth shall be declared what, and whatever we declare loosed on earth shall be held what in heaven? Matthew 18:18

Personal – How have you dealt with someone who has wronged you, in comparison to the above scripture?

9. What does Jesus say will happen if two of you join your voices on earth to pray for anything whatsoever? Matthew 18:19

10. What must we do in order to receive anything from the Lord? Matthew 7:7, John 15:7

11. Who is present when two or three are gathered in his name? Matthew 18:20

Personal – With whom have you joined your voice in prayer this week, and what has been the result?

FIFTH DAY   **READ PSALM 95:1-2, 6-9**

("Let us acclaim the rock of our salvation.")

Read and meditate on Psalm 95: 1-2, 6-9.

What is the Lord saying to you personally through the Psalm?

How can you apply this to your life?

SIXTH DAY   **READ ALL OF THE COMMENTARY**

EZEKIEL 33:7-9

This passage tells us that God will hold us responsible for not speaking out in defense of his name to those who violate his teachings. We cannot say that it is not our responsibility to speak out because we are not qualified. Ezekiel tells us that God has called us to warn the wicked man of his wrong doings or to face up to the responsibility of his death.

Today there is a strong emphasis to turn the other way concerning wrong doing. A major philosophy of today seems to be, that if it does not affect me, why should I complain. For example: the rate of crime is staggering in many countries; the breakdown of the family is accepted as a price of progress. A tremendous financial profit is being made today in the areas of pornography, child pornography, prostitution, drugs, alcohol, smoking, and abortion.

Scripture tells us the wages of sin are death (Rom. 6:23), yet we remain incredibly silent with our Christian response to this barrage of filth. The essence of all sin is self, and it is the gratification of self that is tearing countries apart. The result of sin is death, and if we do not believe this, take a look around our communities and see the effects of sin. Many times the deaths and horror from AIDS are the results of drugs and immorality that can be passed on even to innocent victims in blood transfusions. Children are born infected with the dreaded disease through no fault of their own.

The rate of abortions has climbed to about 70 million a year worldwide. There has to be an end to the millions of people becoming zombies through the use of drugs and alcohol. Cigarettes kill more people than drugs and alcohol combined, and yet there is a silence in the Christian world. Silence indicates to many a degree of acceptance of the conditions.

I pray that you speak out in the name of Jesus and protest the wrongdoing that is going on in your own heart, your family, your community and your country.

ROMANS 13:8-10

St. Paul calls us to a complete sense of freedom in that we owe no man anything except our love. Jesus gives us his commandment, "Love one another as I have loved you." (John 13:34). Jesus went further when he tells us all to love God with our whole heart, mind, and spirit and to love our neighbor as ourselves.

To many people today that does not offer much, especially when self-esteem, self-image or self-love have never been established. There are millions of people walking around who do not feel that self-worth or feel they are worthy of being loved. Jesus knows that and consequently he said, "Love one another as I have loved you." You are so precious, and so valuable, that God sent his only begotten son to die on the cross at Calvary just for you.

Jesus loves us completely and unconditionally, and he loves us wherever we are. The incredible part of this statement is that he loves us to the extent that he will not leave us as we are. He will transform you if you will let him. Right now he is knocking at the door of your heart while you are reading this study (Rev. 3:20). Try to look for a picture showing Jesus knocking on the door and you will see something very powerful. There is no door handle on the door; it opens only from within. He will love you with an everlasting love. People perish simply because of the lack of knowledge of who he is and of his great love for them (Hosea 4:6).

We are told that God is love and that we love him because we learn that he has loved us first. God is love. Love is patient. Love is kind. Love bears all things. Love believes all things. Love is hope. Love endures all things, and love is the fulfillment of the law. Jesus tells us that if we live in him and keep his commandments, then he will live in us (John 15:7). To love your neighbors as yourself really means that God loved you so much that he died for you. We have to die to ourselves and be willing to do whatever it takes to help anyone who is in need of God's love and mercy.

MATTHEW 18:15-20

The Gospel message tells us today that we are to go to our brother and tell him of his fault of sinning. Many ask today, "Who is my brother?" Jesus tells us in scripture that all who do the will of his Father are his brother, sister and mother (Mark 3:35). You can lovingly confront our brother or sister in Christ, if they are suffering or in pain but it should be done privately. (A wound will fester if it is not tended or healed right away.) If they listened to you and the problem is not resolved, then you know that the problem does not lie with you, it allows you to forgive that person so that he may become healed.

Today, bitterness and divisiveness rage among Christians because of misunderstandings. We are told in Scripture that we will be insulted because of our Christian beliefs and conduct and whoever is called on to suffer should not be ashamed but to give thanks and glory to God (1 Peter 4:16). We are not called to judge the pagans or unbelievers, rather we are called to confront the "brother in the Lord" who is living in sin. This can be done only in love and in accordance with Scripture.

Jesus tells us that even our love of family is not to come between him and ourselves. Also Jesus tells us that he is always present in our midst. Whenever we come together to pray in his name, our requests will be honored by his Father in heaven. We need to remember that to pray in his name means to be completely immersed in prayer with him. His name is all-powerful, all-knowing, and all-healing. Scripture tells us that every knee shall bend and every tongue shall confess that Jesus Christ is Lord (Phil. 2:11). To pray in his name means to have released all unforgiveness toward others. It means to confess all unrepented sins. To pray in his name means to remove all the blocks towards healing within ourselves.

When we pray in his name, whatever we bind on earth will be bound in heaven, and whatever we loose on earth will be loosed in heaven (Matt. 19:18). Then in Jesus' name we can bind the evil in one of our sinful brothers, and in Jesus' name loose upon that person the power of the Holy Spirit. Joy, peace, love - the Holy Spirit brings all that heavenly power and faith. In Jesus' name the honor and glory of the Father are accomplished. We can be an expectant pray-er every time we pray in Jesus' name because we have his Word on it (Matthew 18:19-20).

Application

The first reading tells us that we are responsible for speaking out in faith, and we are called to address the sinful actions of others. The second reading tells us that love is not love until it is freely given away to others, without any conditions. The Gospel tells us to confront one another lovingly in the name of Jesus when their conduct is out of order.

This week, speak lovingly but frankly and privately, to one of your loved ones who is not walking with the Lord. Remember, your silence may indicate that you agree with that person's actions.

TWENTY-FOURTH SUNDAY IN ORDINARY TIME - CYCLE A

BEFORE YOU BEGIN

Pray and ask God to speak to you through His Holy Spirit. "THE PARACLETE, THE HOLY SPIRIT WHOM THE FATHER WILL SEND IN MY NAME, WILL INSTRUCT YOU IN EVERYTHING, AND REMIND YOU OF ALL THAT I TOLD YOU." (JOHN 14:26)

FIRST DAY   **Reread last week's readings.**

1.   What was a helpful or new thought from the readings or from the homily you heard on Sunday?

2.   From what you learned, what personal application did you choose to apply to your life this week?

SECOND DAY   **READ SIRACH 27:30-28:7**   **FIRST READING**

("Forgive your neighbor's injustice.")

1.   What are hateful things, and what does the sinner do with them? Sirach 27:30

2.   What are we to keep in mind, and what does man's anger not fulfill? James 1:19-20

3.   What will the vengeful suffer, and for what reason? Sirach 28:1

4.   Who says, "Vengeance is mine: I will repay? " Romans 12:19

5.   If we forgive our neighbor's injustice, what will happen, when we pray? Sirach 28:2

6.   What did Jesus say to the Father as he was dying on the cross? Luke 23:34

7.   In whom has God forgiven us? Ephesians 4:32

8.   If a person nourishes anger against another person, what can he expect from the Lord? Sirach 28:3

9.   What are the questions asked in verses four and five of Sirach 28?

10. What are we to set aside, what are we to remember, and from what are we to cease? Sirach 28:6

11. Who are we not to hate, whose covenant are we to remember, and what are we to overlook? Sirach 28:7

Personal – Pray and ask the Lord to reveal to you any anger you may be harboring against anyone. What gives you the strength to forgive when you were innocent and unjustly treated?

THIRD DAY **READ ROMANS 14:7-9** **SECOND READING**

("While we live we are responsible to the Lord.")

1. What does not one of us do? Romans 14:7

2. What example did Jesus give us to follow on how to live, and what is no slave greater than? John 13:12-16

3. While we live, to whom are we responsible? Romans 14:8

4. When we die, as what do we die? Romans 14:8

5. To whom do we belong in both life and death? Romans 14:8

6. The slave called in the Lord is what, and how have we been bought? 1 Corinthians 7:22-23

7. Why did Christ die and come to life again? Romans 14:9

8. Who is set apart by God to judge both the living and the dead? Acts 10:36-42

9. What is the blessed and only ruler called? 1 Timothy 6:15

10. What must every tongue proclaim to the glory of God the Father? Philippians 2:11

Personal – In what way have you submitted to the Lordship of Jesus Christ? Is it partial or total submission? How has this submission been visible to your family, friends, schoolmates, or work acquaintances?

FOURTH DAY **READ MATTHEW 18:21-35** **GOSPEL**

("My Lord, be patient with me and I will pay back in full.")

1. Who was speaking, and what did he ask the Lord? Matthew 18:21

2. When Jesus told his disciples how to pray, what did he say to do regarding forgiveness? Matthew 6:12

3. What was Jesus' reply to forgiving seven times? Matthew 18:22

4. To what may the reign of God be compared? Matthew 18:23

5. As the king began his auditing one was brought in who owed him a huge amount of money, what did his master order in payment of the debt? Matthew 18:24-25

6.   What did the official do and say? Matthew 18:26

7.   With what was the master moved, and what did he do? Matthew 18:27

8.   What did that same official do when he met a fellow servant? Matthew 18:28

9.   What did his fellow servant do and say, and what did he have done with him? Matthew 18:29-30

10.   When his fellow servants saw what had happened, what was their reaction, where did they go, and what did they do? Matthew 18:31

11.   When his master sent for him, what did he say to him? Matthew 18:32-33

12.   What did he do in anger? Matthew 18:34

13.   What did Jesus say his Heavenly Father would do, and what are we to do? Matthew 18:34-35

14.   What judges the thoughts and reflections of the heart? Hebrews 4:12

Personal - For what major flaw in you did Jesus die on the cross and forgive you? What major flaw do you need to forgive in a brother or sister? Be specific.

FIFTH DAY   **READ PSALM 103:1-4, 9-12**

("Not according to our sins does he deal with us.")

Read and meditate on Psalm 103:1-4, 9-12.

What is the Lord saying to you personally through the Psalm?

How can you apply this to your life?

SIXTH DAY   **READ ALL OF THE COMMENTARY**

SIRACH 27:30-28:7

"Father, forgive these people, they do not know what they are doing (Luke 23:34)." Jesus asked his Father to forgive the people who were putting him to death. God answered that prayer by opening up the way of salvation to everyone.

Today's passage reveals to us that vengeance for us comes from the Lord only (Romans 12:19). We are told that mercy will come only to those who show mercy and that we will be pardoned for our sins in the same measure that we pardon those who have sinned against us.

You and I do not ever have to refuse mercy to anyone, because we have been forgiven by Jesus Christ whose death paid the price of our redemption. His blood has washed us clean.

Because he has forgiven us, we can forgive others. The pain of being hurt physically, emotionally, sexually, or even spiritually, can be so devastating that it seems vengeance is more justifiable. Sometimes it seems more logical just to run away from the pain inside.

As you are reading this, let Jesus come into your heart and let him go to the point of the pain in your entire being. Say, "Come, Holy Spirit, give me the power to forgive as my brother Jesus forgives." He will heal you and renew your mind (Romans 12:2). He will take up residence in your heart and he will give you a heart of flesh in place of that heart of stone. He will be your rock, your fortress, your refuge (Psalm 91). He will anoint your head with healing oil, and you will dwell in his house forever (Psalm 23).

We will learn to give mercy because he resides in our temple (1 Corinthians 6:20). We will pardon those who have injured us because we have been pardoned for all of our sins (Matt. 6:12). Let us remember to be quick to hear, slow to anger, and slow to speak (James 1:19, 20) for the wrath of a man does not show righteousness to God.

ROMANS 14:7-9

The only person who was ever born to die for us was Jesus Christ. He lived and died for all mankind. He died for all of the sinners in the world. His death paid the price that freed humanity from the bondage of Satan.

All mankind did not decide to accept his incredible gift, and consequently, we see a tremendous conflict between good and evil. For God so loved the world that he gave his only Son, so that everyone who believes in him might not perish but have eternal life (John 3:16).

Jesus was born to be the suffering servant of mankind and to be its Lord and Savior. Today we see many people who live in the belief that it is their own talents and drive that determines their fate. We see many cultures who claim we have to be tough and independent to get ahead. Meekness is confused with weakness in many parts of our society. Love of God, family and country is considered by some to be sentimental foolishness.

Jesus called us to be foot washers in the world (John 13:3-17). He called us to be servants to our neighbors and to love one another as he has loved us (John 13:34). He tells us our freedom has been bought at a high price, and that price was his blood (1 Corinthians 7:22-23). He calls from us a submission to him and a sub-mission to one another. We are to think of others first.

We are to put on the mind of Christ (Phil 2:2-11). We are called to live for Christ because he has died for us so that we might live forever. He is our Lord and when we die we will spend eternity in his loving presence.

I encourage you to stop what you are doing right now, get down on your knees, and confess that Jesus Christ is the Lord of your life. He stands at the door of your heart. Open that door and invite him in, and let him heal you today (Rev. 3:20).

MATTHEW 18:21-35

We are told in today's Gospel that if we do not forgive those who have offended us, neither will God forgive us of our offenses to him. In the days of Christ there was a Jewish custom that a person had to forgive someone only three times for having offended you. It was considered acceptable to demand punishment on the fourth offense.

Peter thought he was being very generous by suggesting to forgive someone seven times. He was startled to hear Jesus tell him that, in effect, we should always forgive those who repentant, no matter how many times they ask.

Today's story tells us the serious consequences that awaited those who could not repay their debts. It was not uncommon to see a debtor remain in prison for the remainder of his life. Think about that for a moment. Not one of us is capable of paying off our own debt to God. Jesus Christ had to die on the cross for us, and he paid the ransom for our sins with his life. If we were at any time to be judged as to how well we paid off our own debts, heaven would be empty.

How many times have you asked the Lord to forgive you and you received his forgiveness in the beautiful Sacrament of Reconciliation? How many times did you then go on to fall to the seduction of temptation. God, in his incredible mercy, has put no limit on the number of times we are allowed to fall.

The road to eternal life would be empty and very long if God limited us to only a limited number of times to be forgiven. We have a God who loves us so much that he stands knocking at the door to our hearts, patiently waiting to come in to heal us as well as to forgive us (Rev 3:20).

Today, Jesus impresses us with the fact that forgiveness is a decision, and it is a decision to love. Jesus tells us in the last sentence of today's parable that his Father will do to us what we do to others (Matt. 18:35). Jesus tells us in Scripture that whatever we do to the least of his brothers, we do unto him (Matt. 25:31-41).

Jesus has shown us that his actions back up his words. While dying on the cross he looked up at his Father and said, "Father, forgive them for they do not know what they are doing." (Luke 23:34) My dear brothers and sisters in Christ, we are called today to do no less, and that is to forgive others who have offended us.

Application

The first reading shows us that vengeance comes from God, not from us. The second reading tells us that humility belongs to the character of Christ. The Gospel reveals that forgiveness is not an option for the Christian, it is a requirement that we extend it to others as God has extended it to us.

This week, approach a family member, friend, or co-worker against whom you hold a grudge, and ask them to forgive you. Holding on to any resentment, bitterness or unforgiveness towards them is what you ask in forgiveness. Remember, through forgiveness comes healing.

TWENTY-FIFTH SUNDAY IN ORDINARY TIME - CYCLE A

BEFORE YOU BEGIN

Pray and ask God to speak to you through His Holy Spirit. "THE PARACLETE, THE HOLY SPIRIT WHOM THE FATHER WILL SEND IN MY NAME, WILL INSTRUCT YOU IN EVERYTHING, AND REMIND YOU OF ALL THAT I TOLD YOU." (JOHN 14:26)

FIRST DAY   **Reread last week's readings.**

1.   What was a helpful or new thought from the readings or from the homily you heard on Sunday?

2.   From what you learned, what personal application did you choose to apply to your life this week?

SECOND DAY   **READ ISAIAH 55:6-9**   **FIRST READING**

("Let him turn to the Lord for mercy.")

1.   Whom do we seek while he may be found? Isaiah 55:6

2.   What must we do while he is near? Isaiah 55:6

3.   With what must we seek the Lord? Jeremiah 29:13-14, Deuteronomy 4:29

4.   What are we to let the scoundrel do, and the wicked man? Isaiah 55:7

5.   To whom must the scoundrel and the wicked turn, and what will be given to them? Isaiah 55:7

6.   In what is our God generous? Isaiah 55:7

7.   What has the Lord done with our sins, and what is he asking us to do? Isaiah 44:22

8.   What are the Lord's thoughts and ways not like? Isaiah 55:8

9.   As high as what are his ways above our ways and his thoughts above our thoughts? Isaiah 55:9

10.   What does God do, and what does he not do? Numbers 23:19

Personal - In what way have you experienced the greatness and mercy of God? In what way has he revealed to you that his way is far superior to the way you thought something should be done? What did you do when he revealed this to you?

| THIRD DAY | READ PHILIPPIANS 1:20-24, 27 | SECOND READING |

("For, to me, `life' means Christ, hence dying is so much gain.")

1. Who is writing this letter, and to whom is he writing? Philippians 1:1

2. What does Paul firmly trust and anticipate? Philippians 1:20

3. In what does he have full confidence? Philippians 1:20

4. Of what does Paul not dare to speak when trying to win the Gentiles to obedience by word and deed? Romans 15:18

5. What does "life" mean to Paul, and what is dying? Philippians 1:21

6. What is the life Paul lives, of what is his human life, and in whom is his life? Galatians 2:20

7. If we are to go on living in the flesh, what does that mean? Philippians 1:22

8. To what is Paul attracted, and from what does he long to be free? Philippians 1:23

9. What is the more urgent, and for whose sake? Philippians 1:24

10. How are we to conduct ourselves, and if we do this, what will be clear? Philippians 1:27

Personal – What do you prefer, to live or die? Why? What spiritual insight has the Lord revealed to you personally in this reading? How can you apply it to your life?

| FOURTH DAY | READ MATTHEW 20:1-16 | GOSPEL |

("Thus the last shall be first and the first shall be last.")

1. The reign of God can be compared to the owner of an estate who went out at dawn to do what? What did he reach with the workmen for the usual daily wage, and then, what did he do? Matthew 20:1-2

2. When the owner came out about midmorning, what did he see? What did he say to them? What did he say he would pay them? Matthew 20:3-4

3. What did the owner find at noon and mid-afternoon? What did he say to those he found in late afternoon? Matthew 20:5-6

4. What did they say to the owner, and what did he tell them to do? What did the owner of the vineyard say to his foreman? Matthew 20:7-8

5. When those hired late in the afternoon came for their pay, what did they receive? What did the first group suppose? Matthew 20:9-10

6.   What did they receive, what was their complaint to the owner, and what was his response? Matthew 20:11-13

7.   What did the owner tell them to do, and what did he intend to do? Matthew 20:14

8.   In Matthew 20:15, what two questions did he ask the workers?

9.   What do envy and anger do? Sirach 30:24

10.   How does God give to all? James 1:5

11.   Who will be first, and who will be last? Matthew 20:16

Personal - How do you see yourself, as the one receiving much for little done or as receiving little for much work done? How do you feel about this, and how do you deal with your feelings? Go to the Lord and repent of any envy you may have been holding. Seek the Sacrament of Reconciliation this week.

FIFTH DAY   **READ PSALM 145: 2-3, 8-9, 17-18**

("The Lord is gracious and merciful.")

Read and meditate on Psalm 145: 2-3, 8-9, 17-18.

What is the Lord saying to you personally through the Psalm?

How can you apply this to your life?

SIXTH DAY   **READ ALL OF THE COMMENTARY**

ISAIAH 55:6-9

This passage tells us that first we seek his kingship and then all else will be added (Matt. 6:33). The desire to seek his will is a gift of grace from God. We are called to yield to that gift and then respond to it in faith. The Jews had a prayer called the "Shema" (Deut. 6:4-8) that supported this revelation.

We are called to relate the Word of God in our daily lives. God has emphasized the importance of parents to teach Scripture to their children. The church and Christian schools can not always be used to escape this responsibility. Today eternal truths are most effectively learned in the loving environment of a God-fearing home, just as in the time of Moses.

Jesus tells us that loving God with all of our heart, soul and mind is the greatest command and to love our neighbor as ourself is the greatest rule of all. These two commands of his encompass all of Scripture.

We need to know, study and live out his daily Word so that our ways will be his ways. He will reveal his holy will to us, but we have to hunger and thirst to seek for him, for he is a gentle and loving God who seeks us more than we seek him. He stands always ready at the door to our heart, waiting for us to let him come in (Rev. 3:20).

What is really incredible is that he wants to come in and dine with us. In the early Bible days, the act of eating with someone was a very special sign of friendship. You did not eat with just anyone. Jesus wants to become intimate with us. He wishes to reside in our temple (1 Cor. 6:20). He rushes in and he does everything. All we have to do is open our hearts and let him in. That is why his thoughts and ways are not like ours, because he wants only to heal and love us.

PHILIPPIANS 1:20-24, 27

This was not to be Paul's final imprisonment in Rome. He knew that he could be either released or executed, and it was in this atmosphere that he was filled with joy. The secret of Paul's joy while in prison was his personal relationship with Jesus. Today people desperately want to be happy, but are tossed and turned by their daily successes, failures, and inconveniences. In other words, they are looking to the wrong source for their joy. To those who do not believe in God, life on earth is all there will be for them. So as the television commercial states, they go for the "gusto," or try to get as much as they can as quickly as they can.

Paul saw life as developing eternal values and telling others about Jesus Christ, and this is what a messenger of the king is called to tell his people. We are that messenger. We are that prophet and like Paul, we will have to tell others that money, popularity, power and prestige are only temporary values in this world. Similar to Paul, we are to speak out boldly for Christ and to become more like him in the way we live out our daily lives.

Paul sees dying as more superior than living, because he knew that in death he would be spared from the troubles of the world and would see Christ face to face (1 John 3:2,3). To be ready to die is to be ready to live for Christ. It is only when we die to ourselves and put on the "mind of Christ" that we are really able to live (Phil. 2:5-11). Once we know our purpose in life is to love others as Christ has loved us, then we are free to serve. Then, and only then, can we devote our life to what really counts without the fear of dying.

MATTHEW 20: 1-16

Today's Gospel is not concerned with rewards but with salvation. It is a powerful teaching about the incredible gift called grace that God gives to us. The story is not quite how we earn our way to heaven, because that would be impossible. Jesus clarified the membership rules of the kingdom of heaven. Entrance to heaven is by God's grace alone.

In today's story, God is the estate owner and the believers are those who work for him. In early Christianity there were many who felt superior because of heritage or favored positions, just as today. There were those who felt superior because they had spent so much time with Christ and knew so much about him. The message in this story was a reassurance of God's grace to the new believers.

We should not resent anyone who turns to God in the last moments of life, because, in reality, no one deserves eternal life. Many people we do not expect to see may be in the Kingdom. The thief who repented on the cross will be next to Jesus (Luke 23:40-43) as well as the people who have believed and served God all of their lives.

Think for a moment about your life. Do you resent God for allowing all those outcasts and sinners into heaven, and those who turn to him at the last moment of their lives? Are you ever jealous of what God has given to someone else? I challenge you to reflect on God's gracious gift of grace in your life. Focus on the benefits given to you and give praise and thanksgiving for what you have received. He has given you eternal life (John 3:16). He has loved you so much he died for you. He has given you another chance to love every time you begin a brand-new day.

If you do not have any friends, then invite him into your heart to be your friend. (John 15:13-15). He will change your life immediately, and you will, in return, change others with your joy and testimony (Matt. 28:19). Jesus is our owner, our shepherd, and our Savior, and he wants us to be healed and made whole (John 10:10).

The bottom line is – the generous gift of God's grace and our follow through on it are what allows us to be eligible to enter heaven. The result of accepting that grace in faith will be shown by the way we live our lives on earth.

Application

The first reading tells us to first seek the kingship of God and then all else will be given unto you (Matt. 6:33). The second reading tells how personal relationships with Christ can bring joy and peace even in very difficult circumstances. The Gospel tells us how grace and our response to it bring us into heaven.

This week, show how you value yourself, your family, your school and your work associates by being very generous with your time, money, and talent. Some examples: Spend time with someone who is sick or lonely, financially help someone you know who is struggling, share with someone a talent or a gift that you have. Remember, grace is the presence of God in your relationship with others.

TWENTY-SIXTH SUNDAY IN ORDINARY TIME – CYCLE A

BEFORE YOU BEGIN

Pray and ask God to speak to you through His Holy Spirit. "THE PARACLETE, THE HOLY SPIRIT WHOM THE FATHER WILL SEND IN MY NAME, WILL INSTRUCT YOU IN EVERYTHING, AND REMIND YOU OF ALL THAT I TOLD YOU." (JOHN 14:26)

FIRST DAY   **Reread last week's readings.**

1.   What was a helpful or new thought from the readings or from the homily you heard on Sunday?

2.   From what you learned, what personal application did you choose to apply to your life this week?

SECOND DAY   **READ EZEKIEL 18:25-28**   **FIRST READING**

("Is it my way that is unfair, or rather, are not your ways unfair?")

1.   What do we say about the Lord's way? Ezekiel 18:25

2.   What is the question asked in Ezekiel 18:25?

3.   How does the judge of all the world act? Genesis 18:25

4.   When a virtuous man turns away from virtue to commit iniquity and dies, what causes it that he must die? Ezekiel 18:26

5.   If a wicked man, turning from the wickedness he has committed, does what is right and just, what shall he preserve? Ezekiel 18:27

6.   What is right and just? Psalm 119:137,144

7.   Fill in the following blanks: Since the wicked man has turned away from _____ the sins which he has committed, he shall surely _____, he shall not die. Ezekiel 18:28

8.   Read the following Scriptures and write out what causes you to turn around.
     Numbers 32:15 _____ Deut. 5:32-33 _____
     Psalm 34:14-15 _____ Acts 3:19 _____.

Personal – Have you ever felt you were being treated unfairly? What caused the unfair treatment, and what was the result? What has caused you to turn to the Lord?

THIRD DAY	**READ PHILIPPIANS 2:1-11**	**SECOND READING**

("Jesus Christ is Lord.")

1. What does Paul say is owed to him in Christ? What can love bring, and what does fellowship in the Spirit bring? Philippians 2:1

2. How can they make his joy complete and in what is the one love united? Philippians 2:2

3. Who enables us to live in perfect harmony with others, and of what is he the source? Romans 15:5

4. How are we **never** to act, and how should we think of others? Philippians 2:3

5. For whom are we to show interest, and what must be our attitude? Philippians 2:4-5

6. How must we estimate ourselves? Romans 12:3

7. In what form was Jesus, and with whom did he **not** deem equality? Philippians 2:6

8. What did Jesus do? What form did he take, and in whose likeness was he born? Philippians 2:7

9. In what way did he humble himself by accepting death on a cross? Philippians 2:8

10. What did God do to Jesus, what did he bestow on him, and what must every knee do at the name of Jesus? Philippians 2:9-10

11. In the heavens, on the earth, and under the earth every tongue must proclaim what to the glory of the Father? Philippians 2:11

Personal - In what ways do you show those in your family, your friends, your schoolmates, or your co-workers that you see them as more important than yourself?

FOURTH DAY	**READ MATTHEW 21:28-32**	**GOSPEL**

("No, I will not; but afterwards he regretted it and went.")

1. Who is asking about the man with the two sons, and where is Jesus speaking? Matthew 21:23

2. With what did the man approach his elder son, and what did the son say and do? Matthew 21:28-29

3. When the man came to his second son and said the same thing, what was his reply? Matthew 21:30

4.   After the second son said he would not go, what happened to him?
     Matthew 21:30

5.   What produces repentance without regrets? 2 Cor 7:10

6.   Who did they say did what the father wanted? Matthew 21:31

7.   Who did Jesus say was entering the kingdom of God before them? Matthew 21:31

8.   What did the entire populace receive from John, and what did the Pharisees and
     the lawyers fail to receive? Luke 7:29-30

9.   When John came preaching a way of holiness, what did they not do? What did the
     prostitutes and tax collectors do? Matthew 21:32

10. Even when the chief priests and elders saw them putting their faith in him, what
     two things did they fail to do? Matthew 21:32

Personal – How can you relate to the Scripture verse, "No, I will not, but afterwards he regretted it and went." Matthew 21:30. Share a specific incident.

FIFTH DAY   **READ PSALM 25:4-9**

("Guide me in your truth and teach me.")

Read and meditate on Psalm 25:4-9.

What is the Lord saying to you personally through the Psalm?

How can you apply this to your life?

SIXTH DAY   **READ ALL OF THE COMMENTARY**

EZEKIEL 18:25-28

In the days of Ezekiel some of the people of Judah believed they were being punished for the sins of their ancestors, rather than for their own sins. Ezekiel is bringing home the reality that everyone is responsible for their own sin.

Today, we hear many people trying to shift the blame of their sinfulness on to others. It is true that we often suffer from the effects of sins committed by those who came before us. It is also true that we can not use their mistakes as an excuse for our sins.

Ezekiel shows us that God is not only a God of love, but he is also a God of perfect justice. His love which is perfect causes him to be merciful to those who recognize their sinfulness and turn back to him. God hates sin and will not tolerate it, and he will not wink at those who willfully sin.

We all like to hear that God is love, but we become a little uncomfortable when we hear he is also a God of justice. We are called to love one another as God has loved us (John 13:34). This means we are not to retaliate or brood over wrongdoing against us. For many, a common response to a difficult circumstance is to say, "That isn't fair." In reality, God is perfect justice because he is perfect love.

Many of us turn to the Lord because we finally realize that we can not make it through life without the protection and love of Jesus Christ. We must remember that it is not God who must live up to our ideas of fairness and justice, but it is our responsibility to live up to God's standards. We are challenged not to look for loopholes in God's law, instead we are to decide to work toward living up to his standards. We do that through prayer, scripture, sacraments and fellowship in the church.

PHILIPPIANS 2:1-11

Paul is exhorting the members of the community to be humble and Christ-like to each other. Today we would do well to take to heart this very message. To be humble is a gift that is like a precious stone which never loses its value. To be humble is to put others first and ourselves second.

Today, there is much talk about the need for a healthy self-esteem. Paul tells us in Scripture not to go too far in self-love. There are many people who think too little of themselves and some who think too much of themselves. The key to an honest and accurate evaluation is knowing that the basis of our self worth is in our identity in Christ.

Apart from Christ we are not worth a great amount by eternal standards. In him our worth as creations of God is priceless. We must always evaluate ourselves in God's eyes and not in the world's eyes. Many people today, including Christians, live only to make a good impression on others or to please themselves. This self-centered type of living sows the seeds of discord.

Paul is calling for spiritual unity by asking the Philippians, as well as us, to love one another and to work together with one heart and purpose. When we work together and care for the problems of others, we are living out the example of Christ by putting others first. This is what brings unity in a marriage, a family, a congregation, a parish, a nation and, finally, the whole world.

Being humble means having a true perspective of ourselves (Romans 12:3). It does not mean that we should put ourselves down. We realize that we are all sinners saved by God's grace and we have a tremendous worth in God's kingdom. We can place ourselves in Jesus' hands and humbly let ourselves be used by him to spread his Word and share his love with others.

MATTHEW 21:28-32

The way we live our lives is truly what we profess to believe. The way we treat others is truly the way we profess our faith in God. Scripture tells us that if we say we love God and hate our brother, then we are liars.

The parable of the two sons strikes at the very heart of what is wrong in today's society. Many people pretend that they are following Christ. They say it and even sing it in some songs, but their lives do not prove it. The Pharisees gave the impression that they were very obedient to God's will by keeping all the external signs of their religion. We have that today in our society. We have those who make great financial contributions but live with their own set of values. We can fool others about our inner intentions, but it is dangerous to pretend to obey God when our hearts are distant from him. God knows the intentions of our hearts. Our actions must always match our words.

In today's Gospel passage we see the first son say, "no," then regrets his action and becomes obedient to his father. True repentance means being sorry for our sins and to change our behavior. Paul tells us that occasionally God uses sorrow in our lives to help us turn away from selfishness and to come back to God. Compare Peter's remorse and repentance with Judas' bitterness. Both of these men denied Christ. One repented and was restored to faith and service. The other ended with his life in disgrace.

Let us, as Jesus did, be obedient and humble in our relationships with others (Phil. 2:2-11). Jesus calls us to love one another as he has loved us (John 13:34). He also tells us that he will abide in us if we keep his commandments (John 15:7). Jesus gave us his two greatest commandments, "Love your God with all your heart, mind and spirit, and love your neighbor as yourself." We can do this only when we are obedient to God's word. Remember, we are all sinners and we are saved only by God's grace and not by our own deeds.

Application

This week's first reading tells of being accountable for your own sins. The second reading reveals the power of humility which brings unity. The Gospel tells us that actions speak louder than words.

This week, let us show our accountability in what we say and do by not being selfish. The cure for selfishness is servanthood, which is being like Christ. Do something beautiful for God by doing something pleasing for members of your family, school and work area. Do not let them know your intentions. Show others that your actions in humility and caring are what you really believe and live. When you say "yes," mean it; and when you say "no," ask yourself, "What would Jesus say at this time?"

TWENTY-SEVENTH SUNDAY IN ORDINARY TIME – CYCLE A

BEFORE YOU BEGIN

Pray and ask God to speak to you through His Holy Spirit. "THE PARACLETE, THE HOLY SPIRIT WHOM THE FATHER WILL SEND IN MY NAME, WILL INSTRUCT YOU IN EVERYTHING, AND REMIND YOU OF ALL THAT I TOLD YOU." (JOHN 14:26)

FIRST DAY   **Reread last week's readings.**

1.   What was a helpful or new thought from the readings or from the homily you heard on Sunday?

2.   From what you learned, what personal application did you choose to apply to your life this week?

SECOND DAY   **READ ISAIAH 5:1-7**   **FIRST READING**

("What more was there to do for my vineyard that I had not done?")

1.   For whom and for what shall we sing in Isaiah 5:1?

2.   What does my friend have, and what kind of a hillside is it on? Isaiah 5:1

3.   What did he do with it, what did he build within it, and what did he hew out? Isaiah 5:2

4.   Who are the true vine and the vine grower? John 15:1

5.   When he looked for the crop of grapes, what had it yielded? Isaiah 5:2

6.   Between what two things must the inhabitants of Jerusalem and the people of Judah judge? Isaiah 5:3-4

7.   How did the vine turn out to the Lord? Jeremiah 2:21

8.   What did he mean to do with his vineyard? Isaiah 5:5-6

9.   Who is the vineyard of the Lord of hosts, and who are the cherished plants? Isaiah 5:7

10.   The Lord looked for judgment and justice, but what did he see and hear? Isaiah 5:7

Personal – List some of the things the Lord has done for you in cultivating and preparing your soil. What kinds of fruit are you bearing?

THIRD DAY   READ PHILIPPIANS 4:6-9   SECOND READING

("Dismiss all anxiety from your minds.")

1. What are we not to have at all, and in everything, how are we to make our requests known to God? Philippians 4:6

2. What does anxiety do to a person's heart? Proverbs 12:25

3. What are we to do with all our worries? 1 Peter 5:7

4. How often and for whom are we to pray? Ephesians 6:18, 1 Timothy 2:1

5. What does the peace of God surpass, and what will it do to our hearts and minds in Christ Jesus? Philippians 4:7

6. When Jesus left to go to the Father, what did he tell his followers he would leave with them? John 15:26

7. What keeps a nation in peace? Isaiah 26:3

8. About what eight things are we to think? Philippians 4:8

9. About what are we to seek and think? Colossians 3:1-2

10. What does Paul tell the Philippians to keep on doing, and who will be with them? Philippians 4:9

Personal - Evaluate your thinking for the last 24 hours. What did you think about the eight ways to find peace taken from Philippians 4:8?

FOURTH DAY   READ MATTHEW 21:33-43   GOSPEL

("The very stone which the builders rejected has become the head of the corner.")

1. What did the property owner do to the vineyard he planted, and to whom did he lease it? Matthew 21:33

2. What did the property owner do at vintage time, and how did the tenants respond? Matthew 21:34-35

3. What did the property owner do a second time, and how were the slaves treated? Matthew 21:36

4. Whom did he finally send, and how did he feel they would treat him? Matthew 21:37

5. What did the tenants say when they saw the vineyard owner's son? Matthew 21:38

6. Whom has God made heir of all things? Hebrews 1:1-2

7. How have we become heirs in hope of eternal life? Titus 3:4-7

8. What did the tenants do to the son? Matthew 21:39

9. What was the question Jesus asked in Matthew 21:40, and what was their reply? Matthew 21:41

10. From what did Jesus ask if they read? Who is the stone which the builders rejected, and what has he become? Matthew 21:42, Acts 4:10-11

11. Who made this stone the cornerstone, and how do we find it? Matthew 21:42

12. For this reason, what will happen to the kingdom of God? Matthew 21:43

Personal – In what way has Jesus become the keystone in your life? He is either an obstacle or the keystone for you to succeed in this life and the next. Read 1 Peter 2:4-8 and repent of the times you have rejected the Lord.

FIFTH DAY   **READ PSALM 80:9, 12-16, 19-20**

("A vine from Egypt you transplanted;")

Read and meditate on Psalm 80:9, 12-16, 19-20.

What is the Lord saying to you personally through the Psalm?

How can you apply this to your life?

SIXTH DAY   **READ ALL OF THE COMMENTARY**

ISAIAH 5:1-7

Today's passage tells us that God's chosen nation was to "bear fruit," to carry out his work, and to uphold justice. It did bear fruit, but the fruit was sour and wild. We see in Scripture that the way to identify a tree or a person is by the kind of fruit it produced (Matt. 7:20). This was a powerful story about God's people and how he prepared everything for their benefit, and how they were very careless in taking care of what God had given to them.

Today, we need to take a look at our own vineyard. Jesus' blood prepared our soil. His death gave us the right of becoming an heir to the vineyard. How have we spaded our vineyard? How have we taken out the rocks and weeds in our life?

Lately, have you checked the fruit that is growing on your vine? Is it being deprived of spiritual nourishment by being in the shadow and coldness of sin? Do you give your vineyard plenty of sunlight through Sacred Scripture, the Sacraments and church fellowship? You may want to check the fruit in your vineyard and make the necessary corrections.

The vine is Jesus and we are the branches. We cannot do anything without the vine (John 15:1). We are in the full protection of the vineyard owner when we are giving praise and glory to his Son, Jesus. People will judge us on the kind of fruit that we bear. The fruits of the Spirit are love, joy, peace, patience, kindness, generosity, faith, mildness and self-control.

Since we have accepted Jesus Christ as our Lord and Savior and live by the Spirit, let us follow in the Spirit's lead (Gal. 5:22, 23, 25). Let our grapes never become sour or wild. Let us not ever be boastful or challenging or jealous toward one another.

PHILIPPIANS 4:6-9

In today's reading we are encouraged to worry about nothing. Imagine never having to worry about anything! It seems like an impossibility. We all have worries on the job, in our homes, or at school, but today, Paul's advice is to turn our worries into prayers. Scripture tells us that anxiety depresses a person's heart (Prov. 12:25). We only are required to look around in our society and see how much competition and anxiety there is in the area of work.

We are told in Scripture to cast all of our cares on to the Lord, because he cares about us (1 Peter 5:7). We keep our eyes on what is so temporary, instead of on what is eternal (Col 3:1-2). We are called to become pray-ers and the light of the world will drive away the anxiety and darkness (John 8:12).

We must never forget that God's peace is different from the world's peace (John 14:27). We do not find his peace in positive thinking, in absence of conflict, or even in good feelings. Real peace can come only when we know that God is in control. When we seek his kingship first, all else will fall into place, and we will experience his peace (Matt. 6:33). His peace is our destiny, and because of his peace we know that victory over sin in our lives is indisputable.

You can receive his peace at this moment if you will renew in faith your commitment to him. Let him come into you right now and feed your hungry and unstable heart (Rev. 3:20). He promised that he would never leave us orphans and that he will never leave us. His peace surpasses all understanding because it is a peace of love.

You might be asking, "How do I achieve that peace?" What we bring into our minds determines what comes out by our words and actions. Paul tells us to fill our minds with thoughts that are true, good and right. If you are having impure thoughts and daydreams, then examine what you are bringing into your mind because of television, movies, books and magazines. You need to read, study and put into action God's Holy Word every day. Ask the Lord Jesus Christ to help you right now to free you of the "stinking thinking" and help focus your mind on what is proper and pure. Remember, try to fill your mind with thoughts of the Lord that are pure and true and see your anxiety disappear. You will have peace that surpasses all understanding.

MATTHEW 21:33-43

In this parable Jesus is showing the chief priests and the elders the incredible patience and mercy of God. To his chosen people God has given a fertile and productive vineyard for their homeland. He did all of this to prepare them for the future Messiah. All he asked of them was their cooperation. But, as we see in this story, they had other plans. They wanted their kingdom on earth and they wanted it now. Does this sound familiar?

God was extremely patient with his people. He sent them many prophets to bring them into a state of repentance, and they abused them, ignored their warnings, and even killed a few of them. God finally sent his only begotten Son to earth in human form. His Son lived among them and preached a message of love and peace. He offered them his Father's mercy and pardon. Instead of accepting his offer, they committed an even greater sin. They killed the Son of God by crucifying him on the cross as a criminal.

The people's plan backfired because Jesus' death brought life to the world and opened up the gates of God's eternal home for all nations and races. He was trying to get them to see that they were like the people in the story, when he asked them if they had ever read the Scriptures. Jesus told them this so that they could repent even as he was telling them. They did not see themselves as the greedy tenants or the murderers of the prophets. They blinded themselves to God's justice. (God's justice is that he hates sin, and whatever happened to the chief priests and elders will happen to unfaithful Christians.)

Jesus has set up a new vineyard and we have been called to work in it. Are we working honestly and devotedly? Is our life producing good fruit so that it will feed others? Jesus gives us that chance to repent and to let his grace come into our lives and become faithful tenants.

We can say thank you to our heavenly Father and ask him to help us, through his Holy Spirit, to keep us on the right path. Jesus wants us to repent. He wants us to change and to enjoy his vineyard. He wants us to make the vineyard enjoyable for others. We can still put ourselves right with God. Let's do it now; tomorrow may be too late.

Application

This week's first reading reveals that a tree or a person is judged by the fruit it produced. The second reading shows that peace comes from filling our mind with thoughts that are pure, good and true. The Gospel shows how God is merciful and patient, and to ignore God is to lose our soul for eternity.

This week, show others that the fruit you are bearing is good fruit, by being especially kind and supportive to someone who is very unkind or non-supportive to you. Do not let this person know your intentions.

Also, this week, try to be a righteous example to someone in your family, school, or at work, by inviting them to read with you a passage from Scripture that is good, pure, and wholesome.

Finally, show someone your Bible Study and tell them what virtue it is bringing into your life. You may very well be an instrument of the Lord that will help them dismiss some anxiety and help them find the peace that surpasses all understanding.

TWENTY-EIGHTH SUNDAY IN ORDINARY TIME - CYCLE A

BEFORE YOU BEGIN

Pray and ask God to speak to you through His Holy Spirit.
"THE PARACLETE, THE HOLY SPIRIT WHOM THE FATHER WILL SEND IN MY NAME, WILL INSTRUCT YOU IN EVERYTHING, AND REMIND YOU OF ALL THAT I TOLD YOU." (JOHN 14:26)

FIRST DAY   **Reread last week's readings.**

1. What was a helpful or new thought from the readings or from the homily you heard on Sunday?

2. From what you learned, what personal application did you choose to apply to your life this week?

SECOND DAY   **READ ISAIAH 25:6-10**   **FIRST READING**

("The Lord God will wipe away the tears from all faces.")

1. Who will the Lord of host provide for on this mountain? Isaiah 25:6

2. What will the Lord provide? Isaiah 25:6

3. What will he destroy on this mountain, and where is it woven? Isaiah 25:7

4. What will the Lord destroy forever? Isaiah 25:8

5. Who has passed from death to life? John 5:24

6. What will the Lord God wipe away from all faces? Isaiah 25:8

7. Who will lead us to life-giving water? Rev 7:17

8. What will the Lord remove from his people? Is 25:8

9. On that day, what will be said, and about what shall we be glad and rejoice? Isaiah 25:9

10. For what reason did the Father send his Son into the world? 1 John 4:14

11. On what will the Lord rest his hand? Isaiah 25:10

Personal – In what way have you passed from death to life here and now? In what way have you experienced some of heaven here on earth? How can you apply this Scripture passage in wiping away the tears in your life?

THIRD DAY   **READ PHILIPPIANS 4:12-14, 19-20**   **SECOND READING**

("I have the strength for everything, through him who empowers me.")

1. In what circumstances does Paul know how to live? Philippians 4:12

2. In what other way does he know how to live, and in every circumstance and in all things, what is the secret Paul learned? Philippians 4:12

3. What does Paul do when ridiculed and persecuted? 1 Corinthians 4:11-13

4. For what does Paul have strength, and where does he get it? Philippians 4:13

5. Why would Paul rather boast of his weaknesses? 2 Corinthians 12:9

6. What did Paul say it was kind of the Philippians to do? Philippians 4:14

7. How are we strengthened with power? Ephesians 3:16

8. Why did the Lord stand by Paul and give him strength? 2 Timothy 4:17

9. According to whom and with what will God fully supply us? Philippians 4:19

10. What is God able to make abundant for us, and for what reason? 2 Corinthians 9:8

11. To what does the kindness of God lead? Romans 2:4

12. What is given to our God and Father? Philippians 4:20

Personal - Where do you seek the strength to get through your day? Upon whom do you rely when you have a problem? What is your response when you are ridiculed or persecuted?

FOURTH DAY   **READ MATTHEW 22:1-14**   **GOSPEL**

("Many are invited, but few are chosen.")

1. How did Jesus speak, and who was listening to him? Matthew 22:1, Matthew 21:45

2. To what did Jesus compare the kingdom of heaven, and for whom did he have it? Matthew 22:2

3. What happened when the king invited the guests to the feast? Matthew 22:3

4. When the king sent his servants out a second time and told them everything was ready, what did some of them do? Matthew 22:4-6

5.   What was the king's reaction, and what did he do? Matthew 22:7

6.   When the feast was ready, who were those not worthy to come, and whom did he send his servants to invite? Matthew 22:8-9

7.   Who filled the hall, and when the king came, what did he see? Matthew 22:10-11

8.   With what has the Lord clothed and wrapped us? Isaiah 61:10

9.   In whom have we clothed ourselves? Galatians 3:27

10.   How did the king address the man without a wedding garment, and how did the guest react? Matthew 22:12

11.   What did the king tell his attendants to do with the man? Matthew 22:13

12.   How many are invited, and how many are chosen? Matthew 22:14

13.   What three things are those who follow the Lord? Revelation 17:14

Personal – When you meet with the Lord on a daily basis, how are you clothed? How have you feasted on his Word? How have you been faithful in carrying it out among your family, friends and co-workers or school friends?

FIFTH DAY   **READ PSALM 23:1-6**

("Beside restful waters he leads me.")

Read and meditate on Psalm 23:1-6.

What is the Lord saying to you personally through the Psalm?

How can you apply this to your life?

SIXTH DAY   **READ ALL OF THE COMMENTARY**

ISAIAH 25:6-10

The message in this reading came from a prophecy about 700 years before Christ came to earth. Isaiah described the result of that coming of the Messiah in the beautiful imagery of a bountiful banquet. In this banquet all those who took part would find everlasting happiness and contentment. Isaiah was referring, of course, to heaven, the second and final stage of the messianic kingdom. In heaven, desires will be pleasant and happiness will be fulfilled. The reality is that whatever Isaiah foretold, Jesus brought to pass.

Jesus destroyed the power of death by dying on the cross for us, and in his death we are given victory over death. There is no more veil of fear from death because of Jesus' victory for all those who believe in him. Jesus, through his death, made us his brothers and sisters and co-heirs of heaven with him. Because of

Jesus, you and I have been accepted as God's adopted children. Heaven is ours for the taking. For us, God the Father invented it, God the Son has earned it, and God the Holy Spirit is always ready to help us obtain it. We, in our human minds, can not really describe what heaven is like or even perceive what it looks like.

Scripture tells us that, "Eye has not seen, ear has not heard, nor can man ever comprehend what God has in store for those whom he loves" (1 Cor. 2:9). Today's message is a message of hope and eternal freedom from pain, sickness, imprisonment, persecution, and death. Once again, it brings the hope and joy of being in eternal union with all of our relatives, friends and saints of God.

We may do well to meditate on what heaven will be like and to see this life as it really is - a journey. Sometimes our journey is unpleasant or difficult and, for some, very short. This journey is our route back home to our permanent home with God. Many people are mistaken and think this world is the only one and, therefore, fail to travel on the path he has laid down for us on our journey. God is waiting for us to enjoy our eternal banquet with him. Let us not be foolish and journey the wrong way and miss the banquet.

PHILIPPIANS 4:12-14, 19-20

Today, many people have great difficulty being content with what they have, where they are, and who they are. Are you content in any situation you face? St. Paul tells us in today's readings that he knew how to be content whether he had much or little. He tells us that the secret of contentment was having Christ's power in his life. Paul was content because he saw life from God's point of view. He focused on what he was supposed to do, not on what he felt like doing.

We can all learn to be content with life if we try to rely on God's promises and Christ's power. If you have great needs and always seem to be discontent, ask God to remove these desires and teach you to be content in every situation. There is a tremendous message in our society today that says, think only about number one. People are congratulated for being loners and doing things their way. We have lost much of the humility that Christ calls for us in our daily lives.

Paul had his priorities straight and was grateful for everything that God gave him. He knew God because he talked to him, he read Sacred Scripture, and he worshiped him. We need only to look around in our communities, and, many times, even in our own families, and see that the desire for more or better possessions is really a longing to fill an empty place in our own life. We need to reflect on what we dream about when we feel empty inside. Scripture tells us the answer lies in our perspective, our priorities and our source.

You can dismiss your anxiety by praying when these thoughts are invading your mind. Fill your mind with things that are good, solid, pure, and right with God. This will bring you a peace that nothing in this world can match or even understand (Phil. 4:6-8). Your source for this incredible power is Jesus Christ. He is the source that will supply all your needs, not all your wants. We always must remember that God will meet our needs, but he may not always meet them in this life. Christians suffer and die and God does not always intervene to save or spare them. In heaven, where sin and death have been permanently destroyed, our wants and needs will be abundantly supplied for eternity.

MATTHEW 22:1-14

A tremendous revelation is made to us in today's Gospel, and that is, God wants you and me to join him in his eternal heavenly banquet. He has sent us invitations in many, many ways. Have you accepted his invitation? In the culture of the people in today's story, there were two wedding invitations given. The first asked the guests to attend; the second announced that all was ready and to come right away. You are invited to let Jesus come into your heart and let him become the Lord of your life. Some day the Lord will call you to come home, and if you have accepted his invitation, you will enjoy his banquet forever. If you did not accept his invitation, "You will be left out in the outer darkness where there is weeping and gnashing of teeth" (Matt. 22:13).

The custom was to put on a special garment supplied by the host at the wedding banquet, and to refuse the robe would be an insult to the host. Jesus, in telling this story, is speaking of the garment of righteousness needed to enter God's banquet in the kingdom. The robe is our acceptance of Christ as our personal Lord and Savior. It is a picture of total acceptance in God's eyes, given to every believer by Christ.

Christ has provided this garment for everyone, but each person has to choose to wear it in order to enter the king's banquet (eternal life). For us, Jesus won the right to wear this robe of righteousness by his dying on the cross and rising from the dead. We are allowed to wear this special garment, not because of our merit, but totally because of his incredible gift of grace to us. Many people have heard about Christ inviting us to his banquet, but for various reasons they are too busy to listen to, reflect upon and accept his invitation. It is true, many are called but only a few are chosen.

Take this time, right now, and thank him for choosing you and for offering you such a precious garment. If you have not accepted his invitation to his banquet (eternal life), fall on your knees right now and tell him that you want him to come and take up residence in your heart. He will bring out one of his special garments and place you next to him in a special place of honor. Your whole life will be changed when you realize that because of him, you have been called to be one of his chosen ones.

Application

The first reading reveals to us a message of eternal freedom from pain and death. The second reading shows us that the secret of contentment is having Christ's power in our lives. The Gospel invites us to let the Lord Jesus come into our hearts and become the Lord of our lives.

This week, share with a family member, work or school associate, where you obtain your strength. Share who is the source of your power. Be bold and introduce to the people around you the gift of being chosen. You do not need to preach, but you do need to witness. Share with your spouse how God supplies your needs in Christ Jesus. Then listen to the reply. Listen!

TWENTY-NINTH SUNDAY IN ORDINARY TIME - CYCLE A

BEFORE YOU BEGIN

Pray and ask God to speak to you through His Holy Spirit. "THE PARACLETE, THE HOLY SPIRIT WHOM THE FATHER WILL SEND IN MY NAME, WILL INSTRUCT YOU IN EVERYTHING, AND REMIND YOU OF ALL THAT I TOLD YOU." (JOHN 14:26)

FIRST DAY   **Reread last week's readings.**

1.   What was a helpful or new thought from the readings or from the homily you heard on Sunday?

2.   From what you learned, what personal application did you choose to apply to your life this week?

SECOND DAY   **READ ISAIAH 45:1, 4-6**   **FIRST READING**

("I have called you by your name.")

1.   What does the Lord say to Cyrus, and what does he grasp? Isaiah 45:1

2.   What does the Lord say he has done for Cyrus, and what has Cyrus done for the Lord? Isaiah 45:1, Isaiah 44:28

Personal – What have you done for the Lord, and what has he done for you?

3.   Who are God's chosen ones, and how have they been called? Isaiah 45:4

4.   What does God give Cyrus even though Cyrus did not know him? Isaiah 45:4

5.   What are we not to do and for what reason? Isaiah 43:1

6.   Where is our name written? Isaiah 49:16

7.   Who does the Lord say there is none other besides him? Isaiah 45:5

8.   Even though we do not know him, what does he do for us? Isaiah 45:5

9.   Why does the Lord arm those who do not know him? Isaiah 45:6,14

10. What does the Lord use to bring his message to Balaam? Numbers 22:28–35

Personal – What and how have you been anointed? What is the message you are to bring to your family, friends, schoolmates, and work acquaintances?

("For our Gospel did not come to you in word alone,")

1. With what and in whose names are Paul, Silvanus, and Timothy greeting the Church of Thessalonica? 1 Thessalonians 1:1

2. How do we receive grace? John 1:16–17

3. What did Jesus tell his disciples he would be leaving them? John 14:27

4. How is Paul remembering the Church of the Thessalonians, and how often does he give thanks for them? 1 Thessalonians 1:2

Personal – This past week, how often did you thank God and pray for the specific church in your area, your parish, and your diocese?

5. What work of _____, labor of _____, and endurance in _____ were they calling to mind, and before whom is it done? 1 Thessalonians 1:3

6. How does God feel about the Church of Thessalonica, and what has he done for them? 1 Thessalonians 1:4

7. What four ways did the Gospel come to them? 1 Thessalonians 1:5

8. The Gospel is the power of God for the salvation of everyone who does what? Romans 1:16

9. What was further proof to the Church of Thessalonica of Paul, Silvanus, and Timothy's message? 1 Thessalonians 1:6

10. What did Christ Jesus display in Paul, and for what reason? 1 Timothy 1:16

Personal – In what way have you spread the Gospel message in word, power, the Holy Spirit, and with conviction to those around you? Be specific, and share with someone.

FOURTH DAY   **READ MATTHEW 22:15-21**   **GOSPEL**

("Then repay to Caesar what belongs to Caesar, and to God, what belongs to God.")

1. What did the Pharisees go off and plot? Matthew 22:15

2. Who was a Pharisee, and how is he described? Acts 5:34

3. Whom did the Pharisees send to Jesus with the Herodians? How did they address him, what did they call him, and how did they say he taught? Matthew 22:16

4.   What does Jesus say about himself? John 14:6

5.   With what is Jesus not concerned, and what does he not regard? Matthew 22:16

6.   What does God not have and accept? Deuteronomy 10:17

7.   What was Jesus' answer to the question, "Is it lawful to pay the census tax to Caesar or not? " Matthew 22:17-19

8.   What did Jesus call the Pharisee's that were questioning him? Matthew 22:18

9.   When we walk in the truth, with whom do we not stay? With whom do we not consort? Psalm 26:3-4

Personal - How do you know who the hypocrites are in your life? Read 1 Timothy 4:1-3 and see one of the traits of a hypocrite in Verse 2.

10.   What did Jesus say to them, and what did they reply? Matthew 22:20-21

11.   What did Jesus say to repay to Caesar, and what did he say to repay to God? Matthew 22:21

Personal - How have you been able to discern what you are to give to Caesar (your government)? What are you to give to God?

FIFTH DAY   **READ PSALM 96:1, 3-5, 7-10**

("Tell his glory among the nations,")

Read and meditate on Psalm 96: 1, 3-5, 7-10.

What is the Lord saying to you personally through the Psalm?

How can you apply this to your life?

SIXTH DAY   **READ ALL OF THE COMMENTARY**

ISAIAH 45: 1, 4-6

This is the only place in the bible where a pagan ruler is called "anointed." God is the power over all powers, and he anoints whom he chooses for his special assignments. Cyrus' kingdom was the largest of the then-known world. God chose Cyrus to be the instrument in his plan. Cyrus would allow God's city of Jerusalem to be rebuilt, and he would set the exiles free without expecting anything in return. There were very few kings of Israel or Judah that had done as much for God's people as Cyrus.

This is a tremendous show of God's sovereignty over all people. He had chosen this pagan king to be instrumental in restoring God's chosen people to their homeland. Cyrus was a disciple of the pagan god called Bel-Marduk. This religion was very active in prostitution and child sacrifice. Its adherents worshiped in Babylon, and the god's name stood for weather, war, and sun god.

The title "anointed one" was used for priests, prophets, and kings in the Old Testament. Every Christian is anointed priest, prophet, and king through the sacrament of Baptism. We need to ask ourselves what we have done with our gift of anointing. Do other people see us as one who sacrifices our wants to help others? Do we attend church regularly and receive the Holy Eucharist on a regular basis? Are we proclaiming God's Holy Word like a prophet in our families, at school or work? Do we rule in our home, school, or job, like a king who is compassionate, just and very merciful?

We come back to the question of why would God anoint someone like Cyrus? He was a pagan, and the Lord not only anointed him, he also armed him. The Lord subdued nations before him. He opened many doors for Cyrus and, as a result, Cyrus became very popular. Through Cyrus, the Lord has shown that nothing is outside of the scope of his power.

The power of the Lord is not to be denied to anyone. Your name is engraved in the palm of his hand (Isaiah 49:15), and he will work through you if you will let him. Cyrus did not even know who God was. Balaam's donkey knew who he was, and finally, even Balaam understood the message that "there is no one else beside me," said the Lord (Numbers 22:28-35).

Do people see the power of God working in you? Do you see the power of God working in your life? Stop now and ask him to allow you to experience his love and gentleness. God is our fortress, refuge, and rock (Psalm 91).

1 THESSALONIANS 1:1-5

Thessalonica was the place of the first Christian church in Greece founded by Paul in about 50 A.D. However, Paul had to leave in a great hurry because his life and the lives of his companions were threatened (Acts 17:1-10). Paul made a brief visit there later, and the new believers were growing fast and firm in their new faith. Paul wrote this letter to answer some of their questions, and he commended them on their faithfulness to the Good News. Timothy and Silvanus were of great help to Paul in getting the new church on its feet.

Thessalonica was the capitol of Macedonia and was one of the wealthiest cities in the region. The city was allowed self-rule and with that came many pagan religions and cultural influences that seriously challenged the faith of the young Christians there. Persecution only made the believers stand even more committed to their faith.

The power of the Holy Spirit changes people when they believe in God's Holy Word. When we tell others about Jesus, we must depend on the Holy Spirit to open their eyes and convince them that they need salvation. This is what happened in Thessalonica. We must remember, his power changes people, not our cleverness or persuasion. Without the work of the Holy Spirit, our words are meaningless.

The Good News produced a powerful effect upon the Thessalonians. Whenever and wherever the Word of God is heard and obeyed, lives are changed. We must always remember that Christianity is more than just a collection of interesting facts; it is the power of God for salvation to everyone who believes. Paul told them our very lives were further proof (Vs. 5). They could see that what Paul, Timothy, and Silvanus were preaching was true, because they lived it. Does your life confirm or contradict what you say you believe?

MATTHEW 22:15-21

The Pharisees were a religious sect of Jews who aimed to keep the Mosaic law in all of its strict interpretations. They had many followers among the elite, and they kept strictly aloof from the ordinary people. They were opposed to Christ from the beginning of his public preaching because he came to "call sinners" and he associated freely with them.

Jesus calls the Pharisees hypocrites because, while they pretended outwardly to be strictly religious, they were lacking true religion in their hearts, love of God and neighbor, and humility. Jesus clearly tells them and us with his answer to "Give to Caesar what is Caesar's and give to God what is God's," that the government has a right to expect obedience and cooperation in all things that tend to the material welfare of the state, provided the spiritual welfare of the members is not impeded by the government. This is where the hypocrisy that Jesus speaks about is so common. Many people try to figure out ways to cheat the government out of the tax money that is due. People will justify their actions by making all kinds of excuses about why the government does not need the money.

Jesus tells us that we have to be truthful in all matters of our lives. We are called to be truthful in our relationships with our families, in our jobs and with our government. Cheating on income tax is a very common form of acceptable hypocrisy. Jesus also tells the Pharisees that putting the law above the common good of the people is also hypocritical. Jesus knew very well that they were trying to trap him, but he still did not shy away from his conviction of being truthful. A hypocrite is a person who is deceitful and who depends on lying. He appears to be a so-called "good person," but is loaded with sinful intentions. Jesus really spoke out strongly against hypocrites.

You and I have to choose between God's laws or man's laws (Acts 5:29). We need to show that the way we live is the way we believe. Our example of loving God and loving our neighbors as ourselves will be the strength of all nations.

Application

This week's first reading shows that God will use anyone to fulfill his plan for his people. The second reading shows that a strong faith is needed to endure persecution and death. The Gospel reveals that Jesus came for the sick, lonely, and oppressed, and he deflated the hypocrites with their trickery.

This week get involved with a project, such as the pro-life cause, that affects your community. Invite someone from your school or work to go with you. Share your feelings with someone close to you about your discoveries working on that project.

THIRTIETH SUNDAY IN ORDINARY TIME – CYCLE A

BEFORE YOU BEGIN

Pray and ask God to speak to you through His Holy Spirit. "THE PARACLETE, THE HOLY SPIRIT WHOM THE FATHER WILL SEND IN MY NAME, WILL INSTRUCT YOU IN EVERYTHING, AND REMIND YOU OF ALL THAT I TOLD YOU." (JOHN 14:26)

FIRST DAY   **Reread last week's readings.**

1. What was a helpful or new thought from the readings or from the homily you heard on Sunday?

2. From what you learned, what personal application did you choose to apply to your life this week?

SECOND DAY   **READ EXODUS 22:20-26**   **FIRST READING**

("If he cries out to me, I will hear him; for I am compassionate.")

1. Who shall we not molest or oppress, for what reason, and who is saying this? Exodus 22:20, Exodus 20:22

2. Whom shall we not wrong? Exodus 22:21

3. Who executes justice for the orphan and the widow? Deuteronomy 10:17-18

4. What will the Lord do if ever we wrong the widow or orphan? Exodus 22:22-23

5. Who was oppressed, how were they oppressed, and what happened to them even though they were oppressed? Ex. 1:11-14

Personal – In what way have you experienced oppression in your life, and in what way have you oppressed others?

6. If we lend money to one of our poor neighbors, how shall we not act towards them? Exodus 22:24, Leviticus 25:35-37

7. If we take our neighbor's cloak as a pledge, when shall we return it to him, and for what reason? Exodus 22:25-26

8. If he cries out to God, what will God do, and for what reason? Exodus 22:26

9. How does the Lord act if we return to him? 2 Chronicles 30:9

10. How are we to act toward one another, and for what reason? Ephesians 4:32

Personal - Look up in the dictionary the meaning of compassion. In what way can you show mercy and compassion to someone close to you? Follow through and do it; then share with someone.

THIRD DAY   **READ 1 THESSALONIANS 1:5-10**   **SECOND READING**

("And you became imitators of us and of the Lord.")

1.   The Gospel did not come to us in word alone, but also in what with much conviction? 1 Thessalonians 1:5

2.   In what may we abound by the power of the Holy Spirit? Romans 15:13

3.   Whom did the Church of Thessalonica imitate, and how did they   receive the word? 1 Thessalonians 1:6

4.   "So be imitators of God, as beloved children." How are we to live, and whose example do we follow? Ephesians 5:1, 2

5.   As the Thessalonians imitate God, Paul, Silvanus, and Timothy, what do they become? Why did they do this? 1 Thessalonians 1:7

6.   What has sounded forth from the church of Thessalonica, not only in Macedonia and in Archaia, and where else, so that Paul has no need to say anything? 1 Thessalonians 1:8

7.   From what did they turn in order to serve the living and true God? 1 Thessalonians 1:9

8.   Whom are they awaiting from heaven, and from what does he deliver us? 1 Thessalonians 1:10

9.   For what did God not destine us, but for what did he destine us to gain? 1 Thessalonians 5:9

10. How can we store up wrath for ourself, and how does God repay everyone? Romans 2:5-8

Personal - Are people imitating you in your walk with the Lord? How are you bringing the power of the Holy Spirit to others? List the people you have tried to imitate.

FOURTH DAY   **READ MATTHEW 22:34-40**   **GOSPEL**

("You shall love the Lord, your God, with all your heart with all your soul, and with all your mind.")

1.   When the Pharisees heard that Jesus had silenced the Sadducees, what did they do? Matthew 22:34

2.   How may we silence the ignorance of foolish people? 1 Peter 2:15

3.   What did one of them, a scholar of the law, do to test Jesus? Matthew 22:36

4.   What did Jesus say was the greatest and first commandment? Matthew 22:37-38

5.   What is the second commandment? Matthew 22:39

6.   What was the first commandment given to Moses by the Lord?
     Deuteronomy 6:4-5

7.   What will we do if we love Jesus (God)? John 14:15

8.   How does God demonstrate or prove his love for us? Romans 5:8

9.   What is a new commandment that Jesus has given, and how do we demonstrate
     our love for God? John 13:34

10. What depends on these two commandments? Matthew 22:40

Personal – How can you demonstrate your love for God with someone in your family, friends, school or business who appears to be steeped in sin?

FIFTH DAY   **READ PSALM 18:2-4, 47, 51**

("Extolled be God my Savior.")

Read and meditate on Psalm 18: 2-4, 47, 51.

What is the Lord saying to you personally through the Psalm?

How can you apply this to your life?

SIXTH DAY   **READ ALL OF THE COMMENTARY**

EXODUS 22:20-26

God's warning to the Israelites not to treat strangers unfairly comes through loud and clear. They well remember that they themselves were once strangers in Egypt. It is not easy coming to a new environment where you feel alone and out of place. Today's reading shows how the Hebrew law protected the poor and less fortunate. God tells us that the poor, the powerless, and the aliens are very special to him, and they are not to be mistreated. In today's reading we see a cloak being used as collateral for a loan. In Hebrew law cloaks were one of an Israelite's most valued possessions. Most people owned only one and it was used as a blanket, a sack to carry things, a place to sit, and a pledge for a debt, as well as for clothing.

We need to take a long look at the way we treat refugees and immigrants who come into our country. Our sensitivity to their struggles and our expression of God's love to them are clearly stated by our actions.

We see that God is very clear on what happens to those who mistreat the poor, the widows, and the orphans. The challenge upon us today is to turn our concern and resources to help those less fortunate than ourselves.

Much of the tragedy in our society today is the exploitation of the poor. We need only look around and we can see widows, orphans and elderly trying desperately to survive. Instead of being helped, many are forced into homelessness or into homes they cannot afford. They receive little or no health care, and many have little food available to them and their families. God warns us very clearly what he will do to those who abuse and oppress them.

A call to repentance needs to come into the hearts of the people, and a renewal of our covenant with God has to take place. We need to look at the poor and oppressed with the eyes of Jesus Christ. If we turn to the Lord and seek his will, he will bless us and our families. He will bless and honor us for loving his poor. Remember, what we do to the least of our people, we do unto him (Matthew 25:31-46).

1 THESSALONIANS 1:5-10

St. Paul continues to praise the Thessalonians, not only for their faith and courage, but for their Christian lifestyle. Suffering for his faith was not new to St. Paul, and the Thessalonians gladly accepted their sufferings in imitation of Paul and Christ, who had died for them. The spirit with which they accepted and lived the faith was an example to other young Christian communities in Greece.

Today's reading was about people who turned from believing in idols to belief in the living God. Today much of religion is rhetoric and young people see right through it. Idolatry is out of control in many nations, and the gods of money, power, and pleasure have many people struggling in bondage.

There are some Christians who still live by and stand up for their Christian principles, thank God; but they are too few and far between. We need millions of sincere, active, spirit-filled Christians to stem the flood of materialism and worldliness which is upon us. The failure of Christians to live out their beliefs is what gives the anti-God movement its fuel.

We need to look at ourselves and ask what kind of Christian role model we are in our community. Am I imitating Christ and bringing others to him? Do I spend time alone with him in prayer and reading his Word? In order to be an imitator of him, I must do these things daily. There are those around us who are looking for the light and the truth. We have that light and truth. We are called to give that light to the world of darkness. Do we dare refuse to help our brothers and sisters who are in darkness and risk losing our own eternal salvation?

MATTHEW 22:34-40

This Gospel reading seems to reveal the intentions of the Pharisees trying to catch Jesus in some legalistic or political error. The Pharisees and Sadducees had many disputes among themselves about this question. There were over 600 laws and they often tried to ascertain which were the more important ones.

Jesus was asked what was the greatest commandment in the law of Moses. Jesus quotes from Deuteronomy 6:5 and Leviticus 19:18. By keeping these two commandments a person keeps all of the Law. They summarized the ten commandments. Yet, we see Jesus telling them and us that if we really love God and our neighbor, we will keep the commandments without any great problem. Jesus tells us what we can do, rather than to worry about what we can not do. We show how much we love God by keeping his commandments. We love God with our mind and heart, soul and body.

Today the world is trying to keep up with being it's own conscience and it's own code of conduct. We are told in Scripture that filling our minds with thoughts that are of the Lord is how we love the Lord with our minds (Phil. 4:8). We know that the Spirit of the Lord within us is greater than the spirit that is in the world (1 John 4:4). This is loving God and our neighbor with all of our strength, and that strength is the Holy Spirit.

We are called to love God with all of our heart, and it is with the heart of Jesus that we love others as he has loved us (John 13:34). We can not say we love God and hate our neighbor; if we do then we are liars (1 John 3:20). Jesus sums it all up on how to love others the way he loves us when he says, "Whatever you do to the least of my brothers and sisters, you do unto me" (Matthew 25:31-46).

Application

The first reading shows God's intense love for orphans, widows, and the oppressed. The second reading reveals that the core of Christianity is in the witness of its believers. The Gospel brings home the power of loving God and neighbor completely.

This week, before you speak, ask yourself what would Jesus say in this situation. Before you do anything, ask yourself what would Jesus do in this situation. God is love and we should try imitating him in what we say and do. Then we will be not only loving and obedient to his commandments but also capable of loving others as he has loved us.

THIRTY-FIRST SUNDAY IN ORDINARY TIME – CYCLE A

BEFORE YOU BEGIN

Pray and ask God to speak to you through His Holy Spirit. "THE PARACLETE, THE HOLY SPIRIT WHOM THE FATHER WILL SEND IN MY NAME, WILL INSTRUCT YOU IN EVERYTHING, AND REMIND YOU OF ALL THAT I TOLD YOU." (JOHN 14:26)

FIRST DAY   **Reread last week's readings.**

1. What was a helpful or new thought from the readings or from the homily you heard on Sunday?

2. From what you learned, what personal application did you choose to apply to your life this week?

SECOND DAY   **READ MALACHI 1:14-2:2, 8-10**   **FIRST READING**

("For a great king am I, says the Lord of hosts.")

1. Who is cursed? Malachi 1:14

2. Who have gone out into the world and have not acknowledged Jesus Christ as coming in the flesh? 2 John 7

3. What will be feared among the nations? Malachi 1:14

4. What does it mean to fear the Lord? Proverbs 8:13, 2 Corinthians 5:9-11, Revelation 14:7

5. For whom is this commandment? Malachi 2:1

6. What two things will cause the Lord to send a curse upon us? Malachi 2:1-2

7. What three things will give us life? Deut 30:19-20

8. From what have we turned aside, what have our instructions caused, and what have we made void? Malachi 2:8

9. What has the Lord made us and for what reason? What do we show in our decisions? Malachi 2:9

10. What are we now to do, and who shows no partiality? 2 Chronicles 19:7

11. What are the three questions asked in Malachi 2:10?

Personal – How do you show your fear of the Lord to those around you? Do you show partiality to just those who are nice to you? Reflect on this and ask the Holy Spirit to show you how you can restore any broken relationships. This week attend the Sacrament of Reconciliation for the grace needed to do this.

THIRD DAY   **READ 1 THESSALONIANS 2:7-9, 13**   **SECOND READING**

("..., we proclaimed to you the Gospel of God.")

1. Who is speaking, to whom are they speaking, and what were they able to impose on them? 1 Thess 1:1, 1 Thess 2:7

2. How were they among the Thessalonians? 1 Thess 2:7

3. Paul asks the Corinthians, what kind of spirit do they prefer? 1 Corinthians 4:21

4. What did Paul, Silvanus, and Timothy have for the Thessalonians, and what were they willing to share with them? 1 Thessalonians 2:8

Personal – How do you share the Gospel of God with your family and friends? Do you share yourself and how the Gospel has affected your life?

5. What do Paul, Silvanus and Timothy recall to the brothers, and what did they proclaim? 1 Thessalonians 2:9

6. For what are we to work, and what is the work of God? John 6:26-29

7. What do we give God unceasingly? 1 Thessalonians 2:13

8. What is the will of God in all circumstances? 1 Thessalonians 5:18

9. What did the Thessalonians receive from hearing Paul, Silvanus, and Timothy? From whom did they not receive it? 1 Thessalonians 2:13

10. The Word of God is at work in those who do what? 1 Thessalonians 2:13

11. Who are those who believe? 1 John 5:1-5

Personal – How is God working in you, and how are you working in the world?

FOURTH DAY   **READ MATTHEW 23:1-12**   **GOSPEL**

("...and those who humble themselves will be exalted.")

1. To whom did Jesus speak? Matthew 23:1

2. Who have taken their seat on the chair of Moses? Matthew 23:2

3. Where must we all appear? 2 Corinthians 5:10

4.   What are we to do and observe, what are we **not** to follow, and for what reason? Matthew 23:3

5.   What did the Lord order those who preach the Gospel to do? 1 Corinthians 9:14

6.   What do the Scribes and Pharisees do to people, and what do they not do? Matthew 23:4

7.   For what are their works performed, and what do they love? Matthew 23:5-7

8.   What do they like to be called, what are we not to be called, and for what reason? Matthew 23:7-8

9.   Who is our teacher? John 14:26

10.   Who do we have only one, what are we not to be called, and what must the greatest among us be? Matthew 23:9-11

11.   What will happen to him who exalts himself, and what will happen to him who humbles himself? Matthew 23:12

12.   Jesus tells us to come to him. What does he say to do, and what does he say he is? Matthew 11:28-30

Personal – In what ways, in your family and with friends, are you practicing what you preach? What has the Holy Spirit taught you this week, and how have you shared this by word and deed?

FIFTH DAY   **READ PSALM 131:1-3**

("…, I have stilled and quieted my soul like a weaned child.")

Read and meditate on Psalm 131:1-3.

What is the Lord saying to you personally through the Psalm?

How can you apply this to your life?

SIXTH DAY   **READ ALL OF THE COMMENTARY**

MALACHI 1:14-2:2, 8-10

Malachi gives a clear, strong rebuke to the people and the priests for neglecting their part in the covenant with God. He is really strong about the person being cursed who lives a life of deceit. Malachi was the last Old Testament prophet and he preached about 430 B.C. Isaiah and Jeremiah had left exciting prophecies for Israel and they had not come true as of yet, so apathy had set in and the nation did not feel good about itself.

Malachi saw many of the sins still being committed that caused the downfall of Israel. Malachi never wavered from his position of truth, and God's first message to Malachi was, "I have loved you very deeply." It is a message of hope to all people in stressful times of their lives.

Because the government was corrupt and the economy was poor, many people probably assumed that God just did not like them. God loves all people because he made them. God warned his priests about not leading the people into sin because of the example of their own lives. The worship of God had lost its vitality and had become more of a business for the religious than a heart-felt vocation.

Some people find it very hard to just confess what is wrong in their life and try to justify why they are doing the things that they do. This deceit spreads throughout their families and into the communities. We must remember that we can not lead others if we ourselves are stumbling blocks in the way of people searching for God. Jesus certainly was strong against community leaders who were not living the Gospel as well as they preached it. We need only to look at some of the spiritual and political leaders and see how much damage has already been done by not practicing what they preach.

Today that danger is even more present because of the humanistic attacks on lives of those who believe in Jesus. We who are called into spiritual leadership must remember that we are not fighting our neighbors, families, or congregations. No, we are fighting against the dark forces of Satan himself. The weapons against Satan are the sword of the Spirit (Word of God, teachings of the church, sacraments, and prayer). It is very important that you always have your own personal armor. We all need to be people of prayer and as we enter into battle, let our battle cry be "Pray, Pray, Pray, Pray."

1 THESSALONIANS 2:7-9, 13

We are told that love is kind and gentle (1 Cor. 4:7) and in today's reading we see that being expressed in the way Paul practiced his ministry to the Thessalonians. Life was very hard in those days and gentleness was not often a respected quality.

In many places in today's world, we see power and assertiveness getting more respect than gentleness and kindness, even though none of us like to be bullied. Gentleness is love in action; it is being considerate, and meeting the needs of others. It is being humble, listening to others talk, and being able to learn from them. Gentleness, in many prisons or in some military camps, is taken as a sign of weakness.

Paul is telling them that only through gentleness can we really imitate Christ. He also shows that gentleness is an essential trait for both men and women. We all need to have a gentle attitude in our relationship with others. Paul shows the value of honest hard work by his trade as a tent maker (Acts 18:3). He certainly deserved to be financially supported by the people, and, yet, he taught and did not want to be a burden to the new believers. He shows us how loving parents would treat their children, and that is how he felt toward them.

We are to help and encourage new believers in the journey of faith. They need to see in us that gentleness that was in Paul. By his words and example, Paul encouraged the Thessalonians to live in ways that would bring joy to God. We need to look at our own life style and see if there is anything going on that would embarrass God. What do people think of God, when they see the way you live your life?

MATTHEW 23:1-12

Matthew proclaims very strongly Jesus' description of hypocrites. Jesus tells about religious leaders who told the people how to obey rules that they themselves did not obey. Jesus did not condemn what they taught but what they were, and they were hypocrites. They did all the right things at the right time and at the right place. They carried around a little prayer box so that people would see it and be impressed with their holiness. Jesus was exposing the hypocritical attitude of the religious leaders because they knew Scripture but they did not live it. Many of the Pharisees were more concerned about looking holy than being holy.

We have that today with many people giving external signs of a belief that is very shallow. We are all called to be holy and a holy man is not recognized because of a title. A holy man is one who possesses the fruits of the Spirit. If our desires are leading us to possess the fruits of the Spirit, such as love, joy, peace, patience, kindness, goodness, faithfulness, gentleness, and self-control, then we know the Holy Spirit is leading us. Today, many people, like the Pharisees, know God's Holy Word and attend church services regularly, but they do not let it change their lives. We hear people in many lands say that they follow Jesus, but do not live by his standard of love. We are called, today more than ever, to make sure our actions match our beliefs.

The Pharisees desired very strong places of leadership in the church as well as leadership in the community. The danger is when the desire for the position grows stronger than the submission to God's will. Jesus was not against leadership, but against leadership that serves itself, rather than others. Jesus challenged society's norms then, and he continues to challenge them today. To our Lord Jesus Christ, real greatness comes from serving others in the giving of self. We need to remember that service keeps us aware of other's needs, and Jesus came as a servant.

Application

The first reading shows us that truth is the only way to become free. The second reading reveals the importance of gentleness. The Gospel shows us the power of being a servant.

This week, let the fruits of the Spirit be evident in you. Each morning pray that the Holy Spirit will lead you in each one. At night, check how well you are using your fruits. Be generous giving them all away and God will replenish you. Ask someone to evaluate you.

THIRTY-SECOND SUNDAY IN ORDINARY TIME - CYCLE A

BEFORE YOU BEGIN

Pray and ask God to speak to you through His Holy Spirit. "THE PARACLETE, THE HOLY SPIRIT WHOM THE FATHER WILL SEND IN MY NAME, WILL INSTRUCT YOU IN EVERYTHING, AND REMIND YOU OF ALL THAT I TOLD YOU." (JOHN 14:26)

FIRST DAY   **Reread last week's readings.**

1.   What was a helpful or new thought from the readings or from the homily you heard on Sunday?

2.   From what you learned, what personal application did you choose to apply to your life this week?

SECOND DAY   **READ WISDOM 6:12-16**   **FIRST READING**

("He who watches for her at dawn shall not be disappointed.")

1.   What is resplendent and unfading, readily perceived by those who love her, and found by those who seek her? Wisdom 6:12

2.   In what did Jesus advance? Luke 2:52

3.   With what two things are reputable men filled? Acts 6:3

4.   In anticipation of men's desire, what does wisdom do? Wisdom 6:13

5.   Whose name has Jesus made known, and what will Jesus make known? John 17:25-26

6.   What will happen to those who watch for wisdom at dawn? Wisdom 6:14

7.   What should we not reject, and what makes a man happy? Proverbs 8:32-34

8.   What is the perfection of prudence, and how can we be free from care? Wisdom 6:15

9.   Who is wisdom seeking? Wisdom 6:16

10.   Who is most worthy of honor? Hebrews 3:3

11.   In what way can we live a life worthy of the calling we have received? Ephesians 4:1-3

Personal – Look back to when you made your First Holy Communion and write down on a piece of paper the ways you have grown in wisdom since then. When you awake in the morning, ask the Holy Spirit for wisdom. Make a conscious effort to seek after her this week.

THIRD DAY	READ 1 THESSALONIANS 4:13-18	SECOND READING

("Thenceforth, we shall be with the Lord unceasingly.")

1. Who would have you be clear about those who sleep in death? To whom are they speaking, and for what reason? 1 Thessalonians 1:1 4:13

2. From where do we derive our hope? Romans 15:4

3. What do we not have when we are without God in the world? Ephesians 2:12

4. If we believe that Jesus died and rose, what will God do? 1 Thessalonians 4:14

5. What helps us believe that Jesus is the Messiah, the Son of God, and what gives us life? John 20:30-31

6. What will those who live, who survive until his coming, be without?
    1 Thessalonians 4:15

7. What will the Lord do at the word of command and with what sound? What will happen to those who have died in Christ? 1 Thessalonians 4:16

8. If we obey the commands of Jesus, what will he do? John 14:15-16

9. After those who have died in Christ rise, what will happen to the living, the survivors? 1 Thessalonians 4:17

10. With what are we to console one another? 1 Thessalonians 4:17

Personal – What do you know about the personality of God that makes you look forward to being with him unceasingly?

FOURTH DAY	READ MATTHEW 25:1-13	GOSPEL

("Keep your eyes open, for you know not the day or the hour.")

1. To what can the reign of God be compared? Matthew 25:1

2. What were they like? Matthew 25:2

3. How are we not to act, and what are we to try to discern? Ephesians 5:15-17

4.   What did the foolish bridesmaids, in taking their torches, not bring, and what did the sensible ones bring? Matthew 25:3-4

5.   What happened to the bridesmaids when the groom delayed his coming, and what happened at midnight? Matthew 25:5-6

6.   What did the foolish bridesmaids say to the sensible ones, and what was their reply? Matthew 25:7-9

7.   What happened when the foolish bridesmaids went off to buy some oil, what happened to the sensible ones, and what was barred behind them? Matthew 25:10

8.   What happened when the other bridesmaids came back, and what did the master say? Matthew 25:11-12

9.   What is the moral to the story? Matthew 25:13

10.   What will every eye see, even those who pierced him? Revelation 1:7

Personal - In what way have you been preparing for the coming of the Lord? Do you have a reserve of oil so that the light you are carrying stays lit day and night?

FIFTH DAY   **READ PSALM 63:2-8**

("O God, you are my God whom I seek,")

Read and meditate on Psalm 63:2-8.

What is the Lord saying to you personally through the Psalm?

How can you apply this to your life?

SIXTH DAY   **READ ALL OF THE COMMENTARY**

WISDOM 6:12-16

The book of Wisdom was written about 150 B.C. It was written in Greek, and was, therefore, excluded from the Jewish canon. We have been told in this reading that wisdom is recognized by those who love the truth and seek true knowledge. The man who searches for true wisdom and really hungers and thirsts for it will not have far to seek. Today wisdom is ever present to the man or woman who seriously and prayerfully thinks on life and its value.

Today's reading really brings us to that age-old question, "What is truth?" Jesus tells us that he is the way, the truth, and the life. Today some people are like a hitchhiker hoping someone will give him a ride. When asked where he was going, he said, "I don't know." When questioned where had he been? He again answered, "I don't know." People like this are on a journey that goes only from the cradle to the grave. Their main purpose in life is to fit into these short years all the pleasures that this world has to offer. The rise of secularism in our countries has brought about a tremendous decline in the moral and spiritual life of millions of people. Today many people want to fit as much fun and leisure as possible into their life.

There still is a high degree of apathy, apostasy, and anarchy in our struggling group of nations. Much of this humanism, self-gratification, and my-way theology has had an enormous impact on the concept and lifestyle of the Christian family.

We have had 21 centuries of Christianity from which to learn the clear meaning of life which Christ's life, death, and resurrection brought into the world. This true knowledge, this true wisdom is within the reach of all peoples. We need to use our gifts, which have come from God, and reach out to those around us. Let us respond to his call with prayer, study, and action (liturgy, penance and Holy Eucharist). They will know we are Christians by the way we share our life and time and give spiritual support.

1 THESSALONIANS 4:13-18

In this reading, Paul wants the Thessalonians to know that death is not the end of the story for Christians. They were very much concerned about what would happen to their fellow believers who had died before Christ returned. Paul states to them that when Christ returns all believers, both dead and alive, will be reunited, never to suffer or die again. Paul also reveals to us a teaching that was given to him by Christ or passed along by word of mouth by the apostles to other Christians.

These words of Paul were a tremendous help to the Thessalonian people, and they challenge us today to comfort and encourage one another when one of our loved ones has died. The same love that unites believers in this life will unite others when Christ returns and reigns forever. We must always remember what we are told in Scripture, "For God so loved the world, he gave his only Son so that anyone who believes in him shall not perish but have eternal life." (John 3:16).

Because Jesus came back to life, so will all those who believed in him. Every faithful Christian, both living and dead, will enjoy the reward of being in the full presence of the living God for all of eternity. Think about what will happen on that tremendous day of judgment. All believers in Christ who are dead will rise from their graves. All believers who are alive will be lifted into the clouds and meet Christ. We do not need to despair when a loved one dies or even when world events take a dark turn for the worse. God will turn our sorrows into triumphs, our poverty to riches, our sickness into health, our pain to glory, and our defeat into victory.

All of God's children will stand once again united in the incredible presence of God. We will be safe and secure for all eternity. Paul gave great hope and comfort to the people with the promises of the resurrection. Today you and I are called to comfort and reassure one another with this great hope. Let us always remember the "Good News" is a message of hope and the message of "Jesus."

MATTHEW 25:1-13

Jesus tells us in today's reading that it is very important to be prepared for his return and to live in his commandments until he comes. We are taught through the story of the ten bridesmaids that accountability will be expected of all believers with no exceptions. We are taught that every person is responsible for his or her own spiritual condition. Jesus is telling what will happen on that day of his return to some of those whom he has chosen and to whom he had given every opportunity to reach their one and only goal.

The bridesmaids in the story were chosen for a great honor, and they were expected to be ready when the celebration began. The bridesmaids were generally intimate friends of the bride who went through a lot of trouble to prepare for the occasion, and yet, through carelessness, were found unworthy to share in the festivities.

Jesus describes this incident to bring home to his listeners the need to be constantly prepared for his return. The invitation that Christians receive is the Sacrament of Baptism. The Christian starts on the road to heaven and he gets his invitation to the heavenly nuptials, but this is only the beginning. He is expected from the time of reason to prepare himself by living in accordance with God's law. "Abide in me and keep my commandments and I will abide in you." (John 15:7)

To abide means to take up residence or to live with or in another. We are to live in Christ by keeping his commandments and that means to love him with all our heart and soul, mind, and strength. We are also to love our neighbors as ourself.

The call will come for each one of us, and we will be held accountable for our lives and our preparedness. Do not be like the foolish bridesmaids who did not plan and then through carelessness missed the great event. Today, fall on your knees and pray for the Holy Spirit to let his fire fall upon you. Let the Lord have your offering of a contrite spirit, a heart that is humble and contrite (Psalm 51:13). It is up to you, filled with the grace of the Holy Spirit, to decide where you will be found on the last day. Will you be with the wise bridesmaids or with the foolish ones?

Application

The first reading revealed that truth is the core of wisdom and knowledge. The second reading showed the strength of being able to hope. The Gospel shows us that we are to prepare and act on our preparations.

This week, at the end of every day, evaluate your actions and their results. Be accountable and honest with yourself. See how you are walking with the Lord. Write down what the Lord is saying to you regarding your accountability to him. He will help you to take action to be prepared for anything.

THIRTY-THIRD SUNDAY IN ORDINARY TIME – CYCLE A

BEFORE YOU BEGIN

Pray and ask God to speak to you through His Holy Spirit. "THE PARACLETE, THE HOLY SPIRIT WHOM THE FATHER WILL SEND IN MY NAME, WILL INSTRUCT YOU IN EVERYTHING, AND REMIND YOU OF ALL THAT I TOLD YOU." (JOHN 14:26)

FIRST DAY   **Reread last week's readings.**

1.   What was a helpful or new thought from the readings or from the homily you heard on Sunday?

2.   From what you learned, what personal application did you choose to apply to your life this week?

SECOND DAY   **READ PROVERBS 31:10-13, 19-20, 30-31**   **FIRST READING**

("The woman who fears the Lord is to be praised.")

1.   When one finds a worthy wife, what is her value far beyond? Proverbs 31:10

2.   What does a worthy wife's husband entrust to her, and what kind of a prize does he have? Proverbs 31:11

3.   What is the married man busy doing, and what does this mean? 1 Corinthians 7:33

4.   How should the wives be toward their husbands, and who is the head of the wife? Ephesians 5:23

5.   How should a husband love his wife? Ephesians 5:33

6.   What does a worthy wife bring her husband? Proverbs 31:12

7.   What does she obtain, make, and do with her hands? Proverbs 31:13 31:19

8.   To whom does she reach out her hands and extend her arms? Proverbs 31:20

9.   What is deceptive and fleeting, and who is to be praised? Proverbs 31:30

10.   Of what is the fear of the Lord the beginning, and who greatly delights in his commands? Psalm 111:10, Psalm 112:1

11.   What is she given for a reward, and what praises her at the city gates? Proverbs 31:31

Personal - If you are a wife, what gives you value in your relationship with your husband? If you are a husband, how do you show love to your wife? To all children, young and old, how can you help a husband and wife by sharing what you have learned in this lesson?

THIRD DAY	**READ 1 THESSALONIANS 5:1-6**	**SECOND READING**

("...let us not be asleep like the rest, but awake and sober.")

1. What do we not need to write you, and how is the day of the Lord coming? 1 Thessalonians 5:1-2

2. Who knows the day or hour of the Lord's coming? Matthew 24:36

3. Just when people are saying "Peace and security," what will fall on them? What will it be like, and will there be any escape? 1 Thessalonians 5:3

4. What will the coming of the Son of Man repeat? Matthew 24:37-42

5. What are we not in, that the day should find us off guard and like a thief? 1 Thessalonians 5:4

6. In whom is there no darkness? 1 John 1:5

7. Who is the man who claims to be in the light but is still in the dark? 1 John 2:9

8. Of what are all of us children? 1 Thessalonians 5:5

9. What should we not be, but what two things should we be? 1 Thessalonians 5:6

10. What is another reason for staying sober and alert? 1 Peter 5:8

Personal - If the Lord Jesus were to come right at this moment, what would you change in yourself if you had the time?

FOURTH DAY	**READ MATTHEW 25:14-30**	**GOSPEL**

("Come, share your master's joy.")

1. What did the man going on a journey hand over to his servants, and to what was it in accordance? Matthew 25:14

2. What did the disciples do, and to what was it in accordance? Acts 11:29

3. What did the man disburse to the three servants before going away? Matthew 25:15

4. What did the two men do who received the larger amounts, and what did the one who received the smaller amount do? Matthew 25:16-18

5. After a long absence, the master came home. What did he do, and what did the servants who have received the five thousand and the two thousand say and do? Matt 25:20-23

6. What was their master's response, what three things did he say about his servants, and of what did he put them in charge? Matthew 25:21-23

7. To what kind of people must we hand on what we have heard? 2 Timothy 2:2

8. What is it like to depend on a faithless man? Proverbs 25:19

9. In what do the first two servants share? Matthew 25:21, 23

10. How may we have Jesus' joy? John 15:9-11

11. What did the man who received the thousand say about his master, and what did he do out of fear? Matthew 25:24-25

12. What did his master say to him, and what did he have done with him? Matthew 25:26-30

13. What casts out fear, and with what does fear have to do? 1 John 4:18

14. In what should we not grow, and whom should we imitate? Hebrews 6:12

Personal – In the measure of faith that God has granted you, share how it has grown in the past six months. Have you been sharing it with those around you? Which of the servants do you see as similar to you?

FIFTH DAY **READ PSALM 128:1-5**

("Happy are you who fear the Lord.")

Read and meditate on Psalm 128:1-5.

What is the Lord saying to you personally through the Psalm?

How can you apply this to your life?

SIXTH DAY **READ ALL OF THE COMMENTARY**

PROVERBS 31:10-13, 19-20, 30-31

Today's reading is a somewhat unusual reading in the sense that it is a testimony of praise to the ideal wife. This is rather rare in the Old Testament because in the culture of that time women played a minor role in public, civil or religious life. The real power in today's message is in the power and praise of a wise and faithful wife.

We see in this reading a woman who is faithful first to God, then to her husband, and finally to her children. She is in perfect order as we are told in Scripture (1 Cor. 11:3). Today's reading gives tremendous encouragement to the Christian mothers of all ages. The ideal woman of today's Scripture is still the ideal wife and mother of today's real-life world. Much of our society has rejected the sacred role of wife and mother, and as a result, we have tremendous destruction in the role and place of the family.

An ideal wife is a woman of strong faith, character, and great compassion. Many people think that the ideal woman in the Bible was shy, servile, and completely domestic. This is not so. The ideal woman is one who puts God first in her life and has been blessed with many gifts and talents. Her abilities, intelligence, strength, and integrity do not come from her amazing achievements, but as a result of her reverence of God.

In our society, where physical appearances count for so much, it may surprise us to realize that a woman's appearance is never mentioned. Her beauty comes entirely from her character. We are assaulted by television, movies, magazines, and books that a woman has to look like a beauty queen in order to be accepted. Today's reading encourages a woman to be all that she can be. These qualities when coupled with fear of the Lord, lead to enjoyment, success, honor, and worth.

1 THESSALONIANS 5:1-6

Efforts to determine the date of Christ's return were foolish then and they are foolish today. We hear different people claiming to know when the Lord will be coming back, and some even describe the time, place, and the action that will accompany the return. Do not be mislead by anyone who claims to know.

We have been told in today's reading that no one knows, and that even the believers will be surprised when it happens. Paul tells us that the Lord will return suddenly and unexpectedly. We are told by Paul to be ready. We should plan our lives as if we were going to live on earth forever and live our lives as if this were the last day.

Suppose Jesus were to return today. How would he find you living your life? Are you ready to meet him and say, "Lord, I have decided to follow you and I am ready to go with you?" The day of the Lord is a future time when God intervenes directly in world affairs. The day of the Lord will include both punishment and blessing. Christ will judge sin and set up his eternal kingdom. We who believe in God are children of the light and we do not have to be afraid of that moment of judgment. We have the light of the Gospel - the illumination of the true faith.

If we continue to live and practice our faith in that light, the coming of death will not be in the darkness. We shall spiritually be prepared for it. We are called to keep awake and be sober. This means being prepared by living our Christian faith every day. You still have time to choose Christ, or the world, to be the center of your life. If Jesus came today, what would you wish you had changed? Then change it now!

MATTHEW 25:14-30

In today's Gospel we see that the master divided the money among his servants according to their abilities. No one received more or less than he could handle. If he failed, it could not be because he was overwhelmed. Failure could come only from laziness or hatred toward the master. God gives us time, abilities, and other resources, and he expects us to invest wisely until he returns. We are responsible for using well what God has given us, and we will be held accountable.

The real issue is not how much we have, but what we do with what we have. Jesus is going to return, and for us to serve God does not mean that we have to quit our jobs. It does mean that we have to diligently use our time, talents, and treasure to serve God completely in whatever we do. For some people, it may mean changing professions. An example would be someone who is in a career that participates in abortion. Another is someone who works in the media where pornography is a common product. For most, it means doing our daily work in a manner that gives reverence to God.

The last man in today's story was thinking of himself only, by playing it safe and protecting himself from his hard task master. In the end he was judged for his self-centeredness. We need to really heed the message of this last part of today's Gospel. We must not make excuses to avoid what God has called us to do. We are caretakers, not owners. When we ignore or abuse what we are given, then we are rebellious and sinful. We might do well to remember that the wages of sin is death (Rom. 6:23).

Application

This week's first reading reveals that real beauty is in the character. The second reading shows that we must live a life of preparedness. The Gospel tells us that God rewards faithfulness.

This week, point out and praise the character of your "ideal" wife or mother. Be specific and let her know how you feel about her internal beauty. Take time out to talk with your wife, take her out of the house. Bring her a special gift (flowers, candy, etc.). Let her experience your love for her by being there for her. Don't make jokes about her (age, weight, etc.) and don't criticize her in public. God will reward your loyalty, your courtesy, and your loving your very special "ideal" wife. Visit your mother as she grows older, whether she is in her own home or in a convalescent home. She will experience being loved more by your presence than by your presents.

THIRTY-FOURTH SUNDAY IN ORDINARY TIME – CYCLE A

BEFORE YOU BEGIN

Pray and ask God to speak to you through His Holy Spirit. "THE PARACLETE, THE HOLY SPIRIT WHOM THE FATHER WILL SEND IN MY NAME, WILL INSTRUCT YOU IN EVERYTHING, AND REMIND YOU OF ALL THAT I TOLD YOU." (JOHN 14:26)

FIRST DAY 　　　　　　　　　**Reread last week's readings.**

1. What was a helpful or new thought from the readings or from the homily you heard on Sunday?

2. From what you learned, what personal application did you choose to apply to your life this week?

SECOND DAY 　　　　　**READ EZEKIEL 34:11-12, 15-17** 　　　　　**FIRST READING**

("I myself will give them rest, says the Lord God.")

1. What does the Lord God say he will do when he finds himself among his scattered sheep? Ezekiel 34:11-12

2. What will he do to those who were scattered when it was cloudy and dark? Ezekiel 34:12

3. What did God do when we were in the power of darkness? Colossians 1:13

4. Who does the Lord say will pasture his sheep and give them rest? Ezekiel 34:15

5. Who does Jesus say he is? John 10:11, 14

6. Whom will the Lord seek out, whom will he bring back, whom will he bind up, and whom will he heal? Ezekiel 34:16

7. What did the Son of Man (Jesus) come to do? Luke 19:10

8. Whom does the Lord heal? Isaiah 61:1

9. What does the Lord do to the sleek and the strong, thus shepherding them rightly? Ezekiel 34:16

10. Who is singled out in this world to shame the strong? 1 Corinthians 1:27-28

11. Between what does the Lord God judge? Ez 34:17

Personal - How have you been healed by the Lord, and in what way has he brought you back when you went astray? What wounds has he bound up in you? Spend a few minutes in thanksgiving to the Lord.

THIRD DAY	READ 1 CORINTHIANS 15:20-26, 28	SECOND READING

("Just as in Adam all die, so in Christ all will come to life again.")

1. From what has Christ been raised, and of whom is he the first fruits? 1 Corinthians 15:20

2. To what will he who raised Christ bring your mortal bodies, and how will he do it? Romans 8:11

3. Whom will God bring forth with Jesus from the dead? 1 Thessalonians 4:14

4. How did death come, how did the resurrection of the dead come, and what is the proper order? 1 Corinthians 15:21-23

5. To whom did Adam listen, and what did God forbid him to do? Genesis 3:17

6. To whom did this single offense bring condemnation, and what did a single righteous act do? Romans 5:18

7. Who will come down from heaven at the word of command, what will happen to those who have died in Christ, and what will happen to the living? 1 Thesselonians 4:16-17

8. When the end comes what will be destroyed, and what will be handed over to God the Father? 1 Corinthians 15:24

9. How long must Christ reign, and what is the last enemy? 1 Corinthians 15:25-26

10. Where is Christ seated, and of what is he the head? Ephesians 1:20-23

11. Through what has Christ robbed death of its power and brought life and immortality into clear light? 2 Timothy 1:10

12. When all has been subjected to the Son, to whom will he then subject himself, and why? 1 Corinthians 15:28

Personal - In what way has fear of death been destroyed in you? Check off on the list below those to whom you have been listening when making decisions: mother, father, wife, husband, daughter, son, friend, pastor, God's Word.

FOURTH DAY	READ MATTHEW 25:31-46	GOSPEL

("I assure you, as often as you did it for one of my least brothers, you did it for me.")

1. When the Son of Man comes in his glory, who will escort him; where will he sit, and who will be assembled before him? Matthew 25:31-32

2.   How will those assembled be separated? Matthew 25:32-33

3.   How does one receive his recompense, good or bad? 2 Corinthians 5:10

4.   What will the king say to those on his right and for what reason? Matthew 25:34-36

5.   What kind of fasting does the Lord desire? Isaiah 58:6-7

6.   Who is the virtuous and the one who shall live? Ezekiel 18:7-9

7.   What did the just man ask the Lord, and of what did the king assure him? Matthew 25:37-40

8.   How does Jesus say we discover who we are, and when we welcome others, whom do we also welcome? Matthew 10:39-40

9.   What will the king say to those on the left, for whom is the everlasting fire prepared, and what did they neglect to do? Matthew 25:41-43

10.   What does God's Word say about faith? James 2:14-17

11.   What will those on the left ask, and what will he answer? Matthew 25:44-45

12.   What will happen to those who neglected one of the least ones, and what will happen to the just? Matthew 25:46

Personal – In what ways have you given food to the hungry and drink to the thirsty? This week, have you welcomed a stranger, clothed the naked, comforted the sick, and visited those in prison? Pray and ask the Lord to reveal to you those in your everyday life who fit into these categories. Ask him how you might respond to them.

FIFTH DAY   **READ PSALM 23:1-3, 5-6**

("Beside restful waters he leads me;")

Read and meditate on Psalm 23:1-3, 5-6.

What is the Lord saying to you personally through the Psalm?

How can you apply this to your life?

SIXTH DAY   **READ ALL OF THE COMMENTARY**

EZEKIEL 34:11-12, 15-17

Today's reading is a powerful prophecy given by God to Ezekiel over 500 years before Christ came on earth. This prophecy was fulfilled to the letter in Christ. Jesus founded the new sheepfold, the new chosen people, and the kingdom on earth. We see in this passage that God himself would be their shepherd. He would replace the earthly shepherds that had failed in their duty. He described the relationship between his people and himself under the image of sheep and shepherd.

This reading is a tremendous comfort. We can be assured that God will sovereignly take over as pastor of the scattered flock. When our leaders fail us, we must not despair, but turn to God for help. We must never forget that he is still in control and can turn even this tragic situation over to produce good for the kingdom. (Rom. 8:28)

Jesus tells us that he is the Good Shepherd and that he knows his sheep and they know him. He constantly seeks out the lost and brings back the strayed and disillusioned. We need only to listen to his call in the darkness of our soul. The sheep know the shepherd's voice very well. We need to know our shepherd's voice also. We can do this by spending quiet time alone with him each day and listening to him speak to us. We need to be still and realize that he is our God, our shepherd, our savior, our refuge, our rock, and our strength (Psalm 46:10 and Psalm 91).

A good shepherd always takes care of his flock and he feeds them before he eats. He notices each one and immediately binds up any wounds. He heals the sick by giving them his love, skills and attention. We need to take all this into our heart. Today, in many places, there are shepherds who have abandoned their flock, while others are abusing and even killing their flock. We can pray for our brothers and sisters who are going through this time of terror. We know that one day the Good Shepherd, Our Lord Jesus, will return and he will heal the wounded, raise the dead, and will destroy the arrogant, fat, sleek, false shepherds (Ezekiel 34:16).

1 CORINTHIANS 15:20-26, 28

Today's passage from 1 Corinthians tells us that death came into the world as a result of the sin of Adam and Eve. Today many people say, "How can we be declared guilty of something Adam did so many centuries ago?" So many people today think it is not right for God to judge us because of Adam's sin, yet each of us confirms our solidarity with Adam by our own sins. We seem to be made of the same stuff, prone to rebel, and we are judged for the sins we commit.

Because we are all sinners, what we need today is not fairness; no, what we need is mercy. Paul tells us that Christ, through his dying and rising, paid the ransom for what Adam did. We who believe have become Christ's brothers and sisters and share in his resurrection. Because Christ did rise from the dead, you and all who believe in him can face tomorrow without fear. We all can face eternity because Christ will conquer the ultimate enemy and that is death. Christ's role is to defeat all evil on earth. He defeated sin for us with his death on the cross. In the final days he will defeat Satan and all evil. World events may seem totally out of control, and justice may be very hard to find, but God is in control. God has allowed evil to remain for a time until he sends Jesus back to earth again. Jesus will present to the Father a new and perfect world. Death need have no claim on us.

Jesus tells us in 1 John 4:4 that the Spirit in us is greater than he that is in the world. We have the church, sacred Scripture, and the sacraments. The source of truth is Jesus Christ, and he is the same yesterday, today, and forever (Hebrews 13:8).

MATTHEW 25:31-46

Today's Gospel strikes at the very core of what we say we believe. To say that we believe is proved by how we act. To talk with the Lord does not mean to walk with the Lord. When we walk with the Lord we walk in the dark, dangerous, lonely corners of oppressed and beaten people's hearts.

One day God will separate his obedient followers from the pretenders and unbelievers. We are called to treat all persons whom we encounter as if they are Jesus, and this is no easy task. What we do for others demonstrates what we really think about Jesus' words to us - feed the hungry, give the homeless shelter, visit the sick and imprisoned. You will be observed by others, and will your actions separate you from the pretenders and unbelievers? Jesus used sheep and goats to show the division between believers and unbelievers. Sheep and goats often grazed together but were separated when it came shearing time.

Today's Gospel describes acts of mercy that we all can do every day. They are simple acts freely given and freely received. We have no excuse to neglect those in deep need, and we can not hand over this responsibility to some agency. Jesus demands personal involvement in caring for the needs of others. Many people might say that they do not have the opportunity to visit a prison or hospital, work in a soup kitchen, or even a shelter for the homeless. Some even say that they do not have the special talents needed for this, but Jesus really lays it on the line when he says, "What you do to the least of my brothers and sisters, you do unto me."

We get the power to do this through the Holy Spirit who anoints us to feed the hungry, set the captives free, and give sight to the blind (Luke 4:18). This could be right in your own family and the hunger might be for Christ; the prison might be their humanistic minds. The blindness may be their inability to see the truth which comes from God's Holy Word (John 8:32). We can and we must, through the Holy Spirit, set our children free.

Application

This week's first reading reveals the Good Shepherd is Christ. The second reading assures us that even in turmoil God is still in control. The Gospel shows us that all of us can do God's holy works of mercy.

This week pick out a particular work of mercy and give of yourself to another person. Maybe write to a prisoner or a person in a hospital. Visit a shut-in or someone who lives alone. Bring a meal to an elderly person or a sick friend. Spend a few hours at a soup kitchen. Volunteer some time in a thrift shop that uses its donations and sales to help others in need. If you look real closely, you might just see Jesus smiling at you and saying, "Thank you, my faithful servant."

IMMACULATE CONCEPTION - CYCLE A-B-C

BEFORE YOU BEGIN

Pray and ask God to speak to you through His Holy Spirit. "THE PARACLETE, THE HOLY SPIRIT WHOM THE FATHER WILL SEND IN MY NAME, WILL INSTRUCT YOU IN EVERYTHING, AND REMIND YOU OF ALL THAT I TOLD YOU." (JOHN 14:26)

FIRST DAY   **Reread last week's readings.**

1.   What was a helpful or new thought from the readings or from the homily you heard on Sunday?

2.   From what you learned, what personal application did you choose to apply to your life this week?

SECOND DAY   **GENESIS 3:9-15, 20**   **FIRST READING**

("He will strike at your head, while you strike at his heel.")

1.   Who called to the man, and what did He ask him? Genesis 3:9

2.   Whom did Jesus come to call? Mark 2:17

3.   Why did the man hide himself? Genesis 3:10

4.   With what are we longing to be clothed? 2 Corinthians 5:1-3

5.   What did God ask the man? Genesis 3:11

6.   What did the man say about the woman, and what did he do? Genesis 3:12

7.   What did the Lord ask the woman, and who did she say tricked her? Genesis 3:13

8.   What was Paul's fear that the serpent may corrupt in the people of Corinth? 2 Corinthians 11:3

Personal - When you lose the peace of God within you, whom do you blame? Who is responsible?

9.   What did the Lord say to the serpent, what did he say he would put between the serpent and the woman, and at what would he strike? Genesis 3:14-15

10.   To what are we to be wise, and what will crush Satan under our feet? Romans 16:19-20

11.   What did the man call his wife, and for what reason? Genesis 3:20

Personal - In what way can you protect your mind and thoughts from the evil one?

THIRD DAY **READ EPHESIANS 1:3-6, 11-12** **SECOND READING**

("...so that we might exist for the praise of his glory.")

1. Who is blessed, and with what has he blessed us? Ephesians 1:3

2. What two things does the Father show toward us? 2 Corinthians 1:3

3. How did God choose us to be before him, and when did he choose us? Ephesians 1:4

4. How do you become holy and without blemish? Ephesians 5:25-27

5. How did God destine us for adoption, and with what was it in accord? Ephesians 1:4-5

6. To whom did he give power to become children of God? John 1:12

7. What are we to praise? Ephesians 1:6

8. How were we chosen, and how does God plan and guide all things? Ephesians 1:11

9. What happens to those who are called according to his purpose, and how are we predestined? Romans 8:28-29

10. For what purpose do we exist? Ephesians 1:12

Personal – When things work out for your good, to whom do you give the glory? In what way do your actions show that you have been chosen by God?

FOURTH DAY **READ LUKE 1:26-38** **GOSPEL**

("May it be done to me according to your word.")

1. Who was sent by God to a town of Galilee named Nazareth, and when was he sent? Luke 1:26

2. To whom was he sent, and what was her name? Luke 1:27

3. What did the angel say to Mary, and what was her reaction to this greeting? Luke 1:28-29

4. What did the angel tell her not to do, and what did he say would happen to her? Luke 1:30-33

5. What did Jesus say to his disciples, and what cast out fear? Matthew 14:27, 1 John 4:18

6. What was Mary's response to the angel telling her she would conceive and bear a son? Luke 1:34

7. Who did the angel say would come upon Mary, who would overshadow her, and what would the child be called? Luke 1:35

8. What did the angel tell Joseph not to be, and how did he tell him the child was conceived in Mary? Matthew 1:20

9. What did the angel tell Mary about Elizabeth, and what did he say about God? Luke 1:36-37

10. What was Mary's response, and what did the angel do? Luke 1:38

Personal – What specific plan does God have for your life? Have you responded as Mary did, "May it be done to me according to your word?" Think and pray about this.

FIFTH DAY   **READ PSALM 98:1-4**

("The Lord has made his salvation known,")

Read and meditate on Psalm 98:1-4.

What is the Lord saying to you personally through the Psalm?

How can you apply this to your life?

SIXTH DAY   **READ ALL OF THE COMMENTARY**

GENESIS 3:9-15, 20

Nothing really prepares us for the presence of the devil serpent in the garden. The ancient word "Nahash" brought fear into the hearts of the Israelites because they were forbidden to attend any type of liturgy that involved snake worship upon pain of violating the covenant. The mention of a serpent would identify something evil in the minds of the pious Israelites. The word Nahash and evil were synonymous and the serpent's entrance into the garden brought sinful pollution.

This reading shows us how the serpent was cleverly working his way into new territory, and it shows the existence of evil forces outside the sphere of mankind. We see that God does not crash-in at people with death and punishment. In fact, God places himself on the side of people in the ongoing battle against the serpent.

The message of hope in this passage is that God always remains on man's side. Sin, evil, and Satan are always the enemy of God and man. God states that Satan will be crushed by our Lord and Savior Jesus Christ. The good news is that Jesus has won for us the victory of eternal life. He defeated Satan on the cross at Calvary. We are assured of this because scripture tells us that it is so (John 3:16). God is with us, on our side, to save us from sin. If God is with us, who can be against us? In today's passage the Messianic promise of ultimate salvation has been announced.

EPHESIANS 1:3-6, 11-12

Paul wrote this passage from inside the walls of a Roman prison. He had been a Christian for nearly thirty years, and he had taken three missionary trips and established churches all around the Mediterranean

Sea. Ephesus was a commercial, political and religious center for all Asia Minor. The temple of the pagan Greek goddess Diana was located there. It is in this environment that we hear about blessings and heaven.

What is heaven? Heaven is where God is, and blessings mean all the good things that God has given to us, such as salvation, the gifts of the Holy Spirit, and the power to do God's will. We can enjoy these blessings now if we live in an intimate relationship with Jesus Christ.

Paul tells us that God chose us to emphasize that salvation depends totally on God. We are not saved because we deserve it, but because God is gracious and freely gives it. There is no way to take credit for our salvation, or to find room for pride. God chose us, and when we belong to him through Jesus Christ, we are transformed from sinner to a life of grace. God has adopted us as his own children through the sacrifice of Jesus Christ (Romans 8:17). When you feel that your life is not worth much to anyone, remember that you are special in God's eyes, a precious present that brings him great joy. God has offered salvation to you, and when your life seems chaotic, rest in this truth: Jesus is Lord, and God is in control.

LUKE 1:26-38

In the old covenant, Jerusalem was the center and symbol of God's union with his people. In the new covenant, the symbol is no longer a city, but a person, and she is Mary, the Mother of God. She seals the covenant's beginning with the free gift of herself in love.

Mary was young and poor, all characteristics that, to the people of her day, would make her seem very unlikely to be chosen as the Mother of the long-awaited Messiah. But God chose her for one of the most important acts of obedience he has ever demanded of anyone.

You might feel that your situation in life today makes you an unlikely candidate for God's service. Do not limit God's choices, he can use you if you, like Mary, trust in him. Mary's honor of being blessed to become the Mother of God brought her much pain and ridicule. Her peers would gossip about her; her fiance would come close to leaving her; her Son would be tortured and murdered on a cross as a convicted criminal. But through Mary, her Son would become the world's only hope, and this is why Mary has been called by countless generations "Blessed among women." Her submission led to our salvation.

If your blessings lead to sorrows, think of Mary, and wait patiently for God to finish working at his plan. Think of a small young teen-age girl who understood little and trusted much, and said humbly, and yet courageously, that she was a humble servant of the Lord, and he could do with her whatever was in accordance with his Holy Word (Luke 1:38).

Application

The first reading shows us that God is always on man's side, and Satan and sin are always the enemy. The second reading reveals that a blessing is something that God has given you: life, salvation, family, friends, etc. The Gospel shows courage is made up of obedience and trust.

This week let yourself, like Mary, experience being in accordance with God's word. Take time every day this week to pray alone as she did throughout her life, to study God's Holy Word, and to do what is necessary in work and school for you. Remember each day to take time to relax and enjoy yourself for a few moments. Develop each day a discipline of prayer, study, work, and leisure. God has chosen you, and you, like Mary, can say, "Yes, Lord, do with me whatever is in accordance with your Holy Word."

CHRISTMAS – CYCLE A-B-C

BEFORE YOU BEGIN

Pray and ask God to speak to you through His Holy Spirit. "THE PARACLETE, THE HOLY SPIRIT WHOM THE FATHER WILL SEND IN MY NAME, WILL INSTRUCT YOU IN EVERYTHING, AND REMIND YOU OF ALL THAT I TOLD YOU." (JOHN 14:26)

FIRST DAY **Reread last week's readings.**

1. What was a helpful or new thought from the readings or from the homily you heard on Sunday?

2. From what you learned, what personal application did you choose to apply to your life this week?

SECOND DAY **READ ISAIAH 52:7-10** **FIRST READING**

("Your God is King")

1. Whose feet are beautiful and what does he announce? Isaiah 52:7, Romans 10:15

2. What are we not to be afraid to cry out? Isaiah 40:9

3. Why do the watchmen shout for joy? Isaiah 52:8

4. What are the watchmen never to do? Isaiah 62:6

5. What are we to do together and for what reason? Isaiah 52:9

6. Why does God comfort and encourage us? 2 Cor 1:3-4

7. Whom does the Lord redeem? Psalm 34:23

8. What has the Lord done with his holy arm and in the sight of whom? Isaiah 52:10

9. What will all the ends of the earth see? Isaiah 52:10

10. What is to be known upon the earth, among all nations? Psalm 67:3

Personal – To whom have you been announcing peace and good news? How do people see the joy and salvation of the Lord upon you?

THE BREAD OF LIFE CATHOLIC BIBLE STUDY

THIRD DAY   **READ HEBREWS 1:1-16**   SECOND READING

("Let all the angels of God worship him.")

1.   How did God speak in times past? Hebrews 1:1

2.   How does God speak to us now, what did he make him, and what did he do through him? Hebrews 1:2

3.   What came to be through him (Jesus)? John 1:3-4

4.   Of whom is Jesus the reflection and perfect copy, and by what are all things sustained? Hebrews 1:3

5.   When Jesus accomplished purifications from sins what did he do? Hebrews 1:3

6.   How did Jesus accomplish this purification? Col 1:15-20

7.   What has Jesus inherited, and to what is he far superior? Hebrews 1:4

8.   Because Jesus humbled himself becoming obedient to death, what did God do to him? Philippians 2:8-9

9.   What are the questions asked about angels, and what does he say about his first born? Hebrews 1:5

10. Who is ruler of the kings of the earth and who loves us? Revelations 1:5

Personal – How have you been sustained by God's Mighty Word and how have you worshipped his Son Jesus this past week?

FOURTH DAY   **READ JOHN 1:1-18**   GOSPEL

("And the Word became flesh and made his dwelling among us,")

1.   Who was in the beginning? John 1:1,14

2.   Who did Jesus say he was to the Father? John 10:30

3.   Who was in the beginning with God and what was this life that came to be through him? John 1:2-4

4.   What has the darkness not overcome? John 1:5

5.   Who came for testimony, to what did he testify, and what did he say about himself? John 1:6-8

6.   What does the true light do, how did the world come to be, and who did not accept him? John 1:9-11

7. To those who did accept Jesus what did he give them power to become, in what did they believe, and how were they born? John 1:12-13

8. Who can enter the kingdom of God? John 3:5

9. What has not been revealed and what will happen to us when it is revealed? 1 John 3:2

10. When the Word became flesh what was he full of? John 1:14

11. What did John say about Jesus, what came through Moses, and what came through Jesus? John 1:15-17

12. Who has revealed the Father to us? John 1:18

Personal – What has Jesus revealed to you about the Father?

FIFTH DAY   **READ PSALM 98:1-6**

("The Lord has made his salvation known.")

Read and meditate on Psalm 98:1-6

What is the Lord saying to you personally through the Psalm?

How can you apply this to your life?

SIXTH DAY   **READ ALL OF THE COMMENTARY**

ISAIAH 52:7-10

In today's passage God urges his people to draw comfort from past history and to look forward to a greater exodus. He is telling them that it is time to shake off the grief and lethargy that has overtaken them. There is the sound of Good News that God is about to escort his people home, to Jerusalem, God's holy city, the city with God's temple. But the people experienced desolation instead of prosperity, and destruction instead of liberty. The people suffered terribly because of their sins, but God promised to restore Jerusalem as a holy city.

God reigns, and today he still is very much in control. Today's verse states how beautiful are the feet of those who bring good news of peace and salvation (v.7). How beautiful are the feet of those who go forth and preach the Gospel of Jesus Christ (Rom. 10:15). How welcome are those who bring the message of hope to a broken, hopeless, segment of our world.

God's great message of salvation must be through us to others so they can have the chance to respond to the "Good News". How will our loved ones hear it unless we take it to them. How will the nations hear it unless someone takes it to them? God is calling us to take a part in making his message known in our family and our community. Think of one person who needs to hear the good news, and think of something you can do to help him or her hear it. Then you go out and do that act, in Jesus' name, as soon as possible.

HEBREWS 1:1-6

The letter to the Hebrews was written to a group of Jewish Christians who appeared to be having second thoughts about Jesus Christ being their long-awaited Messiah. They should have been a community of mature Christians by this time; instead, they seemed to be sort of withdrawn and inward-looking in their spiritual walk. They needed a strong reminder that what they now possess in Christ is far better than what they had before they became Christians.

This passage begins with a tremendous affirmation of Jesus' divinity. Through Jesus, God has made his supreme and final revelation of himself to man. Jesus is the living embodiment of the character and majesty of God. Jesus has dealt with the problem of human sin by sacrificing himself on the cross and paying the ransom for all mankind with his blood. He is now at God's side in the position of supreme power. The angels, whom the Jews came very close to worshipping themselves, worship Jesus Christ. They are spiritual beings and they are to serve and glorify God himself.

The people were well versed in scripture and whether through doubt, persecution, or false teaching, they seemed to be in danger of falling away from their Christian faith. This danger is very much present in today's world. There is much false teaching today and many so-called "Shepherds" are just wolves in sheep's clothing. We need to stay in fellowship, pray, and to study God's Holy Word, and follow the teachings of our church. Take the time this Christmas season to thank the Lord for bringing his light into your heart and bringing about a better relationship with him. Remember, it is Jesus birthday, and the present he wants most is YOU!

JOHN 1:1-18

This passage clearly shows that what Jesus taught and what he did are tied inseparably to who he is. In today's reading John shows Jesus as fully human and fully God. Although Jesus took upon himself full humanity and lived as a man experiencing all the emotions that all of us have, he never ceased to be God who has always existed. This is the truth about Jesus, and the foundation of all truth. If we cannot or do not believe this basic truth, we will not have enough faith to trust our eternal destiny to him. This is the reason John writes this Gospel, to build faith and confidence in Jesus Christ, so that we may believe he truly was and is God in the flesh (John 20:30-31).

Jesus' life brings light to mankind, in his light we see ourselves as we really are: sinners in need of a savior. We fall on our knees, and like the shepherds at the little cave in Bethlehem, we too give praise and glory to the light of the world, our Lord and Savior Jesus Christ. The wise men followed the light of a star to see the light of the world. When we follow Jesus, the light of the world, we can avoid walking blindly and falling into sin. He lights the path ahead of us so we can see how to live. He removes the darkness of sin from our lives, and if we have allowed the light of Christ to shine in our lives this Christmas season, then we will never stumble in the darkness.

As the world celebrates the birth of Christ, let yourself be reborn spiritually. Through faith in Christ this new birth changes us from the inside out - rearranging our attitudes, desires and motives. Have you asked Christ to make you a new person on Christmas day? This fresh start is available to all who believe in him. Merry Christmas.

Application

The first reading tells us how beautiful are the feet of those who go forth and proclaim God's Word. The second reading shows that encouragement and discipline lead to a stronger commitment to God. The Gospel reveals Christmas as a time of new birth, a time of giving your life over to God.

This week, give those you love the greatest present you could give them for Christmas. How beautiful are your feet as you go forth and gift them with the gift of your presence, of your love, of salvation by bringing them to Christ. Remember, it is Christ's birthday, and the presents should all be for him, and he only wants you!

OCTAVE OF CHRISTMAS – CYCLE A-B-C
FEAST OF MARY, MOTHER OF GOD

BEFORE YOU BEGIN

Pray and ask God to speak to you through His Holy Spirit. "THE PARACLETE, THE HOLY SPIRIT WHOM THE FATHER WILL SEND IN MY NAME, WILL INSTRUCT YOU IN EVERYTHING, AND REMIND YOU OF ALL THAT I TOLD YOU." (JOHN 14:26)

FIRST DAY   **Reread last week's readings.**

1.   What was a helpful or new thought from the readings or from the homily you heard on Sunday?

2.   From what you learned, what personal application did you choose to apply to your life this week?

SECOND DAY   **READ NUMBERS 6:22-27**   **FIRST READING**

("The Lord bless you and keep you!")

1.   To whom was the Lord speaking, and to whom did he tell him to speak? Numbers 6:22-23

2.   Who was Aaron, and what did the Lord say to Moses about him? Exodus 4:14-16

3.   About what was Moses to speak to them? Numbers 6:23

4.   What six things were included in the blessing? Numbers 6:24-26

5.   Who will be blessed? Proverbs 28:20

6.   What brings wealth? Proverbs 10:22

7.   Who was blessed by the Lord, what did he do for her, and what was her response? Luke 1:46-55

8.   What has the Lord given us? Psalm 118:27

9.   Who did Jesus say he was? John 8:12

10. What shall be invoked upon the Israelites, and what will the Lord do? Numbers 6:27

Personal - In what way have you blessed a family member or a friend? What do others see shining forth from your face?

THIRD DAY READ GALATIANS 4:4-7 SECOND READING

("…God sent the Spirit of his Son into our hearts, crying out, 'Abba, Father!'")

1. Under what was God's Son born? Galatians 4:4

2. What did God's Son do? Galatians 4:5

3. What happens to everyone who believes in Jesus? John 3:16

4. Who did the law come through, and what did Jesus bring? John 1:17

5. Who are the children of God, and who bears witness that we are? Romans 8:14-16

6. What proof do we have that we are his children? Galatians 4:6

7. To whom did he give the power to become children of God? John 1:12-13

8. Why are the children of God not known to the world? 1 John 3:1

9. What are we no longer, and what has he made us? Galatians 4:7

10. With whom are the children of God joint heirs? Romans 8:17

Personal – In what way have you cried out to "Abba," Daddy, this week? What have you inherited from God? What are your parents leaving you as an inheritance, or what are you leaving your children as an inheritance?

FOURTH DAY READ LUKE 2:16-21 GOSPEL

("And Mary kept all these things, reflecting on them in her heart.")

1. When the shepherds went off in haste, who did they find? Luke 2:16

2. Why did Mary lay her firstborn Son in a manger? Luke 2:7

3. What did the shepherds do when they saw the child? Luke 2:17

4. What was the reaction of those who were told the message? Luke 2:18

5. What amazed or astonished the people listening to Jesus? Matthew 7:28-29

Personal – What have you seen and made known to others since you have been studying God's Word?

6. What did Mary do? Luke 2:19

7. What did Mary do when Jesus became lost and then told her he was about his Father's business? Luke 2:49-51

Personal – What have you personally pondered in your heart that God revealed to you, and how have you followed Mary's example?

8.   How did the shepherds return? Luke 2:20

9.   What was the reaction of the paralytic and the people upon the healing? Luke 5:25-26

10. What happened on the eighth day, and to whom had the name been given? Luke 2:21, Luke 1:31

11. What has his name done for us? Acts 4:12

12. To what is the name Jesus inherited far superior? Hebrews 1:3-4

Personal – What name has been given to you, and of what is it a reflection?

FIFTH DAY   **READ PSALM 67:2-6, 8**

("…may he let his face shine upon us.")

Read and meditate on Psalm 67:2-6, 8.

What is the Lord saying to you personally through the Psalm?

How can you apply this to your life?

SIXTH DAY   **READ ALL OF THE COMMENTARY**

NUMBERS 6:22-27

When Mary said, "Generation after generation shall call me blessed of God," she was recognizing and accepting the gift God had given her (Luke 1:48). If Mary had denied her incredible position, she would have been throwing God's blessing back at him.

In today's reading we are being shown that a blessing was one way of asking God's divine favor to rest upon others. All of God's blessings had their fulfillment in the coming of Christ on earth. Mary received the fullness of these promises and blessings when she said, "Be it done unto me according to thy Word." At that very moment she conceived Jesus Christ in her womb. As proof of this blessing we have the angel Gabriel's words as he salutes her as "full of grace." She has the full friendship of God, and no man or woman had ever received the fullness of God's blessing until then.

A blessing conveys that God will (1) bless and protect, (2) be pleased because of us, (3) be gracious, merciful, and compassionate to us, (4) show favor to us, and (5) give us peace. When we ask God to bless us and others, we are asking him to do these five things. We will have the full friendship of God as we ask him to bless others as well as ourselves.

Today, on this special feast, let us thank God for all the blessings that he has given Mary, the Mother of God. We have all profited through her blessings; and the title, Mother of God, that the church confirmed in her regard at the Council of Ephesus in 431 AD, demonstrates all this.

GALATIANS 4:4-7

In today's reading Paul uses the example of slavery to show that before Christ came and died for our sins, people were in bondage to the law. By becoming enslaved to the law, people thought they could be saved. At just the right time, God sent Jesus to earth to die for our sins, and we who were once slaves are now God's very own children with an intimate relationship with him. For centuries the Jews were wondering when their Messiah would come, but God's timing was perfect.

We may sometimes wonder if God will ever respond to our prayers, but we must never stop trusting or give up hope. At the right time, he will respond to us. Jesus was born of a woman and was subject to God's law and fulfilled it. His death brought freedom for us who were enslaved to sin so we could be adopted into God's family. Under the Roman law, an adopted child was guaranteed all legal rights to his father's property. As adopted children of God, we share with Jesus all rights to God's resources.

As God's heirs, we can claim what he has provided for us; which is our full identity as his children. The Old Testament was based on the law, but was only a shadow of things to come. Christianity is the fulfillment of the Old Testament. Christianity is the reality, and the reality is God has become man, and man is now free and has been adopted into God's family as rightful heirs to the kingdom.

LUKE 2:16-21

What a tremendous sign of comfort and hope it is when we read that the first visitors to lay eyes on the long-awaited Messiah were simple, hard-working, uneducated, common folks called shepherds. Even in birth Jesus has shown us the ultimate in humility, and his choice of those who were part of his birth experience were of humble origins themselves.

Can you imagine the thoughts that flowed through Mary's head as she observed the shepherds coming to pay homage to her Son? She certainly was aware of the power and beauty of the angels singing praises of glory to God to their new born king. The Jewish custom was when a new child was born the local musicians would come by and sing some congratulatory songs. Mary had, not earthly musicians to sing to her son, but she had a choir of angels to fill the air with heavenly sounds.

On this very special day, we can honor Mary in her blessed role as Mother of God. God himself honored her by making her the mother of his Son. Jesus, in one of his last acts on this earth before dying on the cross, made his mother our mother. It was through no merit of her own that she earned this dignity. This honor was given as a sheer gift of God. When we honor her, we are in fact thanking God for his gift of her to us.

Application

The first reading explains that a blessing is God giving someone his protection and direction. The second reading tells how the Old Testament was a time of preparation, and the New Testament was a time of the reality of God entering into human history as a human being named Jesus. The Gospel reveals Jesus beginning his life on earth humbly, and in humility he went to his death on a cross for us.

This week, let the humility of the shepherds be your model of conduct during the Christmas holidays. Bring to your family, friends, and co-workers, the gift of listening, the gift of gentleness, and the gift of humility. Mary was a role model for the whole world, for both male and female.

ASSUMPTION - CYCLE A-B-C

BEFORE YOU BEGIN

Pray and ask God to speak to you through His Holy Spirit. "THE PARACLETE, THE HOLY SPIRIT WHOM THE FATHER WILL SEND IN MY NAME, WILL INSTRUCT YOU IN EVERYTHING, AND REMIND YOU OF ALL THAT I TOLD YOU." (JOHN 14:26)

FIRST DAY   **Reread last week's readings.**

1.   What was a helpful or new thought from the readings or from the homily you heard on Sunday?

2.   From what you learned, what personal application did you choose to apply to your life this week?

SECOND DAY   **READ REVELATION 11:19; 12:1-6, 10**   **FIRST READING**

("Her child was caught up to God and his throne.")

1.   When God's temple in heaven was opened, what could be seen, and what was happening? Revelations 11:19

2.   What was in the ark of the covenant? Hebrews 9:4

3.   What did Jesus say would happen before the persecution? Luke 21:5-12

4.   What appeared in the sky, who was clothed with the sun, the moon under her feet, and twelve stars as a crown on her head? Revelation 12:1

5.   What was happening to the woman? Revelations 12:2

6.   What did God say to the woman after she sinned? Genesis 3:16

7.   What was another sign that appeared in the sky? Revelations 12:3

8.   What did the tail of the dragon do, who did it stand before, and what was it about to do? Revelations 12:4

9.   To what did the woman give birth, what was he destined to do, and what happened to him? Revelations 12:5

10.   Where did the woman go, and what happened to her? Revelations 12:6

11.   What did a loud voice in heaven say, and who was cast out? Revelation 12:10

Personal - How has Satan been accusing you, and how has God protected you from him?

THIRD DAY **READ 1 CORINTHIANS 15:20-26** **SECOND READING**

("The last enemy to be destroyed is death.")

1. What has Christ done, and what is he to those who have fallen asleep?
   1 Corinthians 15:20

2. What did God the Father give us in his great mercy? 1 Peter 1:3-4

3. What will happen to our mortal bodies, and how does it happen? Romans 8:11

4. How did death come, and how did the resurrection of the dead come?
   1 Corinthians 15:21

5. How did death come to man? Genesis 3:17-19, Romans 5:12-18

6. Just as in Adam, who dies, in Christ, who is brought to life? 1 Corinthians 15:22

7. In what order are they brought to life, and then what happens?
   1 Corinthians 15:23-24

8. How long must he reign? 1 Corinthians 15:25

9. What is the last enemy to be destroyed? 1 Corinthians 15:26

10. What did Jesus Christ do? 2 Timothy 1:10

Personal – How have you faced the fear of death in your life? Have you been able to overcome that fear through Christ's resurrection?

FOURTH DAY **READ LUKE 1:39-56** **GOSPEL**

("He has thrown down rulers from their thrones, but lifted up the lowly.")

1. Who traveled to the hill country to a town of Judah, whose house did she enter, and who did she greet? Luke 1:39-40

2. What did the baby do that was in Elizabeth's womb, with what was she filled, and with what did she cry out? Luke 1:41-42

3. What was Elizabeth's response? Luke 1:43-44

Personal – What is your response to the presence of God in your life?

4. What did Elizabeth say for what was Mary blessed? Luke 1:45

5. What did Mary say her soul proclaimed, and in what did her spirit rejoice?
   Luke 1:46-47

6.   Who and what is the joy of my soul? Isaiah 61:10

7.   What has the Lord looked upon, and what would all ages call her? Luke 1:48

8.   What does God do for the lowly? Psalm 113:7

9.   What has the mighty one done for Mary, what does she say about his name, and to whom is his mercy? Luke 1:49-50

10.   What has he shown, what has he done with the arrogant of mind and heart, and the rulers? Luke 1:51-52

11.   What has he done with the lowly, the hungry and the rich? Luke 1:52-53

12.   What has he done to Israel, and to what was it according? Luke 1:54-55

13.   How long did Mary remain with Elizabeth, and then where did she go? Luke 1:56

Personal - How can you identify with Mary's lowliness? In what way has God lifted you up, or in what way has he brought you down?

FIFTH DAY   **READ PSALM 45:10-12, 16**

("They are borne in with gladness and joy;")

Read and meditate on Psalm 45:10-12, 16.

What is the Lord saying to you personally through the Psalm?

How can you apply this to your life?

SIXTH DAY   **READ ALL OF THE COMMENTARY**

REVELATION 11:19; 12:1-6, 10

John was writing this passage for a persecuted church to take heart. The woman stands for God's faithful people (the church) and Mary, the Mother of Christ, the Messiah. The pain of childbirth refers to the sufferings of the early church, the flight into the desert is also a description of pain. The sun covering the woman is an image of the glory of Mary, the mother of the Messiah. The powers of evil are represented by a dragon who fights bitterly to kill the Messiah at birth but fails.

Jesus ultimately fulfills his mission by dying on the cross for the sins of the world and triumphantly returns to the throne of God. Mary also has triumphed in her role of obedience and humility. The dragon bent on destruction is Satan, and we are reminded that the struggle of Christians today is part of a much greater conflict.

The message of today's reading is that although Satan is strong and powerful and his attack is fierce, his time is short. He has been overpowered by Christ. God's people at all times and everywhere are under his sovereign protection. This reading brings out the closeness between Christ our Messiah and his blessed Mother. Mary was chosen from all eternity to be the Mother of God. She was intimately connected with her Son in the completion of this divine plan. Satan directed much opposition to Mary, but she was triumphant in her mission here on earth. We celebrate Mary's assumption into heaven because we believe that, after Christ, she occupies the next highest place of glory.

1 CORINTHIANS 15:20-26

In today's reading Paul is proving that we shall all rise from the dead one day. The Christian converts of Corinth were not denying the resurrection of Jesus Christ, but the resurrection of the body. Paul was very strong and clear in his reply that if you denied the resurrection of the body, then you have denied the resurrection of Jesus Christ. In fact, you have emptied the Christian message of its truth and the Christian life of its reality.

Paul goes on to tell them that one of the basic doctrines of the Christian faith which they have accepted was Christ's resurrection. Paul tells them that if it is for this life only that we hope, we of all people are most to be pitied. This means that if there was no resurrection for us then Christianity can gain us nothing but the grave.

It is very important today that the center of Christian teaching, which is Christ died, was buried, was raised from the dead, and appeared again on earth, be believed. Christ's burial emphasized the reality of his dying. Christ then was raised from the dead by God and left an empty tomb. Christ then appeared to many leaders of the church. Jesus' resurrection is a promise of the future to all those who die. The final enemy is death, and Christ defeated death on the cross at Calvary.

The Good News is a message of hope, and Paul tells the Corinthians and us that, like Christ, we too will rise one day and be with him in a new incorruptible body. The foundation of the church is being the bearer and the repository of the Good News. We are told that no man can have God for his Father unless he has the church for his mother. Mary is the mother of all of us who are "church," and we celebrate her being raised up to be with her Son and Messiah, Jesus Christ.

LUKE 1:39-56

Today's Gospel shows us something about the kind of woman through whom God chose to fulfill his purpose. Mary, upon hearing the incredible news about her aged relative, Elizabeth, becoming pregnant, sets out on a four or five day journey south. The meeting becomes a meeting of special joy and significance because they both had so much to share.

The power of their thoughts and feelings emerge very strongly in Elizabeth's benediction and Mary's hymn of praise. The gift of blessedness makes a powerful impact on Mary. To her was granted the blessedness of being the Mother of the Son of God. Her heart must have been bursting with joy at so great a privilege. Yet, that very blessedness was to be a sword to pierce her heart. It meant that one day she would see her only Son hanging on a cross.

Many times, to be blessed and chosen by God means a crown of joy and a cross of sorrow. We must come to know that God does not choose a person for ease and comfort and selfish joy. He chooses one to do a task that will take all one's head, heart and hands. God chooses a person in order to use him or her. It is the mystery of blessedness that it confers on a person both the greatest joy and the greatest task in all the world. We will do well to remember that Jesus Christ came, not to make life easy, but to make men great.

We celebrate today that "all ages have come to call her blessed." She saw nothing in herself but a maid-servant who understood little, but trusted and obeyed completely. Let us all assume her holy attributes of gentleness, humility and obedience, and we too will be blessed.

Application

The first reading reveals the Spirit within us is stronger than he that is in the world (1 John 4:4). The second reading showed that a Christian is born to live forever. The Gospel reveals that a blessing is a gift from God to you, and for others.

This week can be a time of great joy and possibly even a time of great pain for you. You can ask God to bless you with a spirit that hungers and longs for him. You will be opposed by many distractions when you decide to submit yourself to Christ.

Each day, make time alone to pray to Jesus. Read a passage of scripture and meditate on it, and then, like Mary, be submissive to someone who is near you. That means, putting that person first. It might mean ridicule or even rejection. Remember, blessedness is loving others, not yourself. Jesus died for you and this makes you blessed too.

ALL SAINTS DAY - CYCLE A-B-C

BEFORE YOU BEGIN

Pray and ask God to speak to you through His Holy Spirit. "THE PARACLETE, THE HOLY SPIRIT WHOM THE FATHER WILL SEND IN MY NAME, WILL INSTRUCT YOU IN EVERYTHING, AND REMIND YOU OF ALL THAT I TOLD YOU." (JOHN 14:26)

FIRST DAY   **Reread last week's readings.**

1. What was a helpful or new thought from the readings or from the homily you heard on Sunday?

2. From what you learned, what personal application did you choose to apply to your life this week?

SECOND DAY   **READ REVELATION 7:2-4, 9-14**   **FIRST READING**

("They prostrated themselves before the throne,")

1. What was seen coming up from the east, what was he holding, and to whom did he cry out in a loud voice? Revelation 7:2

2. On whom has God the Father set his seal? John 6:27

3. With what were you sealed as the first installment of your inheritance towards redemption? Ephesians 1:13-14

4. What were the angels told not to damage until the seal was put upon whose foreheads? Revelation 7:3

5. How many had been marked, and from where were they? Revelation 7:4

6. Who were standing with the lamb, and what were they doing? Revelation 14:1, 3

7. What was John's vision, before whom did they stand, and what were they wearing? Revelation 7:9

8. From whom did they say salvation comes, and where is he seated? Revelation 7:10

9. What did the angels standing around the throne do? Revelation 7:11

10. As the angels worshipped God, what did they exclaim? Revelation 7:12

11. What did one of the elders speak up and say, and who were the ones wearing the white robes? Revelation 7:13-14

12.   What did the blood of Jesus do for us? Hebrews 9:14, 1 John 1:7

Personal – How often do you worship the Lord during the day in practice for the time you will spend in eternity worshipping him?

| THIRD DAY | READ 1 JOHN 3:1-3 | SECOND READING |

("What we shall be has not yet been revealed.")

1.   What has the Father bestowed on us, what might we be called, and why does the world not know us? 1 John 3:1

2.   How do we become a child of God? John 1:12, John 3:16

3.   What did Jesus make known to us, and for what reason? John 17:25-26

4.   What are we now, what has not been revealed, and what will happen when it is revealed? 1 John 3:2

5.   What does Jesus do to our bodies? Philippians 3:20-21

6.   Why should we remain in Jesus? 1 John 2:28

7.   What is happening to us, and how is the veil lifted? 2 Corinthians 3:14-18

8.   What does everyone do who has this hope based on him? 1 John 3:3

9.   How do we make ourselves pure? 1 John 2:5-6

10.   What is pure and true? Psalm 19:10

Personal – How have you become more like Jesus this past week? Be specific.

| FOURTH DAY | READ MATTHEW 5:1-12 | GOSPEL |

("Blessed are you when they insult you and persecute you
and utter every kind of slander against you because of me.")

1.   Where did Jesus go when he saw the crowds, and who came to him? Matthew 5:1

2.   What did he do with the disciples, what did he say belongs to the poor in spirit and those who are persecuted for the sake of righteousness? Matthew 5:2-3, 10

3.   What will happen to those who mourn and to those who are meek? Matthew 5:4-5

4.   Where is God's dwelling, and what will he do? Rev 21:3-4

5.   In what shall the meek delight? Psalm 37:11

6.   What will happen to those who hunger and thirst for righteousness and to those who are merciful? Matthew 5:6-7

7.   Over what does mercy triumph? James 2:13

8.   Who will the clean of heart see, and who will be called the children of God? Matthew 5:8-9

9.   Whose heart is clean? Psalm 24:4-5

10.   Who is to rejoice and be glad, for what reason, and who was persecuted before them? Matthew 5:10-12

11.   What happened to those who proclaimed the name of Jesus, and what was their reaction? Acts 5:40-42

Personal – In which of the beatitudes do you find yourself blessed? In what way have you been persecuted for your faith by your family, friends, work associates or school friends?

FIFTH DAY   **READ PSALM 24:1-6**

("The Lord's are the earth and its fullness;")

Read and meditate on Psalm 24:1-6.

What is the Lord saying to you personally through the Psalm?

How can you apply this to your life?

SIXTH DAY   **READ ALL OF THE COMMENTARY**

REVELATION 7:2-4, 9-14

This reading shows John is seeing a vision of the last terrible day and in particular the great tribulation which is to come. During the tribulation there will be a final assault by all the forces of evil and a final devastation of the earth. But before this time of horror and devastation comes, the faithful are to be sealed with the great seal of God so they may survive it. It is not that they escape from experiencing it, but that they may survive it.

A seal on a scroll identified and protected its contents. God places his great seal on his followers, identifying them as his own and guaranteeing his protection over their souls. This is why we have the Sacrament of Baptism, and it shows how valuable we are to him. Our physical bodies may be beaten or even destroyed, but nothing can harm the souls of those marked by God.

We see the seal of God that is placed on the forehead of the believers is the exact opposite of the mark of the beast (Revelation 13:6). These two marks place the people in two very distinct categories. There are those owned by God and those owned by Satan. Satan is always trying to imitate the great works of God.

The number of believers in today's passage symbolizes completeness. All God's followers will be brought safely to him. You will always be protected from spiritual harm when Jesus is Lord and master of your life and soul, and not even death can separate his love from you (Romans 8:39).

1 JOHN 3:1-3

As believers, our self-worth is based on God's love for us and that he calls us his children. To belong and to be loved is the deepest need there is in a human being. The numbers in the mental hospitals and prisons would be drastically reduced if the people in those places really had a good self-image.

We are God's children now, not just sometime in the distant future. We are children of the king, and we are heirs to his kingdom of heaven. We have been adopted into God's family through the sacrifice of our Lord Jesus. To be called a child of God is a great privilege, and yet, we are not just called children of God; we are the children of God. By nature a man is a creature of God, but it is by grace that he becomes a child of God.

The Old Testament tells us that the Israelites are the covenant people of God. In the New Testament, by a deliberate act of adoption on the part of God, the children enter into his family. We become his children in the intimate and loving sense of the term only by an act of God's initiating grace and the response of their own hearts in the Sacrament of Baptism.

When we become children of God, our life has only just begun. We will continue to grow in the image and likeness of God by following the teachings and examples of Jesus Christ. We can do this through the power of the Holy Spirit and the loving guidance of the Catholic Church. One day you will be face to face with "ABBA," your heavenly Father and your Loving Savior Jesus Christ, and what a wonderful joy it will be when he says to you, "Welcome, my obedient, loving child."

MATTHEW 5:1-12

This passage reveals to us the Christian attitude of being. Jesus is not calling his disciples to live in such a way that they will be blessed. He is in fact saying that because they are living in accordance with God's will, they are already blessed. Blessed means being joyful, and this is a joy that no man or circumstance can take away.

This passage begins with Jesus sitting down as he began to preach. This was a signal that what he was saying was an official message, a message that was to be heard and responded to. When a Jewish rabbi was teaching officially, he sat to teach. We speak today of a professor's chair, and the Pope only speaks "Ex cathedra" from his seat.

We hear Jesus say blessed are the poor in spirit, for theirs is the kingdom of God. The Jews had four levels of being poor. The first was just being unable to make ends meet, second was having no power, third was having no influence, and finally, having no earthly resources whatsoever and putting their whole trust in God. The Jews described the word poor as the humble and hapless man who puts his whole trust in God. This really means blessed is someone who realized his own helplessness and put his whole trust in God. He will become completely detached from things and will become completely attached to God. The man who is poor in spirit is the one who has realized that things mean nothing and that God means everything.

Do not think that poverty is a good thing. Jesus would never call living in slums, not having enough to eat, and poor health as being blessed. The poverty which is blessed is the poverty of the spirit. The kingdom of heaven awaits the one who realizes that God is his real treasure. Are you that person?

Application

The first reading shows that God has placed his great seal on all of his believers through baptism. The second reading tells us that adoption means being selected and God chose you to be his child. The Gospel reveals that nothing can separate us from God's love, not even death (Romans 8:39).

This week, let yourself be completely poor in spirit. Let your attachment be only to people, not things. Look in your closet and see what clothes you do not really need and then give them to the poor. Look at your financial picture and see what you can cut out of your spending and give that expense to the poor.

Look at how you spend your time. Is it mostly for your benefit? Try to see where you can give more time to others in need. Mother Teresa says, "Unless life is lived for others, it is not worthwhile." Blessed are you because you are poor in spirit (Matthew 5:3).